D0886561

MANUFACTURING INEQUALITY

THE WILDER HOUSE SERIES IN POLITICS, HISTORY, AND CULTURE

The Wilder House Series is published in association with the Wilder House Board of Editors and the University of Chicago.

David Laitin, *Editor*
George Steinmetz, *Assistant Editor*

EDITORIAL BOARD

Leora Auslander
Prasenjit Duara
Ira Katznelson
William Sewell
Theda Skocpol
Susan Stokes

A complete list of titles in the series appears at the end of the book.

MANUFACTURING INEQUALITY

*Gender Division in the French
and British Metalworking
Industries, 1914–1939*

LAURA LEE DOWNS

Cornell University Press

Ithaca and London

This book has been published with the aid of a grant from the University of Michigan, Ann Arbor.

First published 1995 by Cornell University Press.

⊛ The paper in this book meets the minimum requirements
of the American National Standard for Information Sciences—
Permanence of Paper for Printed Library Materials, ANSI Z39.48-1984.

Library of Congress Cataloging-in-Publication Data

Downs, Laura Lee, 1955–
  Manufacturing inequality : gender division in the French and British metalworking industries, 1914–1939 / Laura Lee Downs.
     p.   cm. — (The Wilder House series in politics, history, and culture)
  Includes bibliographical references and index.
  ISBN 0-8014-3015-1 (alk. paper)
     1. Sexual division of labor—France—History. 2. Sexual division of labor—Great Britain—History. 3. Metalworking industries—France—History. 4. Metalworking industries—Great Britain—History.   I. Title.   II. Series.
  HD6060.65.F8D69   1995
  306.3′615—dc20   94-46958

To the memory of
Edna Wylie Gilman

Contents

Acknowledgments

This book has been a long time in the making, and I have acquired many debts. It is a great pleasure to express my gratitude for the generous support I have received along the way. Nearly two years of research in London, Coventry, and Paris and some release time from teaching were made possible by a Bourse Chateaubriand from the French government, a President's Fellowship from Columbia University, a Whiting Fellowship, a Mellon Postdoctoral Fellowship at Columbia University, an American Council of Learned Societies Research Fellowship, and summer travel grants from the Council on European Studies and the Office of the Vice President for Research at the University of Michigan.

Archivists in both France and Britain helped me to locate documents, and lugged volumes of material to and from my desk each day. In between trips, I received much advice and assistance, and, at the Union des Industries Métallurgiques et Minières (UIMM), a tiny cup of espresso at four o'clock each day, warming the late afternoons of a gloomy Paris winter. I thank in particular Isabelle Brot of the Archives d'Entreprises in the Archives Nationales, Mme Bordes at the UIMM, Mlle Vernholes at the Ecole des Surintendantes, Thérèse Doneaud at the Union Féminine Civique et Sociale, M. Suriano at the library of the Paris Chambre de Commerce, Howard Gospel and Leslie Hannah at the London School of Economics, Richard Storey at the Modern Records Centre in Warwick, and the staff at the Coventry District Engineering Employers' Association. I also thank the Engineering Employers' Federation, the Services Photographiques at Thomson-Houston, and the Groupement des Industries Métallurgiques, Mécaniques et Connexes de la Région Parisienne for opening their rich collections to me.

Many scholars and colleagues have read and commented on various parts

ix

of the book. Patrick Fridenson, Sabine MacCormack, David Mayfield, Robert Moeller, and William Sewell read the entire manuscript and kept me from the shoals of error; Miriam Bodian, Mary Dearborn, Alice Echols, Geoffrey Eley, Elizabeth Faue, Diana Fortuna, Thomas Harrison, Susan Johnson, Pieter Judson, Susan Juster, Valerie Kivelson, Kathryn Oberdeck, and Dror Wahrman commented on particular chapters and, equally important, provided that spiritual sustenance of lively intellectual debate and good friendship on which any scholarly endeavor rests. But there is no one to whom I am more indebted than Robert Paxton, who read the manuscript through several drafts. Each time, his insights proved crucial in shaping and clarifying the argument. Perhaps his most vital contribution to this work, however, lies in his capacity to inspire by his own unostentatious example, practicing history with a deep sense of political and moral responsibility.

One often hears of the frustration and disappointment that dog a first-time author as she seeks to get her manuscript published. But I have no such tales to tell, for Peter Agree's enthusiastic support of this project made the notoriously trying process of publishing a first book into a genuine pleasure. Cornell's anonymous readers read the manuscript with extraordinary care and offered challenging and thoughtful criticisms for which I am heartily grateful. I owe special thanks to Margaret Lourie, who helped with the painful task of trimming back detail so that the lines of argument might emerge more clearly. Donald LaCoss assisted mightily in preparing the index. And Barbara Salazar did a superb job of editing the manuscript.

Chapter 4 draws heavily on my article "Women's Strikes and the Politics of Popular Egalitarianism in France, 1916–18," in Lenard Berlanstein, ed., *Rethinking Labor History: Essays on Discourse and Class Analysis,* copyright © 1993 by Illinois University, and is reprinted here with the permission of the publisher. Similarly, passages in chapters 5 and 7 previously appeared in two articles. The first, "Between Taylorism and Dénatalité: Women Welfare Supervisors and the Boundaries of Difference in French Metalworking Factories, 1917–1935," in Dorothy O. Helly and Susan M. Reverby, eds., *Gendered Domains: Rethinking Public and Private in Women's History,* copyright © 1992 by Cornell University, is reprinted here with permission of the publisher. The second, "Les Marraines élues de la paix sociale? Les surintendantes d'usine et la rationalisation du travail en France, 1917–1935," appeared in *Mouvement Social,* no. 164 (July-September 1993): 53–76, and is reprinted here with the permission of the editor. Finally, material in chapter 8 previously appeared in two articles: "Industrial Decline, Rationalization, and Equal Pay: The Bedaux Strike at the Rover Automobile Company," *Social History* 15, no. 1 (January 1990): 45–73; and "Women Assemble," in *Social History* 17, no. 1 (January 1992): 150–55. I thank the editors for permission to use this material here.

Like most scholarly projects, this one emanates from concerns that are at once political and personal. I therefore dedicate the book to my grandmother Edna Wylie Gilman, whose own working days at the Midvale Steel and Ordnance may well have resembled those of the women described in these pages.

L.L.D.

Abbreviations

AEU	Amalgamated Engineering Union
AN	Archives Nationales, Paris
APP	Archives of the Prefecture of Police, Paris
ASE	Amalgamated Society of Engineers
BAS	*Bulletin de l'Association des Surintendantes*
BDIC	Bibliothèque de Documentation Internationale Contemporaine, Nanterre
BMD	Bibliothèque Marguerite Durand, Paris
BMT	*Bulletin du Ministère du Travail*
BSGF	*Bulletin de la Statistique Générale de la France*
BUG	*Bulletin des Usines de Guerre*
CDEEA	Coventry District Engineering Employers' Association
CGT	Confédération Générale du Travail
CNFF	Conseil National des Femmes Françaises
DLB	*Dilution of Labour Bulletin*
EEF	Engineering Employers' Federation
GIMM	Groupement des Industries Métallurgiques, Mécaniques et Connexes de la Région Parisienne
GIRP	Groupe des Industriels de la Région Parisienne
IWM	Imperial War Museum, London
MRC	Modern Records Centre, University of Warwick
NFWW	National Federation of Women Workers
NUVB	National Union of Vehicle Builders
NUWSS	National Union of Women's Suffrage Societies
OWD	Out-of-work donation
PP	Parliamentary Papers
PRO	Public Records Office, London

T&G	Transport and General Workers' Union
TUC	Trades Union Congress
UFCS	Union Féminine Civique et Sociale
UIMM	Union des Industries Métallurgiques et Minières

MANUFACTURING
INEQUALITY

Introduction

In the summer of 1917 a Scottish lady who was "prominently" engaged in welfare work among women munitions workers remarked that "the Kaiser handed British women an opportunity which their own fathers and brothers and mothers and husbands had ever denied them."[1] This book is an exploration of that opportunity, of the shape and extent of the new fields that opened to women in metalworking.[2] It proceeds from the observation that although World War I did not herald a new age of economic equality for women, as some middle-class feminists hopefully asserted, the departure of male factory workers for the front did create genuine opportunities for women in well-paid "men's" industries, particularly metalworking. Moreover, these gains did not entirely evaporate with the Armistice. The demand for arms production had permanently altered the technology and organization of the industry in ways suggesting that at least some women would continue to work in it after 1918.

But alongside the story of new opportunities for women stands a related narrative: a tale of employers who hastily restricted that opportunity even as they introduced women into their factories. And together, the two tell a third story, that of the origins of a new sexual division of labor within the metalworking industries of England and France. Thus, while the pressures

[1] "Fair Play for Women," *People's Journal*, 27 January 1917, in Imperial War Museum (hereafter IWM), Press Cuttings Box on Trade Unions, 1917.
[2] Metalworking embraces the iron and steel industries, machine building of all varieties, automobiles, bicycles, airplanes, electronics (lampmaking, radios, batteries, and the automobile accessory trades), and small metalworking (chain- and nailmaking, screw cutting, cutlery, hollow ware and file cutting). Some branches, notably autos and airplanes, include processes that involve working with fabric or wood, but these workers generally worked within the same integrated production process as those who machined parts or assembled the bodies.

I

of war production drew women across the boundary that had defined prewar metalworking as a world of men, the sexual division of labor did not simply crumble in 1914. Rather than seize the opportunity to cut labor costs by abandoning the principle of gender division, employers in both England and France chose to reconstitute that boundary within the labor process itself. Gender was thus transformed from a principle for excluding women into a basis for dividing labor within a newly fragmented production process.

Manufacturing Inequality is a comparative study of the complex historical process whereby metals employers in two distinct national and cultural settings first brought women into their factories, then reorganized work processes and managerial structures in efforts to accommodate women to the workplace and the workplace to this new source of labor. It begins in the spring of 1915, when the crisis of protracted industrial war drew thousands of women into the previously male world of metalworking. Pressed by the sharply spiraling demand for weapons at the very moment when much of their traditional workforce had left for the front, employers found themselves experimenting with new technologies of work even as they introduced female workers en masse. What is perhaps most significant here is how similarly French and British employers responded to this challenge. Despite differences in political culture, in industrial organization, even in level of industrial development, employers in both countries strove to assimilate the simultaneous transformations in technology and personnel by integrating a new distinction, that of gender, into an existing system of skill differences. These men reorganized productive hierarchies and allocated tasks between the sexes in accordance with their understanding of the ways in which male–female difference manifested itself on the assembly line or at the machine. The result was a structure of inequality that was taken to be both inevitable and economically rational, anchored in the solid bedrock of "natural" difference and articulated through a newly gendered language of job skill.

It is not entirely surprising that employers should have recast notions of skill to embrace distinctions of gender, for in early-twentieth-century Europe, workers' "innate" ability to perform different kinds of work (especially skilled work) was understood to be intimately linked to the structure of shop-floor authority. Together these technical and social aspects of skill formed the inherently gendered bases on which a rational factory order could be founded. And yet the very move by which employers sought to comprehend and contain the new female workforce—defining women as a particular kind of labor within an existing system of skill divisions—had the unintended effect of ensuring that wartime changes in the sexual division of labor would endure well past the Armistice. For if the wartime experience had linked women contingently with the new technologies, employers then cemented this connection more durably by enshrining it in the language of job skill.

Since the publication of Heidi Hartmann's ground-breaking essay "Capitalism, Patriarchy, and Job Segregation by Sex," scholars have tended to frame studies in women's labor history with an eye toward identifying either capitalism or patriarchy as the prime source of working women's oppression.[3] However, the quest to assign analytic priority to one system or the other carries the hidden presumption that capitalism and patriarchy are pure structures: despite their unsavory alliance against women workers, each has remained unpolluted by the other.[4] My research challenges this hermeneutic of segregation, for the difficulties posed by artificially separating patriarchy from capitalism emerge with especial force and clarity in the history of metalworking after 1914. Thus employers in both England and France constructed female labor as a distinct and significant category in relation to the newly fragmented labor process, classifying women workers in terms of their technical capacity to perform involved, rapid, or repetitive work, and not in terms of their domestic roles outside the factory gates. This is not to say that ideas about women and domesticity played no role in the restructuring of metalworking after 1914. On the contrary, the ideology of gender difference arrived in the war factory bearing the familiar message that whatever else women might do or be, they were above all domestic beings. Once inside the factory, however, the principle of sexual division became yet another party to broader struggles

[3] Heidi Hartmann, "Capitalism, Patriarchy, and Job Segregation by Sex," in Zillah Eisenstein, ed., *Capitalist Patriarchy and the Case for Socialist Feminism* (New York, 1979). See also Hartmann, "The Unhappy Marriage of Marxism and Feminism: Towards a More Progressive Union," in Lydia Sargent, ed., *Women and Revolution* (Boston, 1981), for a discussion of how patriarchy, defined as a system of social relations generated entirely outside the workplace, interacts with capitalism's need for a hierarchically structured labor force to produce a sexually segregated workforce. Sylvia Walby, *Patriarchy at Work* (Minneapolis, 1986), offers a thorough introduction to the scholarship on theories of patriarchy and women's work.

[4] Hartmann's "dual systems theory" has been criticized as logically inelegant (see, for example, Veronica Beechey, *Unequal Work* [London, 1987]). Yet feminist scholars have found it difficult to build useful theoretical alternatives, for, as Ava Baron put it, "how one forges such a synthesis, creates that integration, dissolves the hyphen between patriarchy and capitalism is not self-evident": Ava Baron, ed., *Work Engendered* (Ithaca, 1991), p. 18. Thus, in the early 1980s, labor historians did some excellent work within the dual systems model (Ruth Milkman's *Gender at Work* [Urbana, Ill., 1987] is especially noteworthy here). But instead of moving forward through the problematic choices that the capitalism-or-patriarchy antinomy offers, many women's historians shifted away from efforts to "gender" the language of class (and vice versa) and turned to poststructural explorations of language, identity, knowledge, and subjectivity. Consequently, much of the work done in women's labor history continued to be framed in the capitalism-vs.-patriarchy dualism. It is only in works published since 1990, notably Miriam Glucksmann's *Women Assemble: Women Workers and the New Industries in Interwar Britain* (London, 1990) and Sonya Rose's *Limited Livelihoods: Gender and Class in Nineteenth-Century England* (Berkeley, 1992), that scholars have begun to challenge this hermeneutic of segregation, though from a rather different perspective than the one adopted here. See Ava Baron's very useful Introduction to *Work Engendered* and Rose's *Limited Livelihoods*, chap. 1, for fuller discussions of these issues. On the "linguistic turn" in women's history, see Jean Wallach Scott, *Gender and the Politics of History* (New York, 1988).

over wages, shop-floor authority, and the redivision of labor. In the course of these struggles, gender acquired new, technical meanings that bore little direct relation to any broader discourses on women's and men's social roles in an extrinsic domestic order. Ideas about gender difference thus traveled in a technical idiom within the "hidden abode of production."[5] Here femaleness meant dexterity and speed within a "scientifically" ordered work process, whereas maleness signified a clumsier brute strength but also an exclusive capacity to gain mechanical understanding of the overall labor process, and so to rise to positions of technical and moral authority on the factory floor.

It is not sufficient, then, to assert that metals employers simply imported into their factories the gender divisions familiar outside the halls of production. Rather, these men's conviction that gender forms a salient, stable, and meaningful distinction in human character and capacity entered into and emerged transformed from the process whereby work was restructured during and after World War I. Far from constituting a set of ideas and practices outside the rational economic practice of capitalist employers, patriarchy was thus partially constitutive of that practice—an integral element in the system of technical and social relations that governed metals production after 1914. Treating patriarchy and capitalism as discrete systems simply hinders our ability to comprehend a structure of inequality that workers and employers alike understood and experienced as a seamless entity.

Employers' certainty that the labor process could not be reorganized without recourse to the principles of sexual division points to one deeper issue with which this book is centrally concerned: the meaning that gender difference acquired on the metals factory floor after 1914.[6] In the cultural context of early-twentieth-century Europe, none doubted that gender was relevant to ordering production, for sexual division stood as a foundational principle of social order. This division was so familiar as to be hardly articulable: women

[5] The term is Karl Marx's in *Capital*, trans. Ben Fowkes (London, 1976), 1:279. Marx's investigation of the social relations of production in the "hidden abode of production" proceeds from the premise that I also adopt, that the technical and social relations of labor are completely interdependent. Hence ideas about social difference, in this case gender, are less a brake on pure economic reason than a crucial element in the factory's productive hierarchies. See William Reddy, *The Rise of Market Culture* (Cambridge, 1984), for a very different approach to the problem of what market language does and does not tell us about the societies that have created and deployed such language.

[6] On gender as a category in historical analysis see Scott, *Gender*; Mary Poovey, *Uneven Developments* (Chicago, 1988); Jacquelyn Dowd Hall, "Disorderly Women: Gender and Labor Militancy in the Appalachian South," in Ellen DuBois and Vicki Ruiz, eds., *Unequal Sisters* (New York, 1990), 298–321; Denise Riley, *Am I That Name?* (Minneapolis, 1988); Barbara Taylor, *Eve and the New Jerusalem* (New York, 1981); Jane Flax, "Postmodernism and Gender Relations in Feminist Theory," *Signs* 12, no. 4 (1987):621–43; Sandra Harding, "Feminism, Science, and the Anti-Enlightenment Critiques," in Linda Nicholson, ed., *Feminism/Postmodernism* (New York, 1990); also Sandra Harding, "The Instability of the Analytic Categories of Feminist Theory," *Signs* 11 no. 4 (1986):645–64; and Rose, *Limited Livelihoods*.

belonged to the private, domestic, and notionally unpolitical sphere, men to the public world of work and politics. The realm of family stood outside the stream of history as something originary, natural, and given. It was ruled by the "eternal" rhythms of nature and enjoyed a certain moral purity, excluded as it was from the ethical dilemmas and violence that inevitably attend participation in the struggles of history. The public world of work was productive, social, conflictual, historical, and political. Productive (i.e., public) activity was the mode through which the human individual could develop and change. But it was a world of men; no matter how many women turned up in this realm, they were always seen to be on a pilgrimage back to the home. "A boy's career is bound up in his work," explained a British metals employer in 1918, "whereas the average woman looks on her work merely as an incident in her career . . . her work is not her life . . . she is merely spending her time usefully until marriage brings her the fulfillment of her life."[7]

Within the private world of home and family, labor was perceived as cyclical and repetitive, offering no scope for the progressive unfolding of character and intelligence. Further, such work was performed for love, not money, and was organized by domestic divisions of labor that were rooted in the "biologically" determined hierarchies of age and gender. Their apparent grounding in nature's design meant such divisions were not open to contest, and conflict in this narrow, definitionally harmonious little world, though endemic, was understood to be against nature.

Because metalworking was an almost exclusively male activity before 1914, it affords an excellent opportunity to explore what happens when the ideology of sexual division—an ideology that still took the form of a domestic–public division in the early twentieth century—is used to order relations in a realm where there are no domestic tasks per se. When the principle of sexual division was applied in the microcosm of the metals factory, those managers who applied it, and those workers who had to live by it, wrangled over the placement of the line separating men's from women's work. But the existence of the line itself stood largely unchallenged. Rarely did either party to the labor–capital polarity ever question the presumption that the process of producing metal parts embraced tasks that were, a priori, the province of male versus female labor. The idea of sexual division as a fundamental distinction in social space and human character thus exerted a powerful influence over employers' understanding of women as labor power.

After 1914, the conviction that gender difference defined crucial distinctions in technical capacity emerged with sudden, sharp force in the metalworking

---

[7] Testimony of Alfred Herbert, machine-tool manufacturer of Coventry, PP 1919, Cmd. 167, *Appendices of Evidence to the Report of the Committee on Women in Industry*, pp. 54–55.

factories of England and France. In part, this conviction rose out of the circumstances of war, which juxtaposed dramatic changes in the technology and organization of work with the sudden influx of women into this quintessentially male trade. More specifically, the army's insatiable demand for weapons forced employers in both nations to replace the old craft methods and technologies with a more mass-production organization of work, grounded in the "rationalization"—that is, the subdivision, routinization, and mechanization—of formerly skilled jobs. At the same time, war destroyed the old sexual division of labor, pressing thousands of women upon an industry that had hitherto all but excluded them. The new technical division of labor was thus expressed as a sexual division of labor from its inception.

What is most significant here is the way in which a discourse on gender difference intersected with the wartime process of industrial rationalization. Indeed, it is precisely in the convergence of gender ideology with that rationalization process that the distinctiveness of this investigation lies. After all, the nineteenth century had seen significant transformations in the sexual division of labor in several major industries.[8] But it was in the wartime and postwar metalworking trades, the machine-building industries that lie at the very heart of the modern economy, that shifts in the gender division of labor overlapped with the structural transformation that contemporaries termed the "rationalization" of industry. Hence, as women poured into the war factories, employers in both nations linked their advent directly to the concomitant redivision of labor, drawing upon ideas about sexual difference in an effort to make sense of the rapid changes in technology that the crisis in war production had forced upon them. The new workers soon became inseparable from jobs requiring speed and monotonous repetition. Once in place, the connection of women to fragmented repetitive work was to enjoy a long life in the metalworking industry.

After 1914, then, employers in both England and France articulated their conviction that gender signifies particular technical abilities in the context of rapid changes in the organization of work. At each point where gender ideology met with the process of industrial rationalization, new sexual divisions of labor arose, divisions invested with a highly technical conception of the meaning of gender difference. What is one to make of employers' steadfast

[8] See Rose, *Limited Livelihoods*, for an especially illuminating discussion of the carpet weaving and stocking knitting trades in mid-Victorian Britain. On the broader issue of the industrial transformation of work in the nineteenth century, see Patrick Joyce, *Work, Society, and Politics: The Culture of the Factory in Later Victorian England* (New Brunswick, N.J., 1980); also Patrick Joyce, ed., *The Historical Meanings of Work* (Cambridge, 1987); Elinor Accampo, *Industrialization, Family Life, and Class Relations* (Berkeley, 1989); Patricia Hilden, *Working Women and Socialist Politics in France, 1880–1914* (Oxford, 1986); William Rosenberg, "The Democratization of Russia's Railroads in 1917," in James Cronin and Carmen Siriani, eds., *Work, Community, and Power* (Philadelphia, 1983).

loyalty to the principle of sexual division in the context of war, where such divisions might have been dispensed with altogether? Neoclassical models, in which capitalist rationality is understood as socially neutral, driven solely by the pursuit of profit, compel one of two conclusions: either cheap female labor imposed additional "social" costs that male labor did not (separate washrooms, perhaps additional supervisors), and restricting women's employment was therefore a rational (i.e., cost-efficient) solution; or discrimination against cheap labor represented a failure of managerial reason.[9]

This book challenges the first proposition by observing that women's rate of employment in metalworking tripled, even quadrupled their prewar level of participation between 1914 and 1939. And this expansion does not simply reflect the short-term impact of war; on the contrary, after the sharp fluctuations of wartime mobilization and postwar demobilization, the percentage of women metalworkers in both countries settled around 10 percent—about double their prewar rate of 5 to 6 percent—and then proceeded to expand steadily, reaching some 15 to 20 percent by 1939.[10] The significant expansion in women's peacetime employment suggests that employers' labor strategies were far more complex than the blanket presumption of additional overhead charges can encompass, that an expanding conception of the specific abilities and value of women as metalworkers outweighed any possible outlays on separate changing rooms or toilet facilities.

And what of the alternative explanation, that employers' ability to recognize the benefits of cheap female labor were filtered by the perceptual veil of their attachment to a gender-divided universe? Certainly their allegiance to the notion that women and men constitute qualitatively distinct categories of labor shaped and ultimately limited their deployment of cheap female labor. But as the case of metalworking in the early twentieth century reveals, it is ultimately less helpful to view ideas about gender difference as a baffling screen separating capitalist reason from a firm and knowable reality than to see such ideas as an integral aspect of employers' economic reasoning. Hence the revised sexual divisions of labor and newly gendered understanding of job skill that emerged after 1914 were not solely the products of employers' distorted and overly narrow vision of women's capacity for this kind of work, although such visions did play a part. Rather, the rationalization of the labor

---

[9] Neoclassical models (e.g., human capital theories) and their radical critiques (e.g., theories about split or segmented labor markets) all understand the rationality of economic man (*sic*) as rigorously distinguishing pure material interest from social ideas; the latter can never be grasped as anything other than a troubling distortion of the former. For an important statement of the neoclassical position, see Gary Becker, *Human Capital: A Theoretical and Empirical Analysis with Special Reference to Education*, 2d ed. (New York, 1975). See also Becker's *Economics of Discrimination* (Chicago, 1971) and *Economic Analysis of the Family* (Dublin, 1986).

[10] See Laura Lee Downs, "Women in Industry, 1914–1939: The Employers' Perspective" (Ph.D. thesis, Columbia University, 1987).

process represented a deep structural shift in the nature of capital investment, away from traditional forms of skill and the apprenticeship of workers and toward investments in technology and equipment. This structural transformation could be realized only through negotiation and struggle with skilled craftsmen, whose expertise was still required to effect and institutionalize these changes but whose shop-floor power and position were nonetheless put at risk by the fragmentation and deskilling of work that rationalization entailed. The new gender division of labor is thus more usefully understood as the outcome of bitter struggles with these men over wages, skill, labor deployment, and the nature of shop-floor authority; of conflicts over an entire rationalization process of which women were both the harbingers and the avatars. In each of these struggles, perceptions of gender difference played an integral part.

In the context of early-twentieth-century metalworking, then, ideas about social difference, in this case differences of gender, were partly constitutive of social (i.e., productive) order in the factory. Far from obstructing the industrialist's clear perception of his own best interest, such ideas formed an integral aspect of that capitalist rationality. The centrality of social ideas to employers' reasoning about industrial production is reflected in the vocabulary of social being, difference, and social order being used to render intelligible the carefully articulated and highly differentiated hierarchies that these men implanted and reconfigured on the factory floor. This vocabulary is perhaps best characterized as Aristotelian, in the sense that it firmly links social being to social order, in this case to the productive order in the factory.[11] Such Aristotelian language was by no means the sole idiom employed in interwar metals factories, for employers drew equally on the language of political economy—a language of efficiency and of justice in the distribution of material goods: capital, wages, resources, labor. But the language of political economy is neutral on the issue of who fills what slots in the horizontal division of labor and in the vertical hierarchy of command. It is a language of ordered desires emerging from efficiency, an ideal first limned in Adam Smith's *Wealth of Nations*. It is an ideal that employers found hopelessly inadequate when it came to binding individual women and men (and children) to the rigors of factory discipline and the narrow confines of a rigid division of labor. Order did not emerge spontaneously from efficiency; it had to be created, then policed.

In characterizing the social language of factory order as Aristotelian, I do

[11] On the broad currency that Aristotelian conceptions of social being and social order enjoyed in modern Europe, see Maryanne Cline Horowitz, "Aristotle and Woman," *Journal of the History of Biology* 9 (Fall 1976):183–213; Thomas Laqueur, *Making Sex* (Cambridge, 1990); Georges Duby, *The Three Orders*, trans. Arthur Goldhammer (Chicago, 1980).

not seek to make an argument in the realm of the history of ideas, about particular intellectual influences or their transmission over time. On the contrary, what is at issue here is the deeper, less self-conscious level of *mentalités*, of ways of conceptualizing society that are so familiar as to be hardly articulable. I use the term "Aristotelian," therefore, in order to identify a particular and pervasive way of reasoning about the relationship between social order and social being, and to point to the presence of this hierarchical social logic at the very heart of the capitalist enterprise.[12] Aristotle believed that social being (wife, child, artisan, slave, free man, aristocrat) inevitably implies differences in both the quality and the degree of productive and rational capacity appertaining to each category. This conviction then provided the rationale for creating social order through hierarchy. This kind of approach to the problem of welding a coherent and unified order out of diverse human materials appealed to employers, who in the early twentieth century believed that strict hierarchical control was the essential condition of efficient factory production. In the Aristotelian vocabulary, which links social being to productive capacity, employers found a language of hierarchy and command that political economy does not possess on its own, a language of social order and power that allowed them to organize and speak directly about what actually happened in the vertically ordered world of factory production.[13]

The two languages—economic and political, efficiency and order—converged in a number of places, but above all in the vocabulary of skill, which endowed creatures of differentiated social being (male and female, old and young, native-born and colonial) with differential status in the capitalist idiom of efficiency. Skill translated differentiated social beings into differentiated productive beings, enabling employers to construct and reconstruct gender as a meaningful category on the factory floor.

The language of skill was, among other things, a language that sought to grasp the distinction between human activity (voluntary, nonrepetitive, progressive) and the repetitive, involuntary movement of machines. In the shifting discourse on job skill, one can hear employers using the notion of "skill differentials" to discuss the meaning of social difference, and especially sexual difference on the factory floor, for in the factory sexual difference was perceived as articulated in a hierarchically ordered range of workers' attainments, with women at the lower end and men at the higher end of that

---

[12] Further, I suggest that it was this kind of hierarchical social logic, as opposed to a more egalitarian form (Rousseauean or Hobbesian, for example), that underwrote the creation and recasting of socioproductive orders on the factory floor in early-twentieth-century Europe.

[13] In other words, political economy is silent on its own need for an Aristotle-like language of social being, productive capacity, and vertical control. Like any other ideology, political economy mystifies its own true (Aristotelian) predicate—its dependence on a vocabulary of social power that the language of market encounters does not on its own make visible.

hierarchy. Discrimination was thus an integral aspect of order in the "hidden abode of production." It was not an irrational epiphenomenon or periodic failure in an otherwise socially neutral system. Rather, it was constitutive of a productive system built in part on hierarchical distinctions and inequalities among workers.

But this book does not concentrate exclusively on discrimination. In a larger sense, it is about the genesis of the modern factory in the great shift from a craft-based order to a mass-production system.[14] It is about the centrality of women workers and ideas about gender to the construction of this modern, "rational" factory world. In this world, where the idea of job skill translated broad ideas of what it means to be human (vs. animal or machine) into specific, hierarchically ordered technical divisions on the shop floor, the technical and ontological orders overlapped. In other words, a highly conservative language of social being and social order, a language that I believe is fundamentally Aristotelian in origin, coexisted with the more socially neutral language of political economy. As we will see, the numeric logic of the latter acquired social meaning and a discriminatory twist in the case of women. By the same token, the moral reasoning of the language of social being/social order drew added force and authority from the aura of mathematical certainty surrounding the system of political economy.[15] But the two structures did not always overlap perfectly, or rather, their coincidence was easily disrupted. As we will see, wartime rationalization and employers' concomitant gendering of skill laid bare the fragility of their association, dissociating technical skill from moral authority in the case of women workers, and so generating a powerfully felt need for gender-specific managerial interventions, such as the deployment of middle-class women welfare supervisors.

Here, in the arena of labor discipline, lies another axis along which to

---

[14] Anson Rabinbach also argues in *The Human Motor* (Berkeley, 1992) that the rationalization of work at the turn of the twentieth century represents the birth of the modern factory. Here the term "modern" is understood to entail the skilled male worker's diminishing significance, at least in direct production work, balanced by the growing importance of a more detailed division of labor, of unskilled and female workers, and of techniques of social rationalization, intended to monitor and control the unskilled mass more effectively.

[15] Aristotelian rationality (i.e., practical reason) is a way of thinking that links social being with social order so that individuals and the collectivity may realize the good life. Under market capitalism, rationality shifts, becomes the singular, calculating, numeric reason of profit and advantage; a single measuring stick along which the many and different are arrayed and treated as commensurable with respect to the one end: profit. I contend that the old Aristotelian way of reasoning, in which the social is linked to the material, still underlay the new when it came to arranging productive hierarchies in the factory. See Martha Nussbaum, "The Discernment of Perception: An Aristotelian Conception of Private and Public Rationality," in *Love's Knowledge* (Oxford, 1990), 54–105; and Horowitz, "Aristotle and Woman." See also Alisdair MacIntyre, *After Virtue* (South Bend, Ind., 1981); also MacIntyre, *Whose Justice, Which Rationality?* (New York, 1988).

examine the meaning that gender difference held in the early-twentieth-century workplace. Chapters 4, 5, and 7 explore the problems raised by the arrival of persons whom employers understood as not fully rational, and hence lacking an internal principle of self-control. Incidentally, most male workers were also seen as lacking in restraint; the fully skilled craftsman was the only person on the shop floor who escaped the charge. But the indiscipline of working-class women was different from that of working-class men, and demanded different solutions. By the interwar period, employers in both nations had decided that the answer lay in chaining women to a carefully articulated structure of repetitive work. In England, the combination of assembly lines and the Bedaux time-motion management system formed a structure of control that was aimed specifically at women, tailored to their perceived strengths and liabilities. French employers elaborated similar technical structures, all related to the international development of mass production. But French businessmen located the new techniques and technology in relations of authority that had been reshaped by the addition of middle-class women to the managerial hierarchy—women brought in to oversee the health, productivity, and discipline of the new female workforce.

In every respect—deployment, job opportunities, training, wages, and the particular managerial structures within which they were expected to work—employers' broader treatment of women was grounded in the conviction that male–female differences are stable and knowable, and once discerned, have practical relevance for shaping both technical/sexual divisions of labor and vertical relations of authority on the factory floor. At the same time, however, the way employers thought about gender—as a series of noncommensurable polar oppositions (male–female, rational–emotional, initiative–imitative)—created problems for the replication of that stable productive order. Whenever employers tried to pin gender difference to a particular set of oppositions, and so to fix that difference in place, another equally cherished but not necessarily congruent pair would surface and unsettle the first (for example: working-class women are greedy wage hounds who reject a quiet home life; women are repetitive workers by their very domestic "nature"). This messy jostling of ideas about women produced the uncomfortable sense that sexual divisions were perpetually at the edge of breaking down. Hence, while employers could use the mobility of sexual division to their own advantage by replacing expensive or querulous men with cheap, docile women, such substitutions did not necessarily make the industrialists any happier about the overall condition that made them possible. It was a condition in which sexual division was treated as a foundational principle of production and of shop-floor order. Yet that division shifted over time and from place to place in a way that suggested that this fundamental fact of life, bedrock of a factory pecking order, might not be natural and immutable, but rather a construction that required constant reinforcement if it was to endure. As we shall see, employers were prepared to expend a great deal of effort and energy to ensure that it did.

When I first conceived this project, I decided to conduct the research on a comparative basis. This decision grew out of my sense that a phenomenon that transcends national boundaries, such as gender-based job discrimination, should be studied comparatively, so that one might learn something of its operation in different cultural and political contexts. Wartime and interwar France and Britain present a layering of similarity and difference that invites comparative exploration of the interpenetration of productive and social orders in the modern industrial economy. The common pressures of war, mobilization, and industrial rationalization disrupted the prewar productive orders in these two western and capitalist nations, one more industrially advanced than the other. As a result, the core industries that made up the metalworking trades—machine building, iron and steel, automobiles, electronics—were pressed in remarkably similar directions: away from smaller-scale and craft-based systems toward a more fragmented organization geared to mass production; away from skilled and male labor toward less experienced and female labor. In both nations, employers interpreted this dual shift in light of ideas about gender difference, among other things, and reorganized the labor process accordingly. This convergence of understandings produced some similar developments, notably in the gendered language of job skill that arose after 1914. But the reorganization worked itself out in nationally specific ways as well—in the arena of labor management technique, for instance.

Manufacturing Inequality thus adopts a comparative perspective in order to suggest how national culture and differences in state structures defined distinctive routes to what were, in many important respects, rather similar outcomes. The sources I have consulted reflect the interplay of similarity and difference that binds these two national histories over the period 1914–39. Of primary importance are the archives of the employers' organizations for the metalworking industries of France and Britain: the Engineering Employers' Federation (EEF) in Britain and the Union des Industries Métallurgiques et Minières (UIMM) in France. The content and organization of these archives underscore characteristic differences in the structure of industrial authority and in the relative power of trade unions in the two countries. Britain's EEF has organized its records around a full set of verbatim transcripts from industrywide collective bargaining sessions, running continuously from the turn of the century forward. French metals employers, by contrast, generally refused to bargain collectively with their workers, and before the great sit-down strikes of June 1936, the *syndicats* (trade unions) rarely were strong enough to force them to the table.[16] On the other hand, French employers were consistently more concerned with workers' lives outside the factory gates than were their British colleagues. Consequently, both the UIMM and its Paris affiliate (the Groupement des Industries Métallurgiques, Mécaniques et Connexes de la Région Parisienne, or GIMM) gathered and exchanged information on various welfarist and especially pro-natalist provisions. Their allocations and advice, readily dispensed at the works level, were understood to be consonant both with worker pacification and with what many employers saw to be the factory's broader social function: controlling labor while meeting workers' "just" needs.[17]

In their effort to control labor rather than bargain with it, French employers were amply assisted by the local police, who kept close watch on all leftist and syndicalist activity. The book rounds out its account of worker activism and employer repression by drawing on police records, and especially on reports by individuals paid to spy at leftist meetings. These reports are quite rich, as police and paid spies alike took careful note of who attended these meetings, paying particular attention to the women present. They also kept track of who spoke, and sometimes reproduced long passages from the impassioned and often eloquent speeches, always noting the gestures (fist-waving or foot-stamping) and the bravos or hisses with which such oratory was greeted.

Finally, the book develops an important subtheme in its discussion of welfare supervision as a gender-specific form of labor management. Again, the organization of the archives reflects a critical dimension of this national comparison, for welfare supervision disappeared from British metalworking factories soon after the Armistice, whereas it spread rapidly across the interwar

---

[16] The years 1917–22 form the main exception here, when the war government sought to temper rising labor militancy in the munitions plants by urging defense contractors to negotiate with their workers. To this end, Minister of Armaments Albert Thomas instituted a "shop-floor delegate" (i.e., shop steward) system in the war factories, and offered government arbitration for collective bargaining sessions. Neither institution survived the war, for as one representative of heavy industry put it, "the institution of shop-floor delegates threatens France with rule by the Soviets": Archives Nationales (hereafter AN), F7, 13366, Comité des Forges to Ministre de l'Armement, quoted in a police spy report, "Les Délégués d'atelier," Paris, 16 May 1918, p. 4. Between June 1919 and June 1936, the UIMM's Paris local steadfastly refused to bargain collectively with its employees.

[17] Like their British counterparts, the UIMM and GIMM collected detailed information on wage levels, strike activity, and worker "morale." The information was used not to inform collective bargaining sessions but rather to allow these associations to monitor labor militancy and keep regional wage levels as low and as uniform as possible. The *groupement* strategy thus concentrated employers' power against organized labor while preserving the autonomy of individual industrialists. In addition, these associations allowed member firms to pool resources and coordinate paternalistic policies from about 1920 on through a system of regional *caisses*, into which individual firms paid and from which they could then draw funds for the various allocations disbursed. See Downs, "Women in Industry," pp. 563–66, for details.

landscape of France. Accordingly, the French sources can be found in the library of an ongoing institution, the Ecole des Surintendantes d'Usine in Paris, which still trains women for factory-based social work and supervision. The material gathered there reflects this institutional rooting of welfare management in France: a nearly complete run of the *Bulletin de l'Association des Surintendantes*, consisting largely of reports from *surintendantes* on their work in the factories, and a thick dossier of the journals that students kept during their factory *stages*.[18] The material on welfare discipline from British factories, on the other hand, reflects the temporary nature of this strategy in Britain, for it is mixed in with the records and memoirs of other wartime birds of passage—reports of charity work and bourgeois guidance that close definitively in 1919–20, and are housed among the arcana of war in London's Imperial War Museum.

Beyond underlining crucial similarities in the structures governing women's work, then, comparison also permits the exploration of difference, as one national history can be used to interrogate the other. Hence the argument in *Manufacturing Inequality* moves on two levels, emphasizing fundamental similarities in the way gender intersected with structural transformations in the labor process while exploring significant differences in the way this multivalent process unfolded in the two national contexts. The comparison reminds us of the relevance of particular human cultures in the shaping of broader historical transformations—in this case, the gendered genesis of the modern metalworking factory.

---

[18] Students at the school were required to complete a two-to-four-week stint as an ordinary factory worker (the *stage d'usine*) before they could graduate to the job of *surintendante d'usine*. Their experiences are explored in chap. 7.

CHAPTER I

War and the
Rationalization of Work

In March 1918, one Dr. Clothilde Mulon, having been taken around Citroën's new Javel plant on a publicity tour by the management, published her impressions:

First of all to where they make the shell casings. It's an enormous hall with twenty four presses, each surrounded by black demons, male and female, who wield shells of incandescent steel in the flame. . . . In the ovenlike heat, one man pulls a reddened bar from the flame and carries it in a vise over to a woman, who with a single gesture pierces the bar with a powerful awl, as one might plunge a finger into soft clay. Showers of sparks burst forth and catch on the screens. Three seconds pass and the pierced shell tumbles from the vise, hollowed out, as they say. A man lifts it up with long pincers; it is ready to be tempered. He lays it on a moving walkway that carries it to another shop. Twenty-four teams make these same rhythmic movements around twenty-four machines, tongues of flame flare and spread throughout the vast hall . . . a vision of war. . . .

We then move on to see them making shrapnel. At the end of one shop, the lead comes in a single mass; at the other end, it leaves as finished ball bearings. Machines run by women roll, stretch, draw, and wind the lead into wire on enormous bobbins, then cut the wire into ball bearings, which are immediately polished. . . . The ball bearings are now ready to play their part in the killing. . . . Women riding little electric carts carry the ball bearings, all boxed up, to the shop where the shells are filled. . . .

Another shop . . . immense like a railway station, runs on into another great hall, this one with a second story, raised up like a stage, where trains circulate! Four thousand women work in this remarkable workshop, built in six weeks on a site where less than a year ago thirty-eight houses stood. Here in the bustling din . . . workers make the pointed nose cones for the shells, thread the screws, band the shells, etc. The hollowed shell case arrives at one end of the hall, at the other it is finished, inspected, filled with shrapnel of ball bearings, painted red, wrapped, and finally loaded onto a wagon. Great bays separate the rows of machines into avenues, each of those avenues devoted to a different operation, a different type of machine. . . . Such colossal dimensions, the endless bays, the noise, the order, the electric carts, run so swiftly and adroitly by these women, all this contributes to a growing sense of lavishness and wonder.[1]

The vast and streamlined spaces of Citroën's brand-new shell factory had come to represent the apotheosis of wartime efforts to bring modern American methods for rationalizing both space and time to industrial production in France. Observers were enchanted by the very size of new factories like the one on the quai Javel, by their brightly lit interiors, and above all by the organization of these factories, with their continuous flow of materials and finished goods, moved by conveyor belts and electric carts toward a single, culminating point, where the final product was assembled, inspected, and prepared for its departure from the factory. Such carefully laid-out plants presented an enormous contrast to the cramped and ill-lit workshops of prewar England and France, where skilled craftsmen worked according to schedules determined by their own sense of a job, aided by laborers and apprentices rather than semi-automatic machinery. Under the old craft-based division of labor, each shop within a factory performed its part of the job, then sent the piece along to the factory storeroom—none of the tightly integrated sequential flows that Mulon so admired at Citroën.

Mulon's account reminds us that women workers were central to the wartime modernization of industry. By the same token, that process of industrial modernization, variously termed rationalization, Taylorism, and the scientific reorganization of labor, powerfully shaped the industrial work that women performed during and after World War I.[2] In fact, industrial rationalization, as an ideology of progress and as a concrete set of rules for transforming the labor process, was the single, crucial thread winding through women's experience in the wartime and postwar metals factories of France and Britain. Because of the tight connection that developed between female labor and the deskilled, machine-driven labor of the fully rationalized factory, one must begin by exploring the various guises in which Taylorist ideas moved across the Atlantic before 1914.

In the decade before the war, industrialists in both England and France

[1] Clothilde Mulon, "Une Visite à l'usine de guerre Citroën," *La Française*, 2 March 1918.
[2] As Simone Weil observes, the terms "Taylorism," "rationalization," and "scientific organization of labor" were used interchangeably "to characterize the current industrial regime and the changes introduced in the organization of labor": *La Condition ouvrière* (Paris, 1951), p. 296. See also George Humphreys, *Taylorism in France, 1914–1920* (Norman, Okla., 1984); Anson Rabinbach, *The Human Motor* (Berkeley, 1992).

had heard a great deal about the economic miracles that Taylorist systems had wrought on the American factory floor. But European employers remained ambivalent about the American example, unconvinced that it was entirely relevant to European industry.[3] For many European employers, Frederick Taylor's "scientific organization of labor" seemed above all an accommodation to the peculiarities of the United States. The intense and detailed division of labor, the extensive use of automatic machinery, the extraordinary leap forward in productivity that attended the rationalization and deskilling of labor— these were appropriate to a nation that had comparatively few skilled workers and an abundant and polyglot horde of unskilled workers, a nation whose potentially vast home market could absorb the enormous output generated by factories such as Henry Ford's.

But Europe was different. Markets here were narrower, more oriented toward customized and luxury production, and workers were, accordingly, more skilled than their American counterparts. American entrepreneurs had had to create an industrial base from whole cloth, relying on work systems such as Taylor's in order to do so, but European industrialists had scant need for such extreme measures. After all, the French and British metalworking factories had developed from densely rooted structures of craft-based and artisanal production.[4] Craft was not simply a way to organize machinery and men; it was also a structure of authority, a shop-floor hierarchy in which the fully skilled policed both the work and the comportment of the less skilled. It was not at all clear to most industrialists why one should upset this still profitable and largely self-regulating structure to introduce a costly and unfamiliar work system designed around automatic machinery, unskilled labor, and intensive managerial supervision.

As an ideal type, the fully rationalized factory stood in stark contrast to the craft-centered workshop of the nineteenth century. Under a craft-based productive regime, skilled men planned and executed all the tasks of production in the order that seemed most reasonable to them. Starting with a blueprint (or sometimes drafting the design himself), the craftsman produced each part, using tools of his own making, then filed the individual pieces until they fitted smoothly together. He accomplished each job with little interference from the boss and with the assistance of apprentices and a few unskilled laborers, who cleaned equipment, fetched materials, and helped with the lifting of heavy pieces. The skilled craftsman was likely to work in

[3] Aimée Moutet, "Le Patronat Français et le système Taylor avant 1914," *Mouvement Social*, no. 93 (October–December 1976), pp. 15–49; and Wayne Lewchuk, "Fordism and the British Motor Car Employer, 1896–1932," in Howard Gospel and Craig Littler, eds., *Managerial Strategies and Industrial Relations* (London, 1983), are just two in the legion of works that stress how slowly Taylorism penetrated European managerial practice before 1914.

[4] Craig Littler, *The Development of the Labour Process in Capitalist Societies* (London, 1982).

a small shop, where the layout of equipment reflected no planned productive flow. Within this space he could move about freely, from one machine to another, to his toolbox and then to the fitting bench and back again to the first machine, all according to a logic of the job that he himself determined and by the dictates of his own rhythms. Employers might object to the craftsman's broad discretion over the pace and organization of work, but so long as engineering firms produced so wide a variety of goods, each essentially custom-made, the skilled man remained the indispensable heart of production.

Industrial rationalization was to change all that. Through a detailed subdivision of labor, employers gradually broke down the craftsman's complex task, standardizing parts and mechanizing the various operations so that each individual phase of the formerly skilled job could be performed by cheaper, unskilled labor. These less skilled production workers no longer followed a job through to completion but rather specialized on some narrow aspect of the task; the skilled task of filing and fitting together nonstandard parts, for example, gave way to the less skilled job of simply assembling machine-made pieces of standard dimensions. Those skilled men who remained on the floor no longer produced goods but repaired and regulated the machines of less skilled machine operators. As the variety of work to which any individual was exposed narrowed, managerial control over the labor process expanded. This shift in control, from worker to manager, is reflected in the layout of machine rooms and assembly halls in a modern, rationally ordered factory such as Citroën's. Here the reintegration and ordering of subdivided tasks into a single productive flow lay not with the individual worker but with managerial planners, who determined the order in which these tasks were to be performed and the time necessary to execute each of them.

Since the end of the nineteenth century, French and British employers had been slowly introducing individual Taylorist strategies, intended to reduce labor costs while curbing the autonomy of skilled men. By subdividing and mechanizing entire portions of the labor process, introducing less skilled men and even women to the new jobs, substituting payment by results for a straight hourly rate, and tightening shop-floor supervision, employers sought to achieve a more intensive work effort and to enhance their direct control over the use of time and materials on the shop floor.[5]

[5] On deskilling in prewar France, see Humphreys, *Taylorism in France;* Bernard Moss, *The Origins of the French Labor Movement: The Socialism of Skilled Workers* (Berkeley, 1976); Patrick Fridenson, "France–Etats-Unis: Genèse de l'usine nouvelle," *Recherches,* nos. 32/33 (September 1978); Peter Stearns, *Paths to Authority: The Middle Class and the Industrial Labor Force in France, 1820–1848* (Urbana, Ill., 1978); and Lenard R. Berlanstein, *The Working People of Paris, 1871–1914* (Baltimore, 1984). For England, see Jeffery Haydu, *Between Craft and Class* (New Haven, 1990); Littler, *Development of the Labour Process;* Charles More, *Skill and the English Working Class, 1870–1914* (London, 1980); and Jonathan Zeitlin, "Craft Control and the Division

This multivalent process of gradual transformation had proceeded unevenly across the prewar industrial landscape. Here the newer, consumer-goods sectors (automobiles, bicycles, electrical goods) always led the way, thanks to their larger, more standardized product markets. By 1914 the French and British metals industries hovered somewhere between fidelity to the old-fashioned craft organization and a cautious turning toward the new mechanized work systems imported from America. The distinction between the old methods and the new cut across the industrial landscape in various ways. In France, industry was sharply bifurcated. All across Paris, small shops, organized more or less along craft lines, continued to function in the shadow of enormous modern plants where employers were experimenting with serial production techniques.[6] Here, then, the division between the old ways and the new largely coincided with the distinction between large and small. It was, after all, more cost effective for the large employer to switch over to mass production; economies of scale could hardly affect workshops with only ten to twenty employees. By contrast, it was the medium-sized firm that dominated the British industrial landscape. In such factories, an employer might well have subdivided and mechanized some phases of the labor process, but the nature of British markets (small-batch, customized building) and organized resistance by skilled men to such incursions on their craft ensured that the new "American" techniques were generally introduced in partial and piecemeal forms only.

The idea of craft thus remained the industrial center of gravity in prewar Europe; any "Taylorization" proceeded around the edges of this craft-based order. This caution reflected employers' conceptions of good order and profitability as much as skilled men's dogged refusal of Taylor's "brutal and inhuman" system.[7] Employers' explicit valuing of craft skill stands as one of the most peculiar yet significant features of the rationalization process in this

---

of Labour: Engineers and Compositors in Britain, 1890–1930" (Ph.D. thesis, University of Warwick, 1981).

[6] Aimée Moutet emphasizes the importance of small shops in French metalworking, and their retarding effect on Taylorism's conquest of the industry: "Patrons de progrès ou patrons de combat?" *Recherches*, nos. 32–33 (1978), p. 449. During the war, some of these small shops closed their doors while others survived by subcontracting to larger firms. Even in 1921, then, after a war that encouraged bigness and spelled the death of many a small firm, 91.6 percent of all metals factories in the Paris region employed fewer than twenty persons. By the same token, over 25% of the labor force was employed in 0.5% of the factories, concentrating tremendous power in the hands of a few large industrialists (Renault, Citroën, et al.). See Bertrand Abhervé, "La Grève des métallurgistes parisiens de juin 1919" (mémoire de maîtrise, Université de Paris VIII, 1973), p. 36.

[7] The term is from Alphonse Merrheim, head of the Fédération des Métaux, from his essay on the evils of Taylorism published hard on the heels of an anti-Taylor strike at Renault: "Le Système Taylor," *La Vie Ouvrière*, pt. 1, 20 February 1913, pp. 210–26, and pt. 2, 5 March 1913, pp. 298–309.

period. Even as these men inaugurated the kinds of systematic changes that spelled the final destruction of craftwork in the metalworking factory, they continued to vaunt the skill of craftsmen, "the most deeply appreciated artisans in engineering."[8] This was more than mere snake oil in the face of skilled men's resistance to the wholesale overturning of custom, wages, and work loads in their trade. On the one hand, Taylor's scientific reorganization of labor permitted employers to cheapen the labor process, leveling skills by the fragmentation and mechanization of formerly complex tasks. On the other hand, Taylorism also reduced the value of labor, for within a deskilled labor process, labor itself was deskilled and degraded, the technical capacities of the skilled man replaced by mere speed and manual dexterity on the part of unskilled, unknowing operatives.

The progress of Taylorism/rationalization in prewar metalworking was hindered not only by managers' ambivalence but also by the resistance of organized craftsmen, who at first were quite hostile to Taylor's system of "scientific slavery." In the end, the British resisted rationalization more successfully than the French, in part because the entire craft-based system was already eroding in antebellum France. Not that French industrialists had dispensed with the need for skilled labor; on the contrary, from the 1890s on through the interwar period, employers' eternal complaint was that skilled men were in such short supply. Yet well before the outbreak of war, the industry as a whole was moving away from a purely craft-based labor process, pressed in part by the lack of skilled workers.[9] Apprenticeships in France were thus comparatively brief, lasting no more than two to three years (in contrast to five or six in Britain). Moreover, the selection and training of apprentices, still controlled by skilled craftsmen in Britain, had shifted into the hands of employers and state officials in France. By 1914 the French worker's route to advancement ran through either employer-controlled programs or the municipal technical schools, where local employers often wielded decisive influence.[10]

[8] Georges Calmès, "Note sur l'utilisation de la main-d'oeuvre féminine," *Bulletin des Usines de Guerre* (hereafter *BUG*), 31 July 1916, p. 112. Bernard Moss writes of the contradictory pulls in French managers' fin-de-siècle strategies: "The structural crisis [which he locates at the turn of the century] was defined in terms of two opposite features, the proletarianization of skilled workers and the survival of skill": *Origins of the French Labor Movement*, p. 159.

[9] Peter Stearns notes that the "reduction of the responsibilities of skilled workers, substituting rules and foremen, was attempted earlier [in France] than in England or the United States in terms of the stage of industrialization involved": *Paths to Authority*, p. 87; and Patrick Fridenson locates the struggle for control of the work process in France between 1880 and 1920: "France–Etats-Unis," p. 387. On the survival of craft control in Britain see Zeitlin, "Craft Control"; Haydu, *Between Craft and Class;* Gospel and Littler, *Managerial Strategies;* Littler, *Development of the Labour Process;* More, *Skill and the English Working Class;* and G.D.H. Cole, *Trade Unionism and Munitions* (Oxford, 1923).

[10] PP 1915, Cd. 8187, *Report on the Output of Munitions in France* (December 1915), p. 6. In fact, the report asserts that French industry did not appear to have a recognized apprenticeship system "except in the higher branches of the engineering trade. . . . Labour is being specialised

The steady erosion of craft control in France sharply narrowed the base from which labor could mount effective resistance to Taylorism. Hence on the eve of war, Alphonse Merrheim, head of the Fédération des Métaux, denounced Taylorism in terms that matched the most vehement fulminations of British labor, calling it "the most ferocious, the most barbaric" system of work yet hatched by the bosses, a brutal system that dehumanized workers, rendering each an "automaton ruled by the automatic movements of the machine."[11] But without the level of shop-floor control over production enjoyed by their British counterparts, French workers were in no position to persuade their employers to take their view into consideration.

Given the ambivalence of employers, the antagonism of workers, and the initial costs of implementing Taylorist strategies, it is not surprising that it took a war of unprecedented ferocity to shake the foundations of craft in the European metalworking industries. Here the systematic interventions of an unusually powerful wartime state were crucial in driving and shaping a change that few employers were prepared to contemplate.

Organizing the War Economy in France

Women first came into the metalworking factories of Britain and France when their governments officially recognized that, contrary to popular expectation, the war was not destined to end by Christmas. Germany's swift and devastating invasion of the industrially rich northeast forced this recognition on the French almost immediately; the British had the luxury of pondering the unexpected turn of events into the winter of 1915, a luxury that was to have important consequences for the organization of England's defense industries. France's most acute need was to raise arms output at a time when some of its most productive land lay under occupation.[12] Ammunition stocks were perilously low, and as the German army advanced deeper into France, General Joseph Joffre pressed the Ministry of War to increase the output of shells from 84,000 a week to 700,000.[13]

---

and workpeople are permitted to specialise in more skilled operations as they show ability." On the decline of apprenticeship in late-nineteenth-century France, see Gérard Noiriel, *Workers in French Society in the Nineteenth and Twentieth Centuries* (Oxford, 1990), p. 87.

[11.] Merrheim, "Le Système Taylor," pp. 212 and 224.

[12] In a matter of days, France had lost 75% of its coke and coal, 81% of its pig iron, 63% of its steel, 75% of its sugar production, nearly all its textile mills, and a good deal of rich farmland as well. Moreover, most of France's coal mines and the most modern machine-tool plants were located in the northeast. See L. Baclé, "La Destruction systématique par les Allemands des usines métallurgiques du nord et de l'est de la France," *Bulletin de la Société d'Encouragement pour l'Industrie Nationale,* November–December 1920, p. 830; and Arthur Fontaine, *French Industry during the War* (Hew Haven, 1926).

[13] See Gerd Hardach, *The First World War, 1914–1918* (Berkeley, 1981), p. 88.

With the declaration of war, the French government called for people of all political stripes to set aside their differences, to join together in "sacred union" and rally to the cause of national defense.[14] In early September, as the Germans approached Paris, the newly formed government of "sacred union" fled hastily southwest to Bordeaux. Here industrialists and bureaucrats met to define the structures that would govern arms production for the rest of the war. On 20 September, Minister of War Alexandre Millerand summoned representatives of the major banks, railroads, and mining and metallurgical industries, including members of the Comité des Forges, heavy industry's powerful lobbying association, in an effort to secure their active cooperation in the drive to raise arms output.[15] By the end of the conference, Millerand had shifted prime responsibility for weapons production from the state arsenals to private firms, which he grouped into twelve regional associations, each under the direction of a powerful local industrialist. He selected Louis Renault to oversee production in the Paris region, perhaps the most important center for armaments outside the occupied northeast.[16]

Each association was to direct all aspects of arms production in its region: to allocate raw materials (particularly steel, which was in short supply) and defense contracts among local firms, and to verify and coordinate all contracts. In addition, Millerand asked that these men monitor the region's overall industrial resources, to ensure that plant and personnel were being used to their fullest capacity.[17] Henceforth the Ministry of War (and later the Ministry of Armaments) would function as middleman between army and industry, distributing contracts to the several associations and facilitating production by supplying labor, raw materials, and cash or credit for plant expansion

[14] The "sacred union" took formal shape in the Chamber of Deputies on 4 August as men of the left, center-right, and center solemnly forged a government of national defense embracing all parties. Later that evening the Chamber voted this new executive the quasi-dictatorial powers it requested, then prorogued "for the duration." A few days earlier, the popular Socialist deputy Jean Jaurès had been gunned down by Raoul Villain, a mentally unbalanced young nationalist. The shock of his death helped precipitate a domestic political truce that bound working class to bourgeoisie in a national crusade against the German threat to the Republic. See Philippe Bernard, *Le Fin d'un monde, 1914–1929* (Paris, 1975).

[15] On the Comité des Forges see John Godfrey, *Capitalism at War: Industrial Policy and Bureaucracy in France, 1914–1918* (Leamington Spa, 1989); Richard Kuisel, *Capitalism and the State in Modern France* (Cambridge, 1981); Charles Maier, *Recasting Bourgeois Europe* (Princeton, 1975); and Henry Peiter, "Men of Good Will: French Businessmen before the First World War" (Ph.D. thesis, University of Michigan, 1973).

[16] Gilbert Hatry, *Renault, patron absolue* (Paris, 1982), chap. 6. In January 1917 Renault turned the wartime regional association into a formal metals employers' association, the Groupe des Industriels de la Région Parisienne (GIRP), precursor to the GIMM. The Paris region included the city of Paris and the departments of the Seine (embracing the *proche banlieue*), Oise, Seine-et-Oise, and Seine-et-Marne.

[17] William Oualid and Charles Picquenard, *Salaires et tarifs, conventions collectives et grèves: La Politique du Ministère de l'Armement et du Ministère du Travail* (Paris, 1928), pp. 48–49. Oualid was a member of Thomas's staff at the Ministry of Armaments and an old *normalien*.

to those firms under contract. For the first year of the war, the short-run considerations of France's most powerful businessmen determined policy in the defense plants.

No one from the Confédération Générale du Travail (CGT) was called to the discussions at Bordeaux, and labor had no part in any of the broad agreements that set the terms of employment in the defense plants (*usines de guerre*).[18] Labor's exclusion from the settlement reached at Bordeaux was symptomatic of the larger, long-term problem entailed in placing such sweeping authority in a network of employer-directed associations. Under the terms of the agreement, these associations wielded enormous power: to set production policy in the defense plants and, more generally, to shape industrial conditions in their respective regions. Moreover, as the twelve regional leaders were drawn almost to a man from the Comité des Forges, the Bordeaux scheme effectively empowered this preponderant organization to operate as a monopoly in the state's name.[19] It was an arrangement that, in the words of Philippe Bernard, allowed industry to "combine patriotism and profit in an easy partnership."[20] As the wartime state would soon discover, this authority was not easily displaced—not without risk to the entire war effort.[21]

At first industry was not always ready to absorb additional labor. Lack of steel, coal, and iron compounded the formidable logistical problems involved in converting and expanding plant for arms production, and government policy did little to ease the confusion. As one inspector recalled, during the initial panic the Ministry of War offered a contract for shells to any workshop, no matter how small or inefficient, so long as it had a lathe.[22] After Bordeaux, the Comité des Forges used its control of scarce raw materials to gradually impose order on this chaos. But the order that the Comité brought to the metals industries was by no means neutral. By directing contracts and raw materials to the larger, better-equipped firms, the Comité pursued a policy that promoted industrial concentration in the name of greater efficiency. Large firms such as Renault and Delaunay-Belleville simply grew larger, while small shops were forced to group together or subcontract to a larger neighbor in order to obtain the necessary supplies.

Ultimately the structures of war production spurred a full-scale transforma-

---

[18] The CGT was a national umbrella organization for local unions (*syndicats*) in all trades. This loose confederation embraced only a portion of the labor movement, however, as some locals, especially the Catholic ones, rejected its overtly revolutionary stance.

[19] Kuisel, *Capitalism and the State*, p. 35.

[20] Bernard, *Le Fin d'un monde*, p. 26.

[21] See Godfrey, *Capitalism at War*, and Hardach, *First World War*, on the formidable authority that the Bordeaux agreements placed in the hands of arms manufacturers in wartime France.

[22] Lt. Col. Réboul, *La Mobilisation industrielle* (Paris, 1925), p. 158.

tion of the industrial landscape around Paris. Not only were large producers favored over small, but government policy invited new producers to enter the market and try their hands at turning out shells. Industries sprang up overnight, drawn by the promise of unlimited demand and by the ministry's generous policy of paying out one-third of the delivery price in advance.[23] The industrial suburb of Boulogne-Billancourt, just across the Bois de Boulogne from Paris's opulent Sixteenth Arrondissement, grew from 20 factories to 104 over the course of the war. But the most dramatic and certainly the most famous example of this spectacular growth was Citroën's new Javel plant, which rose rapidly under the shadow of the Eiffel Tower. Citroën began construction in the winter of 1915. By the following August, eight of the twelve hectares on the once-barren quai Javel had been covered with vast new assembly halls and machine shops. All were devoted solely to shell production, and 500 women (21 percent of the total labor force) were already hard at work inside them.[24]

The army's demand for a fairly narrow range of goods in vast quantity reinforced the trend toward industrial concentration and pressed firms to specialize. The circumstances of wartime demand thus combined with the Comité's policy to bring a new order within the factory walls of the Parisian metals industries, one that favored the transition from a craft-based to a mass-production organization of work. But the hasty construction and conversion of plants did not always result in a quality product. Throughout the fall of 1914, the General Staff reported a rash of shells that were exploding prematurely, sometimes as many as thirty a day, blowing up in the faces of the luckless poilus charged with loading the artillery.[25] In addition, the government policy of advancing one-third of the delivery price resulted in a string of widely

[23] In the spring of 1915, for example, Louis Renault received advances amounting to Fr 3.48 million, while Delaunay-Belleville garnered Fr 7.3 million (AN, 94 AP, 71, Fonds Albert Thomas, "Avances aux industriels, 1915–1917").

[24] By 1918 the Javel plant employed 11,700 workers, nearly half of them women. The government promoted this dramatic industrial development with advances for plant expansion, usually 20% of the projected cost, and Paris emerged from the war as the major center of metals production. By 1921 nearly one-third of all metalworkers—over 400,000 out of some 1.37 million—were employed in the Paris region, and firm size had risen as well; the number of firms employing over 100 workers had increased from 228 in 1906 to 530. See Statistique Générale de la France, *Résultats statistiques du recensement général de la population effectué le 6 mars 1921*, vol. 2 (Paris, 1925), secs. 1–5. See also AN, F22, 536 for details on industrial expansion during the war. On the expansion of Boulogne and Citroën, see Henri Sellier, *Paris pendant la guerre* (Paris, 1926), p. 10, and Sylvie Schweitzer, *Des engrenages à la chaîne: Les Usines Citroën, 1915–1935* (Lyon, 1982), p. 56. See Charles Sabel, *Work and Politics* (New York, 1982), for the economics of such "dual markets," in which small and large firms coexist, the latter meeting the stable component of product demand while the former handle the unstable, fluctuating component.

[25] Réboul, *Mobilisation industrielle*, p. 28. See also Godfrey, *Capitalism at War*, p. 208.

publicized scandals and accusations of war profiteering.[26] Some industrialists delivered only a fraction of what they promised, while others delivered defective goods, produced on the cheap, like the prematurely exploding shells. And of course there were some who simply pocketed their advances and skipped town.

In May 1915 the cabinet established a separate Undersecretariat of Artillery within the Ministry of War, naming the right-wing Socialist Albert Thomas to head up the new, quasi-autonomous division. Perhaps Thomas would succeed where Millerand had failed in curbing abuses and asserting more direct and effective control over private arms suppliers. The undersecretariat's arrival signaled a new phase in the industrial mobilization, in which the government was to adopt a far more activist stance in organizing arms production. Thomas was concerned with ensuring both a steady supply of cheaper munitions[27] and better working conditions to those laboring in the *usines de guerre*. After his appointment, the government reversed the practice of dispersing work across a plethora of small shops and joined the Comité des Forges in concentrating production in the larger, more efficient firms.

Thomas soon found that his main point of leverage in contests with industry lay in his expanding control of the labor supply, an authority enhanced by the extensive powers that the undersecretariat gained through the Dalbiez Law of 17 August 1915. The law regulated employers' access to their main source of labor power at the time, the mobilized soldier-workers whom the army had "loaned" to the war industries. In the initial scramble that followed France's victory at the Marne, the army had allowed industrialists to tour the depots and select skilled metalworkers, who were then recalled and stationed in the factories that had requested them. Returned to their peacetime occupations, though not necessarily to their former employers, these men remained on mobilized status and built weapons under the shadow of military discipline.[28] After August 1915, however, employers' visits to the depots ceased; henceforth the undersecretariat regulated the supply and distribution of mobilized men through its Labor Control Board, which mediated between the arms factories, the army, and, eventually, the municipal labor exchanges, where nonmobilized workers, including women, were recruited.

The board was staffed by a roving team of labor controllers drawn from

[26] After the war, Gaston Gros published some of the more spectacular tales of profiteering and corruption in his infamous *République des coquins* (Paris, 1934).

[27] According to Bernard, Thomas deliberately chose to keep profit as the central motive for arms production, and excluded all levies on profits (unlike Lloyd George, as we shall see).

[28] Hardach, *First World War*, p. 85. Alfred Rosmer, *Le Mouvement ouvrier pendant la guerre*, vol. 1 (Paris, 1939), offers a compelling eyewitness account of the conditions under which these conscripts labored.

the Civil Labor Inspection Corps. The controllers were themselves mobilized men, officers all, who formed a kind of shadow factory inspectorate, but with extra powers. Most important, they controlled the flow of mobilized labor, and could grant or refuse an employer's request in accordance with their determination of the firm's need for skilled workers. This power gave the labor controllers an expansive role in deploying labor and setting work conditions in the war factories.

Under military law, mobilized workers were forbidden to strike and often prevented from organizing as well. Rather, the labor controllers monitored their wages and hours, received complaints, and watched over their "habits and deportment" outside the factories. But the controllers' ultimate purpose was to reduce the number of mobilized workers in the *usines de guerre* by transferring them from jobs and factories where they were no longer needed and forcing their replacement with women and other civilians. Under this policy of systematic substitution it became difficult to separate the nonmilitarized workers from the mobilized, and the labor controllers' authority rapidly extended outward to embrace the women and civilian men they had recruited through the local labor exchanges.[29]

With control over the allocation of labor resting squarely with the undersecretariat, the government was at last in a position to counter the control of arms production handed over to private industrialists at Bordeaux.[30] After six months of near silence on the organization of war industry, Thomas and his labor controllers were at last asserting a governmental voice in the organization of war production, removing skilled men from jobs that could be performed by less skilled and female workers, and occasionally intervening on the issues of wages, hours, and working conditions.

Rationalization as Industrial Reform

The main architect of state policy in the war factories was undoubtedly Albert Thomas himself. Under his guidance, the output of 75-millimeter shells rose from 13,500 to 212,000 a day and that of 155-millimeter shells rose from

[29] At the start there were 40 officers in the corps. By January 1918, 66 officers roamed the *usines de guerre*, aided by 392 assistant controllers: William Oualid, *The Effect of the War upon Labour in France* (Paris, 1923), p. 155. Oualid goes on to note that although the Dalbiez Law (1915) explicitly dealt with mobilized men only (nearly 50% of the workforce in December 1915, under 30% by the end of 1918), the law enabled Thomas's controllers to exert "decisive influence over the disposition of the entire body of workers." Hence, by 1916, controllers were receiving complaints from women workers as well as mobilized men.

[30] AN, F22, 538, Henri Sellier, "L'Organisation du placement des ouvrières dans les usines de guerre."

405 to 45,000 a day.[31] Thomas's success prompted the cabinet to enhance his powers in December 1916, transforming the undersecretariat into the full-fledged and free-standing Ministry of Armaments.[32]

As undersecretary, then minister of armaments, Thomas blended a kind of reformist right-wing socialism with neo-Jacobin patriotism. For him, war and socialism were close kin; they shared "the spirit of sacrifice and self-abnegation, the consciousness of collective duties . . . the subordination of all particular interests to the common interest, the assent to discipline and social organization, the will to give all for the good of the nation."[33] In this pure and disciplined collectivism Thomas discerned the lineaments of a new France that would emerge cleansed and purified by the flames of war, coordinated and modernized by the need to organize and increase arms production.

Thomas's industrial policies thus evolved as much out of ideological conviction as from the immediate exigencies of war. From the outset he strove to balance industrial concentration, efficiency, and continuous technical improvement with careful attention to the wages and conditions of labor in the *usines de guerre*. In the notion of industrial rationalization, or Taylorism, the undersecretary found a concept that linked the two wings of his nascent industrial plan, a vision that suggested that technical modernization might travel in tandem with higher wages.

War made such Taylorist changes financially feasible, thanks to the ministry's generous pricing policy. Further, Thomas and his associates explicitly encouraged employers in "the most perfect utilization possible of the efforts of each worker through the use of the Taylor system," not merely as a means to the end of winning the war but as an end in itself.[34] As far as these men were concerned, the mechanization and "scientific" reorganization of work would improve not only output but also working conditions, and they pressed employers to intro-

---

[31] B. W. Schaper, *Albert Thomas: Trente Ans de reformisme social* (Assen, 1959), p. 111.

[32] Pierre Renouvin, *Les Formes du gouvernement de guerre* (Paris, 1925).

[33] Albert Thomas, "L'Esprit de guerre et l'avenir de la France," speech delivered to the workers at Le Creusot, April 1916, in *BUG*, 1 May 1916, p. 3. Thomas's staff published the *BUG* weekly and distributed it to defense contractors free of charge. It contained informative articles on new work technologies, the expanding and successful deployment of women in munitions, training programs for women, designs for expanded plant and welfare facilities, etc.

[34] *BUG*, 8 May 1916, p. 11. Aimée Moutet argues that the war not only forged a social consensus around the notion of permanently raising national efficiency but implanted the structures whereby that increase could be realized, "integrat[ing] Taylorism into the general organization of the factory at the same time that it revealed to industrialists the possibility of obtaining greater efficiency [in the quality and in the output] of the directly productive departments by means other than simple mechanization or recourse to piecework systems. Thus, Taylorization provides an organizational framework that is indispensable to mass production": "La Première Guerre mondiale et le taylorisme," in Maurice de Montmollin and Olivier Pastré, eds., *Le Taylorisme* (Paris, 1983), p. 73. See also Kuisel, *Capitalism and the State;* Godfrey, *Capitalism at War;* Maier, *Recasting Bourgeois Europe;* Patrick Fridenson, *Histoire des usines Renault*, vol. 1 (Paris, 1972), and "France–Etats-Unis."

duce labor-saving devices (lifting tackle, moving belts) and more automatic machinery as part of a broader campaign to increase "national efficiency." Thomas and his staff believed that higher productivity would flow inevitably and painlessly from a more rational deployment of material and human resources, and not from any increased exploitation of labor; in the brave new world of the rationalized factory, mechanization would render work less laborious, and so less degrading and more humane. The scientific organization of work thus constituted a social vision as well as an economic one, an end to class conflict through collaboration in the effort to raise national output.[35]

The labor leader Léon Jouhaux and his reformist fellow travelers agreed with the men at the ministry: the installation of a rational order in the factory, answering to the rigorous and nonpartisan criteria of science, would improve efficiency and eliminate waste, raising output while lowering unit costs. The benefits from this badly needed industrial modernization could then be returned to all participants in the form of higher wages for labor and greater profit for the employer.[36] This kind of "laborist" productivism resonated all too closely with the technocratic dreams of the bureaucrats who had gathered around Thomas, men who hoped that the war would spur France forward into a new age of prosperity and industrial expansion.

The episodic and impressionistic data scoured from French war factories make it seem very likely that skilled men may not have agreed with Jouhaux's sanguine assessment of shop-floor changes after 1914, which often arrived not in the beneficent guise of science but rather in the blunt, harsh form of speedups and rate cutting. Unlike their British counterparts, however, French craftsmen were in no position to mount an effective rear-guard defense of prewar practices. French unions, notoriously weak before the war, had collapsed with the mobilization, while the suspension of protective legislation and the prevalence of mobilized men in the defense plants multiplied employers' disciplinary force several times over.[37]

---

[35] Yves Lequin points out that the state's intervention in industry did not produce the rational modernization of Thomas's reforming vision; rather, it "facilitated the exacerbation of worker exploitation . . . the workday was almost always extended, wages were cut and in every way devalued by the swift rise in prices, the pace of work was accelerated by the extension of piecework": "La Rationalisation du capitalisme français: A-t-elle lieu dans les années vingt?" *Cahiers d'Histoire de l'Institut Maurice Thorez*, no. 31 (1979), pp. 116–17.

[36] See Jules Ravété (anarchosyndicalist from Roanne, in the Loire) "Une Défense de la méthode Taylor," *La Vie Ouvrière*, 5 March 1914, pp. 257–67, for a prewar statement of the argument that Taylorism reduces the brutality of factory labor. See also Gary Cross, *A Quest for Time: The Reduction of Work in Britain and France, 1840–1940* (Berkeley, 1989); Rabinbach, *Human Motor;* and Nicholas Papayanis, *Alphonse Merrheim: The Emergence of Reformism in Revolutionary Syndicalism, 1871–1925* (The Hague, 1985).

[37] ". . . Throughout the war, at a time of unprecedentedly rapid and large-scale organizational change, French workers had no institutional means within the firm through which they could make their influence felt and protect their interests. . . . Freed from pre-war legal constraints, armed with unprecedented disciplinary powers, and unopposed by any form of effective union

By casting hyperproductivity as patriotic duty, the politics of war gave broad currency to the Taylorist reorganization of work.[38] But employers, driven more by the pressure of circumstance than by visions of industrial utopia, rarely inaugurated the kinds of deep, systematic changes that Frederick Taylor had preached. (Citroën's Javel plant is the exception that proves the rule.) Taylor's original conception paired shop-floor change with a reorganization of management, away from an old-fashioned hierarchical command structure and toward functionally distinct yet interlocking departments (control, marketing, research and development). Wartime "Taylorism" was less comprehensive and more focused on the production process itself. Employers subdivided and mechanized tasks, and labor was specialized accordingly. If they had the time and resources, industrialists then reorganized the redivided work, so that tasks succeeded one another in a logical flow. On rare occasions, different phases of this opened-out labor process were then reintegrated by mechanized conveyor belts. The most consistently applied aspect of Taylor's system was the piece-rate wage, which attached workers' earnings directly to the speed and accuracy with which they produced.[39]

Nonetheless, much of what passed for the "scientific" reorganization of work in the war factories was often nothing more than what one scholar has termed "the most brutal and archaic forms of overexploitation."[40] Armed with exceptional disciplinary powers (especially over mobilized workers) and freed of most legal constraints, thanks to the state of seige, employers raised output not only through technical improvement but by extending the workday and slashing piece rates. As we will see, employers often piloted these restructuring projects on women. Recently arrived on the metalworking factory floor, women were unfamiliar with the work and with prewar shop traditions. Their inexperience combined with their uniformly low rate of wages (averaging half to two-thirds of the male rate before 1917) to render them especially vulnerable to the speedups and rate cutting that spread throughout the industry after 1914.

Thomas was aware that the politics of war production fostered such abuses, and that women were particularly easy to exploit. Nonetheless, he frowned

organization, French employers were able to carry through extensive restructuring of work organization for war production on terms entirely of their own choosing": Duncan Gallie, *Social Inequality and Class Radicalism in France and Britain* (Cambridge, 1982), p. 232.

[38] Moutet, "Première Guerre mondiale," p. 67.

[39] In fact, one can use the spread of piece rates to track the progress of Taylorist strategies before the war. By the early 1890s, 30% of France's industrial workers were paid by the piece: Bernard Mottez, *Systèmes de salaires et politiques patronales* (Paris, 1966). During the war, the piece rate was extended to all but the most highly skilled and laborers, who continued to be paid a straight time rate. In its most common form, the piece-rate wage consisted of a low base rate (dependent on a minimum output) with a fluctuating bonus paid for all pieces above the minimum.

[40] Lequin, "Rationalisation du capitalisme français," p. 117.

on women's efforts to improve conditions by striking. Improving labor's lot was all well and good, so long as the improvements came through state intervention, not from the workers' own initiatives. A dedicated partisan of the sacred union, Thomas regarded the war factory as a site of intensive and continuous production, where a strike was a blow against the national defense and the pace of work was feverish and unrelenting. Joffre's "miracle of the Marne" had halted the German advance, but it hardly eased the sense of crisis surrounding the invasion. Should munitions workers of either sex take matters into their own hands, Thomas was prepared to unleash the state's considerable repressive force against them.

Nonetheless, Thomas did lend his patronage to workers' demands for improvements in wages and conditions, dispensing reforms from the center as befitted his neo-Jacobin ethos of centralist war socialism. In 1916 he created a Committee on Women's Work, which designed a series of reforms, most of them related to protecting and preserving women's roles as mothers, and the minister used every means at his disposal to press these reforms on defense contractors. In January 1917 the ministry established a set of minimum wage rates that narrowed the gap between male and female rates from 31 to 18 percent.

Thomas's efforts on behalf of labor entailed not only monitoring conditions through his labor controllers but consulting with syndicalist leaders as well. Alphonse Merrheim and Léon Jouhaux soon became regular figures at the ministry, meeting frequently with Thomas and his associates to discuss wages, conditions, and problems of labor supply, in particular the question of female labor. But their role remained purely consultative. Unlike their British counterparts, French syndicalist leaders never gained a formal voice in labor policy-making, and Thomas retained full control over the disposition of labor in the *usines de guerre.*

Despite his concern for workers' welfare, then, Thomas's policies ultimately reinforced the sharp reassertion of managerial power that war, invasion, and the Bordeaux agreement had brought to France. The pressure to raise arms output, though hardly less urgent in Britain than in France, would produce quite the opposite result there, strengthening the institutions of trade unions and shop stewards, through which workers—especially skilled men—could defend their interests in the face of a radical restructuring of work.[41]

Reorganizing British Industry for War

With the declaration of war, domestic divisions in Britain seemed to evaporate as easily as they had done in France. Previous commitments to proletarian

---

[41] See Gallie, *Social Inequality,* chap. 12.

internationalism foundered under the wave of popular opposition to German militarism, and the labor movement joined ardently in the national cause. Thousands of trade union men volunteered for the army while their leaders hastily abandoned plans for a general strike in the autumn. It seemed that all England had been swept into a kind of informal sacred union. "Strikes were called off 'for the duration,' " a British historian reports. "The women's suffrage agitation was called off, and Home Rule was put in cold storage."[42] Only the Independent Labour Party clung to its internationalist ideals, standing aloof from the patriotic upsurge and from the rest of the labor movement until the end of the war.[43]

Unhurried by the pressures of invasion, Lord Kitchener soon raised a volunteer army (only in 1916 was conscription introduced) that the Ministry of War managed to field and equip by drawing on traditional sources of supply: a combination of government arsenals and private arms factories on the ministry's official list of suppliers. Only in the winter of 1915 did such expedients begin to seem inadequate, as orders for shells and machine guns fell sharply into arrears. The unrestricted voluntary enlistment of skilled men had left manufacturers with a shrunken workforce at the precise moment when demand for munitions began to soar beyond all prewar calculations. Lacking sufficient skilled labor, arms manufacturers could not even deliver the goods on time, much less contemplate expanding production. Threatened with a serious shortage of munitions, the government stepped in and began to regulate directly both the supply of labor and the organization of production in the munitions industry.

Britain's historic commitment to maintaining a pared-down "nightwatchman" state might lead one to anticipate even less state intervention in the nascent war economy than in traditionally more *étatiste* France. Yet paradoxically, quite the opposite was the case. The government emerged from Britain's own Bordeaux Conference, the Treasury Conference of 19 March 1915, with far greater control over its industrial partners than was ever enjoyed in France. Moreover, from the outset all negotiations and agreements about arms production in Britain were tripartite, with the voices of organized (especially skilled) labor and state officials weighing in on the vital issues of wages and the organization of work. The power to determine conditions in munitions work was not symmetrically apportioned among the three parties, and tripartism by no means assured labor an equal voice in these arrangements. But government policy ensured that the national interest would at no time appear

[42] Mary Anderson, *Women at Work* (London, 1942), p. 81.
[43] Of course, many people opposed Britain's entry into the conflict, including an important part of the NUWSS (National Union of Women's Suffrage Societies) leadership, who left the organization en masse in 1915 to pursue the pacifist cause. See Johanna Alberti, *Beyond Suffrage: Feminists in War and Peace, 1914–28* (London, 1989), pp. 38–70.

coterminous with the industrialists' private pursuit of profit, as it did in France. Both state and union officials would remain decisive presences in British defense factories throughout the war, exerting a visible influence over the conditions and wages that women confronted there.[44]

This three-way partnership reflects the liberal proclivities of state officials, who desired above all to prevent wartime controls from interfering unduly with the pursuit of "business as usual."[45] But it also reflects the enduring importance of skilled craftsmen, who continued to organize and execute the basic work of production in most engineering shops. Skilled men's power rested on two mutually reinforcing phenomena: the strength of their trade unions, especially the Amalgamated Society of Engineers (ASE), and the industry's continued orientation toward building for a narrow market in custom-made machinery and equipment. War, recession, and the eventual widening of the product market would force a gradual reorientation toward mass production. Until the market for customized equipment dried up, however, investment in skilled men rather than in expensive, automatic machinery remained a cheap and flexible alternative for the majority of firms.[46]

The industry's continued reliance on skilled men reinforced the strength of the ASE, enabling the union to defend craftsmen's high wages and preponderant role in production to a degree that was simply not possible for the weaker *syndicats* in France. Of course individual foremen loomed large on the factory floor in France, and it was their skill that determined their ascent to this lofty role. But these men acted more as managerial envoys, since ultimate responsibility for organizing production was shifting increasingly away from the factory floor toward the managers and directors.

From the outset, then, British employers' efforts to reorganize industry for war depended on their success in securing the full cooperation of skilled craftsmen, a fact that is underscored by the term most often used to describe

---

[44] The difference in the roles that organized labor played in setting the terms of munitions production in the two countries was not lost on working-class leaders in France: "The [British] consulted the labor organizations, discussing wages and work conditions with their representatives, and requisitioned the factories, limiting employers' profits to 10 percent [above their prewar average] while requiring them to pay the union wage rate. The [French], by contrast, summoned only the employers. They placed orders in the hands of the Comité des Forges and left it to the Comité to distribute them": Fédération des Métaux, "L'Action patronale et l'union sacrée," *L'Union des Métaux,* May–December 1915.

[45] The phrase is from Lloyd George's memoirs, quoted in Hardach, *First World War,* p. 77.

[46] British employers often exercised authority indirectly through their craftsmen, who directly managed the work of laborers and apprentices. This remnant of the old subcontracting system had survived the phasing out of the system itself after about 1870. See Littler, *Development of the Labour Process,* and William Lazonick, "Production Relations, Labor Productivity, and Choice of Technique: British and U.S. Cotton Spinning," *Journal of Economic History* 41 (September 1981). For further information on skill and the organization of work in France and Britain, see Gospel and Littler, *Managerial Strategies,* and Patrick Fridenson, "The Coming of the Assembly Line to Europe," in *Sociology of the Sciences* 2 (1978): 159–78.

wartime reorganization in Britain: the "dilution" (that is, fragmentation) of skill. Whereas French discussions of scientific reorganization focused attention on the transformation of the whole—work processes, entire factory spaces, even the structure of industry itself—the British notion that war production rested ultimately on "diluting" skill tended to bring British discussions back to the impact such changes had on the skilled worker.

Employers' earliest stabs at dilution followed the pattern of prewar efforts to cut labor costs by subdividing and mechanizing portions of the labor process, and placing unapprenticed women and men on those new jobs. Skilled men had energetically resisted these efforts, for deskilling threatened both the craftsman's wages and his control of the work process. Sometimes the craft unions obstructed the introduction of new methods and machinery *tout court*, but their premier tactic had been to instruct members to "follow the machine"; they would admit mechanization and redivisions of labor in the name of progress, but then refuse to allow employers to reap the full benefit of deskilling by insisting that all the fragmented bits of formerly skilled jobs be performed by fully skilled men, at the full craft rate. Before the war, employers had alternated between overriding and accommodating craftsmen on the machine question, acting out of the knowledge that, progressive mechanization notwithstanding, these men retained a crucial role in the production process.

By 1914 the ongoing struggle over mechanization and deskilling had produced a labor process that combined skilled and unskilled phases, nearly all of which remained in the hands of skilled craftsmen. Technically speaking, then, many processes had already been subdivided and simplified, and the substitution of unskilled labor for craftsmen on this work would be a relatively simple and straightforward matter, should the political constellation of forces on the factory floor shift. The war provided that shift, for with the mounting pressure to produce weapons, skilled men were simply too rare and valuable a commodity to waste on routine jobs that could just as well be performed by untrained women and men. Under the patriotic aegis of war, employers hoped at last to break the craft monopoly on production work.

On 1 October 1915 *The Engineer* announced:

> The fact of the matter is really not that women are paid too little—or much too little—but that men are paid too much for work which can be done without previous training. High wages are paid on the false assumption, now almost obscured by trade union regulations, that it takes long to learn the craft. . . . The whole argument of high wages, based on long training, has been carried by the board. (p. 319)

As it turns out, the employers' journal had overstated the case, and wartime arrangements did not break the craftsmen's power. On the contrary, these men's cooperation was essential to the extensive retooling and shop conversion needed to place the peacetime industry on a war footing, and most employers recognized that fact. The days of following the machine, however, were well and truly over.

From the autumn of 1914, then, skilled men directly faced the undercutting that they had managed to block before the war. Throughout that first winter of war, the men fought a doomed battle against employers' "dilution" of skill through the introduction of unskilled and female labor into their shops.[47] Then, in mid-March 1915, Chancellor of the Exchequer David Lloyd George invited employers and trade union representatives to meet with him at the Treasury to negotiate a binding settlement on dilution that would cover work in both private industry and the public arsenals. At the end of the day, he had secured the official cooperation of organized male labor in implementing "such changes in working conditions or trade customs as may be necessary with a view to accelerating the output of war munitions or equipment."[48] Henceforth, skilled men were legally bound to accept dilution, not only by covenants within the trade but by the laws that covered the land in time of war. In addition, the unions formally relinquished the right to strike on all war work, and accepted government arbitration in the event of a dispute.[49] In return, skilled men received the government's solemn guarantee that it would "use its influence to secure the restoration of previous conditions in every case after the War."[50]

If the Treasury Agreement clipped the wings of skilled labor in its campaign to maintain the engineering industry as skilled male terrain, it also confirmed the skilled man's pride of place in the industry. In giving the craft unions a partnership, however junior, in setting the terms that would govern war

[47] In the autumn of 1914 skilled men at the Vickers arms factory resisted employers' efforts to introduce women in unskilled jobs usually done by craftsmen. That November the Engineering Employers' Federation (EEF) and ASE signed the Crayford Agreement, the first wartime compromise on women's work in the engineering industry. Disputes and stoppages continued until the March accords on dilution were reached. For details on all these agreements, see G. D. H. Cole, *Labour in Wartime* (London, 1915) and *Trade Unionism and Munitions;* and Matthew Brown Hammond, *British Labour Conditions and Legislation during the War* (New York, 1919).

[48] Clause 4, Treasury Agreement, quoted in Cole, *Trade Unionism and Munitions,* p. 72.

[49] Not that there were no strikes in munitions after 1914—far from it. As early as 1915, shop stewards in the North (Clydeside) were leading craftsmen in strikes against the introduction of women and unskilled labor in "their" shops. By 1917, the shop stewards had been transformed from the dues-collecting functionaries of prewar days into the leaders of a grass-roots protest against dilution and the conscription of skilled men into the military. The shop stewards' movement was, ultimately, a revolt against the ASE leaders—the men who had assented to the dilution scheme in the first place. See James Hinton, *The First Shop Stewards' Movement* (London, 1973).

[50] Clause 5, Supplementary Treasury Agreement, quoted in Cole, *Trade Unionism and Munitions,* p. 74.

production, Lloyd George underscored the important role that they continued to play in organizing and directing the labor process. The enduring importance of craft and trade union in Britain created a continuity in male personnel and structures of labor defense that found no parallel in France. Indeed, both government and employers courted the craftsmen's cooperation, knowing it would be essential to the expansion and smooth operation of wartime industry.

Such overtures were unnecessary in the case of less skilled and female labor. As it happens, Lloyd George did invite representatives of the unskilled unions (Workers' Union, Transport and General Workers Union) to the Treasury that day, but it was a purely formal gesture; they participated in the accords as silent signatories only. The only organization excluded altogether, even from such passive participation, was Mary MacArthur's National Federation of Women Workers (NFWW).[51] The NFWW had several thousand members already at work in the munitions factories, yet Lloyd George's failure to invite MacArthur struck no one as odd or significant, least of all Mary MacArthur herself, who conceded that after all, "the trade belonged to the men and they laid down, in consultation with the Minister, the terms upon which women should be admitted."[52]

In June 1915 the wartime cabinet put Lloyd George in charge of a newly created Ministry of Munitions, with broad statutory powers over labor and over industries deemed essential to the war effort. The new minister strove to build an organization imbued with the pragmatic can-do philosophy that in his view animated Britain's great business leaders. Within weeks he had recruited more than 90 industrialists—nearly half the total staff of 200 at the fledgling Ministry of Munitions.[53] Under Lloyd George's energetic leadership, they immediately set to work organizing a controlled economy: requisitioning raw materials (and occasionally industrial plant), allocating labor, and developing a set of incentives that would encourage private manufacturers to produce in accordance with the exigencies of war.

Lloyd George's ministry operated in two domains: the semipublic "national factories" and the growing network of "controlled establishments," private firms that were building weapons under government contract. The national factories were a peculiar hybrid of public and private. The government either

[51] The general unions of unskilled workers also organized women in the metals and munitions industries. The Workers' Union was especially active in this department, and in 1913 had already led a successful strike of semi- and unskilled metalworkers (male and female) in Birmingham and the surrounding "Black Country." See Richard Hyman, *The Workers' Union* (Oxford, 1971).

[52] Quoted in Barbara Drake, *Women in the Engineering Trades: A Problem, a Solution, and Some Criticism* (London, 1917), p. 112.

[53] Hinton, *First Shop Stewards' Movement*, p. 29. By March 1916 the 200 had become 4,758; by June 1917, 12,190, nearly half of whom were women. See John Fairlie, *British War Administration* (New York, 1919), p. 107.

requisitioned or rapidly erected these enormous installations, then appointed directors, drawn from private metals and munitions firms in the area.[54] They were not intended to survive beyond the Armistice, at least not in their semipublic form. At the end of 1915, seventy such factories were in operation; by the end of the war, more than two hundred. The national factories were veritable pioneers in introducing standardized and mass-production techniques to British industry. By 1916, many thousands of women had found employment in these massive, highly modern plants, for it was here that government schemes for the dilution of skilled labor were most thoroughly and faithfully applied.

By February 1917 the controlled establishments included some 4,285 private firms working on arms contracts and therefore bound to produce within the strictures of the nation's Munitions of War acts.[55] The acts placed a strict upper limit on war profits, which could not exceed 20 percent of their prewar average, and laid down minimum wages and working conditions for the thousands of women and men who flocked to munitions plants after 1914. Lloyd George could designate any factory engaged on war work a "controlled establishment." This designation empowered the ministry to intervene in all aspects of war production: wage fixing, shop discipline, welfare and working conditions, and, most important, the organization and deployment of labor.

Officials at the Ministry of Munitions were far less interested than the French in Taylorism's long-term potential for industrial renovation. Concerned above all with the immediate and pragmatic goal of raising arms production, these men spoke comparatively little about the role that wartime changes might play in restructuring industry after the war. They nonetheless pressed hard on arms contractors, pushing for a swift and radical reorganization of work so that weapons output might rise as rapidly as possible. To this end, the ministry offered generous financial assistance (loans, grants, and cash advances for retooling and expansion), supplemented by the technical advice contained

[54] Local management boards (embracing men from local government, industry, and the occasional trade union) organized the facilities, then appointed the directors.

[55] In February 1917 the controlled establishments employed about 2 million workers. After the spring of 1915 the number of controlled establishments soared: from 345 in August 1915 to 1,000 in October 1915 to 4,300 in the summer of 1916, and finally to about 6,000 by the end of the war. Ninety-five percent of these firms had not produced weapons before the war, so the government grants and loans for expansion and plant conversion, new machinery, and welfare facilities were critical to their participation in arms production. See Humbert Wolfe, *Labour Supply and Regulation* (Oxford, 1923). The Defence of the Realm Act (DORA), passed in August 1914, gave the government broad powers of economic control, including the right to requisition industrial plant deemed essential to the war. Amendments in March and June 1915 refined the state's economic authority, empowering civil servants to set priorities in production and to recruit and deploy labor. The Munitions of War acts followed in July 1915, 1916, and 1918.

in its *Dilution of Labour Bulletin*. This heavily illustrated newsletter contained information on new machinery, shop reorganization, the dilution of skilled work, and techniques of scientific management—information that would become much more interesting to employers as their contingent of women workers grew. Finally, Lloyd George dispatched an army of "dilution of labor officers," factory inspectors who reviewed working conditions and enforced the terms of the munitions acts. The officers were to ensure that employers used their skilled men sparingly, "that no skilled man [would be] employed on work which [could] be done by semi-skilled or unskilled male or female labour."[56] Any employer found flouting the ministry's guidelines or the terms of the acts was liable to a heavy fine. But British bureaucrats shared French reservations about undue meddling in the market, and so exercised their command with some caution. One member of the ministry later recalled the "subconscious resistance" that the very idea of deliberately organizing industry for war production encountered in a government "committed to the doctrines of free trade and individualism."[57]

Such ministerial squeamishness about trespassing on the market did not extend to the regulation of labor, however. With the declaration of war, the government immediately followed the French example, suspending all legal limitations on working hours and overtime, and eleven- or twelve-hour days rapidly became the rule.[58] The first Munitions of War act (July 1915) compounded the loss of legal protection by outlawing all strikes on war work and restricting labor mobility through a system of "leaving certificates." These certificates, signed by employers, affirmed that workers had left their jobs with the employers' consent. Without this slip of paper, workers had to sit idle (and wageless) before another employer could take them on. Intended to prevent employers from poaching workers and bidding up wages in the scramble for labor, the hated certificates effectively chained workers to their current jobs, no matter how ill paid or unsatisfactory. Employers, too, were enjoined to avoid lockouts, and, like labor, accept government arbitration in the event of a dispute. But in a period of essentially unlimited demand, the

[56] Ministry of Munitions, Central Labour Supply Committee, Circular L5, *Report on Dilution of Labour*, quoted in Cole, *Trade Unionism and Munitions*, p. 93. Cole's Appendix B provides the text of the munitions acts.

[57] E. M. H. Lloyd, *Experiments in State Control* (Oxford, 1924), p. 22.

[58] The British workweek was already shorter than the French in the decades preceding the war. In 1900, metalworkers worked (on average) 53.7 hours per week in Britain and 63–66 hours in France. The British workweek remained 5 to 10 hours shorter during the war, thanks to the half-day Saturday, which French workers did not achieve until June 1917, when women munitions workers struck en masse to demand *la semaine anglaise*. Cross, *Quest for Time*, gives a detailed account of labor's struggles to reduce working hours in France and Britain during the late nineteenth and early twentieth centuries.

ban on work stoppages weighed far more heavily on labor than it did on capital, and the government's slow and clumsy arbitration procedure offered scant compensation for workers' wholesale loss of rights.

The wartime government thus stripped workers of their usual means of resisting exploitation, casting such resistance as unpatriotic, even sabotage against the national war effort. This redefinition was institutionalized in a system of special munitions tribunals, where the disobedient could be prosecuted for the least infraction of the work rules.[59] Fifty years later, Lilian Miles, who made explosives for White & Poppe of Coventry, still remembered how harsh the tribunal's enforcement could be. One morning a young shell filler inadvertently carried a match into the danger shed. For this breach of the rules she was hauled before the tribunal "and she had twenty-eight days without the option of a fine. . . . She didn't have a say. They just said 'twenty-eight days.' They took her away . . . to prison . . . to Winston Green."[60] In the effort to guarantee the flow of arms to the front, the government had lent unexpected reinforcement to the employers' disciplinary arsenal, augmenting the ordinary modes of shop discipline—fines and dismissal—with its own formidable sanctions.

Ministerial hesitation over state intervention thus combined with the sense of urgency surrounding war production to create a system of uneven control, which weighed far more heavily on labor than on private industry.[61] On the factory floor, this ambivalence translated into a lack of conviction about enforcing minimum wages for women and the unskilled in the controlled establishments. It also ensured that the recruitment and training of women workers would be a haphazard, ill-organized affair, oriented neither to the demands of war, as understood by the Ministry of Munitions, nor to the needs of individual women for a comprehensive industrial education. Despite these defects, however, the system that gradually evolved gave the British government more effective control over the shape and direction of war production than its French counterpart would ever enjoy. It allowed the Ministry of Munitions to oversee the terms and conditions of work in private industry while keeping a fairly tight hold on defense costs and on the benefits that accrued to arms manufacturers. As the war ground on, these precautions would help the British government to avoid the sharp drop in morale that

[59] By July 1916 the tribunals had prosecuted 5,354 cases and reviewed 15,210 applications for leaving certificates: Fairlie, *British War Administration*, p. 115.

[60] Imperial War Museum (hereafter IWM), Sound Records Dept., Lilian Annie Miles, "War Work, 1914–1918," accession no. 000854/04, typescript, p. 13.

[61] Indeed, Gail Braybon terms the system of labor control "authoritarian," and Jonathan Zeitlin observes that it verged on "industrial conscription." See Braybon, *Women Workers in the First World War* (London, 1981), p. 59; and Zeitlin, "Rationalization and Resistance: Skilled Workers and the Transformation of the Division of Labor in the British Engineering Industry, 1830–1930" (B.A. thesis, Harvard University, 1977), p. 152.

plagued the French, who soon grew weary of the all too accurate tales of arms profiteering.

Dilution and Labor Substitution in France and Britain

Throughout the first winter of war, engineering firms in both countries struggled to raise arms output while using prewar methods and a division of labor that relied heavily on skilled men. The first women recruited to metalworking were brought in to assist in this largely unreformed labor process, replacing laborers and hastily promoted apprentices on tasks that demanded little experience or skill. It would be another six months before industrialists inaugurated the kinds of systematic changes that, in their eyes, permitted more extensive employment of women.

Employers' initial production strategies thus rested on preserving, even increasing, their contingents of skilled men. Women remained peripheral; though hired in increasing numbers, they were brought in only to supplement the core of skilled male labor. Both governments briefly encouraged this strategy: the French by allowing industrialists to recall mobilized metalworkers to their factories, the British by issuing "trade cards" to shield skilled men from service in the trenches.[62] But industrialists soon found the limits of labor and production policies based solely on conserving a dwindling force of skilled men. By mid-1915 they were already "economizing" on skill, dividing complex jobs into their component phases, mechanizing as many of those elements as possible, and distributing the fragmented tasks to a host of new workers, most of them women.

Women usually started on simple machine work, minding presses or lathes as they more or less automatically turned out a long series of standardized parts. Employers organized the unskilled machine tenders into gangs of ten to fifteen workers and placed them under the supervision of a single skilled

[62] By August 1915, when the Undersecretariat of Artillery used the Dalbiez Law to forbid further recalls, mobilized men constituted just under 50% of the entire munitions workforce in France. After Verdun, these men began to flow back toward the front, as military inspectors began to comb all able-bodied men out of the factories. By April 1917, only 35% of munitions workers were mobilized; a year later, the proportion had fallen to 30%. See John Horne, "L'Impôt du sang: Republican Rhetoric and Industrial Warfare in France, 1914–1918," *Social History* 14, no. 2 (1989): 201–23. See also Hardach, *First World War*. In Britain the chemical and engineering industries lost 16 to 24% of their largely skilled prewar workforce during the first year of fighting alone: Wolfe, *Labour Supply and Regulation*. Hence when conscription began in January 1916, the Ministry of Munitions issued trade cards to some million skilled men to protect them from the draft and keep them at work in munitions. As the war chewed up men, however, the ministry was forced to allow skilled men to be conscripted as well. On the trade card scheme, see Hinton, *First Shop Stewards' Movement*.

man. The craftsman ground the tools, set the machines for each new operation, and corrected any jams or misfeeds that the operator herself could not handle. Newcomers to the gang learned their work not from the craftsman but from the more experienced hands on the team.

The changed organization of work had an immediate and dramatic impact on the statistics of women's employment. The Parisian metals industry tripled its contingent of women workers during the first year of war, from between 8,000 and 9,000 women in 1914 to about 30,000 the following summer.[63] By December 1915, women formed nearly one-fifth of the metalworking labor force in the nation as a whole.[64] The figures for Britain trace a similar trajectory, with women's participation in metalworking rising from about 6 percent in 1914 to 11.4 percent in the summer of 1915 to 17.8 percent in July 1916.[65]

By extending the division of labor and employing inexpensive female labor on the new tasks, employers lowered their unit costs while raising output many times over. Despite these apparent advantages, however, few were prepared to carry the reorganization of work and substitution of women beyond the point reached in 1915–16. Though many industrialists had complained of skilled men's resistance to the subdivision and mechanization of work before the war, few were prepared to replace men, especially skilled men, with inexperienced women on so grand a scale. This reluctance was a product less of hidebound conservatism than of their common-sense perception that in a time of wildly fluctuating demand, it was safer to invest in skill than to sink their capital in the expensive changes in plant and machinery required for the extensive deployment of unskilled labor. No one knew how long the war would last, and employers could effect changes in production runs and shop organization only with the craftsman's expert assistance. Any industrialist's long-term future thus depended on retaining these flexible human instruments of production.

Nonetheless, the governments of both nations pressed their suppliers to push ahead, combining patriotic exhortation with coercion. Thomas used his powers over France's labor supply to force the desired changes. In the summer of 1916, as Verdun swallowed troops by the thousands, he forbade men's employment outright on entire classes of work, including all operations involved in producing shells for the army's main tactical weapon, the 75 gun.[66]

---

[63] *Bulletin du Ministère du Travail,* July–August 1915, pp. 180–81 (hereafter *BMT*).

[64] *BMT,* January–February 1918, p. 4, gives 19% for December 1915. Senator Paul Strauss gave 17% as the December 1915 figure: "Discours de M. Paul Strauss," *BUG,* 20 May 1916, p. 20.

[65] Adam Kirkaldy, *British Labour, 1914–1921: Replacement and Conciliation* (London, 1921), pp. 3, 107.

[66] AN, 94 AP, 348, Fonds Albert Thomas, circular to industrialists, 20 July 1916. Between November 1915 and November 1916 the ministry sent out ten circulars encouraging the employment of women. The circular of 20 July 1916 received the most attention, as it explicitly banned men's employment in any job included in a ten-page list.

Except for jobs requiring the heaviest labor (manipulation of the very largest shells), all unskilled work was reserved exclusively for women, as were a number of semiskilled jobs involving smaller pieces. By August his labor controllers began to enforce the policy, patrolling the factories and removing mobilized men from the specified list of jobs. The ministry reinforced its stringent labor economies by extending technical advice and financing for reorganizing, mechanizing, and deskilling work.[67] The results were striking: once the ministry stepped in, the recruitment of women to the war factories surged forward. Between January 1916 and January 1917 the number of women in private munitions plants rose 3.5 times; the numbers in state factories rose nearly 2.5 times.[68] After 1917 the numbers continued to rise, although the rate of increase slowed somewhat. In Paris alone the number of women metalworkers rose from some 44,000 in July 1915 to over 100,000 in the spring of 1918.[69] By 1917–18, women accounted for 30 percent of all metalworkers in the Paris region and 25 percent of the national metalworking labor force; before the war they had made up a bare 5 percent of that labor force.[70]

Dilution succeeded equally well in Britain, where the numbers of women employed in private engineering firms soared from 170,000 in 1914 to 518,000 by the summer of 1917 and 597,000 by 1918. Of these workers, 363,000 directly replaced men.[71] When the lure of patriotic gesture and short-term profits failed to draw employers' cooperation, Lloyd George stood as ready as Thomas to force a far-reaching dilution of skill. The policy, proclaimed in the first issue of the Ministry's *Dilution of Labour Bulletin,* was to confine skilled men to work that could not be "efficiently performed" by less skilled labor, and to confine less skilled men to jobs that were too heavy and laborious for women.[72]

[67] In addition, the state offered its own good example: by the second year of the war, thousands of women had already found work in state arsenals. In its July–August 1915 issue (pp. 180–81) the *BMT* notes 14,162 women employed in the arsenals by the summer of 1915 (4,800 of whom had been working in the arsenals before the war).

[68] *BMT*, January–February 1918, p. 6.

[69] *BMT*, May–June 1919, p. 457.

[70] As many as 80% of workers employed by some large firms were women. The trajectory of expansion ran as follows: taking the employment figures for January 1914 as its base (100), the Ministère du Travail found that over half (58%) of these women had been thrown out of work in the initial weeks of war. The following summer, before Thomas's ministry had begun actively to recruit women, the index figure had risen to 225. Once the state stepped in, the index leaped forward: 590 by July 1916, peaking at 733 in July 1917, then falling back to 677 in July 1918. The latter figure reflects a slowing of production due to shortages of raw materials and the last great German offensive in the spring and summer of 1918. See *BMT*, November–December 1918, p. 473. See also Laura Lee Downs, "Women in Industry, 1914–1939: The Employers' Perspective" (Ph.D. thesis, Columbia University, 1987), p. 549.

[71] Kirkaldy, *British Labour*, p. 2. A further 247,000 were employed in government arsenals, bringing the wartime employment of women in metalworking (private and public) to 844,000.

[72] *Dilution of Labour Bulletin,* October 1916, p. 6 (hereafter *DLB*). The Ministry of Munitions distributed this publication gratis to all national factories and controlled establishments. It

With the progressive withdrawal of skilled men from production, wartime rationalization in both countries at last achieved its most fully realized form: formerly skilled jobs were broken down into their component phases, often as many as twenty-two separate tasks.[73] Most of these tasks were mechanized and distributed among a host of women and men with little experience, each of whom executed only one or two of the component tasks in continuous, repetitive motions. These workers were arrayed in such a way that one task fed logically into the next. When they were gathered at their work stations, the group formed a kind of loosely bound "collective worker," producing in short order what an individual craftsman had taken hours or days to turn out before the war. Job fragmentation thus extended the work process across the factory floor; operations that had been spatially contained under a more craft-based organization now fanned outward in long chains of repetitive taskwork. As the work process expanded outward, the job of coordinating and managing the newly subdivided labor process fell to the skilled men who, with the assistance of laborers and apprentices, had once handled production jobs from start to finish.

In the name of efficiency, rationalization reduced the variety and range of work performed at every level, narrowing the scope of everyone's job, from unskilled laborer to fully skilled toolroom worker. From the skilled craftsman's point of view, this breakdown and recomposition of work was not a happy development. Under the old shop organization, he could move more or less at will from the concentrated effort of a skilled finishing operation to the more relaxing (if occasionally heavier) tasks of unskilled machine operation: "Processes of this description, at one time, within the recollection of us all, came within the usual work of the skilled man," recalled one older craftsman in the mid-1930s. "When I was in the shop, we used to call it 'currant jam.' " As the easier tasks were progressively sifted out and distributed to others, the skilled supervisor or tool setter was left with only the most onerous and taxing phases; the rhythm that governed his day under the old craft organization was succeeded by a more intensive regime, in which he moved from one laborious or troublesome task to the next, without respite and often without additional compensation.[74]

After 1915, Britain's Ministry of Munitions pressed relentlessly on employers and craftsmen, seeking to extend dilution to its technical limits. The ministry's

---

arrived complete with "process sheets," detailing technical and organizational innovations permitting the extended employment of women.

[73] See Drake, *Women in the Engineering Trades,* for some excellent descriptions of the fragmentation of labor in munitions factories.

[74] Modern Records Centre, University of Warwick (hereafter MRC), EEF, Central Conference, no. 66, Barrow reference, York, 11 June 1937, p. 10; Amalgamated Engineering Union (AEU) representative speaking.

standing army of dilution of labor officers, many of whom were middle-class women, roamed the controlled establishments, ferreting out men who were doing work that women could handle efficiently. In the course of her work, the dilution officer often found that although the ASE had officially lowered the barriers to women's employment at the Treasury Conference, individual craftsmen were keeping up a guerrilla struggle against the invaders on the factory floor. With the option of open protest closed off by wartime legislation, skilled men fought the good fight through a variety of quieter means, from sullen refusal to cooperate to outright sabotage of women's work. In one factory whose management had judged women a failure in shell work (*the* province of women's work par excellence after 1914), the dilution officer discovered that craftsmen had deliberately set the machines wrong, so that women would scrap a prohibitively high percentage of the work. In another factory, the charge hand removed women from shell boring on the specious ground that it was too heavy for them (in the national factories, women routinely handled all phases of shell production, even on the largest bombs); lack of proper tools hampered women's progress in a third shop.[75] Sometimes the men altered their tactics, inviting women to cooperate in limiting output by bluntly instructing them on the finer points of craft restriction. One morning a particularly speedy worker arrived at her lathe to find a note pinned to the bench: "The right output for this machine is 18 [pieces per hour]." She had been pulling out 27.[76] The ministry recommended that employers do their utmost to end this subterranean warfare, as it threatened the flow of weapons to the front.[77]

In theory, overcoming resistance to deskilling harmonized with employers' prewar campaigns to raise productivity and limit craftsmen's control. But sometimes it was the employer's unwillingness to depart too radically from past methods that stood in the way of further rationalization/dilution. These men grew especially evasive when they were urged to use women for skilled or heavy work. One contemporary was struck by employers' "prejudice" against women in skilled jobs, and in 1917 noted that "several firms report that women are not allowed to set their own tools."[78] In the fall of 1916 the ministry embarked on a patient campaign to prove, through repeated demonstration, what employers were inclined to disbelieve on its face—that,

---

[75] All these tales of frustration and woe were reported in *DLB*, February 1917, pp. 54–56.

[76] Kirkaldy, *British Labour*, p. 15.

[77] One firm found that hiring the female friends and relatives of male workers helped to minimize their opposition. The ministry published this helpful hint in *DLB*, March 1917, p. 44. Another firm reported that the men's objections to hiring women in the toolroom crumbled when they read "the Ministry's views [of women toolmakers] in black and white in their 'Bulletin' ": "Process Sheet," *DLB*, February 1917, p. 62.

[78] Adam Kirkaldy, *Industry and Finance—War Expedients and Reconstruction* (London, 1917), p. 46.

given the proper tools and organization, women could execute the most difficult and demanding tasks with speed and accuracy that were in every respect up to the men's standard. To this end, the dilution officers lent employers of little faith highly skilled and experienced women: "demonstrator operatives" who had trained for at least six weeks (sometimes as long as six months) in government schools, then informally apprenticed in factories and workshops as skilled men's assistants, where they learned to execute a range of skilled work—fitting, turning, welding, and toolmaking.

These women were assigned to firms that reported trouble in deploying women and spent several months analyzing the problems (errors in adapting the machinery, craft sabotage, or just plain bad management, as when foremen gave ambiguous directions), then organizing and training the women:

> When I started, there were ten girls, without discipline, without instruction, wasting most of their time, turning out more scrap than work; when I left at the end of the month there were forty-four girls in a better shop with 1d an hour added to their pay, as well as shortened hours, all capable of taking on any filing to templates, riveting, bending, drilling or other simple [i.e., semiskilled] work, and of doing it in good time.

The demonstrator operatives also furthered the ministry's long-range scheme: to extend the ambit of women's employment by steadily upgrading labor. "There was quite a number of enterprising girls willing to be taught more difficult work. By December the girls' benches were responsible for all fuselage clips, besides all parts filed to templates, a great many bending jobs, riveting, small assembly jobs, soldering, etc."[79]

At the end of a typical two-week period in 1917, women dilution officers around the country had sent back to the ministry recommendations for the following labor transfers: 77 skilled men from work where they were no longer needed; 376 women to replace men directly; 560 additional women to be introduced; and 55 women to be upgraded (10 toolsetters, 10 forewomen, 35 toolroom workers).[80] Government policy thus forced industrialists to inaugurate two distinct kinds of change on the engineering factory floor: extensive subdivision, "rationalization," and substitution of women in those sectors and processes where it was technically feasible; and the swift education and upgrading of semiskilled women and men in sectors that remained technically dependent on some level of craft skill.[81]

[79] IWM, Women's Work Collection, Mun. 17/7, Dorothy Poole, typescript account, 1919, pp. 8, 7.

[80] *DLB*, March 1917, p. 77.

[81] Most factories were affected by both kinds of change. As work moved toward mass production, women and men were promoted off the floor and into the toolrooms and specialized production shops around it.

Substitution through changes in the labor process was carried furthest in shells and fuses, where production was reorganized according to a highly detailed division of labor. Thanks to the extreme standardization of the product—the size of the shell was really the only variable—a full-scale turn to mass production was possible within the available technology and feasible because demand was unlimited. The conjuncture of extreme fragmentation in production work with the progressive scarcity of male labor forced an abrupt reversal in a sexual division of labor that had designated this industry an exclusively male preserve before the war. Even in the toolroom—the factory's technical apex—standardization narrowed the range of skilled work demanded. Workers had only to learn to grind and sharpen a fairly restricted array of tools, and with careful training, women could move on to this simple toolmaking as well. By 1917, firms were employing 50 percent, 75 percent, even 95 percent women,[82] and the government could reasonably stipulate in its contracts for shells that at least 80 percent of the operatives employed in executing the contract be women.[83] The state's wartime policy thus reinforced a nascent connection between women and the deskilled process work of mass production, a connection that was to endure well past the Armistice and define a growing arena of opportunity for women workers in the postwar engineering industry.

Government policy also created a pool of highly trained women, some of whom were, by the employers' own admission, on a par with fully skilled men.[84] When craftsmen objected to the rapid upgrading of women and laborers, the ministry hastened to point out that the upgrading aspect of dilution posed no danger to the skilled man's preeminent position within the industry: "These women were to be trained for the purpose of producing munitions;

[82] "In many factories the workers are 95% female, and include every variety of semi-skilled mechanic, 'gauger,' 'examiner,' 'tracer,' clerk and unskilled labourer, together with a minority of women taking the places of fully qualified or skilled tradesmen as 'toolsetters,' 'fitters,' etc., in the toolroom": Drake, *Women in the Engineering Trades*, p. 43. In France, a few factories also used women for essentially all phases of shell and fuse work. By the end of the war, 86.5% of workers in the assembly halls at Citroën's Javel plant were women, as were 80–90% of workers who filled shells. Final inspection of the finished shells was performed exclusively by women at Javel. See Schweitzer, *Des engrenages à la chaîne*, p. 56.

[83] The clause appeared on all government contracts for shells and further specified that the term "operative" included not only unskilled machine tenders but laborers, all production workers, toolsetters, viewers, charge hands, and repair and maintenance staff. See Ministry of Munitions, *Official History of the Ministry of Munitions* (London, 1920–24), vol. 4, pt. 4, p. 78, and *DLB*, January 1917, p. 35.

[84] See testimonial letter from Neville Gwynne (employer at Gwynne's Aircraft, Chiswick, South London, 1919) to Joan Williams, toolroom worker at Gwynne's, appended to her memoir of 1919 in IWM, Department of Printed Books: ". . . you were the only one in the whole works to rise to the elevated position of toolroom hand—a position that only a limited number of men apparently rise to, after going through their five years apprenticeship. The accuracy of your work was extraordinarily good."

not for the sake of educating mechanics. . . . This specialised training was not designed to produce expert engineers or craftsmen but simply persons understanding how to do expertly one particular job."[85] But the craftsmen knew better. As standardization narrowed the range of skills demanded in the toolroom, employers would cast a more receptive eye on the growing host of women trained to perform this work for a wage well below the craft rate. Dilution thus threatened the entire structure of skilled work, as well as the craftsman's monopoly on work in the trade.

The pressure to expand production, then, opened employers to experiments with novel methods. The experience permanently changed the way employers viewed the possibilities for women's employment in the industry. If none was converted to the idea of a wholesale replacement of men by women, many were convinced that the line of demarcation between male and female must shift if the industry was to remain competitive on the world market: "This is work that can and should be done by women and boys and girls, who . . . would quickly learn, and whose pay would be less than that of men. . . . The war itself, as a great economic force . . . is giving their chance to working women. . . . Employment can and will never be the same again."[86]

[85] PRO, Mun. 2/1276, T. Z. Zimmerman, "Report on the Training of Munitions Workers in Great Britain," pt. 2, submitted to the Commercial Economy Board, National Council of Defence, 30 August 1917.

[86] From an article in the *Scottish Law Courts Record,* quoted in Ministry of Munitions, *Official History,* vol. 4, pt. 2, p. 48.

Equal Opportunity Denied

Well before the outbreak of war, around the turn of the century, the contours of the female workforce had begun to shift. Although none could have predicted it at the time, both England and France were to experience a decline in women's overall rate of participation in the paid labor force. But on the eve of war, the first signs of this reversal were barely visible in Britain and still lay fifteen or more years in the future in France. In fact, war brought to a climax the long-term trend toward ever-higher rates of female participation in paid work in France, pushing women's proportion of the paid labor force from 38.2 percent in 1911 to an estimated 46 percent in 1918.[1] At least 35 percent of these women were married—the very women who by the turn of the century had begun to leave the formal paid economy in Britain. Because the decline in women's overall participation in Britain's formal economy had already begun, the war came not as climax but rather as interruption. By 1911, women formed only 29.1 percent of the British workforce, and among them only 13.2 percent were married.[2]

---

[1] Jean-Louis Robert, "Women and Work in France during the First World War," in Jay Winter and Richard Wall, eds., *The Upheaval of War* (Cambridge, 1988), p. 262.

[2] Gail Braybon, *Women Workers in the First World War* (London, 1981), p. 25. To put the comparison in its starkest terms, nearly half (48.8%) of all married women were listed as "employed" in the French census of 1911, as compared with a scant 9.6% of married women in Britain that same year. As Susan Pedersen notes, "Married women, taken as a group, were fully *five times* as likely to be in the labor force in France as in Britain in 1911": *Family, Dependence, and the Origins of the Welfare State* (Cambridge, 1993), p. 71. For the statistics of married women's participation in the labor force, see Tilo Deldycke, H. Gelders, and J.-M. Limbour, *La Population active et sa structure* (Brussels, 1968), pp. 169, 185. Women's higher rate of participation in paid labor in France reflects that nation's gentler pace of industrial development and the persistence of small-scale production in both agriculture and industry. In 1906, fully 60% of France's industrial workforce labored at home or in firms with fewer

In both nations, then, women's participation in paid work, having risen steadily since the mid–nineteenth century, would gradually drop off: after 1900 in Britain, after 1925 in France. In the long run, the war did not disturb that trend. But war did hasten the redistribution of women workers away from traditionally female sectors of the economy—clothing, textiles, domestic service—toward the new consumer goods industries. This shift from declining to expanding trades reinforced the widespread perception that war had wrought permanent change in the economic life of both nations. And it had, but not in the ways in which most people imagined it. In the popular imagination, working women had stepped from domestic obscurity to the center of production, and into the most traditionally male of industries. In truth, the war brought thousands of women from the obscurity of ill-paid and ill-regulated work as domestic servants, weavers, and dressmakers into the brief limelight of weapons production. After the war, some returned to their old jobs, but others stayed on in metalworking, usually moving into the most advanced and profitable sectors of the interwar industry—electronics and automobiles. Their movement out of the shadowland of women's work masked the gradual, longer-term fall in women's overall participation in the paid economy of twentieth-century Europe.

Mobilizing French Women for War

The sudden military mobilization in France sent the economy into disarray. Twenty-five percent of the prewar workforce and nearly half of all economically active males were called up in the initial days of fighting, and 40 percent of those who remained were thrown out of work as shops and factories closed their doors for the duration.[3] Although some businesses gradually returned to a semblance of normal activity over the fall of 1914, others would not reopen until after the peace had been signed. At the very moment their husbands and brothers were leaving for the front, thousands of women found themselves without work. Municipal authorities responded anemically to the crisis, opening workshops where women could earn one or two francs a day

than ten workers. See Michelle Perrot, "On the Formation of the French Working Class," in Ira Katznelson and Aristide Zolberg, eds., *Working-Class Formation: Nineteenth-Century Patterns in Western Europe and the United States* (Princeton, 1986), p. 72. The expectation that working-class women would continue to earn wages after marriage and throughout their childbearing years, formed in the context of small-scale and familial enterprises, continued to govern official policy and broader cultural assumptions regarding women's work well after the onset of large-scale industrial development around the turn of the century. See Jane Jenson, "Gender and Reproduction; or, Babies and the State," *Studies in Political Economy* 20 (Summer 1986): 9–46.

[3] Gerd Hardach, *The First World War, 1914–1918* (Berkeley, 1981), pp. 88–89.

sewing uniforms for soldiers. But even this meager assistance reached only a fraction of the unemployed. In Paris alone, women's unemployment hit 21 percent by October.[4]

Alternative means of support were slim indeed. At Fr 1.25 a day (plus 50 centimes for each child), the separation allowance for soldiers' wives did not approach the bare subsistence level. Even in the low-wage women's trades, a woman of average skill earned twice that amount, and the allowance was always intended as a supplement to wages, not as a substitute for them. Genuine relief would come only in the spring of 1915, when local munitions factories began to hire women in substantial numbers.[5]

The women who entered the metalworking factories were drawn entirely from the working class, cross-class appeals to women's patriotism notwithstanding. Few were strangers to waged work, for in prewar France, some kind of paid employment was nearly universal among the daughters of the industrial proletariat.[6] Although popular images of the *munitionette* focused public attention on the younger recruits, the available data suggest that many older women accompanied these young girls into the defense plants. In fact, a study of four large shell factories around Paris reveals an age structure rather similar to that of the prewar female factory labor force: over two-thirds of the women were between twenty and forty, and nearly half of this age cohort was over thirty.[7] The prevalence of older and married women, by comparison with the increasingly youthful female workforce of Britain, comes as no surprise in view of their high rates of labor force participation before the war. The war industries were to draw many more worker-mothers back into paid employment.

But far from drawing on a housebound "reserve army" of labor, the war

[4] Mathilde Dubesset, Françoise Thébaud, and Catherine Vincent, "Les Munitionettes de la Seine," in Patrick Fridenson, ed., *1914–1918: L'Autre Front* (Paris, 1977). See also AN, F22, 565, Ministère du Travail survey of economic activity in the First District (Paris region), 17 August 1914; and Laura Lee Downs, "Women in Industry: The Employers' Perspective" (Ph.D. thesis, Columbia University, 1987), chap. 2. Ultimately, over 92% of mobilizable males in France—that is, 7.9 million of the 8.5 million men between the ages of 18 and 46—were mobilized in the course of the war.

[5] The transfer of labor to weapons production was neither smooth nor immediate, however, and throughout 1914–15 high unemployment outside munitions coexisted with chronic labor shortage within. In the second year of the war, with over 60,000 women receiving unemployment benefits in the Paris region alone, employers were still complaining that they could not recruit enough women. See AN, F22, 538, Henri Sellier, "L'Organisation du placement des ouvrières dans les usines de guerre," p. 3.

[6] Robert, "Women and Work," p. 262. Nearly 39% of all women worked, in a land where about 30% of the population still worked the land and another 30% belonged to the industrial working class.

[7] The survey covered four shell plants that employed a total of 1,043 women: Marcel Frois (labor inspector for Paris), *La Santé et le travail des femmes pendant la guerre* (Paris, 1926), p. 157.

industries drew somewhere between 80 and 95 percent of their women workers from other, "feminized" sectors of the economy: clothing, textiles, domestic service. Thus, no more than 20 percent had come directly from the home. Women listed their previous occupations (in descending order of popularity) as needlework of every variety, factory work (textiles, printing), commercial jobs (including street peddling), office work, domestic service, and a few miscellaneous professions: nursing, teaching, hairdressing.[8]

Factories in the *banlieue* (suburbs)—site of rapid expansion in metals and electrical goods since the 1890s—were able to draw on a pool of far more experienced workers, for many hundreds of women had worked in these industries before the war, making lamps, batteries, and cables. A survey of ten defense plants in the *banlieue* shows that one-quarter of the women had worked there or in similar establishments before the war. Moreover, nearly half the female labor force was drawn from some kind of industrial background; only 28 percent lacked any previous industrial experience. In Paris proper, where the urban economy relied more heavily on commerce, services, and artisanal production, the figures are very nearly reversed: only 29 percent of women electrical workers and 13 percent of women metalworkers had worked in similar industries before the war; 28 and 17 percent, respectively, came from other industries, while 43 percent in the electronics works and 70 percent in the metals plants came from nonindustrial occupations.[9]

Work in the war factories was heavy, dirty, and laborious, and could be quite dangerous as well; in Paris alone, more than 100 workers were killed by explosions in powder and grenade factories.[10] The hours were long and

[8] André Citroën, "La Vie à l'usine," *Conferencia*, 1918, cited in Sylvie Schweitzer, *Des engrenages à la chaîne: Les Usines Citroën, 1915–1935* (Lyon, 1982), p. 56. In May 1917 Auguste Pawlowski found that of 1,876 women employed in a large shell and fuse factory near Paris, only 319 had previously worked in a factory and only 4 identified themselves as *mécaniciennes de profession;* that is, experienced metalworkers. The vast majority (676) came from the needle trades; 95 others had worked as domestics before the war; 119 had done office work and 154 listed commercial backgrounds. Most of the remaining women were housewives. See Auguste Pawlowski, "La Main-d'oeuvre féminine pendant la guerre," *Revue Politique et Parlementaire,* 10 May 1917, pp. 252–53.

[9] Housewives are lumped into the nonindustrial category, along with laundresses, garment workers, etc. The sample from the *banlieue* covers ten plants, which employed 1,139 women among them. The Paris sample covers four electrical works, with a total of 1,026 women, and eight metals shops, employing 592 women among them. See AN, F22, 534, Ministère du Travail survey, "L'Organisation des crèches," 1918.

[10] Figures for deaths and mutilation are highly uncertain, as the press was heavily censored and appears to have consistently underreported the carnage. When in 1916, for instance, the Billaud grenade factory exploded the press reported 30-odd deaths, but workers at a nearby factory counted 125 corpses being carried from the smoldering sheds, "not to mention the women and children, horribly wounded and transported to the hospital, where they must surely have succumbed": AN, F7, 13366, report from a meeting of the Syndicat des Ouvriers en Ouvrières et Métaux de la Seine, held at the Bourse du Travail on 11 December 1916, p. 4. Jean-Paul Brunet notes that the Pinet-Charnier powder works in Aubervilliers, popularly

women rarely received a warm reception from their male colleagues. Yet financial need was a powerful goad. In an economy where many working-class households relied on two adult incomes, the man had departed for the front and his daily wage of Fr 6–8 had been replaced by the soldier's Fr 1.25. Meanwhile the woman's contribution was either nullified by unemployment or undermined by the rising cost of living. Under the best of circumstances, households that had gotten by on Fr 8–11 a day before the war were now struggling to subsist on Fr 4–5, while the cost of basic goods (bread, coal, rice, cheese, meat, and vegetables) had risen 25 to 30 percent.[11] As the cost of living pushed steadily higher, even those who had hung on to their jobs through the mobilization began to cast a hungry eye toward the powder mills and shell factories, where one could earn twice the normal woman's wage of Fr 2–3 a day.

By the spring of 1915, posters covered the walls of Paris and the newspapers were filled with appeals for more women workers in state arsenals and private industry. Spurred by perduring unemployment in the "nonessential," feminine sectors of the economy and attracted by the promise of higher wages in munitions, women responded to the call with alacrity. Although the official channels—bourses and labor exchanges—had begun to function more effectively under Thomas's labor controllers, unofficial networks were also important. Not only did employers recruit heavily among the wives and daughters of their mobilized workers, but women seem to have heard about munitions work as much by word of mouth as they did from the official advertisements. One young woman, employed in a pharmaceutical lab when the war broke out, recalls hearing of an opening at Ducellier's grenade shop from one of her fellow employees, who was earning Fr 6.50 a day there—more than double the Fr 3 she took home each day from the lab. She applied immediately and got the job.[12]

Material want was certainly a powerful spur. But in a society that evinced little regard for women or its working class, women workers may also have been drawn to the war factories out of a desire to place something in the

---

known as the "death factory," exploded at least twice, in 1915 and 1917: Saint-Denis: La Ville rouge (Paris, 1980), p. 176.

[11] If July 1914 is assigned a base value of 100, prices had risen to 122 by January 1915 and 136 by January 1916: Jean-Louis Robert, "Les Luttes ouvrières en France pendant la première guerre mondiale," Cahiers d'Histoire de l'Institut Maurice Thorez, no. 23 (1977), p. 41. Jean-Jacques Becker notes that complaints and open, sometimes violent protests were far more commonly directed at rising food prices than at wages during the first two years of war in Paris: The Great War and the French People (New York, 1985), chap. 8. See also John Horne, Labour at War: France and Britain, 1914–1918 (Oxford, 1991), p. 395.

[12] Interview with "Mme M," a grenade worker at Ducellier's from 1915 to 1917, then till 1919 a lathe operator producing shells and an adjuster in the aviation shop at Renault, in Mathilde Dubesset, Françoise Thébaud, and Catherine Vincent, "Quand les femmes entrent, à l'usine: Les Ouvrières des usines de guerre de la Seine, 1914–1918" (mémoire de maîtrise, Université de Paris VII, 1974), p. 437.

balance against that negative judgment. Industrial war set the metals and munitions factories at the center of the national defense. By entering this traditionally male industry at the very moment it was catapulted into the public eye, by succeeding at arduous and often entirely new forms of work, and by earning twice the customary woman's wage for their pains, perhaps some women hoped to prove themselves, to stand forward as individuals of some value and importance. As one bullet maker put it, the husband had been the "master" before the war, and the wife had had to live according to his decisions. After 1914, however, "one had a right to a say in the matter, because one worked."[13]

Everyday Life in the *Usines de Guerre*

French women entered the metalworking trade just when the twin pressures of invasion and the rapid rationalization of work produced a steep decline in working conditions. With the declaration of war, the government had proclaimed a state of siege, which remained in force throughout the war. This emergency law curtailed many civil rights—freedom of speech, freedom of the press—and suspended all protective legislation at work: maximum hours laws, prohibitions on nightwork for women and children, laws requiring that dangerous machinery be fenced to protect the operatives. During the first three years of war, women and men in the war factories worked thirteen days at a stretch, on rotating shifts of eleven to twelve hours. On the fourteenth day they rested, in preparation for another grim fortnight.

Conditions in the factories were often deplorable—cramped, ill-lit workrooms with unfenced machinery, insufficient and filthy lavatories, and inadequate medical facilities for treating the all too frequent injuries on the shop floor.[14] Worse, employers ran their equipment continuously and pushed work-

[13] Interview with "Mme X," who worked at the Cartoucherie d'Issy throughout the war and again in the interwar period, after her husband's death (he had been gassed in the trenches and died in 1928), ibid., p. 442. Under the Napoleonic Code, husbands were literally *chefs de famille*. Women acceded to that status during their husbands' absence but relinquished it when the men returned.

[14] Lack of protection, long hours, and the relentless pace of work combined to produce a high rate of rather spectacular accidents, particularly in factories where people worked with explosives. A survey of eight Parisian firms (employing a total of 1,685 women at the time) lists 81 accidents among women workers during November and December 1915 alone: AN, F22, 535, Ministère du Travail, Service médicale de la place, M. le médicin Aide-major Klotz, "Du contrôle médicale des accidents de travail dans les usines de guerre," n.d. The report attributes the high accident rate to women's long (eleven-hour) shifts and the absence of barriers around most machinery. Typical accidents included crushed fingers and hands caught in whirring gears and the overhead belts that drove the equipment. Women who adjusted their lathes without switching them off (and many did, in order to lose as little time—and therefore as little piece-rate money—as possible) were far more likely to lose fingers in the turning parts. One woman was killed while cleaning a press (unfenced, of course) when the

Shellmaking in an unnamed war factory in Limoges, 1917–18, AN, F22, 555.

ers to ever-greater feats of speed at the assembly table or on the machine. By manipulating piece rates and production bonuses and wielding the patriotic goad—"A single minute lost, another death at the front," as the newspapers put it—management pressed workers to sustain this rapid pace.[15] Finally, employers had taken the mobilization as an opportunity to depress wages across the board, slashing mobilized men's rates by some 20 to 30 percent. Perhaps they had hoped that news of the abrupt wage cuts would be lost in the upheaval and dislocation of war. But it did not escape the sharp scrutiny of syndicalist militants in the CGT's Fédération des Métaux, who carefully monitored and publicized each downward revision in rates. Jobs in which men had earned anywhere from Fr 0.80 to Fr 1.20 an hour in 1914 paid only

---

hydraulic accumulator came loose and crashed down, crushing her. The committee recommended shorter hours, more frequent rest periods, fenced machinery, and on-site first-aid stations with accredited factory doctors.

[15] Quoted in Dubesset et al., "Quand les femmes entrent," p. 29.

Fr 0.45 to 0.70 an hour (about Fr 5–7 a day) in December 1915. "For women and juveniles the exploitation is more odious yet, surpassing all that one could imagine."[16] For the least skilled machine tending, on which men earned 45 centimes, women received a mere 35 centimes. On more skilled jobs, a woman might earn as much as 40 or even 50 centimes an hour, but most earned between 35 and 40 centimes, and took home about Fr 3 each day.[17]

In the winter of 1915, a delegation from the Fédération des Métaux approached the minister of war, hoping that the renegade socialist might be moved to step in and ameliorate labor's desperate situation in the *usines de guerre*. Millerand's response was blunt and uncompromising: "We are at war. There are no more workers' rights, no more social laws. There is nothing now but war."[18] It would be some months before Thomas's ministry would alter this harsh stance, not by overturning the state of siege but through carefully chosen interventions on behalf of a beleaguered and increasingly feminized workforce in the *usines de guerre*.

Thus the broader context of women's war work in France included long hours and harsh conditions, all "justified" by the national crisis of invasion and occupation in the east. Within this broader framework, however, women labored under widely variable circumstances in individual war factories. Some went to work in the small, older shops in the city itself. Many of them were filthy, overcrowded, dim, and ill equipped, with nonexistent or dirty lavatories and aging, temperamental lathes that jammed frequently and demanded constant adjustment. For women, who were paid by the piece, being assigned to such a machine was a sore trial indeed. So long as the machine was down, her earnings stopped, and in a workshop filled with such equipment, the enforced idleness could last several hours as one waited one's turn for the attention of a skilled male machine setter. Even when the setter did arrive, women were not paid for the time lost while he reset the tools. Hence they often learned to fix their own machines when they jammed, and some even mastered the more elaborate task of setting up for a new run, so as not to lose wages while they waited for the tool setter.

In the large new works on the periphery or in the *banlieue*, conditions were rather different. Some, such as Citroën's new Javel plant, had been built

[16] Commission Executive des Métaux, "Salaires et travail des femmes. Prélèvements de solidarité," *L'Union des Métaux*, May–December 1915. The 1915 scale for male workers ran from Fr 0.45 to Fr 1.10. Wages above Fr 0.70 were presumably paid to civilian men, whose wages would have been more difficult to slash without repercussions.

[17] Ibid.

[18] Quoted in Philippe Bernard, *Le Fin d'un monde, 1914–1929* (Paris, 1975), p. 23.

with the mass production of shells and a female workforce in mind. Here women worked in vast, airy halls, brightly lit by arching skylights, where production flows had been planned before the machinery and conveyor belts were ever laid down. Moreover, Citroën had installed a widely admired set of "social services" at Javel: large refectory and canteen, well-staffed infirmaries, adequate lavatories and changing rooms for the workers, and crèches and nursing rooms for their children. Each shop boasted brand-new lathes and presses, fresh off the boat from America. Though women were equally dependent on tool setters and foremen—the speed and smoothness with which a machine functioned depended on the quality of the setup—the new equipment was far less persnickety, and mere assiduity usually sufficed to make the basic rate each day.

Yet all war work proceeded under certain common constraints, whatever the condition of the physical plant. The workday was long, starting (on average) at 7:00 A.M. and ending at 6:45 in the evening, with a ninety-minute break for lunch at noon (workers preferred to return home for lunch whenever possible). For most workers, a lengthy commute to and from work added an hour or more to each end of the day, hours spent grappling for a place on the chronically congested trains and trams. The night shift usually began fifteen to thirty minutes after the day shift ended, and continued until 6:15 the following morning. The mid-shift break, taken around midnight, lasted only an hour, and workers stayed on the premises, usually in the workshop itself, to eat their meal. Machinery was rarely switched off during such pauses.

Factories usually rotated the shifts, with women working two weeks on days followed by two weeks on nights. Although some shops observed a half or full day's rest each Sunday, many women worked thirteen days (or nights) at a time before receiving a single day off. Moreover, if an urgent order came in, the foreman would tour the shop, selecting those who would stay on to work overtime (at no increase in compensation) until the order was finished. Spates of 24 or even 36 hours of continuous labor were all too common, especially during the first years of war. On the night shift, one woman reported, "some fell asleep in the WC. If it hadn't been for Sundays [off], three-quarters of us would have died. Some did die."[19]

The fatigue of long hours and heavy labor was exacerbated by the discomforts that inevitably attend the metalworking process. Extreme temperatures and poor ventilation were perennial problems, even in the most modern factories, while every phase of the production process was accompanied by the deafening clash of steel against steel. In 1918 Citroën published a brochure

---

[19] Mme X, in Dubesset et al., "Quand les femmes entrent," p. 441.

celebrating the streamlined beauty of his ultramodern, fully rationalized shell plant at Javel. This self-congratulatory description waxes almost lyrical on the sharp sounds and smells with which women lived and worked each day:

> The factory's entire output ends up in this workshop, where all the operations are completed at prodigious speed, in the midst of deafening noise, punctuated by the rattle of lead balls flowing without interruption, in an atmosphere shaken by the vibration [of pneumatic presses] and filled with the odor of melting resin.[20]

Women on assembly or inspection were allowed to sit as they did their work, but machine operators spent the entire shift on their feet, as did the laborers who carried materials from one site to the next. A woman who turned shells at Renault remembered the war as a time of perpetual exhaustion. The factory had snapped her up because she was large and strong, but after several weeks of ten-hour days spent wrestling with her old and crochety lathe, she had lost thirty-three pounds.[21] Workers' fatigue was exacerbated by the pressure to produce rapidly for the men who waited in the trenches, a pressure that many employers reinforced by periodically lowering the piece rates.

Discipline was strict in the *usines de guerre*. If work began at 7:00 A.M., the factory gates were locked at 7:05. Anyone who arrived later had to wait until the lunch break, and so lost the morning's wages. Once stationed before the machine or assembly table, women were expected to work swiftly and quietly, neither singing nor speaking with those who worked alongside them. If a worker spoiled a piece while machining it, she was usually asked to pay the cost out of her pay packet. Too many spoiled pieces and she lost her job. In Renault's aviation shop, where the limit was two, one woman set her tools badly and spoiled several pieces as a result. She hid them in her locker, but one day she fell sick and someone discovered them. Only an error in the bookkeeping department saved her from losing her job. "It's because you're a woman and a complainer," groused one of her male colleagues. Another grumbled: "They kept you because you're a good-looking broad."[22]

Industrialists, labor controllers, and the men at Thomas's ministry all cast anxious eyes on the frequent and "indiscriminate" mixing of the sexes in defense plants, particularly on the night shift. Such mixing stirred uncomfortable visions of moral order and good work discipline sliding inexorably toward

---

[20] *Une Visite à l'usine André Citroën*, brochure published by the enterprise (Paris, 1918), quoted in Schweitzer, *Des engrenages à la chaîne*, p. 185.

[21] Mme M, in Dubesset et al., "Quand les femmes entrent," p. 438.

[22] Ibid., p. 439.

Women and boys drilling and tapping shells for the 155 gun at Etablissements Simon Frères, Cherbourg, September 1917. AN, F22, 555.

chaos.[23] Employers therefore tried to separate women from men wherever possible, and women sometimes worked in shops, or areas within a shop, where all the production workers were female.[24] The only men to be seen were those who set and regulated the machinery, and, of course, the foremen and shop chiefs. In such cases, the "natural" rule of male over female under-

[23] In his report on unrest at Clément-Bayard, Sous-Lieutenant Baret, labor controller for the Third Military District (northern Paris), devoted some pages to "the moral dangers presented by the promiscuity that reigns in mixed shops," particularly on the night shift: AN, F22, 539, "Compte-rendu relatif aux conditions de travail des ouvrières à l'usine Clément-Bayard," 28 August 1916, p. 4.

[24] This kind of segregation was rarely feasible on the job, but employers seem to have worried less about the well-patrolled factory floor than about the unstructured time in the factory yard as women and men came and went between shifts. Some solved this problem by

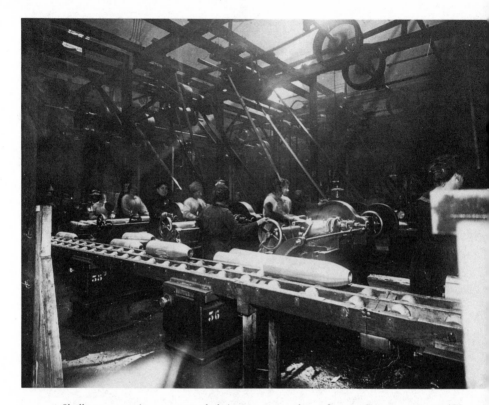

Shells on a moving conveyor belt in an unnamed war factory, France, 1917–18. AN,
F22, 555.

wrote the authority structure on the factory floor, lending a gendered subtext
to the frequent antagonism between production worker and overseer.

Memoirs and oral histories from the war factories abound in evidence of
conflict between women and their supervisors, conflict that sprang in part
from women's technical dependence on these men. Workers complained
bitterly of foremen who took advantage of their powerful position to play
favorites among the women machinists: "Those who were 'in' with the setter
always had their lathe properly set."[25] One of the ways women expressed their

staggering the shifts so that women arrived half an hour after the men and left half an hour
earlier (or later), a practice that allowed women to enter the shops "without fear": AN, 94
AP, 348, Général Perruchon to Mario Roques, "Le Travail des femmes," 1 October 1916, pp.
3–4. Such segregation was typical before the war; good work discipline and good moral order
were indissolubly linked in official minds. See BMT, January 1918, p. 18.

[25] Mme X, in Dubesset et al., "Quand les femmes entrent," pp. 440.

resentment was to accuse these men of being *embusqués*, cowards who hid out in the factories in order to evade the draft.

Government officials were aware of the animosity between women workers and their male supervisors. In the summer of 1916, one of Thomas's staff cautioned industrialists about its negative effects on productivity: "Foremen, team chiefs or group leaders, and male workers should speak correctly and encouragingly to women workers; . . . they will get much more out of these workers with rewards than with punishments."[26] Nonetheless, women did not always receive a sympathetic hearing when they protested their ill treatment at foremen's hands. In the summer of 1916, for example, a worker at Clément-Bayard complained that unwanted attentions from the team chief had forced her from her job. The district's labor controller, Sous-Lieutenant Baret, was instantly suspicious: "It is all too easy to suspect a male worker who in comradeship gives his hand to a woman worker in difficulty." He therefore went straight to the team chief to get the "real" story. Not surprisingly, the chief had quite a different tale to tell. He claimed that the worker in question was in fact habitually late for her shift, and that when he had tried to raise this problem, the woman had flown into a rage, punching and slapping him around. What else could he do but fire her? The chief's account of his own self-effacement before a subordinate rings somewhat false, especially in light of the fact that the firm immediately turned around and rehired the allegedly unruly worker, taking care to place her on a different work team. One wonders what kind of unpleasant behavior the team chief masked in his less than credible rendering of the conflict. But his story was good enough for the lieutenant, who heard in the woman's grievance nothing more than the work of "a malevolent imagination . . . distorting the truth" and stirring up trouble.[27]

Some believed that segregating the sexes would minimize the conflicts between them. Yet it was rarely possible to do so, and when women and men worked side by side at the same or similar tasks, there was no hiding the pay differential that gaped between them. "You make no more pieces than I do," said a woman of her young male co-worker in Renault's aviation shop. "Why do you earn so much more?" (He was paid 11 centimes per piece, versus her 6.) "It's because you're a woman, it's normal," he replied with unruffled aplomb.[28] Women chafed at the manifest unfairness of the system that ruled their wages. Yet the unpleasant discovery of the male production worker's

[26] Georges Calmès, "Note sur l'utilisation de la main-d'oeuvre féminine," *BUG,* 31 July 1916, p. 112.

[27] AN, F22, 539, "Compte-rendu relatif aux conditions du travail," p. 4.

[28] Mme M, in Dubesset et al., "Quand les femmes entrent," p. 438.

relative and arbitrary privilege rarely produced a movement for equal pay. More often it simply reinforced women's certainty that the only way to make up the difference was to redouble their speed. As one woman told the labor inspector: "You really have to hurry in order to earn as much as the men do."[29]

The male–female wage differential was but one distinction among many on a factory floor that was furrowed by such divisions. After rupturing the prewar order on the factory floor, mobilization and the demands of war created a workforce that by 1916 was divided into three roughly equal parts: (1) workers who were new to the industry, including women (about 30 percent in Paris) and foreign/colonial labor (10 percent); (2) civilian men (a little under 30 percent); and mobilized men (29–33 percent). The civilians were men ineligible for military duty for one reason or another—older than 45, unfit (a low standard indeed, as time went on), or noncitizens (generally Belgian refugees).[30] To some extent, each category lived under a rule specific to it. Colonial labor was drawn from the colonial military reserves, and hence subject to military discipline while stationed in French factories. These men (the military did not recruit women from the colonies) were placed in the most arduous and ill-paid jobs, often heavy work in the forges, which were ferociously hot and usually located at some distance from the rest of the works. Their wages dangled perilously close to those of women: about Fr 8 a day in 1916, when most women earned Fr 6–7, and native Frenchmen took home Fr 9–10 for simple laboring, closer to Fr 15 for skilled work.[31]

Renault maintained the physical separation of these men after hours, for they lived in barracks hastily erected by military officials concerned to restrict contact between colonials and the rest of the workforce, especially the women. "We never spoke to them," one woman recalls. Another, who worked at the Issy cartridge plant, remembers being afraid of the Annamites, who gathered in the little woods surrounding the works and uttered menacing cries—"draz, or something like that"—as the women hurried past on their way to work.[32] European women workers (Spanish, Italian, Greek) do not seem to have been segregated from French women; neither, for that matter, were European men. The labor inspectors concurred, however, in judging such women as

---

[29] Woman worker to Pierre Hamp (labor inspector for Albert Thomas), quoted in "Le Quart en moins," *L'Information Ouvrière et Sociale,* 9 May 1918, p. 1.

[30] Belgians may have been classified as civilians rather than foreigners because so many had worked in French industry before the war, or perhaps because so many spoke French and arrived as refugees with the French from the invaded territories in the northeast. See Gary Cross, *Immigrant Workers in Industrial France: The Making of a New Laboring Class* (Philadelphia, 1983). The civilian category also included men who had been drawn to metalworking from other occupations.

[31] See Horne, *Labour at War.*

[32] Mme M and Mme X, in Dubesset et al., "Quand les femmes entrent," p. 439. Horne (*Labour at War*) notes that officials were haunted by the specter of sexual contact between French women workers and colonials, and recorded with evident anxiety the growing number of marriages between them.

clearly inferior, producing on average 20 percent less than French women and utterly incapable, the inspectors reported, of certain kinds of work at which French women excelled, notably serial production and assembly work.[33] The work they did and the wages they were paid, as well as the convictions of their employers, set all foreigners apart from French workers.

In January 1917 ten *munitionettes* from Paris toured the war factories of Britain, the second half of an exchange between the war industries of the allied nations.[34] One of the ten recounted her impressions of the trip in words that suggest that for these women, Britain represented a hope for the future, a contrast with the harsh realities of life in the arms factories of Paris. Each day the *munitionettes* were taken to four or five factories around London "where only women were employed. . . . Everywhere there is air, light, and a constant concern for comfort and hygiene. With understandable pride, they showed us the infirmary, the lavatory, and the refectory." In the refectory the French women were treated to a glimpse of British custom, even in the midst of war: "You know how our neighbors love their tea: it is a ritual for them. The 'five o'clock' is too old a tradition to be broken abruptly. What an amusing spectacle to see, in a factory, women in trousers gathered around the tea table!" In the end, however, it was the civilized structure of everyday life in British factories that seized the French observers:

> Women rarely work more than eight hours and have the 'English week,' that is, they're off on Saturday afternoons and Sundays . . . the cloakrooms are irreproachable . . . the infirmaries are more like little hospitals. In almost every factory there is a lady doctor . . . kitchens and refectories are spotless, to say nothing of the afternoon tea, the hot meals prepared for those on the night shift.

French factories looked quite grim by comparison: "They have more fore-sight than we do, they take thought for the future." All that one could say for French industry was that it appeared more productive; "output in these factories is lower than in ours . . . the series of movements is less carefully regu-lated."[35]

The ten returned to Paris to tell a glowing tale of life in English factories, a tale that constituted, explicitly and by implication, a catalogue of errors and deficiency in French industry: poor conditions, lack of amenities (cloakrooms, lavatories, canteens), long hours, little hope of advancement, strained relations with foremen and shop chiefs. But if the Parisian women were convinced that they had seen the shape of things to come in London's well-equipped

---

[33] *BMT*, January–February 1918, p. 15.
[34] The ten were drawn from Citroën, Panhard, and the state artillery park at Vincennes.
[35] *BUG*, 19 February 1917, pp. 342–43.

Woman worker at the New Gun Factory, Royal Arsenal at Woolwich. Imperial War Museum.

munitions plants, those who toiled outside England's few model factories would have told a rather different story. Women in munitions did enjoy the coveted "English week," but hours were still long, accidents were many, and wages rose too slowly to compensate for the hardship and dangers encountered on shell and fuse work. Had the Ministry of Munitions merely led the Parisian delegation down the proverbial garden path, or was there any truth to the women's sanguine impressions of conditions across the Channel?

British Women at Work in Munitions

When she was very nearly sixteen Isabella McGee left her home in Belfast and traveled to Coventry, hoping to find a job in the munitions industry. The trip was long—first a boat to Holyhead, then a train across Wales to the Midlands. Times were hard, for the war with Germany had thrown hundreds out of work in Dublin and Belfast. Yet that same war also opened up good jobs in English factories; by 1916, all Ireland had heard tales of young girls earning fabulous wages in munitions. So when the British government offered free passage to all Irish women who volunteered for such jobs, Isabella McGee was among the first to make the journey.

No sooner had she landed in Coventry than the government office set her up with a place to live and a new job making explosives at the White Lund factory in nearby Morecambe. The hostel offered unaccustomed luxuries— hot baths, good meals, even maid service—and plenty of entertainment, between the dance hall (complete with piano) and nearby movie theaters. But as Isabella soon discovered, the unfamiliar luxuries of meals and maid service were necessities. When could a woman who worked twelve hours at a stretch for thirteen days straight, moving on and off the night shift as production demanded, find time to cook her own meals or scrub the sheets and floors?[36]

Like many women, McGee began her career filling shells. Her job was fairly straightforward. Each day she stood twelve hours before a press in the explosion room, stemming the shells (that is, filling them with explosive powder) as they arrived on the line.

---

[36] Not every munitions worker made such a happy landing. The Ministry of Munitions' Health of Munition Workers Committee noted in 1917: "Women and girls frequently arrive at munitions centers without luggage or any clothing except what they are wearing and without any money; they are often hungry and thirsty, having had no food on a long journey. The reasons were poverty or exaggerated reports about free lodging and wages in advance": British Health of Munition Workers Committee, memorandum 17, *Health and Welfare of Munition Workers outside the Factory* (London, 1917), p. 4.

I was a press operator, which was pressing the 9.2 shells on a little bogey waggon and it went down so many inches and left room for the TNT bag to fit in. . . . [The shells] come through this trap door and you'd put the lever on to stop it, and then you had to go out in the corridor and there was a kind of machine like a compass and you had to work it up till a certain time on the clock . . . and that brought the bogey up and this stem—it was a big thick steel stem—come down so many inches and that left sufficient room in the shell for the explosion TNT bag to fit in . . . and then you had to turn it back, and when you turned it back then automatically the trap doors went up. And you had to release the bogey that the shell stood on and take it back to the inspection room, and then there was an inspector and he took a gauge and gauged it to see if it was correct, and that's when they used to put the explosion bag into the gas shell.[37]

Working with explosives was dangerous, and employers did not keep anyone on such work for very long. The major ingredients, tetryl (somewhat toxic) and TNT (highly toxic), were volatile powders that seem to have caused some degree of injury and discomfort to all who worked with them. Women who handled the tetryl recall that, at the very least, the noxious powder burned in the nostrils and throat and stung any exposed skin on the hands and arms. "If you had a little scratch on your hand, like a little dig, and you wasn't wearing gloves, you could feel that almost eating your flesh away . . . if it got inside your cut."[38] The tetryl also turned women yellow, head to toe, and gave dark hair a distinctly greenish cast. Lilian Miles, who worked four months on a press at the nearby firm of White & Poppe, shaping the yellow powder into bars, remembers "you'd wash and wash and it didn't make no difference. It didn't come off. Your whole body was yellow . . . but it wore off once you were out of it. It sort of got out of your system, I suppose."[39]

The yellow tint, which won tetryl workers the epithet "canary girls," was an early symptom of toxic jaundice, a disease that ultimately killed more than a hundred munitions workers and caused hundreds of others considerable distress. In the middle of the war, Drs. Agnes Livingstone-Learmonth and Barbara Martin-Cunningham warned employers that working with TNT brought on a host of symptoms, ranging from the merely painful and irritating (sore, swollen throat, persistent cough, rashes and skin eruptions, constipation or diarrhea, nausea, vomiting) to several dangerous, sometimes fatal disorders

[37] IWM, Sound Records Dept., Isabella Clarke (née McGee), "War Work, 1914–1918," accession no. 000774/04, typescript, p. 19. Hereafter page numbers appear in the text.

[38] Ibid., Caroline Rennles (née Webb), "War Work, 1914–1918," accession no. 000566/07, typescript, p. 60. Hereafter page numbers appear in the text.

[39] Ibid., Lilian Annie Miles, "War Work, 1914–1918," accession no. 000854/04, typescript, p. 15. Hereafter page numbers appear in the text.

of the digestive, circulatory, and nervous systems, including blurred vision, drowsiness, memory loss, delirium, convulsions, and coma.[40] Caroline Rennles, who filled shells for nearly a year at Slades Green, outside London, remembers that many women endured low-level poisoning for weeks on end: "Of course, some of the girls used to have stomach pains, the poison used to go in . . . of course, we never had gas masks or nothing like that. Mind you, the manager used to say to us 'Keep your mouth shut,' but of course we used to sing and all that kind of thing and as I say you never used to bother, like" (p. 60).

Tetryl's clearly toxic effects led employers to start switching women off explosives every four to six months, and, in theory, to confine such work to women over twenty-one. "We had to wear pumps," Lilian Miles recalled, "and you had to take all your clothes off in case there was any linen buttons with the tin inside because of explosions, so you had to wear just the . . . uniform . . . and you had cocoa about three times a day. What was in the cocoa we don't know but they reckoned there was something in it for killing the gas" (p. 17).[41] But a few cups of cocoa was no proof against the deadly powder. Not long before the Armistice, Lilian Miles lost her older sister to TNT poisoning.

> Well, she was ill. She went to the doctor. The doctor said that she was under the influence of alcohol because she was falling about. And she couldn't hold herself up. . . . So the doctor told her to come back again when she was sober. . . . Well, I went down to the doctor and I said to him 'She doesn't drink. . . . There's something wrong with her because . . . she's falling about all the while.' And of course she was only nineteen. . . . She died before she was twenty. . . . And they took her to the hospital. And she died in terrible agony. . . . They said that the black powder it burnt the back of her throat away. (p. 18)[42]

So after six months spent filling shells at White Lund, Isabella McGee moved on to the Coventry Ordnance, which had just begun hiring women.

---

[40] "Observations on the Effects of Tri-nitro-tuolene on Women Workers," *Lancet* 2 (12 August 1916): 261–64.

[41] Employers supplied milk or milk-based cocoa to their workers in the hope that it would coat the stomach and so protect the insides of those who breathed in the noxious powders each day. Women who worked with TNT were organized into small teams of six. The explosion rooms or danger sheds where they worked were small buildings set apart from the rest of the factory so that, in the event of an explosion (which was a fairly frequent occurrence; eighty-seven women were blown up in England during the war), the entire factory would not be lost. Before entering the sheds the women had to remove all metal pins, buckles, and buttons (for fear of sparks) and don a special uniform.

[42] Factory doctors were often quite ignorant about TNT poisoning. George Ginns (a foreman at White & Poppe, then at Daimler) remembered that one doctor, puzzled by the yellow stain that spread across the "canaries'" skin, concluded that the women were simply not washing themselves adequately: IWM, Sound Records Dept., Ginns, "War Work, 1914–1918," accession no. 000775/05.

Women filling shells in a danger shed at the national filling factory at Banbury.
Imperial War Museum.

For the rest of the war, she would work here in the gun shop, making the
8-inch howitzers.

When she first arrived at the ordnance, Isabella was put on the night shift,
which she preferred because she could earn more money, and sent to work
under the supervision of Jack Bolton. Bolton was a young man, an ex-soldier
who had been wounded in action and recently released from the army. He
put Isabella to work minding a machine that bored and finished the gun
cradles. The work was routine and, worse yet, ill organized, for Coventry
Ordnance was not yet fully operational. "When we came to the Ordnance
works they hadn't got the machines properly all up and they'd only just built
the new howitzer shop . . . and for a few weeks we had practically nothing
to do but we still got our wages." So while Bolton raced around setting up
the new machines and getting the shop in order, Isabella sat idle at her

Munitions workers in a shell factory, probably in Manchester, July 1918. Imperial War Museum.

machine, reading and crocheting because there was so little work for her to do. After a few weeks, the overtaxed young charge hand came by to inquire about the leisurely pace of things at Isabella's machine. She responded quickly, pointing at another machine on the floor. "Well, there's a machine up there if you'd let me have a go at I think I could manage it" (p. 20). Though somewhat skeptical at the sixteen-year-old's self-confidence, Bolton decided to let her have a try.

The next night, Isabella stood before her new machine, cleaning it down as she tried to divine its inner workings. The new machine, which hollowed out the howitzer barrel, then placed the slinger nut into the gun cradle, was not so simple and automatic as the boring and finishing operations that had episodically claimed her attention since her arrival at the ordnance. So when her more skilled male colleagues offered to help Isabella master the new machine, she happily accepted: "And there was [a] gentleman, called him

Tammy Barnes. . . . And he helped me a lot, and another older gent from Cambridge Street taught me a lot . . . and of course I went on a treat and I learned everything" (p. 4).

The night shift began at five o'clock in the evening and ran straight through until eight the next morning.[43] After cleaning down her machine, "which I always did do first to make the machinery free to handle," Isabella would adjust it to begin the run, hollowing out the inside of the howitzer barrel and placing the slinger nut precisely in the cradle. The setup demanded that she make extremely fine measurements with her gauges and micrometer, in order to determine within a fraction of a millimeter the shape and dimension of the cuts that her machine would make in the metal. "And of course you worked with the gauges in them days, they weren't automatic machines like they are today. When you were getting a job you had to set up with a micrometer and vernier" (p. 5). Once she had established the dimensions of the operation, Isabella had to adjust the machine itself, a job that called for a good deal of strength. "The men were more than good to me . . . because it was them that used to make me these bars of steel to put on the spanners to help me" (p. 4). The steel bars gave her more leverage to tighten the bolts and helped her to steady the machine at the table.

But Isabella's progress did not proceed without a fuss. "Well the men was kicking up in the section because of me doing the job and I wasn't getting the rate" (p. 4). So she applied for the rate, but the bosses told her that she was ineligible because she was underage. When she protested, "I'm doing the same job as them," she was told, "No, but you can't grind your own tools" (p. 5). Isabella then turned to her friend Tammy Barnes, "and of course he took me in with them the week and I was able to grind my own tools and put the lip on it and all the rest" (p. 5). When she reapplied for the rate, management rewarded her efforts with a substantial raise.

But she still was not getting the full rate, for youth and femaleness clung stubbornly to Isabella. "But then I wasn't getting as much money as I should have been getting but it was through no fault of theirs [the men's], it was my own because I was still underage but I was ignorant of the matter" (p. 6). She did not receive the full rate for the job until she joined the Transport and General Workers Union (T&G), which interceded on her behalf and pressed the employers to recognize the justice of her claim.

I still didn't know nothing at all about unions, and there was a Miss Arnold, . . . and she asked me why didn't I form a union among the other girls.[44] There

---

[43] This is fifteen, not twelve hours, but McGee is presumably including time spent cleaning and setting up the machines. That time was rarely booked.

[44] Alice Arnold organized women metalworkers for the T&G throughout the war and into the early 1930s.

Woman worker adjusting her lathe. Imperial War Museum.

was a good many Irish girls there at the time. . . . And I [joined] and they [joined] . . . and it was [Miss Arnold] that come and advised us and told us what we were entitled to and enlightened us as to what to fight for. . . . And [the union] was where they put me right about the rates and that and that's how I got the rate. (pp. 6-7)

As one of two women working in the howitzer shop, Isabella posed a highly visible threat to the men's wages.[45] Indeed, as far as they were concerned, this young woman, performing the work of a semiskilled man for the meager wage normally paid to teenaged girls, was nothing more than a rate-breaker.[46]

[45] Other shops at the ordnance employed hundreds of women, but the howitzer shop, with more specialized production, seems to have employed only Isabella and her "mate" on the day shift, Annie Wall.

[46] The situation was complicated by the fact that although Isabella was doing what could, objectively speaking, be termed semiskilled work—setting up and operating a semi-automatic machine—she was doing it in an environment where fully skilled men might well be doing precisely the same sorts of things.

"When I went to the Ordnance setting up my own machine the men never spoke to me bar this old gentleman . . . and when I asked for the rate the men I felt was up against me" (p. 6). In protesting her placement on the new, "men's" machine, Isabella's co-workers unwittingly inaugurated her informal apprenticeship at the ordnance, for in their outcry Isabella heard the news that her work was the same as theirs, and therefore deserved the same rate. As far as she was concerned, the logic of events entailed her being trained to set up the machine and grind her own tools, so that she might justly demand the rate for the job. But this was not precisely the response her mates had anticipated. By objecting to her working the new machine, the men had hoped to have Isabella returned to the boring and finishing machine, a machine they seem to have accepted as appropriate for women.

Isabella's story thus illustrates one way in which the war was destined to disrupt the prewar system of shop-floor divisions. Further, it reveals that skilled craftsmen were not invariably opposed to such changes, so long as their own rates were not under siege. "And . . . when I got the rate, then of course the men made a bit of noise with their spanners and that" (p. 6). Indeed, Isabella's approach to the problem—learning to grind and set her own tools, then applying for the rate—seems to have led the men in this shop toward some kind of accommodation with less skilled women co-workers. "If they said to me what wages was I getting and I worked with them with the rate, which was them that advised me about the rate, the men were more than good to me afterwards" (p. 18). Clearly, the men's acceptance of Isabella's working the new machine depended in part on her having won the rate such work commanded. But the fact that so few women worked in the howitzer shop probably didn't hurt either. The men accepted this lone pair of young women, so long as they were being paid the rate, and did not view their presence as a harbinger of feminization.

Isabella's accomplishments did not go unremarked by the bosses. One evening the "principal man" of the Coventry Ordnance, Mr. McCarthy, approached Isabella's machine with the words "I only wish we'd thought of this earlier." He then "tapped her on the shoulder," thus signaling that she had been selected for promotion. He watched her grind her tools and promptly pronounced her promotable, on the condition that her counterpart on the day shift, Annie Wall, undergo a comparable examination. "I had a word with her—she was a good operator—and I said, 'Well, Annie, if I can do it you can do it' " (p. 19).

By her seventeenth birthday, then, Isabella not only performed the work of a semiskilled man, she had won the pay and status of one as well. Fifty years later, she still spoke with genuine pleasure when she recalled the job. She had earned "about six times as much as I would have got in Belfast and I didn't work a quarter as hard" (p. 7). Although she no longer remembers the precise amount that turned up in her pay envelope each week, her level of expenditure suggests that, at a time when the government found it expedient to curb exploitation by legislating a minimum of £1 a week for women munitions workers, Isabella took home at least £2 a week. "I used to send my mother a pound a week and my grandmother five shillings a week because she was an old-age pensioner, and the first time I went home she wanted to know how it was I had such nice clothes and such a lot of money; I was sending her money and my mother money and where did it come from?" (p. 7).

Isabella was let go soon after the war ended and returned to her family in Belfast. "We were laid off straightaway as soon as the war finished. We all got free tickets [back to Ireland]" (p. 21). Other women workers remember the joy with which England greeted the peace. "Everybody was out in the street dancing and singing and plenty of drink everywhere," Lilian Miles recalled. "All the pubs had their doors open. There was free beer everywhere" (p. 31). But for Isabella, the Armistice celebrations were a subdued affair, for a friend from home, Julia Miles, had just lost her hand in an accident at White & Poppe's. "Well of course there was detonators and that sort of thing that they were handling and working with . . . when Julia had the hand off they took her to Coventry and Warwick Hospital, and of course that was the week that they were all . . . enjoying themselves when the war was over . . . her losing her hand and me going down to the hospital to see her" (p. 22). But if Julia's injury ended Isabella's war on a sorrowful note, it did not prevent her from looking back nearly fifty years later to recall that it had been "a very happy time" working at the ordnance—"the atmosphere in work and with the people you worked with. There was never no strikes or any trouble of any kind. If you wanted to know anything the men was quite willing to help you" (p. 23).

As in France, war immediately slowed or closed down those industries that were not militarily essential (the garment, jewelry, and other small luxury trades) or that depended on imported materials (cotton textiles). These were industries in which women were disproportionately clustered, and by September about 1 million women—44.4 percent of the entire female workforce—were out of work. Among men, who had the option of joining the army, the comparable figure was 27.4 percent. Male unemployment dwindled rapidly, disappearing altogether by December. But for women, short time and unemployment persisted until the end of April 1915.[47] These women did not have an

[47] Irene O. Andrews and Margaret Hobbes, *The Economic Effects of World War I on Women and Children in Great Britain* (New York, 1921), pp. 22–23. The Labour Party's Central Committee on Women's Employment estimated that in September 1914 the heaviest employers of women were employing (full-time) only 13 to 39% of their peacetime female workforces: 33% in the fur trade, 26% in printing, 13% in boots and shoes, 34% in dressmaking (in the large

easy time, for unemployment benefits were rare, and the munitions industry, locked in the pre–Treasury Agreement struggle over dilution, did not rush to pick up the slack. The sole form of organized relief lay in the "Queen Mary Workrooms," where, for 10s. per week—2s. below the worst wages that prewar sweatshops had to offer—women sewed blankets and uniforms for the military.[48] For most working women, the first year of war was a time of tremendous hardship. Their prospects remained bleak until munitions plants began to hire women workers en masse.

As a young working-class woman, McGee was a typical recruit to munitions work in Britain. Although most of these women were new to metalworking, few lacked the experience of paid work; indeed, more than 90 percent came from working-class households and occupations. Wartime journalists told a glowing tale of duchesses rubbing shoulders with charwomen on the factory floor, of an upsurge in national feeling so powerful that it dissolved the rigid social barriers of prewar England:

> I have seen together, working side by side, the daughter of an earl, a shop keeper's widow, a graduate from Girton, a domestic servant, and a young woman from a lonely farm in Rhodesia, whose husband had joined the colours. Social status . . . was forgotten in the factory, as in the trenches, and all were working together as the members of a united family.[49]

In truth, the munitions factory workforce was far less catholic in its social composition. According to the most generous estimates, middle-class women formed a bare 9 percent of the munitions factory workforce, and not all of these were full-time workers.[50] Many were doing their patriotic duty by joining replacement teams, which came into the factories on weekends to spell the regular shifts. Others were the "women demonstrator operatives," hired directly by the Ministry of Munitions to press dilution on reluctant employers. But most of the middle-class women in munitions were working as welfare supervisors. Middle-class women's participation in the actual work of arms production was thus rather slight in comparison with working-class women's role. But the fact that such women appeared in the factories at all suggests a degree of cross-class participation that, however slight in Britain, was practi-

---

firms; small firms retained only 31%), 39% in the jam and sweets industries, and 18.5% in the furniture and upholstery trades. See Sylvia Pankhurst, *The Home Front* (London, 1932), chap. 4.

[48] This semicharitable organization was funded by the Queen Mary Fund (hence the title) but organized by a group of prominent Labour women, including the trade union leader Mary MacArthur, Margaret Bondfield, Susan Lawrence, and Dr. Marion Phillips.

[49] L. K. Yates, *A Woman's Part* (London, 1918), p. 9. Yates's book is essentially ministry propaganda, intended to sell the idea of war work to both women and their putative employers.

[50] Marion Kozak, "Women Munition Workers during the First World War, with Special Reference to Engineering" (Ph.D. thesis, University of Hull, 1976), p. 122.

cally absent in France. There, none but the working class ever saw the inside of a munitions factory before 1917, when the employers introduced a few bourgeois welfare supervisors. The 9 percent who pitched in (on weekends only, for the most part, spelling absentee workers) did not approach the "equality in sacrifice" that women and men called for in France. Nonetheless, the symbolism of upper-class participation suggests a level of social consensus around the conduct of the war in Britain that was fast disappearing in France.

Despite journalists' delight in the vision of gentlewomen mingling with "the people" in defense plants all across Britain, memoirs and oral histories from the period suggest that class distinctions were by no means buried in those factories where middle-class women found employment. One woman was outraged to learn that doing her patriotic duty entailed working under a man of "inferior station." When he ventured to point out that she had bungled a job, she snarled back: "You're the sort I've been brought up to despise."[51] Clearly, these women carried into the factory a sense of class pride that clashed with the foremen's own elevated position within those gates. The foremen's authority was perhaps rendered all the more tenuous by the fact that many of them had attained their positions only because of war-time upgrading.

Foremen were not the only ones who chafed at the snobbery and condescension of bourgeois war workers. "I can't bear Mrs. So and so, she's so sarcastic—much too sarcastic to speak to *me!*" confided one working-class factory hand. Joan Williams, the skilled fitter in whom she confided, was sensitive to the cross-currents of class and gender on the factory floor: "I could quite understand the foremen preferring to have real working girls under them to the 'War-workers,' who were apt to make much more fuss when displeased and to complain to higher authorities, without being able to be frightened by any threat of dismissal."[52]

In the early twentieth century, working-class women were beginning to leave the paid economy upon marriage as a matter of course. The war temporarily interrupted this long-term trend toward a younger and unmarried female workforce, calling older and married women back to the regular industrial employment that most had abandoned when they married.[53] By 1918, the proportion of women in the national labor force had risen from 29.1 percent

[51] IWM, Department of Printed Books, quoted in Joan Williams, "A Munition Worker's Career at Messrs. G, 1915–1919," typescript, p. 47.

[52] Ibid., p. 47.

[53] But the war did not alter the trend toward young, single women, which persisted through the 1920s, then began to shift back toward older and married women during the 1930s. See Adam Kirkaldy, *British Labour, 1914–1921: Replacement and Conciliation* (London, 1921), p. 30; and Miriam Glucksmann, *Women Assemble: Women Workers and the New Industries in Interwar Britain* (London, 1990), chap. 2, for long-term age structure. Also Downs, "Women in Industry," chap. 3.

in 1911 to 37 percent, and at least 40 percent of these women were married.[54] But if the experience of paid employment was familiar to most munitions workers, the engineering factory was certainly not. As in France, barely 5 to 6 percent of the prewar engineering labor force were women. This figure was destined to rise rapidly, reaching 30 percent or more by 1918, as British engineering factories drew workers from the faltering women's trades—cotton, lace, tailoring, millinery, pottery—from domestic service, and from the growing "reserve army" of women who had retired from paid work upon marriage.[55] In 1917 the Ministry of Labour found that in a sample of 444,000 insured women munitions workers, fully 70 percent had been employed in other trades and occupations when the war broke out.[56]

As in France, regional variations in the pattern of women's work provided employers with labor pools of varying skill and experience. In the Birmingham district, for example, women already made up 30 percent of the local metal-working labor force before the war began. Some made nails and chains at small forges in the smoky old shops that won the region its sobriquet, "the Black Country." Others worked in the new consumer goods sectors—lamps, bicycles, car accessories—in which the demand for semi- and unskilled labor was high. In the coal mining districts of Wales and Northumbria, by contrast, women who worked outside the home were most likely to be employed as servants in the homes of wealthier women.[57]

London was yet another story. Like Paris, the city boasted a largely nonindustrial workforce, with women employed in service industries and semiartisanal trades such as garment-making, printing, and the boot and shoe trade. In the semirural districts on the city's southern perimeter, where new plants sprang up rapidly after 1914, employers recruited strong but industrially inexperienced young women from the farm families in the area. It was not at all unusual for a British employer to prefer such workers, "to get women who have never been on a machine before and train them from the beginning."[58] They made up for their lack of specific experience with their innocence of "bad habits," such as restricting output in order to keep piece rates from

---

[54] Kirkaldy, *British Labour*, p. 30. Kirkaldy suggests that as many as 40 to 60% of war workers may have been married while a survey of nine Glasgow firms employing 2,000 women shows 37% married. "The women have previously been, for the most part, shop workers, domestic servants, *machinists and dress makers, the last two classes being preferred by one firm because of their familiarity with fine machinery,* and by another firm as being a class suffering through lack of employment": Adam Kirkaldy, *Industry and Finance—War Expedients and Reconstruction* (London, 1917), p. 126; my emphasis.

[55] Even those recruited from this domestic "reserve" had probably held regular jobs before marriage, and some continued to work irregularly at a host of casual employments—charring, piecework at home—afterward.

[56] *Labour Gazette,* December 1917; Downs, "Women in Industry." p. 130.

[57] Kirkaldy, *Industry and Finance*, p. 46.

[58] Kirkaldy, *British Labour*, p. 25.

falling. "[I]n a mixed shop the men very soon begin to attain a moral ascendancy over the women and simply make the women do what they want them to do . . . the women have learned in two years the old soldier tricks that the men learned in several generations."[59] By separating these rural "innocents" from the jaded characters who normally dominated the factory floor, employers hoped to weaken the grip of craft control over the pace and methods of work.

Restricting output was a perennial problem in French industry as well, yet I found no parallel strategy in France, no instance in which employers sought out by preference women who lacked industrial experience simply to evade craft control. This difference is perhaps explained by the comparative weakness of trade union organization in French industry. Skilled men were less able to impose a disciplined regime of craft restrictions on their fellow workers, as their resentful yet despairing comments on women's industriousness suggest: "Women's greed for high wages . . . leads [them] to pursue [their] own earnings without regard to corporative concerns."[60] Hence, while French employers also worried about mixing the sexes on the factory floor, their concerns were explicitly moral, focused on the sexual conduct of workers and its impact on overall discipline, and reflect little concern with skilled men as a competing locus of loyalty/authority.

Isabella McGee's tale underscores the confusion that reigned in factories all over Britain during that second year of war, when women first moved into the engineering shops. It seemed that each day some new piece of equipment arrived, while old plant was torn up and shifted around. The ancient, multipurpose lathes were being pressed into reluctant service, turning standardized parts at speeds far in excess of those for which they had been built. Women who entered the factories at this point recall that the confusion made for less than ideal working conditions.

Women normally worked fifty-four to sixty hours a week, though the frequent imposition of compulsory overtime brought many of their workweeks over the sixty-hour mark—short of the seventy-hour weeks prevailing in wartime France, but quite taxing nonetheless.[61] Morning and night, as the shifts turned over, women jostled one another in cramped, crowded cloakrooms, competing for a place at the single cold-water tap as they changed

---

[59] IWM, Women's Work Collection, Emp. 70, War Cabinet Committee on Women in Industry, "Minutes of Evidence," EEF testimony, October 1918, p. F82. One firm solved this problem by firing a group of women who had mastered the "old soldier tricks" and hiring a new crop, all of whom were put to work in their own shop, separate from male production workers (though supervised by male tool setters). See Kirkaldy, *British Labour*, p. 88.

[60] Pierre Hamp, *L'Information Ouvrière et Sociale*, 7 April 1918, p. 1.

[61] The two-shift system was so prevalent that women often worked twelve or thirteen hours a day—every bit as long as their counterparts in France. See PP 1916, Cd. 8185, *Employment of Women*, pp. 4–6.

in or out of oily, grime-coated overalls. Many of the new workshops were little more than sheds, hastily thrown up to protect the machinery from direct assault by the elements. They were damp and ill heated, and in the bitterly cold winter of 1915–16, the women's breath hovered in an icy fog before their faces, while fingers grew stiff and clumsy. In some factories, management encircled the machines with buckets of coke in the vain hope of dispelling the intense cold, but the smoldering coke filled the shop with noxious fumes and warmed only a small area. In factories that lacked canteens (as many did in the early years), workers gobbled their meals on the shop floor, with the evil fumes rising in the frozen air around them.[62]

Conditions soon improved, thanks to a combination of assiduous state intervention and middle-class voluntarism. By the following winter, most factories had expanded their cloakrooms and installed steam-fed radiators and hot water. Canteens had been organized, often by patriotic middle-class women, and many employers added a fifteen-minute tea break to the afternoon shift. Factory yards, churned to muddy bogs during the spring rains, were bridged with raised planks so that workers could cross over to the canteen without sinking ankle-deep in the muck and mire. And employers sometimes installed stools, so that the women might sit for some part of the shift.

As the speed of work increased, so did the rate of accidents—fingers and hands crushed in the powerful and heavy presses, clothing and limbs caught in the whirring belts that drove the machines, burns and eye injuries from shards of hot metal flying up from the lathe, and, of course, the slow poisoning from TNT. These hazards were standard in the munitions and engineering trades, but the war multiplied the accident rate many times over, despite the watchful eye of the Ministry of Munitions.[63] This concatenation of circumstances moved employers to set up first-aid stations and infirmaries on the factory premises, staffed by Red Cross volunteers and the occasional trained nurse. "Men needed the rest-rooms and other accessories just as much as women," observed the ministry's director of health and welfare.[64] Yet it is clear that the presence of women acted as a lever for all these reforms. Employers' perceptions of female difference, reinforced by similar convictions on the part of state officials and concerned middle-class women, thus found

[62] All descriptions are taken from oral histories and memoirs in IWM.

[63] According to one report, 289 women workers were killed in accidents in war factories, 35 of them in a single explosion at the Barnbow national shell factory in Leeds in 1916. IWM, Box 150/34.2.

[64] PP 1919, Cmd. 167, *Appendices of Evidence to the Report of the Committee on Women in Industry,* testimony of Dr. E. L. Collis, p. 206. Employers also incurred "unnecessary expense, nominally for the sake of the women," putting up new buildings and elaborate welfare provisions in order to spend out wartime profits that would otherwise have been skimmed off by the excess profits duty: Kirkaldy, *British Labour,* p. 14.

Women workers leaving the Fuse Danger Building, Woolwich Arsenal, May 1918.
Imperial War Museum.

expression not only in the technical division of labor but in the expansion of
first-aid stations and other welfare facilities after 1916.

Conditions in British munitions plants, then, though perhaps no better at
the outset than those in France, improved steadily during the first eighteen
months of war. By the winter of 1917, when the French *munitionette* delegation
toured the factories around London, their perception that they had arrived
in an industrial utopia was by no means inaccurate, at least comparatively
speaking. The rapid improvement of conditions and the important role played
by the Ministry of Munitions in forcing such changes suggest that the British
government's authority over the defense industries enabled politicians to
forge and maintain a degree of social consensus around the war which simply
could not hold in France. From the outset, Lloyd George had managed to
institutionalize a balance among the interests of labor, employers, and the

state which Thomas never achieved. On the contrary, the state's reinforcement of managerial autocracy in France combined with the imperative to build weapons and carry on the war under German occupation to produce circumstances that workers of both sexes remembered as grueling and inequitable. Worse, political ineptitude only compounded workers' sense of inequality in suffering, as the government failed to keep wages in line with the spiraling cost of living yet allowed arms profits to soar unchecked.

Ultimately the war would become a source of deep social division in France in a way that it did not in Britain. Women's memories of their work in munitions reflect this difference. Where French women spoke bitterly of unending fatigue, harsh working conditions, too little food, and the literal sacrifice of their health to the national defense, British women remembered the war as a break from routine, a time of high wages, a chance to prove themselves at men's work. Of course they, too, recalled hard work, long hours, and chronic exhaustion. Yet these things were accepted as part of a war effort in which all were taking part, in which the burden of sacrifice was distributed more evenly across the social landscape. In France, by contrast, the inequities simply mounted until, by 1917, French workers would cast their harsh working conditions in a larger political critique of the war as a source of gross inequality in fortune, suffering, and sacrifice.

Toward an Epistemology of Skill

As the months of war stretched into years, the extraordinary—women in metal factories, performing heavy or skilled labor—had gradually grown commonplace. An important element in the normalization of women's work was the erection of boundaries delimiting male and female space, masculine endeavors from feminine ones. Indeed, the very process by which women were assimilated into the formerly male world of metalworking rested on the careful reconstruction within the factory of the very sexual division that had barred women from most jobs in the industry before 1914. Establishing these boundaries was clearly important to the men, who feared that cheap female labor might replace them altogether. But it was equally important to the employers, who needed to distinguish male from female in order to identify the kind of labor power that came in female packages. Only then could they deploy those workers most effectively.

At the turn of the century, the metalworking factory floor was already structured along lines of difference—between skilled and unskilled, young and old, native and foreign. These boundaries defined relations of production both horizontally and vertically, fixing particular divisions of labor across the shop floor even as they established the lines of authority within which the divisions were inscribed. Further, as all boundaries were etched along the apparently unitary scale of distinctions in skill, the notion of skill provided workers and managers alike with a single language in which to discuss differences of all kinds—in age, class, and ethnicity—and to connect such differences to the capacity for performing particular kinds of work. Thus capitalist managers' beliefs about the significance of social distinctions often traveled under the rubric of "skill differentials." The war emergency would introduce a new kind of division, female/male, into a factory system that already aligned social differences with distinct roles in the production process.

Shop-floor boundaries were drawn with reference to a concrete if rapidly changing labor process, and so easily assumed the authoritative appearance of "natural" features, intrinsic to the production process. As a result, though workers might struggle bitterly over the precise placement of particular boundaries, they never challenged the principle of division itself, and employers in both England and France retained enormous discretion over the control and organization of work. Indeed, so long as employers and workers upheld the system of division as an inevitable and inescapable fact of factory life, the very boundaries that defined difference and justified inequality would continue to set the terms and establish the limits of shop-floor conflict.

After 1914, employers' ideas about the meaning of gender difference would intersect with the process of industrial rationalization to create a newly gendered discourse on job skill. Skill—that body of knowledge and host of capacities learned from the craftsman—seemed a constant component of labor value in this productive system, the one unshakable reality in factories turned upside down by wartime arrangements. But as wartime rationalization brought the final destruction of craftwork in the metals factory, job skill underwent radical redefinition. At a time when both the division of labor and the boundaries defining the traditional workforce were in flux, employers had to determine anew where genuine skill lay.[1] The language of skill, long used to apprehend and specify differences among men and boy workers, now opened out to embrace and contain the new category of labor, as employers sought to locate women in relation to the existing hierarchy of difference and according to notions of gender complementarity.

The contests over job demarcation that accompanied the new technologies of work reveal the contingent nature of the old shop-floor categories, separating skilled craftsman from unskilled laborer even as they expose the historical pro-

[1] On the question of skill, see Charles More, *Skill and the English Working Class, 1870–1914* (London, 1980); Ava Baron, "The Masculinization of Production: The Gendering of Work and Skill in U.S. Newspaper Printing, 1850–1920," in Dorothy O. Helly and Susan M. Reverby, eds., *Gendered Domains: Rethinking Public and Private in Women's History* (Ithaca, 1992), pp. 277–88; also Ava Baron, "The 'Other' Side of Gender Antagonism at Work: Men, Boys, and the Remasculinization of Printing Work, 1830–1920," in Baron, ed., *Work Engendered: Toward a New History of Labor* (Ithaca, 1991), pp. 47–69; Sonya Rose, *Limited Livelihoods: Gender and Class in Nineteenth-Century England* (Berkeley, 1992); Patricia Hilden, *Working Women and Socialist Politics in France, 1880–1914* (Oxford, 1986); Maxine Berg, "Women's Work, Mechanisation and the Early Phases of Industrialisation in England," and John Rule, "The Property of Skill in the Period of Manufacture," both in Patrick Joyce, ed., *The Historical Meanings of Work* (Cambridge, 1987), pp. 64–98 and 99–118, respectively; Cynthia Cockburn, *Brothers: Male Dominance and Technological Change* (London, 1983) and *Machinery of Dominance: Men, Women, and Technical Know-How* (London, 1985); Ann Phillips and Barbara Taylor, "Sex and Skill: Notes Toward a Feminist Economics," *Feminist Review* 6 (October 1980): 56–79; Barbara Taylor, *Eve and the New Jerusalem* (New York, 1983), pp. 83–117.

cess whereby the new category of "female labor" was constructed. Thus capacities that were defined as skills in the male were often recast as aspects of an essentially feminine nature when they were encountered in women workers—men are individuals, possessed of specific identities; women are creatures suffused by an essential and unitary feminine being; men act and develop in the world, women simply are. The language of skill difference, reforged in a series of wrangles with male workers, the wartime state, and women workers themselves, became one medium for expressing and deploying management's view of the content and salience of gender difference in the metals factory.

Yet the newly gendered discourse was riddled with instabilities, for on the factory floor, gender turned out to be a less stable polarity than employers or workers imagined; female "nature" did not always line up with the strengths and limitations it was believed to entail. Thus while employers frequently spoke about women and skill—of women doing skilled or unskilled work, and of the skills that women acquired or brought with them to the factory floor—what emerges from their wartime experience, and their ingestion of and reflection on that experience, is that mentally, employers could not always align female skills with male skills. As a result, women were not simply slotted into the skill categories already populated by men, even when they performed the same work. As far as metals employers were concerned, women formed a category unto themselves, and with their arrival on the factory floor, the old system of divisions—unskilled laborer, apprentice, semiskilled machine worker, skilled craftsman—would have to be expanded and reconfigured. If rapid change in the labor process entailed drastic change in the content of those old categories—what skilled men did in 1916 was rather different from the labors their fathers and grandfathers performed at the end of the nineteenth century—then women's arrival in the industry heralded a reshuffling of the categories themselves.

Wartime developments thus not only altered the technology and personnel of work but also broadened and reconfigured employers' understanding of what constituted job skill. Further, this shift in understanding was inextricably bound to women's arrival on the metalworking factory floor. After the war, managerial reasoning in light of this experience would produce a newly stratified labor force, articulated (as always) in terms of distinctions in skill. Now, however, the skill differentials embraced women workers as well. The emerging restratification of labor thus rested on a gradual and gendered shaping of skill which began soon after women's first entry into the trade. During the war, elements of this redefinition appeared in discussions of mechanization, industrial rationalization, and the struggles over equal pay. But the logic that was to govern the postwar restratification was articulated most fully in the debates that arose around the issue of training women for skilled work.

Industrial Rationalization vs. Job Training in the War Factory

As we have seen, the fragmentation and recomposition of labor in the war factories gave rise to entirely new forms of work. Some of the new jobs were not terribly demanding; others, however, called for skills of various kinds and degrees: great concentration, manual dexterity, and experience with a wide range of tools, machine and hand-held.

Most munitions work involved the cutting and shaping of metal parts— gun barrels, shell casings—with the later, finishing stages demanding greater skill and precision than the initial "roughing." Indeed, rough cutting was sufficiently blunt and imprecise that automatic machines could perform most of these simpler operations. The machine tender, typically a boy or "youth" in prewar days, simply fed the machine and watched as it shaved the ingot. The more delicate finishing operations (filing and fitting parts together) and the final work of inspection entailed the drilling, shaping, and finishing of metal parts to minute specifications. The qualities required for these highly skilled tasks included strength, "delicacy" (i.e., manual dexterity), accuracy, and independent judgment. Such work also demanded that the worker acquire a general "machine sense"—that is, sufficient familiarity with the equipment to be able to hear and feel how the cutting was proceeding, and so avoid spoiling the piece or jamming the machine. It also called for skill in the hand of the worker, as finishing was simply too precise and delicate for a machine to accomplish on its own.

Hence the disaggregation of craftwork had two important outcomes. First, it created a new setting for craftsmen, who were inexorably withdrawn from directly productive work and reintegrated into the rationalized flow of mass production as foremen and machine repairmen for less skilled production workers. Second, it created a host of new productive tasks, more narrowly defined than the all-around "jobbing" of the old craftworker. Initially compelled by the shortage of skilled men to place women on many of these new jobs, employers in both countries quickly forged a positive connection between women and fragmented, repetitive taskwork. Invariably these men grounded this connection in the notional identity between women's "distinctive" work attributes (swiftness, dexterity, and patience) and the character of subdivided labor.

It was not immediately apparent to employers that the forms of work created by industrial reorganization included jobs that required skill and understanding. In time of war, rationalization presented itself above all as a means to economize on skilled labor. As their interchangeable use of the terms "rationalization" and "dilution" reminds us, employers saw the new methods as resting primarily on the deskilling of craft labor. The fact that women performed much of the rationalized work, from simple machining to complex finishing, made it all the more difficult for managers to perceive the skilled nature of some jobs within the redivided and "deskilled" labor process. In managerial minds, iconic notions of women's domestic activities dovetailed with certain demands imposed by these new forms of work. Those same notions often blinded employers to the fact that much of the new work also required skill, for these men tended to view speed and agility as innate aspects of the female species. As we shall see, it was difficult for them to view women as educable in the same sense as men; that is, as creatures possessing the potential for growth and development.

As a consequence, the substitution of women for men was bound up less with programs of training and apprenticeship, which remained (some) men's route to success in the workshop, than with technical improvements on the shop floor. Indeed, to many employers, such improvements constituted a kind of investment in women, as well as an investment in the more modern methods and equipment that would enable them to compete more effectively in the postwar world. After surveying the opinions of munition employers, one French labor inspector concluded: "One can introduce women into the factory only to the extent that the machinery has been adapted to their capacities . . . the substitution of woman for man is closely dependent on the improvement of the machinery."[2] His statement reflects the tight association that developed in employers' minds between the swift, regular movements of more automatic machinery and what one (male) observer termed the "more continuous, regular, and gentle" movements of women workers.[3] Investing in technology rather than labor had the added advantage of permitting employers to retain control, to guard the greater portion of the investment's value even when labor turnover was high.

As successive redivisions of labor routinized production work, employers began to see a tight fit between the fragmentation and mechanization of work and the character of female labor. On the one hand, rationalization produced jobs that were deemed especially suitable to these workers. As one French employer remarked, "the work of women factory operatives has been reduced to purely manual labor by providing women with machinery whose successive operations demand a predetermined set of movements and no individual initiative."[4] On the other hand, women's "essential being," as

---

[2] AN, 94 AP, 348, "Note II: Le Recrutement de la main-d'oeuvre féminine," n.d. (probably 1916), pp. 3-4.

[3] Gaston Rageot, *La Française dans la guerre* (Paris, 1918), p. 4. Rageot was the drama critic for *La Revue Bleue* and a well-known man of letters in wartime Paris. A conservative republican with strong natalist convictions, Rageot also made frequent contributions to such center-right journals as *Le Temps* and *Annales Politiques et Littéraires*.

[4] Commandant Emile Auguste Léon Hourst, *Le Problème de la main-d'oeuvre: La Taylorisation et son application aux conditions industrielles de l'après-guerre* (Paris, 1917), p. 53.

manifested on the factory floor—gentleness, regularity, assiduousness, timidity, dexterity, swiftness—defined creatures whose bodies and movements were easily assimilated to the automatic movements of the machine.

> Some of these women have gained an extraordinary facility in operating these machines. One hears of women turning out twelve to fourteen thousand pieces in a ten-hour day . . . which means twenty-three pieces per minute. It takes two and one-half seconds to take a metal piece, place it in the notch of the mold, and press the pedal.[5]

The marriage of convenience between women and rationalized work was to endure beyond the Armistice and throughout the interwar period, defining the rapidly expanding realm of light, repetitive taskwork in the metals industries as the peculiar province of women. But Marcelle Capy, a feminist and socialist journalist who worked in a Parisian defense plant in 1917, reminds us that, as in many unions based on expedience, it was the convenience of one party, in this case the employers, that defined the nature and permanence of the bond: "Always repeating the same motions, constantly bending over the same machine, women have gained a tremendous facility. But to understand the mechanics of the machine, to acquire any technical skills, this is forbidden to them."[6]

Ultimately, metals employers would turn away from the possibility of training women for skilled work and opt for adapting the work to women's notional capacities through further subdivision and mechanization. This decision represents more than employers' own limited understanding of what women's capacities as a "class" of labor were. The breakdown and recomposition of the labor process after 1914 entailed a fundamental shift in investment strategy: investment in new technologies and managerial personnel rather than in labor and the education of workers. This structural change could be institutionalized only through negotiation and struggle with those skilled men whose power and position were put at risk by it. As they fragmented previously skilled work into tasks that did not require apprenticeship or some other lengthy education, employers often found it convenient to assign these jobs to women, not only because this course fitted their preconceptions of women's capacities but because it facilitated the renegotiation of skilled men's position and authority on the shop floor.

Thus the gendered understanding of job skill that emerged from the war, in which fragmented or repetitive forms of work were coded "female," represents

---

[5] AN, F22, 555, report from a factory in St-Ouen by M. Lavoisier, departmental labor inspector, "Note sur les perfectionnements apportés aux machines à découper et à emboutir," January 1919, pp. 1–2.

[6] Marcelle Capy, "Pas de professionelles," *La Verité*, 1 February 1918.

Woman working an automatic cartridge machine (for weighing and gauging the cartridge) at the Park Royal plant. Imperial War Museum.

employers' attempt to resolve a difficult and much-fought-over redivision of labor with their skilled men, whose services were still very much needed, if in somewhat altered form. Nonetheless, it must be emphasized that in allocating newly fragmented tasks to women, employers were not simply dumping on women the unpleasant, monotonous work that resulted from the redivision of labor in order to soften their conflicts with skilled men. Rather, this allocation harmonized with employers' understanding of who women are, as labor power, even as it shaped and limited that understanding, raising yet another barrier to the proposition that women could rise to the status of skilled workers. In the end, skilled work, though occasionally performed by women, could be coded only as male. At the same time, the categories of female labor and unskilled labor tended to overlap.

Many of the qualities that were to define women as a distinct source of labor in the metalworking trades were first articulated in wartime debates between state and employers over training women for skilled work. Some of the most heated controversies on the factory floor turned on the question of women's educability—whether they should have access to training, and whether it would make any difference if they did. Job skill seemed like a still point in the midst of a bewildering regime of change in the organization of work; at the very apex of a shifting hierarchy of new workers and new machines, the craftsman of prewar days stood firm. Only gradually did employers and workers come to understand that upheaval in the lower reaches of the skill hierarchy necessarily entailed changes in the meaning of skill itself.

Both British and French employers struggled to define women's abilities in three arenas. First was that of deskilled taskwork, a relatively uncontested field on which women competed with boys for preeminence. Unskilled work was repetitive and exacting but afforded little scope for initiative. A woman in such a job might possess a high degree of manual facility, but she could neither grind her own tools nor adjust her machine for a different run. Mme Clermont, who worked in a Parisian sword factory, recalls the highly particularistic nature of unskilled labor:

It is very curious, but highly subdivided work is completely mechanical. One must produce a lot and from morning to night the woman worker repeats the same motion. There is no call for initiative; it's all in the speed one must acquire. . . . Each does her part in trying to earn as much as possible. I am certain that while she's manipulating small bits of metal, the worker completely forgets that she is part of a larger structure.[7]

---

[7] Quoted in Mathilde Dubesset, Françoise Thébaud, and Catherine Vincent, "Quand les femmes entrent à l'usine: Les Ouvrières des usines de guerre de la Seine, 1914–1918" (mémoire de maîtrise, Université de Paris VII, 1974), p. 79.

Confined to a narrow set of movements, the unskilled worker had no reason to venture beyond them to an understanding of the overall process into which she had been slotted, or even of the machine she operated.

In the second arena, that of semiskilled machining and assembly work, more skilled and experienced women worked alongside semiskilled men. During the war and interwar years, this category of work expanded dramatically, becoming ever more shapeless and diffuse as it grew;[8] a catch-all category containing some jobs that were entirely new as well as the difficult finishing work (welding, hand-fitting) that had been shaved off from craft jobs. On this growing middle ground, work was no longer craft-based. Yet these jobs, though sometimes repetitive, required great concentration and careful execution. Clearly the semiskilled worker, man or woman, had to possess some kind of skill. Consequently, this was the field on which the meaning of skill most visibly shifted. Moreover, the fact that women performed a great deal of this work, and did it very well, placed the issue of gender difference at the core of this shift, and cast the broader reconfiguration of skill in terms of gender.

In the hybrid class of "semiskilled labor" the upwardly mobile woman or man promoted off the floor met the downwardly mobile craftsman, whose skills had depreciated with the advent of mass production. In shell and fuse factories, for example, the "rationalization" of work had routinized not only the work of production but that of skilled tool setters as well, who were called upon to service the same machinery in the same ways—sharpening identical bits and tools, setting the same speeds. Thus it was possible for an operative such as Isabella McGee to learn to set her own machine for a variety of production runs and even to grind and sharpen her own tools. With the turn to mass production, then, the wall separating the skilled from the semiskilled might wear quite thin indeed.[9]

---

[8] Between 1914 and the early 1920s, the proportion of semiskilled metalworkers rose from 20% to 30% of the British engineering workforce. The figures for France are sketchier, but the shifting distribution of skills at Renault, where the proportion of semiskilled labor rose from 26.9% in 1914 to 53.7% in 1925, suggests what the broader shifts for the industry as a whole must have looked like. Over the interwar period, these figures continued to climb, reaching 57% in Britain by 1933 and 67.7% at Renault by 1939. (The figures for France are for semi- and unskilled labor combined, but one can reliably estimate that unskilled laborers made up no more than 10% or 15% of the aggregate figure at each point.) Figures for Britain from M. L. Yates, *Wages and Labour Conditions in British Engineering* (London, 1937), pp. 31–32; for France, see Patrick Fridenson, *Histoire des usines Renault* (Paris, 1972), 1:85; also Alain Touraine, *L'Evolution du travail ouvrier aux usines Renault* (Paris, 1955), esp. pp. 84–87. See also Laura Lee Downs, "Women in Industry, 1914–1939: The Employers' Perspective" (Ph.D. thesis, Columbia University, 1987), chaps. 2, 3, 5.

[9] See Charles Sabel, *Work and Politics* (New York, 1982), chap. 2, for an excellent discussion of the ways in which progressive redivisions of labor alter the mix of jobs and skills and blur the line between craft and semiskilled labor.

Despite genuine erosion, however, that wall held firm, for the semiskilled worker's skills were always job-specific: rooted in particular machines and processes, and in a specific organization of work, and therefore not easily transferred from one firm to the next. Although the semiskilled woman had a firmer grasp of the larger process within which she labored than did her unskilled sister, her knowledges and abilities were more narrow and plant-specific, more bound to the particular than those of the fully skilled craft-worker.

On the third terrain, that of fully skilled craftwork—toolmaking, machine building and design—the skill demanded was uncontested, but women's capacity (and right) to perform this work was most hotly debated. In concrete terms, skilled workers were individuals whose broad experience and abstract understanding of the overall labor process enabled them to perform a wide range of exacting tasks, cutting and fitting metal parts to minute specifications, or designing and building tools and equipment from blueprints and without the aid of automatic machinery. Their grasp of the larger work process also fitted them to direct the work of less skilled workers. Indeed, wartime upgrading progressively withdrew these men from directly productive work, placing them in command of entire shops or removing them from the floor altogether, to the surrounding toolrooms and specialty shops.

During the war, however, few women had the opportunity to rise to fully skilled work, for the vast majority of women workers in both France and Britain learned their work on the job, acquiring new skills as circumstances demanded and always in conjunction with the particular machines and processes that confronted them.[10] Over time, women and men who showed aptitude for engineering and metalwork would move from one machine or process to the next, attaining a considerable degree of skill and proficiency on a broad range of processes and machines. After several months, a worker who had gained this broader experience might be put on a "flying squad," a team of workers adept at all phases of production and therefore able to fill in for an absentee anywhere in the plant.

This kind of movement from one phase of production to the next was more common in small, general engineering firms such as the howitzer shop where Isabella McGee was hired. Here the organization of production was flexible, with women and men working side by side, operating the same machines with the assistance and instruction of a skilled supervisor. In the

---

[10] "We . . . take a girl who does not know anything about this work and put her on the simplest forms of it and teach her to do the work in three weeks to a month. From that she will step up to the different stages, and that is how they are taught": IWM, Women's Work Collection, Emp. 70, War Cabinet Committee on Women in Industry, "Minutes of Evidence," testimony of O. W. Horobin, managing director at Christopher Collins, Ltd. (a lamp and sheet metal firm), Birmingham, October 1918, p. D91.

large shell and fuse factories, where most women were hired, opportunities for learning were far more restricted. Here thousands toiled within a highly subdivided mass-production organization whose shape was determined by the layout of machinery. In this less flexible labor process, managers tended to deploy workers more rigidly, assigning them machines and tasks that many retained until the Armistice.

As the war slowly drained skilled men from the factories, state officials pressed employers to formalize and hasten the upgrading process, to augment the informal apprenticeship of movement from one machine to another with highly focused and intensive training programs, intended to create good semiskilled workers in a matter of weeks. These courses were brief and sketchy by comparison with prewar apprenticeships. Nonetheless, this policy expanded the means by which skills were transmitted in the metalworking industry. Alongside formal apprenticeships, which now proceeded with new haste, appeared a new track for the upwardly mobile male. As the war ground on, women joined them on these new routes to advancement. Entire branches of semiskilled and even skilled work opened to women and men previously excluded from such jobs.

In both France and Britain, then, the war offered women factory workers unprecedented opportunities for learning and advancement. These opportunities were especially plentiful in Britain, where skilled craftsmen continued to play a crucial role in organizing production. Because craft skill loomed so large in the British engineering factory, both the Ministry of Munitions and the National Union of Women's Suffrage Societies (NUWSS) took great pains to organize and finance special courses to train women for munitions work. These interventions gave British employers some opportunity to observe and deploy women who possessed genuine craft skill. In France, by contrast, the government left job training in the hands of industrialists and did not intervene directly to create a skilled female workforce. Consequently, French employers were left to pursue strategies that combined technical rationalization with more haphazard on-the-job instruction of women. The war thus produced large numbers of semiskilled women workers, trained largely through on-the-job encounters with a range of tools and equipment. But the fully skilled woman, formally educated in more "theoretical" areas such as industrial design, was a rare beast indeed.

This national difference at the very apex of the skill hierarchy permits us to observe how slight an impact job training had on the structure of opportunity for women metalworkers over the long term. In 1918, British industry boasted a small corps of trained, highly skilled women. French industry, by contrast, had almost none. By 1920, however, one can discern no meaningful difference in the structure of wages and jobs open to women in the two nations. The fact that women had performed as skilled craftworkers in Britain left no visible imprint on the sexual hierarchy of jobs or on the structure of wages.[11] After 1918, the gateway to advancement off the factory floor closed as firmly in women's faces in Britain as it ever had done in France.

France: The Refusal to Train Women for Craftwork

From 1915 on, Albert Thomas repeatedly encouraged defense contractors to design job training programs for the new female recruits. Thomas's goals were twofold. As the war ate men, it was critical to form a workforce capable of replacing them, skilled and unskilled alike. But the minister of armaments was also impelled by the desire to raise the status of working women, to impart skill—a source of enduring value—to these undervalued and ill-paid workers. From the outset, however, industrialists pursued a more cautious and inexpensive policy: breaking in the new workers by training them on the job. After an initial selection, in which foremen placed women according to the rough-and-ready criteria of physical strength and job history, novices were put before their machines and expected to learn their part (and quickly) from the more experienced women nearby: " 'Just do as I do, *petite*'—and there you have it—all the instruction I would ever receive." So wrote Marcelle Capy in the summer of 1916—a brusque summary of the "training" that most women received upon entering the war factories of Paris.[12]

Firms occasionally institutionalized this procedure by designating a few of their more experienced women as "demonstrator-operatives" and assigning them to train each batch of raw recruits. One could learn quite a lot on the job, if one chose; it was not at all unusual for a lathe worker to learn to set her own tools.[13] But one could never become a fully skilled craftworker this way. No matter how many machines a woman mastered, she remained at best a good semiskilled worker, possessing valuable but narrowly job-specific skills and lacking the ability to make new tools or to work from blueprints.

Clearly, most employers preferred to make their wartime workers into reliable machine operatives.[14] They welcomed whatever practical knowledge and dexterity these workers might gain in the process but rarely took the time to ensure that all acquired such skills in equal measure. Their reluctance

---

[11] Women's memories of skilled work did not fade quite so easily, however, as the formation of the Women's Engineering Society in January 1919 testifies. See Carroll Pursell, " 'Am I a Lady or an Engineer?' The Origins of the Women's Engineering Society in Britain, 1918–1927," *Technology and Culture* 34 (January 1993): 78–97.

[12] Capy, "Pas de professionelles."

[13] Here financial pressure was a powerful goad, for women workers, paid by the piece, could not begin to earn until their machines were adjusted for a particular run.

[14] AN, F22, 538, Henri Sellier, "L'Organisation du placement des ouvrières dans les usines de guerre," p. 7.

stemmed in part from the conditions of war; at any given moment, the pressure to produce weapons made long-term investments in labor—even just a few weeks' training—seem time ill spent.

The brevity and infrequency of wartime "apprenticeships" also reflects the long-term decline of apprenticeship in France.[15] Yet the lack of formal instruction for women workers in France cannot be explained solely by force of circumstance. Once we have taken into account the long-term decline in apprenticeship and fierce pressures to produce, we still find that employers showed particular reluctance to train women. Thus Général Perruchon, one of Thomas's labor controllers, noted with some irritation that "all the instruction being given to men" in Delaunay-Belleville's apprenticeship program "could be given just as fruitfully and easily to women." When he needled the shop chief on this point, he was informed, in a tone of "polite hostility," that the firm preferred to give women "practical instruction on the machines . . . in the workshop itself."[16]

Some employers embraced this policy in the conviction that women were unreliable, a judgment rooted in the observation that in some factories, women had proved to be marginally worse timekeepers than men.[17] Many observers attributed this phenomenon to the "second shift" of household chores that most women had to perform at home. Clearly, shorter shifts would leave women more time for their domestic labors, and after the war, some firms adopted this solution to the problem. But others saw in women's higher rate of absenteeism the mark of an innate and collective instability, of which they

[15] The vast majority of workers in prewar France (about 88%, men and women alike) received no formal training beyond what they picked up on the job. See Bernard Charlot and Madeleine Figéat, *Histoire de la formation des ouvriers, 1789–1984* (Paris, 1985), pp. 139–62; also Gérard Noiriel, *Workers in French Society in the Nineteenth and Twentieth Centuries* (Oxford, 1990), chap. 3. Moreover, workers' descriptions of the apprenticeships in mid-nineteenth-century metalworking factories often bear a striking resemblance to accounts of women's training in the war factories some sixty years later. Jean-Baptiste Dumay describes the apprentices' shop at Schneider's Le Creusot works, where Dumay trained as a turner in 1854–55: "About thirty apprentice turners were grouped together, and each was made to specialize in nuts or bolts that were always more or less identical, for a period of six months, a year, two years, or even more. Through constant repetition, they developed extraordinary dexterity": "Memoirs of a Militant Worker from Le Creusot," in Mark Traugott, ed., *The French Worker: Autobiographies from the Early Industrial Era* (Berkeley, 1993), p. 315. This account places French women's apparent lack of formal training in proper perspective.

[16] AN, 94 AP, 348, Général Perruchon to Mario Rocques, "Le Travail des femmes," 1 October 1916, pp. 1–2.

[17] Where employers complained of absenteeism—and not many did—the difference between women and men lay anywhere between 2 and 7%; that is, if 8% of the men failed to show up, anywhere from 10 to 16% of the women might also be absent. From the evidence, though, it seems employers were just as likely to find women (especially married ones) more reliable, because of their need for the wages. British employers also worried about the women's timekeeping, but these concerns did not take the form of open resistance to training women, undoubtedly because suffrage societies and the government bore most of the cost of these schemes.

found further evidence in the rather high turnover rate among women during the first two years of the war. One employer in St-Denis specified this alleged instability as a classic feminine failure of loyalty to the firm that had educated them: "We do not wish to try to train women because they always go and work for our competitors. In fact, as soon as they've learned their craft, they get themselves hired in the factory where their husband works, or any man who interests them."[18]

The war was a time of tremendous flux among all segments of the workforce not pinned to their jobs by military law. For example, civilian workers of both sexes sometimes tried to reduce the time spent traveling to and from work by transferring from a distant factory as soon as a job opened up in a plant closer to home. Nonetheless, employers persistently viewed women's turnover as more significant than similar mobility among men, seeing in it yet another indicator of their distinctive character as women and as workers.

If the turnover among women stemmed from a feminine tendency to seek out male companionship at work, and not from the highly unstable condition of the Paris labor market during those first two years of war, then the only way to render profitable any investment in such mercurial creatures was to train them "bit by bit and on the job, because it is in the workshop that they learn their habits. . . . [Otherwise] there is no chance of holding onto them."[19] And since women learned rapidly on the job (piecework wage systems make fast learners), they swiftly reached a point where they could produce profitably for the firm. Employers thus shaped their hiring and deployment policies to fit women's presumably fickle natures, hiring them in large numbers but refusing to invest in their training until they had proved themselves worthy of the effort. This predisposition endured well past 1918, creating a barrier to women's advancement which lost all rational basis once peacetime conditions restored a measure of stability to the labor market. What had been a reasonable response in time of war, when women moved unpredictably from one factory to another, continued to structure the factory floor after the Armistice, reinforcing women's confinement to the less-skilled reaches of the labor process.

A rather different disincentive to educating women lay in the fact that some women who arrived in the war factories had already gained skills and experience in previous occupations—skills that enabled them to excel in verification and inspection jobs, where they tested shells and fuses or gauged the quality and dimensions of finished parts with the aid of micrometers and gauges. Although some verification jobs were fairly routine and straightforward, gauging was skilled work. It demanded considerable judgment, experi-

---

[18] Quoted in AN, 94 AP, 348, Général Perruchon, "Note pour M. Rocques," 3 October 1916, p. 2.
[19] Ibid.

ence, and skill in using the instruments and wielding the fine hand tools used to correct flawed pieces. Moreover, the verifier occupied a key post in the labor process, controlling the quality and judging the work of production workers, male and female alike.[20] Yet the fact that this work was often skilled and exacting did not lead employers to install any formalized training. Rather, they took care to distribute these jobs selectively, choosing women who might be presumed to have the right kinds of skills already, skills honed in other occupations: "Those who perform most successfully are former dressmakers and embroiderers. Such work draws on their good taste and delicacy."[21]

In the end, one of Thomas's labor controllers concluded that the majority of employers simply could not envision training women "beyond a certain point. . . . They can be taught certain motions demanding some training, and even a little initiative, but are never initiated into the secrets of the engineering trade."[22] In the rare firms that did establish formal instruction for women, the goal was to create semiskilled workers in a matter of months (five to seven weeks of training plus a few months of experience on the job) rather than gradually, over a year or two of trial and error on the factory floor. But these classes were sparse and graduated only a handful of women—perhaps a few hundred over the course of the war. A woman's "apprenticeship" in the factory was more likely to follow employers' wartime rule: "No superfluous training, but a course limited to the operation that the men and women will be called upon to repeat in the factory."[23] Not surprisingly, the end product was a pool of workers suited only to "the common mechanical tasks of mass production."[24]

Employers' refusal to invest in the training of women thus preserved the sanctity of craft as male terrain, even as their rationalization plans undermined the technical basis of craft. At least one of Thomas's more voluble colleagues at the Ministry of Armaments colluded in this project. Indeed, Georges Calmès (an editor at the ministry's *Bulletin des Usines de Guerre*) went so far as to undermine the minister's repeated pleas for more elaborate training of women,

[20] Despite frequent assertions—by employers and male workers alike—that women were, on the whole, of little "professional value," verification and inspection of all sorts rapidly shifted into female hands in the war factories around Paris. Their swift accession to this delicate and highly responsible work may have rested in part on the fact that although they assessed the work of men, they did not directly supervise them. The reversal of the traditional gender hierarchy, though real, was masked by the physical segregation of production and verification in entirely separate shops, rendering the female verifier's "control" of male labor indirect.

[21] AN, 94 AP, 348, *L'Oeuvre*, a survey by Ennemande Diart.

[22] Ibid., "Note sur le recrutement de la main-d'oeuvre féminine," p. 3.

[23] This was the stated objective of a training center opened in Bordeaux early in 1916: archives of the Bibliothèque de Documentation Internationale Contemporaine (hereafter BDIC), dossier 4.P 1977, Ministère de la Guerre, Direction Générale des Relations avec la Presse, report dated April 1916.

[24] Sellier, "L'Organisation du placement des ouvrières," p. 7.

recommending instead that employers confine women to "an education in motion and maneuver" only.[25] This strategy would not only bring women machine tenders rapidly to their full productive value but smooth the ruffled feathers of skilled men, who eyed the new female labor force with a mixture of hostility and trepidation.

Maintaining the "secrets of the engineering trade" as the special preserve of (some) men would also allow employers to deploy labor in the newly fragmented labor process according to standard gendered templates: under the watchful eye of the male craftworker, the female operative carried out her routine, "mechanical" labors. The vertical (i.e., authority) element in the technical division of labor thus dovetailed neatly with the traditional hierarchy of male over female. To train women as mechanics would only upset this comfortable arrangement, and must have seemed counterproductive to the men who profited from it. Women workers well understood how technical and social authority were intertwined on the factory floor. One group of workers buttressed their plea for more technical training by disputing the proposition that shop-floor authority had to be inscribed within a male-female hierarchy. On the contrary: "A man does not know how to command women the way a woman does, and doesn't dare to demand the same output from them."[26] They did not go so far as to invert that hierarchy and argue for placing women over men. Rather, the utopian vision was one of women working among themselves in a kind of industrial "Herland," untroubled by harassment and ill treatment at the hands of foremen and shop chiefs, abuses of which many women complained.

Job Training in Munitions: The Case of Great Britain

Those ten Parisian *munitionettes* chosen to tour the war factories of London in the winter of 1917 were clearly touched most deeply by the breadth and depth of job training available to British women workers. Indeed, the climactic moment of their ten-day excursion came when none other than Emmeline Pankhurst guided the group on a tour through one of London's munition training centers. "We were amazed. This school trains not only women workers and overseers but also expert forewomen, for whom engineering holds no secrets. . . . Judging a machine's output, setting, resetting, and regulating a lathe are mere games to these women."[27]

[25] Georges Calmès, "Note sur l'utilisation de la main-d'oeuvre féminine," *BUG,* 17 July 1916, p. 95.
[26] "Visite d'ouvrières françaises aux usines britanniques," *BUG,* 19 February 1917, p. 343.
[27] Ibid.

The expertise of their British colleagues gave concrete form to French women's hope that they, too, might advance to more varied, interesting, and well-paid work. Indeed, the sight of women initiating women into the "secrets" of the trade brought latent discontent bubbling to the surface, and prompted the delegation to challenge their employers' easy presumption that women lack ambition and initiative: " . . . like you—we are ambitious. Give us the chance to learn the inner workings of the engineering trade, so that one day we may become overseers and forewomen. The prospect that one might rise through the ranks and so gain a better future is a powerful stimulant."[28]

The ground of British women's industrial expertise surely lay in the plethora of training schools, where women received an intensive introduction to the tools and techniques of their new trade. By the second year of the war, both the Ministry of Munitions and the Women's Suffrage Society had established a network of these training shops, where students spent anywhere from six to twelve weeks (though some courses lasted a full six months) learning the bare rudiments of the trade by doing a range of simple jobs—turning, drilling, sawing, and filing. When the war was over, some 45,000 women—just over 10 percent of the industry's new female recruits—had passed through these training shops.[29] Small though this number may seem in comparison with the total number of women employed (597,000), it is truly impressive in contrast to the mere handful graduated from the employer-controlled technical programs in France.

Of course, not everyone had equal access to the technical schools. Until about 1917, these programs cost women anywhere from 2s. 6d. per week for a six- to eight-week course in the government schools (set up by the Ministry of Munitions) to 10s. 6d. per week for a four- to six-week course run by the London Society for Women's Suffrage. Aside from the question of forgone income, the fees alone placed formal training beyond the reach of most working-class women; only the daughter of a skilled craftsman might muster the resources to attend. In the last years of the war, both the ministry and the suffrage society set aside their fees and offered trainees maintenance allowances as well. While this program enabled poorer women to attend, it still could not compete with the opportunity to earn a minimum of £1 a week immediately upon entry into munitions. Hence the majority of women munitions workers went straight into the factories and received their training on the job. Such training might impart anything from mere manipulative skill on a machine whose inner workings remained obscure to the kinds of

---

[28] Ibid.
[29] Marion Kozak, "Women Munition Workers during the First World War, with Special Reference to Engineering" (Ph.D. thesis, University of Hull, 1976), p. 120.

knowledge and ability gained by an Isabella McGee, who became semiskilled without benefit of previous training or formal apprenticeship.[30]

But formal instruction, however extensive, did not a skilled worker make.[31] Only concrete experience on a variety of jobs could give her a feel for working with different metals, handling tricky fitting and filing, or setting and resetting a finicky machine tool. Access to such broad experience depended largely on the willingness of skilled men, and especially shop foremen, to work with women; to impart the fruits of their experience and to tolerate the broken tools and spoiled pieces that inevitably attend the learning process. Isabella McGee's story reminds us that women's acquisition of skill rested above all on the interest and goodwill of a cooperative foreman. Without Mr. Tammy Barnes, McGee would never have acquired the skills she did; without the protest of the rest of the men (also skilled) and the Workers' Union she would never have gotten the financial reward for her achievement.

Joan Williams, a fully skilled toolroom worker at Gwynne's aircraft engine factory in Chiswick, also recalled the key role her foreman played in her education: "Mr. Baker was only too ready to teach me anything. . . . He was only too delighted if you could do the advanced work and from the first would let me try new jobs, even though chances were I should scrap them." Williams thrived under the tutelage of this gentle young man, whose pedagogical technique included fulsome praise for work well done ("I could not have done it better myself") and patient good humor in the face of a truly appalling mistake. "In those first days he would often come up when the manager wasn't looking and seeing me labouring over the old filing would take the file and do in two minutes what I had not managed in an hour."[32]

Williams moved through a variety of skilled positions at Gwynne's, setting up and instructing on six lathes in the air-pump shop and even taking a turn at the fitting bench (the most highly skilled job in the factory). But she spent most of the war working as a toolroom hand—a job that in normal circumstances required a five-year apprenticeship. It took Williams little more than a year to rise to this position, if one includes the time she spent learning the basics at a Women's Suffrage Society training shop. She hints that she owed her speedy ascent in part to the fact that the normal prewar apprenticeship of five to seven years was actually longer than one needed to

[30] A woman with no previous training needed about two years of varied work on the job to become the equivalent of "a good semi-skilled man": *DLB*, February 1917, p. 54.

[31] Indeed, even those who did receive some formal instruction generally arrived in the factory possessing a level of skill equivalent to that of a good semiskilled worker. This classification came to include women machine setters and those turners, fitters, and toolroom workers who performed several highly skilled portions of the full craft job.

[32] IWM, Department of Printed Books, Joan Williams, "A Munition Worker's Career at Messrs. G, 1915–1919," typescript, pp. 43, 11. Williams, as we have seen, was judged fully skilled by her employer, Neville Gwynne.

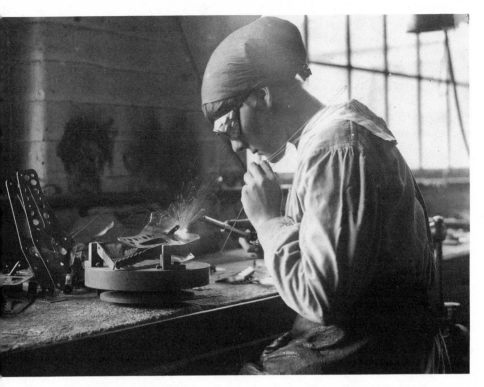

Woman worker welding frame tugs for airplanes in a factory in Birmingham, September 1918. Imperial War Museum.

learn the work.[33] Under the pressure of war, Gwynne's management was forced to shuffle Williams from one job to the next as she was needed, giving her the chance to try her hand at a broad range of jobs over a comparatively short span of time. But Williams makes it quite clear that she owed her success at Gwynne's above all to Mr. Baker's patient and thorough instruction.

By the same token, however, skilled men could just as easily obstruct women's efforts to learn the trade, for, as Williams observed, the sight of women acquiring in a matter of months trade "secrets" to which they had been admitted only gradually stirred jealousy and resentment in the hearts

[33] "The great grievance of the skilled men was the fact that so many men and women came onto skilled work in a short time owing to the exigencies of war when they themselves had had to serve a seven years apprenticeship and had not had the chance of learning their work in a shorter period" (ibid., p. 44).

of all but a stalwart few: "It was hard on the men to have the women coming into all their pet jobs and in some cases doing them a good deal better . . . they were torn between not wanting the women to undercut them and yet hating them to earn as much."[34]

Dorothy Poole, a skilled tool fitter at a large firm outside London, recalled that "over and over again the foreman gave me wrong or incomplete directions and altered them in such a way as to give me hours more work. . . . I had no tools that I needed and . . . it was out of the question to borrow them from the men. . . . My drawer was nailed up by the men, and oil was poured over everything in it through a crack another night." Poole returned the men's rancor in contemptuous tones that suggest a strong class antagonism between this middle-class "lady," who had trained (at her own expense) in a·school run by the London Society for Women's Suffrage, and the working-class men among whom she labored: "They were as undependable and capricious as children, and peace could never be reckoned on for long."[35] Dorothy Poole's lengthy account leaves no doubt that she had a personal knack for speaking down to and antagonizing the people around her. Nonetheless, it is quite evident that the conflict between Poole and her skilled male associates also arose out of the apparent challenge to the working-class foreman's authority which middle-class women's sense of entitlement and self-confidence presented.

Joan Williams was no less middle-class than Dorothy Poole, yet she came up against far less hostility from her male colleagues. Aside from Poole's clearly unpleasant personality, one wonders if Williams may have won acceptance because she was one of a handful of skilled women (five to seven at first, and never more than twenty) employed in their own shop. Segregated both spatially and technically from the skilled men (Williams's tiny shop was responsible for turning and assembling all forty parts for the airplane engine's air pump), the skilled women may not have posed such a clear threat. Certainly a very different atmosphere reigned downstairs on the factory floor, where some thousand women turned out standardized engine parts at the lathe. Here the men's union sought to hedge the women's ambit with elaborate restrictions, hoping perhaps to preserve the skilled man's central position while ensuring that the scope of women's knowledge remained limited. Union rules barred women from sharpening their own tools, and one worker complained of "waiting ages to have her tool sharpened while [the setter] finished the work of his favorite operator" (p. 46).

[34] Ibid., p. 45. Hereafter page numbers appear in the text.
[35] IWM, Women's Work Collection, Mun. 17/7, Dorothy Poole, typescript (1919), pp. 5–6. Hereafter page numbers appear in the text. Poole also worked for a time at Gwynne's before moving on to a much larger works. It was at the second factory that she encountered such stiff resistance.

Women working at the assembly table at the national filling factory at Banbury. Imperial War Museum.

Similarly, Dorothy Poole's encounters with angry skilled men occurred on a job where she worked not in the toolroom but on the shop floor, among hundreds of less skilled women machine operatives. The men harassed other women as well: "They were given the oldest lathes in the shop and it was a continual struggle to get them through their work" (pp. 5–6). Clearly, the sheer numbers of women doing repetitive work roused a level of craft anxiety that was in some ways more acute than that roused by the presence of the odd skilled woman.

It seems, then, that the threat of feminization appeared more potent when large numbers of women took over entire portions of the labor process. This kind of change affected the structure of production in most large munitions factories, but most frequently in shell and fuse work. These shops were exclusively male bastions in prewar days, but by 1916 it was technically possible to mass-produce the bombs by employing semi- and unskilled women on all phases of the highly fragmented production process. Such factories folded together the threat of feminization with that of deskilling to produce the broader danger of craft obsolescence after the war. Under wartime conditions, the fully skilled woman posed a more nebulous threat to craftsmen, the threat of women empowered by the high wages and shop-floor authority (or at least autonomy) attached to skilled work in Britain. It was a dark and disturbing prospect, given its power to invert the "natural" order of gender hierarchy, but so long as she remained a rare creature, the danger could be held at bay.

Job Training and the Gendered Epistemology of Skill

By the end of the war, sustained efforts to train war workers for skilled jobs had produced a handful of women who were working at the level of fully skilled craftsmen. Yet fully skilled work, embracing mastery of a broad variety of processes, machines, and metals and the ability to work from drawings, to design new parts, and (crucially) to direct and supervise the work of others, remained the province of a select few. By themselves, wartime training schemes could impart little beyond the highly valuable but plant- and process-specific skills of the semiskilled worker. The employer then decided whether an individual would be deployed permanently on semiskilled work or be allowed to advance to more highly skilled jobs.

French employers chose pupils from among their more seasoned workers, women who had "demonstrated not only professional aptitude but a taste for factory work."[36] In their view, women who brought to metalworking skills developed in other trades—fine needlework, for example—were the best candidates for education in the finer points of turning, fitting, and drilling. The British, by contrast, declared that higher education—that is, higher class status—constituted the firmest base on which to form a skilled woman worker:

> If you happen to get hold of girls who have been through a high school or had a superior education altogether, you select those girls to do fitting and turning because they have intelligence. You would never dream of putting the ordinary woman who has only got through the lowest classes of the Board School to do fitting and turning. You will put her on labouring or a machine that is absolutely foolproof.[37]

[36] AN, 94 AP, 348, "Note II: Le Recrutement de la main-d'oeuvre féminine," pp. 4–5.
[37] IWM, Women's Work Collection, Emp. 70, War Cabinet Committee on Women in Industry, "Minutes of Evidence," EEF testimony, October 1918, p. F48. For ordinary laboring, employers and state officials sometimes preferred to avoid the more industrially experienced "factory girls" (perhaps fearing that their work experience might include exposure to labor militants) and recruit instead from the ranks of domestic servants and "country girls"—women who had not only the physical strength of the "factory girls" but also "the right sort of

Of course, France had a superabundance of "worker-housewives," married women whose uninterrupted work experience gave them skills that their employers recognized and acknowledged as valuable.[38] England had few such working-class women, but British employers did have access to something the French did not: "educated" women who were willing to go into the factories, master complex work, and perform the semi-and even fully skilled work of engineering. When skilled or delicate work was to be done, British employers turned first to these women. The skilled aircraft worker Joan Williams recalled approvingly that her first boss, a mid-level manager of an entire department, had been "very particular [about] who he took on and though we had girls from all sorts of spheres he never engaged any really rowdy or low class ones who would always be swearing or wanting to carry on with the men" (p. 10).[39]

British employers' preference for "educated" women suggests they held a multitiered vision of the human material available for factory labor. In order to shape a female worker to become the workplace equivalent of a skilled man, one had to begin not with a woman of that skilled man's class but with a middle-class woman:

> We started [in 1914] with the factory girl type, but found her a bad timekeeper, and invariably, if they had had a good week, remained out on Monday. . . . The class of woman we employed [before the war] was very much better . . . more of the type that serve in shops or restaurants, many whose fathers were writers, and girls who failed as pupil teachers.[40]

Higher class status weighed in against lower gender status to produce a human who in value and capacity was presumably equal to the good semiskilled or even skilled (working-class) man.

When we look for the "ordinary" working-class woman's male equivalent, we find him not among the men whom such women married but among their young sons—unformed creatures whose value could not yet be determined. The proof of equivalency here lies in the employers' explicit reshaping

---

temperament and submission to discipline." See PRO, Mun. 4/1276, "Report on the Training of Munitions Workers," n.d., pp. 4–7.

[38] The term "worker-housewife" is Michelle Perrot's in "La Ménagère dans l'espace parisien au xixᵉ siècle," *Nouvelles Annales de la Recherche Urbaine,* December 1980.

[39] His attitude contrasted sharply with that of most foremen working under him, who "preferred this type of girl" (p. 10).

[40] IWM, War Cabinet Committee Minutes, testimony of Melville Smith, manager of the national factory at Abbey Wood, p. D56. The "writer" fathers were undoubtedly clerks rather than novelists.

of wage scales. As the EEF baldly stated in its 1915 directive to member firms, "Female labour undertaking the work of semi-skilled or skilled men shall be paid the recognised rates of the district for youths on the operation in question."[41]

Patterns of labor deployment for teenaged girls suggest that they, too, were roughly equivalent to boys; in fact, employers who sought maximum short-term value from their adolescent labor often hired girls by preference. One British employer had left a skilled man in charge of six troublesome drilling machines, despite the fact that drilling was ordinarily reckoned semi-skilled work. When he was forced to replace that man, he started with a boy (of unspecified age). The machines continued to malfunction and the boy spent a good deal of his time "larking." The problem cleared up only after the employer replaced the boy with a girl of fifteen: "The machines went much better, her delicate finger-tips made her particularly good at grinding fine drills."[42]

From management's perspective, girls already possessed in rather developed form the very virtues—self-discipline and great manual dexterity—that employers hailed in their mothers. The boy was an unknown quantity, with a long and uncertain path stretching between his adolescent self and a future incarnation, in which he might or might not prove a valuable tradesman. (By federation standards, he would not attain adult status until the age of twenty-one.) The girl, by contrast, was a more transparent if perhaps ultimately more limited being. At her eighteenth birthday she would advance to adult status, according to the EEF's wage scales—a stronger, more experienced version of herself at fifteen. It seems that women, like happy families, were all essentially alike, essentially female whether fifteen or fifty.

For most purposes, then, employers treated the "ordinary," working-class woman worker as the equivalent of a teenaged boy. But when it came to job training, the two life forms diverged; because women had less potential for development, they needed intelligence, education, and higher class status to make up for the deficiencies inherent in their sex. "A woman remains a woman and a boy becomes a man," as one feminist observer bitterly remarked.[43]

Employers' vision of the relative educability of boys and women thus rested on the Aristotelian presumption that whereas a boy is an individual in the process of becoming, woman's "nature" is unitary—fixed, eternal, and defined

---

[41] EEF, note to member firms, March 1915, quoted in Barbara Drake, *Women in the Engineering Trades: A Problem, a Solution, and Some Criticism* (London, 1917), p. 17.

[42] Quoted in Adam Kirkaldy, *Industry and Finance—War Expedients and Reconstruction* (London, 1917), p. 25. The employer qualified his praise immediately: "she was of course obliged to call in a skilled man if anything went seriously wrong with the machines."

[43] Drake, *Women in the Engineering Trades*, p. 63.

by her lack of maleness.[44] Even those who praised women for learning their work more quickly than men believed that this agility of mind sprang from absence, in this case of male hubris, rather than from any positive virtue: "They do not pretend to have any knowledge whatsoever about machinery, but the men pretend they have some knowledge . . . and will go their own way. The woman will take all that is told her and she will carry it out."[45] For the vast majority of employers, however, women's lack went much deeper, and prevented them from being initiated into the full range of "secrets" of the trade. They were missing that crucial masculine trait, the "inherited instinct" for mechanical work: " . . . the lads have had a more or less inherited instinct . . . because [they have] knocked about a factory . . . and they know more or less what machines are, and they are able to pick it up . . . whereas a woman has never seen a factory at all."[46] The outcome of social inequality between women and men was thus recast in the biological language of instinct, the bedrock certainties of "nature" being substituted for the fluid structures of social order built on the inequalities of class and gender. The result was a factory hierarchy underwritten by a kind of Aristotelian logic in which men are the only complete creatures, sufficient unto themselves and therefore capable of self-directed activity: "The women of course cannot do every process. A man is a complete unit; the women have to have men assist them."[47]

The author of this statement was head of the Sheffield light steel trades group, an industrial sector in which the capacity for heavy physical labor was

[44] Maryanne Cline Horowitz observes: "It is implied in Aristotle's view that the female is in the fullest sense of the word a 'laborer.' She passively takes on her task, laboring with her body to fulfill another's design and plan, and consequently her contribution to the product is of a secondary nature": "Aristotle and Woman," *Journal of the History of Biology* 9 (Fall 1976): 197. Aristotle's conception of male and female productive capacities/potential registers sharply in the language that employers used to distinguish male and female as labor power. See also Martha Nussbaum, "The Discernment of Perception: An Aristotelian Conception of Private and Public Rationality," in Nussbaum, *Love's Knowledge* (Oxford, 1990), 54–105.

[45] IWM, War Cabinet Committee Minutes, testimony of Major Ovans, manager of five national factories, October 1918, pp. D44–45.

[46] Ibid., EEF testimony, p. F48. If British employers had trouble with the idea that women might equally "inherit" a bent for mechanical work, Joan Williams was more open to observing this very phenomenon among her female colleagues: "The girl who took up the setting-up made a wonderful job of it, although she was only 19, and had not done any work of the sort before coming to the factory. She had the advantage of coming of an engineering family, both her brothers being employed by Gwynne's and two sisters also working in our shop. They were all clever but she was extraordinarily capable and I think few girls can have been so good at setting up; she not only took charge of practically all the centre lathes, but also set up the milling machines and superintended a great deal of the work of the shop" (p. 32).

[47] Ibid., testimony of Mr. Nutt, October 1918, pp. F28–29. This easy slippage between the categorical distinctions of "nature" and those of the social/cultural order is central to Aristotelian social logic, which links essentialized notions of social being to productive capacity.

most highly prized. He therefore concluded that after the war, the incomplete units who should be recruited were not women, who would rarely develop the sheer muscle power needed for heavy forge and steel work, but "lads who will be coming forward for the skilled trades afterwards."[48] Many of his colleagues outside the heavy iron and steel sectors concurred with his reasoning on the relative places of men, women, and boys but reached the opposite conclusion about women's future in the industry. One of the engineering industry's great machine tool moguls, Sir Alfred Herbert, saw a vital role for women in an industry rebuilt along the lines of wartime innovations and redivisions of labor. In this renewed and revivified industry the woman worker would take on a classically feminine supporting role, performing the repetitive and routine labors in the more streamlined work process: "She will relieve the male worker from the drudgery of routine . . . and will give him that fuller scope for development in the higher branches of his trade which every keen and intelligent mechanic desires."[49]

Job training and industrial rationalization could accordingly be seen as very different (often mutually exclusive) kinds of investments in the future employment of women. Throughout the war, employers wavered between the two strategies. Some planned to recover their old markets and restore the old methods, and within this group, a small minority saw training women for skilled craftwork as part of a larger strategy in which cheaper female labor might be integrated into the old productive structure: "The establishment of courses in industrial design, identical to those followed by male apprentices . . . would favor the use of female labor in our industry after the war."[50]

Investments in machine technologies were, by contrast, premised on the idea that postwar industry would conquer new and wider markets for a range of more standardized goods, and so continue to operate along the lines prefigured by wartime rationalization. For many employers, this vision of postwar expansion clearly entailed the continued employment of women on the detailed and repetitive types of labor at which they had proved so able during the war. In May 1917 the British automobile mogul Herbert Austin could declare: "I am so impressed with the possibilities of standardisation that we shall build only one type of car. . . . After the war . . . we shall organise

---

[48] Ibid.

[49] PP 1919, Cmd. 167, *Appendices of Evidence to the War Cabinet Committee Report on Women in Industry*, p. 55.

[50] AN, F22,534, Ministère de l'Armement, Comité du Travail Féminin, "Enquête sur l'organisation des crèches," March–April 1918. This response, from Bréguet, was returned on 8 March 1918. By stressing that the training classes be "identical to those followed by male apprentices, that is, practical design courses enabling them to read plans for making machine parts," Bréguet's managers underscored the skilled nature of the work women might do. The firm backed its testimony by establishing its own courses for women in industrial design. See Downs, "Women in Industry," chap. 5, for details.

as we do now with skilled labour directing a considerable proportion of woman and unskilled workers."[51] Strategies for industrial rationalization thus carved a larger role for women on the shop floor without granting them authority or access to skilled work and high wages.

The fact that in managerial eyes, women workers were always women first shaped their particularity as individuals on the factory floor. In addition, the experience of war reinforced employers' tendency to believe that women were destined for less skilled tasks only, for the wartime coincidence between women's arrival on the metalworking factory floor and the proliferation of highly detailed and repetitive jobs throughout the industry forged a durable link between women and rationalized labor. Employers therefore focused on identifying what was particular to women as a "class" of labor. This procedure required them to overlook all evidence that individual women had performed successfully on craft ("men's") work. The scope of a woman's work was determined not by the training she had received but by a system of labor stratification whose fundamental elements were remarkably similar on both sides of the Channel. This system, elaborated during the war, offered a narrow account of women's capacities and a road map for slotting them into the labor process accordingly.

Thus employers ultimately foreclosed on the possibility of training and deploying women craftworkers. After 1918 they would either return to the prewar technical and sexual division of labor or opt for a more rationalized labor process, with women integrated into the new productive structures. But this choice was not an inevitable outcome, dictated by any evident failure by women to perform well at skilled work when they were called upon to do so. On the contrary, although their opportunities to do so were rather restricted, the available evidence suggests that women accomplished skilled work with no more difficulty than their male counterparts. "They were all really capable," recalled George Ginns, a foreman at Daimler; "you could leave them to the job and there was quite a lot of the girls on capstans and things as good as any men—better than men, in fact, quite a lot of them. And I had about four really good girls on setting automatic machines up as well."[52] Some employers, at least, were well aware of women's capabilities. Their decision to set aside this experience and concentrate solely on the deployment of women within the rationalized labor process emanated from someplace else. Employers in both France and Britain were clearly concerned

---

[51] Herbert Austin, "How I Made Substitution a Success," *System,* May 1917, p. 320.

[52] IWM, Sound Records Dept., George Ginns, "War Work, 1914–18," accession no. 000775/05, p. 26. Ginns remembered lending handbooks on automatic machinery to these four machine setters: "They used to come around to my house on a Sunday and exchange them. The wife never grumbled, I don't know whether she thought anything, but they used to come round and bring the book from the week before and take another one."

with the negative reactions of skilled men to the presence of women who worked beside them on an equal basis. But beyond this concern, employers held a positive conviction that women and men were in every way distinct and complementary beings. Effective labor deployment rested on recognition of this fact.

Wartime pressure to expand the ambit of women's employment repeatedly ran up against employers' conviction that women represented a specific and limited source of labor power. In both nations, such convictions directed their initial deployment of these workers, and restricted their investment of time and energy in training and upgrading them. The French largely avoided the issue by putting few of their resources behind the training of workers of either sex, while the British, ironically, ended up supporting most enthusiastically the training and upgrading of middle-class women—those least likely to remain after the Armistice. But in both nations, employers' conceptions of gender difference, as revealed in the debate over women's educability, shaped their relayering of a workforce already stratified by skill. Where a single hierarchy had defined the prewar factory floor, running from unskilled laborer through fully skilled craftsman, there now stood a more complex structure, whose divisions were grounded in intersecting distinctions of skill and gender.[53]

The Wages of War

From the moment women first entered the war factories, employers paid them according to a rather different set of criteria from those governing the payment of men. They grounded these criteria in a series of propositions about the shape of women's lives and needs outside the factory, about their ability to tolerate swift, repetitive work, and about their a priori status as cheap labor. These propositions were rarely articulated simultaneously. Taken together, however, they sketched a portrait of women workers that dovetailed neatly with the one being drawn in the debate over job training.

[53] The interweaving of skill and gender sometimes found especially vivid expression in the outward form that employers gave to shop-floor hierarchies. The management of one London engineering firm awarded women workers one, two, or three stripes (to be worn on their overalls), depending on their ability and industry. One stripe signified good work and conduct, but carried no authority. Two stripes marked the woman charge hand (authority over one section of the works, subject to the periodic supervision of a skilled man); three stripes conferred authority over more than one section (e.g., a chief gauger). The greatest distinction, however, lay between women employed on women's work and "those women who are doing men's work and drawing men's wages. These superior beings wear a dark brown uniform, to distinguish them from other workers [who wore khaki]." A forewoman, "the highest position of authority that a woman can attain in the shop," wore a blue overall: *DLB*, May 1917, p. 108.

What is most significant about these propositions is that they formed the ground for a wage policy governed by a logic entirely distinct from the one applied to men. Men were paid in accordance with the value of their work; women were paid according to employers' conceptions of who women were. Employers adhered to this fundamental distinction in the basis of male and female wages even during the last two years of the war, when workers of both sexes pressed them to grant a single rate for the job, no matter who performed it. Active intervention by their respective ministries forced industrialists in both nations to grant women significant raises, but employers refused to abandon the practice of grading wages according to the class of labor employed, and so never conceded the principle of a single rate for the job. State officials never challenged them on this point. On the contrary, both Lloyd George and Albert Thomas upheld the principle of separate and unequal wage scales for male and female labor in all of their wartime wage interventions. Their failure to support the demand for a straight rate for the job ensured that gender-based pay differentials would endure in the postwar metalworking industries.

In 1914–15, when women first entered the industry, metals employers paid them according to (or slightly above) what these workers could command in their own, ill-paid sectors of the economy (textiles, domestic service): about Fr 3 a day in France, where women normally commanded Fr 1 to 2 a day, and 12 to 15 s. a week in Britain, where women normally received 10 to 12 s. No matter what kind of job a woman held or how high her output might be, her wages remained about half those paid to men for similar work. Employers thus reproduced in the factory the same mathematical relation between men's and women's wages that had governed the relation between male industry and female industry before the declaration of war.

When employers were pressed on the issue, they invariably cited "the different needs of the sexes" as the justification for women's low rates: "The lower general level of women's wages is the outcome of one of the most fundamental societal conditions, the economic unity of the family. The man's wage is a 'family' wage, the woman's an 'individual' wage . . . " No matter that the majority of male workers were not paid anything approaching a family wage, or that women's wages did not vary according to marital status or number of dependents. When employers discussed women's wages, they insisted that they paid workers of both sexes according to the "conventional needs of a normal member of the class."[54] Melville Smith, who directed

---

[54] Ministry of Munitions, *Official History of the Ministry of Munitions* (London, 1920–24), vol. 5, pt. 2, p. 140. French employers were less likely to advance the "family wage" claim, given the generally lower level of wages in France and the concomitantly high rates of married women's employment. Here a family wage meant a collective income to which both adults contributed. On the family wage in Britain, see Michèle Barrett and Mary MacIntosh, "The

two large metals factories in Birmingham, even speculated that women were "perfectly contented" to be paid "at their own particular rate," despite considerable evidence to the contrary: "I do not think that a woman expects to be paid exactly the same as a man who has responsibilities and a family to keep. [Equal pay] would probably appeal to married women but I do not think to the others." Smith was one of the few employers who actually pursued the logic of a needs-based pay scale for women: "One woman comes to me a little while ago and she said that it was an outrageous thing that she should only have the same money as the other girls, not one were married and she had five children. On the other hand, take a sewing shop where you have a little girl of fifteen who does more than any other woman who is receiving full pay." Having articulated the tension between these two theories of wage payment, however, Smith then dropped the whole question. "We always have those troubles to contend with, but they smooth themselves down alright."[55]

When it came to men's wages, all talk of needs, individual or familial, receded. Now employers spoke of the value of the individual worker's labor to the industry. By introducing women's putatively smaller need for money into the discussion, employers sidestepped the issue of the comparative value of women's work. Thus they refused to answer workers' central objection: that women and men doing similar or identical work were paid according to very different criteria.

But employers did not invoke the question of women's needs solely to mask the fact that they were paying women as little as possible. These men also believed that an accurate assessment of women's "true" needs was essential to keeping them on track and working at maximum efficiency. If a woman's wage edged upward toward a man's, might she not lose the incentive to work, and simply slack off on the job? For this reason, it was dangerous to equalize any element of the wage, even the cost-of-living bonus, awarded to compensate for the drop in real wages caused by wartime inflation. Equal bonuses, one British official explained, would lead to "diminished effort by women, who would be guaranteed earnings greatly in excess of their actual needs."[56]

This man's blunt comment recalls the link that bound women to piecework systems, and the importance of driving these workers to ever-higher feats of

---

Family Wage: Some Problems for Socialists and Feminists," *Capital and Class* 11 (1980): 51–72; also Rose, *Limited Livelihoods.*

[55] IWM, War Cabinet Committee Minutes, testimony of Melville Smith, October 1918, p. D71.

[56] Quoted in Kozak, "Women Munition Workers," p. 188. By November 1918, the cost-of-living bonuses (fixed by the Ministry of Munitions on a national rather than regional basis) totaled 11s. per week for women, 23s. 6d. for men over age 18.

productivity through rate cutting. Herein lay another aspect of women's specificity as a source of labor. If men could not be motivated to work harder this way, women certainly could be:

> We were never able on this particular class of work to get men to cope with it; they would not stand it. Men will not stand the monotony of a fast repetition job like women; they will not stand by a machine pressing all their lives, but a woman will. She will go on with the job till . . . there is no more of that class of work; and then she will find something else equally monotonous.[57]

Thus women were different; more tolerant of monotony and more responsive to incentive payment systems and production bonuses. Indeed, on such repetitive labors, the only motivation left was the struggle to earn as much as possible: "The rule is that a girl on piecework or on a premium bonus system will not only do double the work of a dayworker but she will remain much keener and more interested."[58] Yet if women were essentially repetitive workers by "nature," then why did employers find it necessary to goad them to work ever faster at monotonous tasks by lowering the piece rate?

The manipulation of piece rates and production incentives was one of the most widespread tactics for raising productivity in the war factories.[59] By lowering the wage per piece, employers altered the relationship between effort expended and the expected reward. Workers had to labor far more intensively simply to maintain their earnings, let alone increase them. The way employers applied these incentive systems to women reveals their conviction that the relationship between effort and reward was not the same for women as it was for men. When the Parisian firm of Wilcoq-Regnault substituted women for men on grenade work, the firm started the women at half the male rate. It made no changes in the technology or organization of production; women simply came cheaper than men. Not content with their savings, management decided to push for higher output by cutting the already low base rate (Fr 8 per day) and offering a production bonus of Fr 1 per hundred grenades. The women responded as the boss had hoped: as the rate fell to Fr 7 and then to Fr 6.50 per day (and as the production bonus fell by half), the women went from 350 grenades a day (on a par with the men they had replaced) to 1,200 and finally to 1,700 grenades a day. When management cut the rate

---

[57] IWM, War Cabinet Committee Minutes, testimony of Major Ovans, October 1918, pp. D21, D33.

[58] A Birmingham munitions manufacturer, quoted in Kirkaldy, *Industry and Finance*, p. 129.

[59] In the fall of 1916, Albert Thomas reminded his labor controllers to ensure that defense contractors set the piece rates so as to "encourage both effort and professional skill . . . [for] a poorly conceived wage structure slows production": AN, 94 AP, 348, circular, 27 September 1916.

again, to Fr 5.25 a day, the women went on strike. Wilcoq fired them all and found replacements immediately, all of whom were started at Fr 5.25 a day.[60]

Wilcoq offers a poignant but by no means unique example of the impact that employers' productivist zeal had on women's wages and the conditions of work in the war factories. It was not simply the introduction of new technologies and a redivided labor process that led Wilcoq to push for more output. That the workers were women, and perceived as qualitatively different from men—swifter, more sensitive to changing rates and production bonuses—sufficed to fix management on a new and coercive production policy. As employers searched to find the new limits on workers' output per wage hour, the one bedrock certainty was that women's wages should not rise much above their customary prewar earnings. If new technology, patriotic fervor, or biological advantage (in the form of "nimble little fingers") enabled them to break the rate, then the rate was clearly set too high for such a class of labor. As one British foreman ingenuously remarked: "What can one do when a girl is earning as much as 15s per week except lower the piece rate?"[61]

By 1916, rising protest from workers of both sexes forced employers to reconsider their initial policy and define women's wages in relation not to rates in the ill-paid women's trades but to male rates in the metals and engineering industry. Significantly, it was the lack of a stable sexual division of labor in this industry that drew workers' attention to the blatant inequalities in male and female wages. Women and men, employed side by side on similar, even identical forms of work, had ample opportunity to observe the fruits of gender inequality. For women, the inequity was a galling and unjust reward for their labor. One Parisian shellmaker inveighed bitterly against her employer: "Remember that the men who worked here before us were paid Fr 1.20 and Fr 1.30 per hour and that they produced about half of what we do. . . . We are paid about half a man's wage for producing twice as much."[62] Male workers were no happier with the situation, for they feared (often correctly) that employers were using women to undermine wage levels across the trade.[63] In fact, male trade union leaders in both countries were often the most insistent proponents of equal pay for equal work. Not only did it seem the best way to defend the overall level of wages, but one could always hope that

[60] AN, F7, 13366, police spy report of a meeting of the Union des Ouvriers Mécaniciens de la Seine at the Bourse du Travail in Paris on 27 November 1916, pp. 6–7. The 250 people who attended included a group of women.

[61] PP 1915, Cd. 8051, Ministry of Labour, *Annual Report of the Chief Inspector of Factories and Workshops*, p. 49.

[62] *L'Union des Métaux*, December 1916–February 1917, p. 5.

[63] "After the war . . . the industrialists intend to employ women at low wages": AN, F7, 13366, Jules Bled, secretary of the union of *syndicats* in the Seine (a wartime labor coalition), speaking at a meeting of some 200 workers, mostly women, 14 August 1916, p. 1.

employers would exclude women from the industry altogether rather than pay them on a par with men.

The war had created a favorable political context for these demands, as left-leaning ministers of munitions were anxious to pacify an increasingly restless workforce. Yet the bureaucrats themselves believed that the inferiority of women's wages was not only "traditional" but "quasi-natural."[64] When the call for equal pay at last arose, state officials would support the demand that women's rates be lifted. But they would do so within a larger framework established by the employers' adamant insistence that under conditions of war, with reorganization altering the content of most work, equal pay would be inappropriate.

From the employers' standpoint, it was vital to keep women's rates separate from men's, even when they were performing the same jobs. Only in this way could they preserve the policy of paying wages on the basis of the class of labor employed. The means by which this distinction was maintained were remarkably similar across national boundaries. Employers and state officials divided all war work into three parts: (1) work traditionally performed by women before the war; (2) work that was entirely new to the industry; and (3) work that men had done before the war but that women now performed. No one troubled much about the first category, for here the sexual boundary was fixed and customary. In both nations, it seemed quite reasonable to continue paying the normal (low) women's wage for the region. For the second category, work that was entirely new, employers were to set wages according to the rates paid for similar work in the district. It was the third category that presented the gravest difficulties, and employers usually resolved them by assimilating the third category into the second. All war work was new work, they argued, and therefore open to renegotiation.

French industrialists kept women's wages below men's by arguing that women's work, though seemingly more productive, was in fact more costly than men's. They overlooked the fact that they had changed their methods and equipment in order to reduce their reliance on skilled men and render individual workers more productive, no matter which sex was hired. To hear them talk, one would think that every change had been arranged specially to accommodate the women. All the costs of the new organization, the employers argued, the new equipment and the supervision required for inexperienced operatives—should be deducted from women's pay packets.

Albert Thomas accepted this argument and in February 1916 issued a series of circulars that set policy for the wages of women doing men's work accordingly. On the basis of this kind of reasoning, he then issued a wage list in

[64] Roger Picard, *Le Mouvement syndicale durant la guerre* (Paris, 1927), p. 108.

January 1917 that fixed the male-female wage gap at 15 to 25 percent depending on the task at hand.[65] Though the Thomas list never conceded equal pay, the establishment of clear minimum rates narrowed the wage gap significantly. Semiskilled women saw the differential between their earnings and those of semiskilled men shrink from 45 percent in 1913 to 31 percent in 1916 to 18 percent in 1917.[66]

Once the principle of inequality had been established, however, it proved unshakable. The labor inspector Pierre Hamp observed that employers continued to deduct the costs of tools and setup even from the wages of women who set their own tools.[67] The 25 percent deduction, originally justified by the extra cost of female labor and never levied on similarly inexperienced men, had become part of that "quasi-natural inferiority" that marked women's wages. By the fall of 1917, all talk of the "additional cost" of women had faded away; the Ministry of Armaments simply fixed women's wages at 18 to 20 percent below men's for work that was scrupulously defined as equal:

> Skilled women are those who have passed the same tests demanded of skilled men. For these skilled women . . . the minimum hourly rate will be that established for men; but reduced by Fr 0.15 if the corresponding rate for men is less than Fr 1 and reduced by Fr 0.20 if the male rate is over Fr 1. . . . [For piecework] their hourly rate [will be] Fr 0.10 below that of male workers of the same occupation.[68]

With the principle of labor stratification thus upheld, employers would easily defeat labor's last campaigns for equal pay, in the spring of 1918 and again in May and June 1919, by asserting that semiskilled and female workers could never be conflated with skilled male professionals. "A semiskilled worker [man or woman] is not a professional [i.e., fully skilled] and although he can gain a certain facility in constantly performing the same operation, he profits from that facility in gaining a much greater output and, as a result, a higher

---

[65] AN, 94 AP, 348, Ministère de l'Armement, Direction de la Main-d'Oeuvre, *Tarifs et réglementation des salaires applicable pour les fabrications de guerre de la région parisienne*, 16 January 1917. See also Downs, "Women in Industry," chap. 2.

[66] Madeleine Guilbert, "Le Travail des femmes," *Revue Française du Travail*, November 1946, p. 663. After the war ended, the gap widened again, back to 31% by 1921.

[67] Pierre Hamp, "Le Quart en moins," *Information Ouvrière et Sociale*, 9 May 1918, p. 1.

[68] AN, 39 AS, 914, Ministère de l'Armement, "Décision du 20 septembre 1917," issued 13 November 1917, p. 3. See Downs, "Women in Industry," chap. 2, for a detailed account of skilled occupations (such as wire winding) in which unequal pay governed the labor of women and men who had passed identical tests of "professional capacity." The cost-of-living bonus, granted the following November, was scaled progressively, and was similarly gendered. See AN, 94 AP, 348, Louis Loucheur, "Les Salaires dans les usines de guerre," text of radio announcement, 23 November 1917.

wage."[69] Worse yet, in the union's proposal for a single rate for the job the employers detected the leveling impulse of the masses, "of the vast majority of workers deemed semiskilled, and of women," forcing the hand of the "skilled male elite": "More than ever it is the mass, and the mass of the least competent, that unfortunately tends to make the law," mourned one official of GIMM, the employers' association.[70]

Employers thus clung tenaciously to the system of labor stratification within which the male-female differential was inscribed. When the Fédération des Métaux demanded equal pay, the GIMM countered with wage lists that specified an array of about fifteen skilled and semiskilled occupations alongside two or three rates for women (sometimes only one), always pegged at 30 percent or more below the wage granted to their semiskilled male equivalents.[71] Among other things, this wage structure reflected employers' certainty that women formed a distinct and unitary kind of labor, not to be melded indiscriminately with the several classes of men. GIMM therefore resisted the syndicalists' effort to integrate even the most skilled and experienced women into the (male) categories of skilled professionals, insisting that any such adjustments could occur on an "individual basis" only.

In accepting the employers' dogged adherence to sexually stratified wage scales, Albert Thomas had conceded vital ground in the struggle for equal pay. Indeed, stratification spelled the death of equal pay, a fact that was not lost on the feminist leader Cécile Brunschvicg. No sooner had the minister issued his wage circulars than Brunschvicg took him to task for having failed to contest defense contractors on this point: " . . . why not demand a normal wage for women? Stop compensating employers for the cost [of female labor] and implement a bonus system . . . that would at least leave the woman

---

[69] AN, 39 AS, 914, "Observations de la Chambre Syndicale [employers' association] de la Robinetterie sur les propositions de revision des salaires applicables aux usines de guerre," 15 May 1918, p. 6. In the same dossier, see also Fédération des Ouvriers en Métaux to Ministre de l'Armement, 26 April 1918. For a more detailed discussion of these negotiations, see Downs, "Women in Industry," chaps. 2, 5.

[70] UIMM, 39/21/01, "Reflexions sociales sur la grève des métaux," 3 July 1919, p. 15.

[71] The GIMM lists express stratification through unequal base rates differentiated by age, sex, and skill. Only the production bonus was scaled according to the individual's productivity. Although the federation's request for a revision of the Thomas scale (26 April 1918) demands equal pay for equal work, the specific, industry-by-industry wage demands appended to this document show almost no instances of truly equal pay. Federation leaders, then, must have had almost no hope that GIMM would grant a single rate for the job, and probably the men themselves did not really believe women merited the same pay as a man, no matter how skilled or productive they were. The only workers on whose equality the federation insisted unswervingly were laborers. The wages of laborers of both sexes were based on need, as these workers were considered to have very little "professional value." Hence the demand for equal pay may also have been a tactic to force women from the upper reaches of the industry altogether, based on the not unreasonable presumption that if employers were forced to concede equal pay, they would eliminate women rather than pay them the male rate.

worker with a sense of the true value of her labor; each piece produced should be paid according to what it is worth and not according to who made it." So long as Thomas subscribed to stratification, he, too, was guilty of obstructing equal pay. Brunschvicg thus condemned him for having perverted the equal-pay principle into its opposite: "The French circular [on women's wages] . . . speaks of equal pay only to demonstrate its impossibility, or to show ways to undermine it."[72]

The minister's open admission of unequal pay stood in stark contrast to the British circular on women's wages, which in Brunschvicg's estimation stood firm on the issue of equality. Where the French circular "poses the principle . . . that the cost of tools needed by women workers should be borne solely by the women . . . the English circular . . . formally promises equal pay for equal work. The French circular is addressed to the employers above all. . . . Under the guise of justice, it seeks to present the advantages and warn of the difficulties of using a new labor force."[73] Once again, England stood in French women's minds as a shimmering land of opportunity. Had the English actually done anything to merit this admiration?

In fact, Lloyd George also ended by upholding separate scales of pay for women and men. His scheme took a somewhat different form from Thomas's—a flat minimum rate across the board—and emerged from a more protracted series of negotiations in which trade union leaders, male and female, played active roles. In the end, however, the wage gap between men and women yawned wider in Britain than in France. By 1918, French women's income averaged about 20 percent less than their male colleagues', while British women took home about 33 percent less. Despite the British circular's more open assertion of wage equality, wages in Britain were arrayed on a more sharply graded ladder, with unskilled workers of both sexes earning rates well below those of skilled craftsmen.[74]

The circular to which Brunschvicg referred was the outcome of a long struggle over wage provisions in the Treasury Agreement of March 1915. According to clause 5 of the agreement, women (like other new recruits) were to receive "the rates customarily paid for the job."[75] The EEF immediately interpreted this vague proviso in light of labor stratification, which, as we have seen, equated adult women with adolescent boys. Practically speaking,

[72] Cécile Brunschvicg to Albert Thomas, 1916, typescript in library at Ecole des Surintendantes d'Usine.

[73] Ibid.

[74] The wider wage gap in Britain can be traced to British craftsmen's greater shop-floor power and to a wage strategy that was, overall, defensive and sectional. But it also reflects the lower level of wages in France for both women and men, and the gentler incline of the wage ladders based on skill, age, and gender.

[75] Quoted in G. D. H. Cole, *Trade Unionism and Munitions* (London, 1923), p. 73.

on any given job, women's time rate was fixed at half of men's. The ink had hardly dried on the Treasury Agreement before Sylvia Pankhurst approached Lloyd George, hoping for a more favorable reading of its ill-defined wage clause. The minister responded with a formula that diverged significantly from the EEF's tight-fisted policy: women undertaking the work of men would be paid the same piece rates that the men were receiving before the agreement.[76] The principle of equal piece rates was to become the government's official line on the wages of women employed on men's work. While this policy granted a good deal more toward equality than the employers were prepared to concede at this point, it left untouched all time-based payment systems, including the highly popular premium bonus system (which, though treated as a time-based system, was in fact a complex piece-rate system.) Employers thus continued to pay women on the basis of a time rate fixed at about 50 percent of the male rate.

As the number of women engineering workers multiplied, the ASE began to fear that employers were using the women to undermine skilled wage levels. After all, once an employer had redefined a job as "new work," he no longer felt bound to pay the new occupant, male or female, at the former rate. By the summer of 1915, employers had used this argument time and again to block women's wage demands. In June 1915 the ASE forged an alliance with the women's NFWW, certain that the best means of defending its own position lay in lending its enhanced bargaining power to the women's struggle for equal pay.[77] The new alliance proceeded by measured steps. Rather than demand equal pay from the outset, they approached the Ministry of Munitions to request a decent minimum wage—£1 a week for women employed on work previously undertaken by skilled men. On the work of semi- and unskilled men, they were to be paid piece rates equal to those of the men whom they had replaced.

Lloyd George accepted the NFWW-ASE claim as both reasonable and just, and in the autumn of 1915 issued a circular (L2) setting a minimum wage of £1 a week for all women over eighteen employed on work "not recognized as women's work before the war." The circular also secured equal piece rates for women on semi- and unskilled work (formalizing his earlier interpretation of the Treasury Agreement) and required that employers using the premium bonus system set equal time rates for women and men.[78]

The £1 minimum, exclusive of overtime, ensured a living wage to women,

---

[76] EEF note to member firms, March 1915, quoted in Drake, *Women in the Engineering Trades*, pp. 17, 19.

[77] This decision was reached after the ASE membership voted, by an overwhelming majority, to continue its policy of excluding women and the unskilled from its ranks.

[78] Clauses 8 and 5, circular L2, quoted in Cole, *Trade Unionism*, pp. 89–91. The £1 was paid for a "normal" (forty-eight hour) week. L2 also secured men's overtime rates for women.

even if they failed to make production in the time allotted—something that might happen quite frequently, thanks to poor management or bottlenecks in production. Ten months later, in July 1916, when the ministry finally stirred itself to regulate the wages of women performing what had been defined as women's work before the war (fuses, small arms, and small metal parts), the results were not impressive. Order 447 raised wages for women from 12s. to 16s. a week, and for girls under eighteen from 9s. to 13s. As officials at the ministry later conceded, equal pay was irrelevant for women employed on mere women's work. Here one had only to secure "a living wage." The need to "interpret" the principle of equal pay for equal work arose only in respect to the wages of women employed on men's work, because what was really at issue was "safeguarding the men's established rates of pay."[79]

At first circular L2 was applied in the national factories only; under the terms of the first munitions act, the state had no power to set wages in controlled establishments. As the cost of living rose, employers' refusal to grant the increases grew ever more intolerable. When news of the £1 minimum in national factories reached women working in controlled establishments, they grew positively rebellious, and rumors of threatened work stoppages filled the air. Lloyd George then sought (and received) expanded authority under an amended munitions act that empowered the ministry to set wages and conditions for "dilutees" of both sexes in all munitions works, public and private. Women's basic rates rose instantly from about 15s. to 23s. a week. Those employed on the premium bonus system saw their weekly earnings rise by at least 10s.[80]

The Fabian socialist Barbara Drake hailed L2 as "the foundation of a woman's charter in the engineering trades." Though the circular maintained "the old discrimination in favor of the skilled worker," Drake regarded the £1 minimum as a considerable achievement—and it was. But L2 had not resolved the problem of wages for women on the thousands of new jobs created by wartime dilution. In addition, borrowing a leaf from their French colleagues' book, employers insisted that no matter how much more output women workers attained for the firm, they were more expensive than men because of extra costs for supervision and setting up. In January 1917 the Special Arbitration Tribunal accepted this argument and granted employers a 10 percent deduction from women's pay to compensate for these additional costs. In the end, "not one in a thousand of the scores of women introduced into shell and fuse factories proved a claim to take the *whole* place of a *fully*

---

[79] Ministry of Munitions, *Official History*, vol. 5, pt. 2, p. 7. "The aim of the women's wages section was not to fix them so low as to injure the men, nor so high as to discourage employers from employing them": PRO, Mun. 5/79/340/7, Minister of Munitions to Prime Minister, 30 April 1918 (memo).

[80] Barbara Drake, *Women in Trade Unions* (London, 1920), p. 79.

skilled tradesman."[81] The £1 minimum thus became a standard rate for women, and employers rarely exceeded it.

In setting a minimum rate for women, government officials in both nations hoped to curb some of the worst abuses while protecting the general level of wages until the men returned. As in France, state intervention did win women significant increases within the parameters of labor stratification, and the gap between male and female pay narrowed from 50 percent in 1913 to about 33 percent in 1917.[82] But this defensive strategy, though it generated genuine raises for women, never challenged the practice of paying women on a separate basis from men. Hence British employers also succeeded in keeping the basis of women's pay separate from men's, and so maintained the principle of a rate for the grade of labor employed. Through the last years of the war, feminists and trade unionists would agitate in vain for a rate for the job; once the state had accepted the principle of one rate for men and a lower rate for women, the campaign for equal pay was lost.

There is a relentless circularity to wartime pronouncements on the subject of women's wages; all discussions of the matter seem inevitably to return to their point of departure: women are ipso facto a low-waged source of labor. This circularity reflects a broad acceptance of the notion that women's lower level of wages across the economy signified that women really were workers of lower value than men. It was a durable and profound conviction that the wartime experience could not dislodge. One finds employers and state officials alike recoiling at the spectacle of women earning high wages: "It is not a practical proposition that they should receive the skilled man's rate although this is skilled men's work, because their wages would come to £3 4/-6d for a 54 hour week."[83]

Alongside such convictions traveled an awareness that women's lower wages were central to the economic future of entire segments of the industry. Mr. D. S. Marjoribanks spoke for the entire Employers' Federation when he observed:

> If you are going on the principle that women are going to get equal pay to men you are going to kill the whole [airplane] industry. There are certain classes of work which are essentially women's work and should be paid—I do not say at a prewar women's rate but at a rate suitable to it being women's work. . . . If there is any attempt to put them on to men's rates, you are simply going to destroy a rising industry. . . . It will disappear from England just like the glass work did.[84]

---

[81] Drake, *Women in the Engineering Trades*, pp. 27, 17.

[82] PP 1919, Cmd. 135, *Report of the War Cabinet Committee on Women in Industry*, p. 121.

[83] PRO, Lab 2/243/142/9, memo by Gordon Campbell, assistant controller of Labour Regulation Department, April 1918.

This is where the logic of women's greater cost breaks down, for the airplane industry's ongoing viability rested not on replacing women with men, as the theory of costlier women would imply, but rather on preserving women as cheap labor. The industry would prosper so long as employers could designate entire classes of work as "women's" and pay accordingly.

Women's lower wages thus rested on the existence of something called women's work, and it was, in the words of the machine-tool mogul Alfred Herbert, "work which women can perform a) to the satisfaction of their employer and b) without detriment to their health."[85] If women were paid on an equal basis with men, rising industries and women's own incentive to work quickly would be destroyed. The Birmingham employer Melville Smith pointed out that women were naturally endowed with the ability to work more quickly than men on everything except "physical work." To pay them equally would blunt the force of this "natural" difference: "I think they would bring their rate of production down . . . if you gave them the same rate of pay as men . . . the pay would be more than sufficient for them and therefore they would not have an incentive."[86]

Employers' reasoning on the issue of women's wages was thus riddled by a profound contradiction that declared that women are repetitive workers *by nature,* yet asserted that this "nature" expressed itself only when employers drove women by low rates. Throughout the war and the interwar period, demands for equal pay would hang suspended on this contradiction as it passed unresolved and bound women ever more tightly to the fragmented and repetitive labors of the highly rationalized production process.

---

[84] IWM, War Cabinet Committee Minutes, EEF testimony, October 1918, p. F76.

[85] PP 1919, Cmd. 167, *Appendices of Evidence,* p. 55.

[86] IWM, War Cabinet Committee Minutes, testimony of Melville Smith, October 1918, p. D73. Contemporary feminists were well aware of the contradictions on which unequal pay rested. Yet their efforts to redress the inequities met repeated defeat against the employers' iron law of unequal wages. See Susan Pedersen, "The Failure of Feminism in the Making of the British Welfare State," *Radical History Review* 43 (Winter 1989): 86–110; and Harold Smith, "The Issue of 'Equal Pay for Equal Work' in Great Britain, 1914–1919," *Societas* 8 (Winter 1978): 39–51.

Unraveling the Sacred Union

In the spring of 1917, a sudden, massive strike wave seized the munitions factories of Paris. Commencing in the aftermath of the Pentecost holiday, the movement spread rapidly from factory to factory and from one industrial suburb to the next. Within days, nearly 43,000 metals and munition workers, most of them women, had left their machines to join the crowds that marched along the broad boulevards of industrial Paris. Brief disputes had broken out in individual munitions factories over the previous year, but the May–June movement was by far the most widespread and powerful strike effort since August 1914. After three years of fighting, it seemed that low wages and long hours might undo the "sacred union" that bound working class to bourgeoisie in a crusade against the German threat to the Republic. Within a few short months, political scandal would shatter this domestic truce, but in May and June its partisans still hoped to preserve the fragile unity. Hence employers, police, state officials, and even some trade union leaders collaborated in the effort to end the street demonstrations and get the women back to work as quickly as possible.

The May–June strikes mark an important moment in the history of France's "other front." After three years of relative quiet, muffled by the blanket of sacred union and the many sanctions that state and employers wielded in time of war, the working class was starting to recover its independent voice. Yet historians give this movement a fleeting nod (at best) when they recount labor's fate during World War I. Certainly the police and employers who joined in repressing this movement viewed it as a significant event. The widespread work stoppages threatened the military effort by slowing the flow of arms to the front, while the daily demonstrations constituted the first serious rupture of public order since the war began. Moreover, the strikes followed hard on the heels of open revolt among some 40,000 soldiers along the western front.[1] Although news of the mutiny was carefully suppressed (neither the Germans nor France's British ally ever got wind of it), rumors had traveled back to Paris and circulated among the striking crowds. Police searched vigorously for traitors among the strike movement's "ringleaders," convinced that the link between mutiny and strike was more than casual— that a nefarious force of German agents had fomented the demonstrations on both fronts.

Max Gallo writes that in time of war, with syndicalist militants dispersed across the landscape and unprecedented powers of discipline concentrated in the hands of state and employers, workers' protests over wages and conditions were themselves the critical force that catalyzed labor's revival. Moreover, under the constraints and prohibitions of war, syndicalism would regenerate only through those apparently nonpolitical protests that were tied closely to the concrete conditions of work—struggles that initially were fought almost exclusively by women.[2]

Labor history's classic distinction between "narrow" struggles over shop-floor conditions and the more "political" strike, motivated by broader concerns outside the workplace, thus loses force and clarity in the context of the war. Nonetheless, historians have doggedly fixed their eyes beyond May–June, locating labor's "true" renascence in the spring of 1918, when a predominantly male and explicitly pacifist movement swept the war factories. Those who don't bypass May–June altogether simply shrug it off as the act of an apolitical and wage-hungry female crowd, for whom such serious political issues as the conduct of the war were remote matters indeed.[3] But if French labor first

[1] Guy Pedroncini, *Les Mutineries de 1917* (Paris, 1967). Throughout April and May, collective acts of disobedience shook the very armies that General Robert Nivelle had hurled over the top in a series of suicidal attacks against the German forces along the Chemin des Dames. Pedroncini counts 151 cases, of which 110 were collective demonstrations, and notes that over half the divisions in the entire French army were affected. Soldiers refused to proceed to the front, stacked their weapons, commandeered trains, and steamed toward Paris. The mutinies continued for several weeks and were ultimately ended through a combination of brutal repression (shootings and internment) and concessions (improvement of rations and fairer distribution of leaves). See also Leonard V. Smith, *Between Mutiny and Obedience: The Case of the French Fifth Infantry Division during World War I* (Princeton, 1994).

[2] Max Gallo, "Quelques Aspects de la mentalité et du comportement ouvrier dans les usines de guerre," *Mouvement Social* 56 (July–September 1966): 30, 9. Women accounted for nearly 70% of all strikers between June 1916 and July 1917.

[3] Among those who more or less ignore May–June are Gallo, "Quelques Aspects," and Robert Wohl, *French Communism in the Making, 1914–1924* (Stanford, 1966). James MacMillan, *House-wife or Harlot? The Place of Women in French Society, 1870–1940* (New York, 1981), and Jean-Louis Robert, "Les Luttes ouvrières en France pendant la première guerre mondiale," *Cahiers d'Histoire de l'Institut Maurice Thorez*, no. 23 (1977), pp. 28–65, do not ignore the movement but both contribute to the apolitical reading of these strikes. MacMillan uses the strike to illustrate the regrettable fact that once again women failed to achieve the kind of political maturity demon-strated by permanent, mass adherence to the *syndicats*. At no point does MacMillan question the

recovered its voice in 1917—and the burgeoning protest that followed in the autumn of that year suggests this was indeed the case[4]—then May–June marks an important passage from invertebrate silence to vocal opposition. Had the voice-that first rallied the protest been baritone rather than soprano, perhaps labor historians would not have been so quick to banish this movement to its margins. Their dismissive view of women's protest as preeminently unpolitical closely parallels the opinion of those police and employers who nervously watched and then hastily repressed the movement of May–June 1917.

Organizing Women in the War Factories

As we have seen, French women entered the metalworking industry just when the twin pressures of invasion and the reorganization of work had produced a precipitous decline in work conditions. By the third winter of war, the sense of emergency that infused the war factories had hardly abated. Women continued to work at a grueling rhythm—thirteen days of eleven to twelve hours each, one day's respite, and then thirteen more, perhaps this time on the night shift. Except in the very newest installations, conditions remained execrable, and in these dim and dusty shops, managers pushed workers to labor ever more swiftly and intensively by cutting the rate and increasing the workloads. Women might protest against the speedups; some even refused to work under the new conditions. But by the spring of 1917, the cost of living had risen about 40 percent. For a time, most women simply accepted the doubled pace of work in order to maintain their earnings.

Labor had scant basis on which to resist this pressure, for under conditions of war, shop-floor divisions had multiplied. The isolation of foreign from native, the hierarchical distinction of male over female, the subjection of mobilized men to extreme military discipline—all made it difficult to find a basis for unified protest. Worse yet, the workers most likely to have had prewar connections to the syndicalist movement—mobilized men—faced military courts-martial should they have the temerity to walk out on strike. Finally, police and employers maintained the syndical silence by scattering paid spies

---

relevance of trade union organization at a time when employers refused to receive shop stewards, denied the legitimacy of workers' demands, and even failed to pay the prescribed minimum wage. Alfred Rosmer, a leftist eyewitness to the wartime labor movement, gives the women's strikes a serious and detailed consideration that underscores their crucial role in revivifying labor protest: *Le Mouvement ouvrier pendant la guerre*, 2 vols. (Paris, 1939).

[4] A brief general strike swept the aviation industry in September, and the 3,000 women at the Vincennes cartridge works staged a short, massive demonstration in November.

among the workforce; one source estimates that by 1917, one in every 1,600 defense workers was performing this service on the factory floor.[5]

Invasion and mobilization thus shattered the basis of prewar solidarities and pushed an already weak trade union structure to the edge of the factory floor. The weakened *syndicats* could offer little support to this divided and highly vulnerable workforce, not least because the leadership was itself divided over participation in the war effort. The CGT's reformist majority had followed Léon Jouhaux into eager collaboration with the government; Alphonse Merrheim's Fédération des Métaux had opposed the war from the outset. The federation's refusal of war and sacred union allowed it to hear a tale that the more patriotic CGT could credit only with difficulty: that munitions workers faced exhausting labor, low wages, and a general reassertion of unchecked managerial authority. Ultimately, the federation would form one nodal point around which a viable labor movement could reassemble. In the short term, however, a divided union leadership, in conjunction with the collapse in rank-and-file membership, allowed employers to impose new work regimes without much fear of organized resistance.

Even if the unions had formed a more powerful presence at this time, there is little reason to suppose that they would have extended wholehearted support to women as they struggled to establish decent wages and conditions for themselves. For one thing, syndicalists deeply resented women for working so rapidly. Women's much-touted speed and dexterity won them the title "tool smashers" among their skilled male colleagues. "Because of the speed at which they work . . . the fitters claim that a woman's lathe needs five repairs to every one repair for a man's." In one typical case a woman making shell cases managed in six weeks to raise her output to double that of the men. Not surprisingly, this feat aroused particular hostility: "Having proved her great manual dexterity and her will to break solidarity, [she] pursued her own earnings without regard to corporative concerns."[6]

In syndicalist eyes, women's "excessive" concern with wages bore witness to a greedy and grasping individualism, which could only work against collective efforts to limit exploitation. But in time of war, their productivist zeal was doubly objectionable and doubly threatening, for every increase in efficiency freed more men for duty in the trenches: "The intensification of women's work leads only to men being sent to butchery," Merrheim bitterly remarked.[7]

[5] Mathilde Dubesset, Françoise Thébaud, and Catherine Vincent, "Quand les femmes entrent à l'usine" (mémoire de maîtrise, Université de Paris VII, 1974), p. 30.

[6] Pierre Hamp, in *L'Information Ouvrière et Sociale*, 7 April 1918, p. 1.

[7] AN, F7, 13361, Alphonse Merrheim, quoted in a police report: "2e Réunion des syndicats ouvrier à la bourse du travail," 4 June 1916, p. 1. If women often brought the ardor of the neophyte to their new occupations, they also feared rate cutting and overwork. Dubesset et al., "Quand les femmes entrent," p. 309, mention a strike in mid-October 1916 by twenty-six

The tradition of resisting overwork by limiting output thus took on additional significance, and mingled the politics of war with a nascent shop-floor division between women and their more experienced male colleagues.

If syndicalists feared women's aptitude for the swift, finicky work that multiplied in the redivided and reorganized labor process, they nonetheless saw, quite correctly, that metals employers intended to continue hiring women after the war. Faced with this prospect, union leaders began to argue that women, too, should be drawn into the syndicalist fold, if only as a means of defending the men.[8] They suggested that women might be educated out of their "anticollectivism," that it was the product of women's narrow milieu— home, family, and women's trades—and not an eternal feature of female nature.[9] In 1916 the Fédération des Métaux launched the campaign by organizing a new, desegregated union, the Syndicat des Ouvriers et Ouvrières en Métaux de la Seine, which successfully recruited among the increasingly restive *munitionettes*. By July 1917, women, who accounted for nearly 30 percent of all workers in the Parisian metals and munitions industries, also made up about 30 percent of the region's unionized metalworkers.[10] Yet even this concerted effort to organize women metalworkers was not without its ambiguities. Although Merrheim frequently spoke at Syndicat meetings, the federation as a whole held aloof from this bastard child. Not surprisingly, the organized craft elite were not yet prepared to embrace women as full colleagues.

Despite unpromising circumstances and the enduring animosity of syndicalist militants, women were not wholly without resources in their struggle to carve out a more hospitable space for themselves. During the second year of

---

women lathe workers, demanding that management fire two others who were outproducing the rest. Management was not receptive to the idea.

[8] "Given that to a certain extent women will be called upon to replace men in the factories after the war, it is their duty to join their respective trade unions . . . if they wish to realize their just demands": AN, F7, 13366, Jules Bled, secretary of the Union des Syndicats de la Seine, quoted in a police report: "Une Réunion . . . à Levallois-Perret," 14 August 1916, p. 2.

[9] See, for instance, the labor pamphlet *Le Travail de la femme pendant la guerre*, published by the Comité Intersyndicale d'Action contre l'Exploitation de la Femme (Paris, 1917). The committee was formed in July 1915 and included representatives of the clothing, printing, and metals industries.

[10] Dubesset et al., "Quand les femmes entrent," p. 285. The syndicat was formed in April 1916 by the amalgamation of several federation locals. By midsummer, after a series of successful strikes in the war factories, some 800 women had enrolled in the new *syndicat*. An additional 5,000 women and 450 men had joined by June 1917. By July the organization boasted 10,090 members, 70% of them women. This was a considerable advance over the scant 200 (out of 15,000 members) organized in the federation in 1913. All 200 worked in the state artillery at Vincennes and were organized separately from the men. See Roger Picard, *Le Mouvement syndicale durant la guerre* (Paris, 1927). By the end of the war, women's participation rate in the CGT had doubled, from 8.7% in 1913 to 15% by 1920: Dubesset et al., "Quand les femmes entrent," p. 382.

war, women developed some of these resources as they began to protest openly against the rate cutting and overwork endemic in the munitions industry.

The Resurgence of Protest

Strikes in the war factories were generally brief, lasting two to four days on average, and were for the most part single-sex affairs. Mixed conflicts, though not unknown, were comparatively rare, and aside from the May–June movement, were usually dominated by men. This sexual segregation arose from the conjuncture of two phenomena: (1) these initial struggles rarely spread from the shop where they first broke out, and (2) shops were generally segregated by sex, as employers preferred to separate women and men by workshop wherever possible. Conflicts would remain spatially contained until May–June 1917, when women premiered the tactic of *débauchage:* leaving work with the express intent of calling out support from other shops, industries, and trades—by violence and intimidation, if necessary.

In time, women's strikes acquired a shape and structure that reflect syndicalism's weak links to these workers. The center of the conflict always lay with the strikers themselves, who met daily in local halls—*bourses du travail,*[11] syndicalist meeting halls, and even Boulogne's Mignon-Palace movie house— to formulate their demands, elect delegates, and vote on other matters relating to the struggle. During the briefest stoppages—those lasting but a few hours— the women remained in the shop, arms folded and machines idle, while a small delegation approached the boss. Though workers sometimes stopped to write out formal petitions, the delegation was usually empowered to speak on behalf of the whole. When conflicts dragged on, women were more likely to put their demands in writing. But longer strikes carried the risk of dismissal; so long as the women remained inside, arms crossed before their machines, management could not lock them out. Nonetheless, several of these early strikes did last a week or more, and each time, the women won at least partial victory.

If the strike was to be a long one, the women elected a strike committee,

---

[11] The *bourse du travail* was a distinctively French institution: a local labor exchange, controlled by the *syndicats,* which also functioned as a meeting hall for *syndicats* of all trades in the town, neighborhood, or region. The *bourse* often housed reading rooms and libraries, combining elements of worker self-education with job postings. Most important, the *bourses,* like the syndicat's *maisons communes,* were autonomous, worker-controlled spaces where strikers could meet and formulate demands. See Fernand Pelloutier, *Histoire des bourses du travail: Origines, institution, avenir* (Paris, 1902), and Jacques Julliard, *Fernand Pelloutier et les origines du syndicalisme d'action directe* (Paris, 1971).

which took responsibility for organizing the dispute. The committee wrote up the demands, collected strike funds,[12] approached management or the authorities at the Ministry of Armaments, and made contact with syndicalist leaders at the Fédération des Métaux. The federation lent moral, financial, and organizational support during the more prolonged struggles, using the labor press to publicize the disputes, stir public sympathy, and gather strike funds for these women, "most of [whom] have many children, their husbands at the front, imprisoned or shot."[13] In one case, Merrheim even accompanied the women as they pleaded their case to the director. But in no instance was the trade union present at the outset. Women initiated and directed their own actions, and invited syndical participation only in some cases and only after the conflict had been joined. This pattern would reemerge with a vengeance in the May–June movement.

Frequently women's first concern was to gain direct access to higher management. The relations of production in wartime Paris may have been marked by the reassertion of untrammeled managerial power, but most workers, female and male, experienced this authority not from the director but at the hands of his foremen and shop chiefs. The employer remained a distant figure, unstained by the small daily torments that some of his junior officers wrought in their minor reigns of terror on the factory floor. Many workers of both sexes were convinced that if the director only knew what was going on, he would put a stop to it.[14]

This notion that "the king is good" found its counterpart in the idea that foremen and shop chiefs were the main sources of evil on the factory floor. Women workers, whether on strike or not, often reviled these petty tyrants, and not without reason. In January 1917 the foreman at Malicet & Blin prevented women drillers from circulating a petition for higher wages, claiming that if the women needed a raise, he would give it to them himself. The shop chief then took the petition and promised to pass it along to the director. Eight days later, the woman who started the petition was fired on the pretext

[12] Such funds were rare indeed; most women strikers had no savings or support. Records emphasize women's concern for democratic procedure, in particular their insistence on secret ballots for the strike vote. Records also show that women strikers, like their male counterparts, preferred to act in unanimity.

[13] Fédération des Métaux, "A Puteaux: La Grève de la maison de Dion." *L'Humanité,* 3 July 1916, p. 2.

[14] The notion that remote bosses formed a court of higher justice was by no means confined to women workers. In August 1917, workers at Nieuport, Caudron, and Voisin protested the removal of two wounded war veterans who had been returned to the front after they led a wage protest. The 550 men and 150 women decided to take up a collection for these men and then send a petition not only to the director but also to his mother. See AN, F7, 13366, police report: "Une Réunion des ouvriers . . . des maisons d'aviation Nieuport, Caudron et Voisin . . . à la mairie d'Issy-les-Moulineaux," 22 August 1917, p. 4.

that her work was unsatisfactory. Her entire shift of 321 women stopped work and stormed into the director's office, where they learned that he had never even seen their petition.[15]

The first significant conflict to rupture the labor peace of sacred union came on 29 June 1916, when an entire shop of women gun workers downed tools at the Dion factory. The Dion strike, which was to last eleven days, is in many ways a classic example of the women's strike before the May–June movement of 1917. Dion was a vast works, employing some 4,000 women and men in the various shops and assembly halls. Yet the strike never spread beyond the point where it erupted: the all-female gun shop, where 110 women hollowed barrels and cut gun sights for ten and a half hours a day, eleven hours on the night shift.

Work in the gun shop was minutely subdivided, with women deployed on forty-one separate operations. Each job had its own basic piece rate and a variable production bonus based on the complexity of the operation and the number of pieces produced. A worker's take-home pay thus rested on a complicated set of calculations. Management used this complex system to push for greater output and disguise the fact that the firm had been steadily lowering the basic rates since January.[16]

Near the end of June 1916, the shop chief announced that the work was to be "reorganized": henceforth each woman would operate three machines rather than two. In addition, management proposed to slash the piece rate. It was not the first time that Dion had lowered the rates, but this time the proposed cuts were so deep that workers feared they could not maintain their current earnings even with the heavier workload. The women stopped work immediately and chose a delegation to transmit their grievances directly to their employer, the Marquis de Dion, attempting to by-pass the foreman (there had been numerous complaints of ill treatment at his hands). But the foreman blocked their efforts with words of contempt: "The Dion factory never yields to a strike as a matter of principle. . . . It has never yielded to men and it is even less likely to yield to women."[17]

Even if the women had made direct contact with their employer, it is unlikely that he would have given their case a sympathetic hearing, for the Marquis de Dion ruled his works in the best tradition of France's "divine-

---

[15] After a nine-day strike, the women won the minimum wage of 75 centimes for which they had initially petitioned: *L'Union des Métaux,* December 1916–February 1917, p. 6.

[16] Pay sheets were further complicated by a series of deductions: 1% for tool setting, 2% for a fund to support the families of mobilized men, and variable, episodic deductions for the cost of repairs on equipment and tools. See Rosmer, *Mouvement ouvrier,* 2:115.

[17] Fédération des Métaux, "A Puteaux: La Grève de la maison de Dion," *L'Humanité,* 6 July 1916, p. 4.

right employers,"[18] treating any demand that rose from the factory floor as tantamount to mutiny. Ultimately, the intransigent marquis would yield only to government arbitration, and the Ministry of Armaments dispatched one of its labor controllers to settle the dispute. At that point the strike committee stopped trying to capture the boss's ear and fastened their hopes on the controller.

In letters to the controller, the strike committee stressed repeatedly the themes of overwork, exhaustion, and insufficient wages. Further, the women located their exploitation in the larger context of war, underscoring their own patriotic will to produce weapons and their status as wives or widows of soldiers. Dion's effort to extract more work for less money thus took on a rather unpatriotic coloring:

> Despite all our goodwill, we cannot accept this new organization of work. We are already overtaxed with two machines; we will wear ourselves out more rapidly [with three]. Then we will be accused of soldiering when we fail to produce the maximum, and that means we will get the sack. So it has gone in the past for many of our comrades after each cut in the rate. . . . If management were to consider our painful situation, as widows or wives of patriotic men, surely they would raise our daily rates immediately.[19]

The committee then advanced a set of demands that would soon become standard for women in the war factories: wage guarantees, protection of strikers against victimization, and the request that henceforth foremen treat the women with more respect. The women at Dion also added two requests that testify to the harshness of life in the war factory. They asked (1) that women be given time off during their husbands' leaves from the front, and (2) that if a woman fell sick on her shift, day or night, she not be fired or simply dumped at the factory gates to make her own way home. The record is mute on the resolution of these last two issues, but it does show that the ministry's arbitration brought at least partial victory to the women at Dion. Although the workload was increased, workers were guaranteed their former level of earnings, and management agreed to rehire those it had fired for their participation in the strike.[20]

---

[18] The phrase is Senator Paul Faure's, used to criticize Eugène Schneider's domination of factory and town in Le Creusot; quoted in Donald Reid, "Industrial Paternalism: Discourse and Practice in Nineteenth-Century French Mining and Metallurgy," *Comparative Studies in Society and History* 27 (October 1985): 581.

[19] Quoted in *L'Humanité*, 3 July 1916, p. 2.

[20] Fédération des Métaux, "A Puteaux: La Grève de la maison de Dion," *L'Humanité*, 6 July 1916, p. 4.

Women thus found an unexpected ally in the Ministry of Armaments; unexpected because Albert Thomas's resolute adherence to the politics of sacred union made him intolerant of any industrial action in the war factories. The flow of weapons simply could not be interrupted, no matter what the provocation, and strikers were therefore more likely to receive sharp chastisement than a sympathetic hearing: "Have you thought of the enemy, who never ceases his labors, of your brothers, your husbands who impatiently await the means of defense that you provide them? . . . Be here on the job tomorrow, each and every one of you."[21] At the same time, however, Thomas saw great reformist potential in the centralized mechanisms of state-sponsored arms production. So long as progress was dispensed from the center, he energetically supported the idea of improving wages and conditions in the war factories. Hence, by January 1917—six months after the conflict at Dion was resolved—Thomas was prepared to legitimize women's wage demands (though not their method of obtaining them) by imposing a uniform standard on all defense plants.

The "Thomas scale" of wages was the minister's most important intervention in the war factories, for, as we have seen, it raised the minimum rates for workers of both sexes while narrowing the gap between women's and men's wages.[22] It also rationalized the calculation of piece rates, reducing the complexity and variety that often ruled wages in factories such as Dion's. Thomas imposed his wage list by fiat, hoping the new minimums would bring an end to the growing agitation among (mostly women) metalworkers. In the very short run, he was successful, and the tempo of strikes relaxed in the weeks that followed.[23] But this success was owed as much to coercion as to concession, for in the same decree that established the new wage scale, Thomas had effectively outlawed the strike, enjoining workers and employers to accept government arbitration in the event of a dispute. Although reformists such as Jouhaux welcomed the added strength that arbitration might lend to labor's cause, men such as Merrheim fulminated against the strictures placed on a labor movement that was just beginning to show signs it still lived. Any lull in strikes can probably be attributed as much to compulsory arbitration, that

[21] Thomas addressing a group of women strikers at the Schneider works, Harfleur, 17 January 1917, reported in *La Bataille* (official organ of the CGT), 25 January 1917.

[22] For earlier wage levels, see Rosmer, *Mouvement ouvrier*, 1: chap. 18. See also AN, 94 AP, 348, Ministère de l'Armement, Direction de la Main-d'Oeuvre, *Tarifs et réglementation des salaires applicables pour les fabrications de guerre et de la région parisienne*, 16 January 1917, pp. 19–20. See Madeleine Guilbert, "Le Travail des femmes," *Revue Française du Travail*, November 1946, p. 663, for information on the male-female wage gap over time.

[23] The tempo of strikes slowed but did not abate altogether; on 3 March 1917, for instance, 2,000 women at the Vincennes cartridge plant struck for higher wages. See AN, F7, 13366, police report: "La Grève des ouvrières à Vincennes," 3 March 1917.

"redoubtable weapon against the working class,"[24] as to the improvement in wages. In any event, the relative calm did not last beyond April.

Throughout the spring of 1917, many of the largest employers in the region (Renault, Salmson, Vedovelli) stubbornly refused to implement the widely published "Thomas scale." Wartime inflation had already cut real wages by an average of 23 percent: if 1914 is taken as a baseline of 100, prices stood at 139 in January 1917.[25] As the cost of living climbed ever more steeply that spring, reaching 183 in June, workers of both sexes grew restive and then indignant at employers' failure to grant the new minimums. In view of the increasing severity of conditions that spring, it is perhaps surprising that the strikers held out as long as they did, waiting until the end of May before taking their multiple grievances to the streets.

The Struggle at Boulogne-Billancourt, May–June 1917

On Tuesday morning, 29 May 1917, thirty-eight women workers at the Salmson aircraft factory in Boulogne-Billancourt, an industrial suburb west of Paris, returned to work after the Pentecost weekend. Salmson had expected them back on Monday, but the women had prolonged their holiday by the time-honored working-class practice of observing "*saint-lundi*" (holy Monday). Taking off for *saint-lundi* was a traditional and highly popular means of evading time discipline, and seemed especially reasonable in this situation, for the other big munitions employers in that dense industrial suburb had given their workers Pentecost Monday off. But their late return was just the excuse Salmson had been waiting for. No sooner had the prodigal thirty-eight punched the clock than five found themselves on the street again, walking papers in hand. It seems the shop chief had long since identified them as "troublemakers."

---

[24] From the Fédération des Métaux's blanket condemnation of the decree, voted on 21 February 1917, quoted in Dubesset et al., "Quand les femmes entrent," p. 294. Women's persistence in striking under such conditions indicates the increasing severity of life during that third year of war.

[25] In addition, the array of goods available was sharply reduced by wartime rationing. Flour, bread, potatoes, and other staples were especially scarce, and women who worked long shifts in the war factories had no time to stand in the long lines. Rising food costs were especially serious at a time when, on average, workers spent 64 to 65% of their incomes on food alone. See Michelle Perrot, "On the Formation of the French Working Class," in Ira Katznelson and Aristide Zolberg, eds., *Working Class Formation: Nineteenth-Century Patterns in Europe and the United States* (Princeton, 1986), p. 104. This situation changed little over the interwar period; in 1930, workers were still spending a full 60% of their wages on food. See Gérard Noiriel, *Workers in France in the Nineteenth and Twentieth Centuries* (New York, 1990), p. 136.

Irate at having been singled out in this fashion, the five women departed, only to return later that afternoon with a band of two hundred women behind them—strikers from the Lampes Iris factory, women temporarily laid off from Citroën, and laundresses from the Boulogne district.[26] In the words of one police observer, the five had been "transformed into ringleaders." The group gathered beneath the factory windows and sought to bring out the thousand-odd women who remained at their machines. When this effort failed, they moved on to the nearby Hanriot airplane works and successfully called out the 150 women working there. The throng then proceeded to the local *bourse du travail,* where the Hanriot women signed a petition demanding a substantial wage increase, a half day Saturdays, and Sundays off altogether—the long-sought *semaine anglaise.*[27] Upon returning to the factory, however, the Hanriot women disavowed their action, claiming that the strikers from Salmson had forced them to sign.

The next morning the five returned to Salmson, this time with some thousand striking and unemployed women from various industries in the Paris region.[28] One of the five, Pauline Dantan, carried a red flag, symbol of syndicalist revolt since May Day in 1890, when it had found a permanent place in the working-class iconography of protest. Another waved a banner declaring: "We want our poilus." The other side bore the legend "We demand the English week," blending the politics of war with those of the workplace. The leaders returned to their positions beneath the factory windows. This time their imprecations met with success, and about half of Salmson's women streamed out to join the throng.

Now 1,500 strong, the women turned their force back upon the factory, pushing in the gates and surrounding the shops. Having staged a mass walkout, they now found it expedient to ensure that all work at Salmson ground to a complete halt. So while the main part of the crowd guarded the machines, a delegation approached the bosses to demand that the five leaders be rehired

---

[26] Iris was located in Issy-les-Moulineaux, one of the industrial suburbs on the city's south-western perimeter. A traditionally heavy employer of women, Iris was not under a munitions contract and therefore was unable to guarantee steady employment throughout the war (the firm had no assured supply of raw materials). Citroën was under contract but, like many other defense factories, had to lay off part of its workforce temporarily when it ran out of steel and coal. The presence of laundresses is an interesting harbinger of the shape this conflict would assume—that is, a protest that not only transcended the walls of a single factory but brought out workers (mostly women) of all trades in a kind of festive upsurge that Perrot characterizes as a typical form of protest in France: *Les Ouvriers en grève,* 2 vols. (Paris, 1974).

[27] AN, F7, 13366, police report: "L'Agitation gréviste dans les usines de guerre," 1 June 1917. At a time when the unrealized Thomas scale set women pieceworkers' hourly minimum wage at Fr. 0.85, the strikers demanded Fr 1 per hour.

[28] According to Gilbert Hatry, *Renault: Usine de guerre, 1914–1918* (Paris, 1972), p. 120, the crowd that gathered that morning included women from Thomson-Houston (electrical equipment) and Hanriot; apparently the latter had changed their minds yet again!

immediately.[29] Management responded by letting go the entire workforce, male and female. Undaunted, the women regrouped and marched on several other local defense plants—Hanriot, Farman, Astra, and Kellner—where they garnered some additional force before proceeding to the biggest target, Renault's vast "factory agglomeration," where more than 10,000 workers (4,000 of them women) toiled each day.

Renault's empire was, in some sense, the war factory writ large. The means of repression and organization of production that other employers had adopted in piecemeal or sporadic fashion—huge gates that locked behind the workers each morning, a doorkeeper who kept track of latecomers and enforced the fines for lateness, a liberal sprinkling of paid police informants among the workers, vast mass-production and assembly halls where thousands stood or sat side by side, enjoined to silence as they worked swiftly at a fragmented task whose pace was unrelenting—all these aspects of war production were honed to perfection at Renault. Not only was Renault's staff crawling with police informers, but the streets around the factory were patrolled by the local gendarmerie, assisted by sixty foot soldiers whom management had brought in expressly to maintain order in the works.[30]

The turbulent, overwhelmingly female crowd gathered outside the factory gates. Rumors flew as the strikers called out to their compatriots, urging them to flee the shops and join them in the streets: "At Argenteuil, the men and women stopped work yesterday, except for the Gnôme plant [airplane engines]. But today they've brought the women out of that factory by violence. . . . The soldiers at the front have begun to mutiny and are coming to Paris to support their wives' demands; in St-Etienne, two hundred women [have] been killed by colonial soldiers, the French soldiers having refused to shoot."[31] And of course, Pauline Dantan continued to carry her red flag.

Police, employers, the state, even organized (male) labor were all committed to the notion that this urgent uprising was, like all instances of women's militancy, an unpolitical phenomenon. It sprang from that unstable encounter

[29] This was the last time during the war (the last time that I found, at any rate) that women approached the higher-ups in hopes of redressing injustices and ill treatment suffered at the hands of foremen and shop chiefs.

[30] The use of soldiers to keep order at home and workers at the job grew more common after the women's strikes of May 1917. Indeed, when Georges Clemenceau took over the premiership in September, he held two battalions in reserve solely to keep order among the workers of Paris. See Philippe Bernard, *Le Fin d'un monde* (Paris, 1975), pt. 1.

[31] AN, F7, 13366, police report: "L'Agitation gréviste dans les usines de guerre," 1 June 1917, p. 1. Argenteuil, an industrial suburb north of Boulogne, was also dominated by metals, aviation, and other war industries. All the rumors are found in police dossiers dated 1, 3, and 4 June. The rumors of mutiny at the front (n. 1 above) were a bizarre blend of truth and wishful thinking. The soldiers had many motives, but the desire to support the women's strike demands was probably not at the top of the list. Given the authorities' careful suppression of all news of the mutinies, it is interesting that the women knew of the movement.

between the pragmatic and the demonic that constituted women's character, arising at the conjunction of their practical, appropriately feminine concern with wages and their notoriously "hotheaded," undisciplined natures. These men refused to entertain the possibility that the strike wave might be grounded in a discernible and meaningful set of moral-political affiliations and attachments, a refusal that had significant consequences when it came to suppressing the movement. Hence police and employers duly recorded the language and events of May–June 1917 while giving scant recognition to its clearly political aspect. Nonetheless, this aspect stands revealed in the waving of the red flag and in the language that women used to exhort their fellow workers to lay down their tools: "The poilus will come back sooner, the war will end of its own accord on the day we stop building weapons and munitions of war."[32]

The women at Renault responded with alacrity: 2,000 of them poured onto the streets of Boulogne-Billancourt. These streets, ordinarily patrolled by Renault's private police force, became worker territory, though not without a struggle. At the nearby Place Nationale the largely female crowd came up against a human barrier—municipal police, fortified by Renault's own agents and soldiers. The women surged against this barrier, hoping to swarm back into the works and occupy them. They smashed in the factory windows with their fists, then retreated momentarily to await the lunch break of those women who had not yet come out. At one o'clock the remaining 2,000 had to pass through this agitated crowd on their way to the local canteens and cafés. Few returned for the afternoon shift.[33]

By now the crowd had turned away from the factories and was headed toward Reuilly, where the soldiers charged with maintaining order lived. Women marched on the barracks crying, "Down with the war! Draft dodgers to the front and our husbands will come back!" As they marched, they continued to raise the inevitable cheer: "Vive nos poilus!" The demonstrations at Reuilly reflected a particular kind of protest over the conduct of the war, a protest that distinguished the heroic poilus—those husbands and relatives lost to the trenches—from the cowardly *embusqués* (draft dodgers)—men who had taken dishonorable refuge in the factories. Some of the hated draft dodgers were men with no experience of metalworking (or, indeed, of factory labor at all). Posing as skilled metalworkers in order to escape the front, they had taken advantage of the confusion and grim desperation surrounding the first recalls of mobilized labor. For many women, the *embusqué* became the symbol of unfair privilege: a greedy coward who grew fat and sleek in his

---

[32] AN, F7, 13366, police report: "L'Agitation ouvrière . . . à Boulogne-Billancourt," 4 June 1917, p. 4.

[33] The crowd actively blocked women's reentry into Renault but it did allow the mobilized men to return to work undisturbed.

cushy factory job, watching women perform the hardest labors while their sons and lovers faced death and mutilation.

> Alongside these women workers, who stand toiling at their lathes for a maximum of Fr 6.50, sit men who find it more pleasant to be mobilized in the factories than at the front. In civilian life these are independently wealthy men, rentiers, merchants, and the like, who [now] spend their time verifying pieces. . . . They are paid far more than women for this far less taxing labor. . . . The right thing would be . . . to give their work exclusively to women, and these men, these rentiers, these merchants, these photographers . . . all these *embusqués*. . . who take the places of women . . . might be better deployed elsewhere, and perhaps at the front, if you examined their cases more closely.[34]

But not all mobilized men were such bold *embusqués;* most were indeed skilled metalworkers, including the very foremen and shop chiefs on whom semi- and unskilled women workers depended for the repair and regulation of their machines. As the shell of sacred union cracked apart, tensions between women workers and their foremen, already high by the second year of war, began to emerge into the open. Police and trade union alike reported more than one instance in which the mutual antagonism erupted into an exchange of blows. Most often, the story is one of women using their fists to defend themselves against the foreman's repeated brutality.[35] But sometimes the women themselves took the offensive. Police spies recount the misadventures of "La Boxeuse," who first earned her title at Panhard. The firm eventually dismissed her, presumably for her violent disposition, but in the sellers' market that was wartime Paris, she soon turned up at another factory, where she repeated her antics, this time in the company of two similarly inclined women. The three colluded in relentlessly harassing the foreman, but it was La Boxeuse who finally gave in to the urge to knock him flat.[36]

In attacking the cowardice of the "draft-dodging" craftsmen, women drew a parallel between the politics of war and that of the factory floor, constructing a political vision that implicitly linked their own subordinate shop-floor position to the vulnerable condition of their brothers and husbands, who, under a spurious sacred union, were sacrificed on the battlefield ahead of the syndical-

[34] AN, F22, 539, anonymous worker at Clément-Bayard to Senator Paul Strauss (president of Thomas's newly created Comité du Travail Féminin), 4 August 1916, pp. 2–4.

[35] At Salmson, for instance, a foreman "brutalized" a woman whom he had long tormented while the other foremen and shop chiefs stood by. Only when the woman gave blow for blow did the other foremen intervene. See "La Vie ouvrière: Moeurs de guerre aux usines Salmson," *Le Populaire,* 3 May 1918, p. 2.

[36] Archives of the Prefecture of Police, Paris (hereafter APP), B/a, 1375, untitled report, 9 March 1918. When management tried to dismiss this lively trio, the other workers staged a brief strike on their behalf. The firm refused to rehire La Boxeuse, but it did take back her two more decorous companions.

ist fat cats. Police overheard one group of women sneer that "trade union leaders are disgusting people who earn fat wages while our husbands have gone off to be killed for twenty-five centimes a day."[37] Meanwhile, on the other side of Paris, some 2,500 women downed tools at Delaunay-Belleville and joined their colleagues in the streets, convinced that their factory had become a haven for draft dodgers.[38]

In both cases, women challenged the manifest inequality of sacrifice, at the front and in the factory, which by 1917 seemed to increase daily. This challenge formed part of a larger politics of "equality in suffering," a popular egalitarianism that demanded that the burdens of war be distributed more evenly across the population.[39] By 1916, women all across the city had begun to espouse this vision in protests over food shortages and the mobilization of younger military classes. A handwritten placard posted in a working-class neighborhood on the northeastern edge of Paris on 14 January 1916 proclaimed their vision:

Equality—Equality—Equality
For those who are suffering.[40]

Women workers thus came to understand and express their experience of inequality on the factory floor less through a syndicalist vocabulary of labor–capital polarity than through the wartime language of equality in sacrifice. As the shape and progression of women's strikes reveal, shop-floor divisions intertwined with the politics of war at every level and every turn, and would continue to do so until after the Armistice. One cannot therefore speak with assurance of women's "narrow" concern with wages and conditions versus men's "broader" grasp of war and politics, as though a clear line distinguished the two. Yet historians continue to do so, reflecting in their own work the very categories and convictions by which police, employers,

[37] Ibid., 5 March 1918.
[38] The 2,500 strikers made up nearly 90% of the female workforce at Delaunay-Belleville, which in 1917 stood at 2,800 women (about 30% of the workforce). Conditions were so poor that local newspapers referred to the firm as "a women's penitentiary": Jean-Paul Brunet, *St-Denis: La Ville rouge* (Paris, 1980), p. 176.
[39] See John Horne, " 'L'Impôt du Sang': Republican Rhetoric and Industrial Warfare in France, 1914–1918," *Social History* 14, no. 2 (1989): 201–23.
[40] APP, B/a, 1545, quoted in Dubesset et al., "Quand les femmes entrent," p. 254.
    The poster continues: "Over the seventeen months of this horrible war, not all women have suffered. She whose husband is stationed in the factory has happiness and money; she whose breadwinner has spent those seventeen months in the army has known nothing but misery and privation. . . . *Wives, mothers, sisters, fiancées,* he who has spent seventeen months in the factory should replace him who has languished in the trenches. For Equality and Justice. Demand from your Deputies relief for the *Mobilisés.* Equality for all." According to police, the placard was written "in a woman's hand" and posted on the door of no. 6, Place Martin Nadaud (20th arrondissement).

and male trade unionists characterized as "unpolitical" the sudden menace of women metalworkers surging through the streets, waving the red flag, and demanding that cowardly *embusqués* be sent to replace their own soldier-relatives ("our poilus") at the front.

As a political vision, women workers' egalitarian call to arms recalls the Jacobin idea of a common "tax in blood," levied by the Republican in danger.[41] Yet the women's conception of equal sacrifice to the nation has fallen from view, lost in scholastic distinctions between the narrow archaism of a mere wage movement (all that the undeveloped female consciousness is capable of conceiving) and the more evolved "political strike" toward which mature (i.e., organized, skilled, male, native French) elements in the working population strained after 1914. It is a dubious division, one that undoubtedly rests on the same series of gendered polarities—male–female, rational–irrational, political–sexual—by which police and employers strove to defuse the strike's threat.[42] As the unwitting heirs to this analytic tradition, labor historians have also placed women metalworkers and their strike outside the realm of politics, in this case beyond the bounds of a narrative concerned solely with a single political trajectory: the development of an explicitly pacifist and male-directed protest against the war.

The women's assault on the barracks at Reuilly gave tangible form to official fears that behind the growing strike wave lurked the ever-present danger of defeatism. The many thousands on strike had already shattered both the image and the experience of public order under the sacred union, openly challenging the growing inequities that were sheltered under its patriotic aegis. Now the angry mob of women threatened to spread the pacifist "contagion" to the men in uniform. Official concern turned to genuine alarm when, in keeping with the city's long insurrectionary tradition, the soldiers at Reuilly began to fraternize with the women.[43] Together workers and soldiers marched along the broad avenues, singing popular songs and bits of the "Internationale" in the bright spring air. One journal reported that a large group of young women workers crowded into a café on the rue de Paris, at the eastern

---

[41] John Horne has traced this notion in socialist and left-republican rhetoric after 1914 in " 'L'Impôt du Sang.' " Not surprisingly, the women's conception of egalitarian sacrifice to the nation differed from men's, rooted as it was in the divergent political experience of this disfranchised subset of the citizenry and in the different meanings that sacrifice held for factory workers pure and simple vs. those directly confronted with a stint in the trenches.

[42] Perhaps they hoped that by pronouncing the movement "unpolitical" they might contain its force, extent, and significance. As we shall see, however, these men deployed a further set of oppositions—appropriately feminine dressmakers vs. dangerously masculinized metalworkers, individualistic/selfish women vs. properly social, collectivist men—which threatened to disrupt the vision of unpolitical yet activist women constructed through the first set of oppositions.

[43] In 1789, 1830, 1848, and 1871 revolutionary demonstrations got going in earnest when guards sent to control crowds of women joined them in protest instead.

end of the city, filling all the tables, even those on the terrace, and consuming mountains of foods, "slabs of cold cuts, fistfuls of cherries . . . many glasses of white wine. At the end of the meal, the order was given and the women all rose and departed," leaving an unpaid bill behind them.[44]

The munition strikes of May–June were not the first protest to shake Paris during that weary third springtime of war. Throughout the previous months, increasingly widespread bread rioting bore witness to Parisian women's growing resentment over the spiraling cost of living. Then, in the second week of May, the *midinettes* (dressmakers) from Paris's most fashionable shops struck and took to the posh boulevards around the Opéra. Again the triggering incident was redundancy. On 11 May two women from the Maison Jenny had been told they would no longer be needed for the Saturday-afternoon shift. Enraged, they downed needles and urged their co-workers to join them in demanding the English week (with no reduction in pay) and a cost-of-living bonus of Fr 1 a day. Lifting the tricolor aloft, the marching women (ultimately some 10,000 of them) sang:

> On s'en fout! On aura la semaine anglaise!
> On s'en fout! On aura nos vingt sous![45]

The mid-May strikes of women-doing-women's-work struck a sympathetic chord in the hearts of men across the political spectrum. The rightist journal *L'Eclair* termed the marchers "very rue de la Paix," while socialist militants at *L'Humanité* were overcome by the women's "charm" and appealingly feminine strike tactics: "On the grand boulevards a long parade advances. It's the Parisian dressmakers, blouses fragrant with lilacs and lily-of-the-valley. They run, they jump, they sing, they laugh, and yet it is neither the feast of St. Catherine nor the *mi-carême* [mid-Lent holiday]."[46] Women metalworkers would arouse no such sympathy in the press. Whereas the *midinettes* had pinned on lilies-of-the-valley and waved the national colors, the *munitionettes* waved the red flag of working-class revolt, and generally presented a less gentle and feminine spectacle: "If the young women must claim the English

---

[44] The article continues: "The police watched, as powerless as the rest, and let the strikers move on so that they might quench their thirst in similar fashion a bit farther down the road. Café owners, consider yourselves warned!": *La Seine Départmentale,* 10 June 1917.

[45] Yvonne Delatour, "Le Travail des femmes, 1914–1918, *Francia* 2 (1974): 489. The movement gathered force more gradually than in metalworking; by 14 May only 200 women were out. A few days later, however, the strike had spread to some thirty fashion houses. With 10,000 women out, the entire industry was paralyzed. Workers from other "women's" trades (hats, corsets, shirts, and furs) joined in and Minister of the Interior Louis Malvy (a leftist) finally stepped in to arbitrate. On 22 May the bosses met the women's conditions (including a "no victimization" clause) and work resumed on 23 May.

[46] Georges Montorgueil, "La Victoire des midinettes," *L'Eclair,* 20 May 1917, p. 1; and "La Grève des midinettes parisiennes: Elle tend à devenir générale," *L'Humanité,* 16 May 1917, p. 4.

week, at least they could do so in a more discreet fashion, without parades, or calling in the streets," groused one disgruntled reporter.[47] And the *munitionettes* did indeed present a more menacing aspect, as they smashed windows, fought with *jaunes* (scabs) in the factory yards, yelled threats, and even attacked the police as they strove to restore order.[48] Worst of all, these rough, burly creatures showed scant loyalty to the nation, halting their vital war work with selfish calls for more money, their husbands, and an end to the war. Unlike the *midinettes*, whose movement ended with bourgeois approbation and a peaceful return to work, the *munitionettes* would face arrest, interrogation, imprisonment, and victimization of those identified as ringleaders.

Clearly the May–June strikes were a multivalent movement, erupting as thousands of women were protesting over wages, food prices, and working conditions. The gay assault on local cafés and restaurants might have reflected munitions workers' anger at the pinch of high prices. Or the self-made free lunch, accompanied by singing and dancing, might have expressed a less sharply focused sense of carnival. Having temporarily seized control of the streets around their factories, women and men were perhaps enjoying their brief exercise of power in a society that offered little recognition to women or to its working class. As Simone Weil was to observe nineteen years later, during the sit-down strikes at Renault, the very act of seizing control had transformed the factory from a site of exploitation to a space in which women and men moved throughout the shops with dignity and ease:

> Independent of all demands, this strike is itself a joy; pure and unadulterated. . . . What a joy to walk freely through these shops where one had been riveted to one's machine, to gather in groups, to converse, to eat together. What a joy to hear music, singing and laughter, instead of the relentless clamor of machines, stark symbol of the harsh necessity before which one bends. . . . What a joy to pass before the foremen with one's head held high . . . joy to see them compelled to be our familiars, to fold their hands, to renounce completely all giving of orders.[49]

In 1917 the point was to flee the works altogether, to occupy (and thus reclaim) the streets *around* the factory, transforming those spaces from a locus of police/employer surveillance to a terrain on which workers could meet and move, converse and act without fear of reprisal. Women's brief occupation

---

[47] *Journal des Débats,* 2 June 1917 (a journal of the center/right-center).
[48] At Citroën, where 680 women and 70 men joined the strike, women turned "ferociously" on the gendarmerie, seeking to tear off their uniforms, according to an eyewitness report quoted in Dubesset et al., "Quand les femmes entrent," p. 331.
[49] Simone Weil, "La Vie et la grève des ouvrières métallos," in *La Condition ouvrière* (Paris, 1951), pp. 230–31.

at Salmson, as well as their effort to repeat that trick at Renault, was a means to that end, a tactic for reinforcing the numbers who held the streets.

May–June 1917 thus combined a kind of festive quality with a widespread and mounting sense that things could no longer go on as they were in the war factories. But the sudden agitation that swept the defense plants of Paris that spring was not solely or even predominantly a protest over wages and hours. The war had endowed the already powerful employers with tremendous authority over labor. Moreover, the politics of sacred union guaranteed that these men could exercise their enhanced powers unobstructed by any effective syndical organization. The incident that sparked the protest in Boulogne-Billancourt—the unjust dismissal of the five "troublemakers," arbitrarily singled out and victimized for an infraction that others had also committed—suggests that women's experience of unchecked managerial authority played an important role in triggering the strike.[50] Further, whatever faith women had had in the director as a higher court of appeal against the iniquities of foremen seems to have dissipated over the course of the May–June movement. The strikers thus took their cause not to the director but to the streets of the city.

If the women were all too well aware of their many grievances, management and police officials alike seem to have been utterly obtuse, first stunned, then baffled by the sudden upheaval. "It is incomprehensible, when one considers what high wages we pay [them]."[51] These men agreed that women were "hotheaded" and "undisciplined," prone to such "agitation." The question was why—how had these apolitical creatures ever been moved to such action in the first place? Police and employers both looked to the fearsome "outside agitator"—the only explanation available to them, given their account of women as unpolitical animals.

> From the moment the Salmson women first made contact with the *bourse du travail*, the movement seems to have changed in appearance. Elements who were foreign to metalworking, and to the factory world of Boulogne and Billancourt, intervened with the clear intention of spreading and aggravating the conflict.[52]

Elements "foreign to metalworking" rapidly became elements foreign to France, and a powerful conviction that the real danger lay in *la provocation*

---

[50] As William Reddy has written of the May Day demonstrations among textile workers in the Nord: "The 1890 strike . . . turned into a dramatic denial of deference. . . . [It] was not a bargaining maneuver, it was a gesture in an ongoing struggle over the legitimacy of certain ideas about authority and submission": *The Rise of Market Culture* (Cambridge, 1984), pp. 308–9.

[51] Quoted in "Les Grèves," *Le Petit Journal,* 31 May 1917, p. 1.

[52] AN, F7, 13366, police report: "L'Agitation ouvrière . . . à Boulogne-Billancourt," 4 June 1917, p. 3.

boche led employers to demand that police maintain "a discreet but active surveillance, as active as possible," around their factories, to hold at bay a defeatist contagion whose "foreign origins it is not difficult to discern."[53]

Restoring the Labor Peace

The Paris-wide strike wave, which peaked around the first of June, involved 42,336 munitions workers, nearly 75 percent of whom were women, in more than sixty strike actions.[54] Although these actions did not constitute a full-blown general strike—42,000 workers represented only one-sixth of the total number employed in metalworking at the time—they were by far the most extensive and threatening protests unleashed by the working class since the war had begun. Like previous strikes among women munitions workers, the movement was sudden and sharp, with the metalworkers' union entering in only after the fact, hoping to direct and support the women's action and also to enroll them as dues-paying members. But *syndicat* and *bourse* played only minor roles in May–June 1917. From the outset women took the initiative, opening the protest, developing their own organization and forms of struggle, and formulating their demands with little or no intervention from the formal structures of the labor movement.

By the middle of the month, most of the strikers had returned to work. Poorly paid and lacking access to union strike funds, few women could afford to pass a full week without wages. As they slowly drifted back to the factories, the women took advantage of the fear that their action had implanted in managerial hearts to demand increases in wages and time off. At Renault they circulated a petition demanding a raise of 10 centimes an hour plus a cost-of-living indemnity of Fr 1.25. They promised further direct action if their demands were not met. Unimpressed, management failed to respond, and on 3 June only half of the night shift turned up for work. Renault then conceded the raise, effective 1 July, and suspended all nightwork for women.

The pattern was similar across the city. From 29 May to 4 June, women deserted the factories in droves, joining heartily in street demonstrations and lively confrontations with the police. They then gradually returned to work, armed with specific demands that often took the form of written petitions. The petitions usually called for some kind of improvement in wages, along with Sundays off and a half-day on Saturdays. At the level of wages, the strikes

---

[53] AN, 39 AS, 914, A. Dutreux, Administrateur-Délégué, S.E.V. (Société Anonyme pour l'Equipment Electrique des Véhicules), to Commissaire de Police, Issy-les-Moulineaux, 31 May 1917, p. 1.
[54] Delatour, "Travail des femmes," p. 488.

were a roaring success, and employers all over the city conceded the long-overdue improvements. When employers could not come to terms with the women, the Ministry of Armaments stepped in and arbitrated, usually granting the minimum levels that Thomas had set the previous January. In the favorable conjuncture of the war with tight labor markets and a sympathetic minister of armaments, women's self-organized direct actions proved highly effective, winning far more in the way of wages and conditions than the still-cautious *syndicats* were prepared to demand. Most employers, however, refused to grant Saturday afternoons off and none would meet women's initial demand that the "ringleaders" and "troublemakers" be rehired.

By mid-June order had been restored through a combination of concession and repression, as police and employers collaborated in identifying and purging ringleaders of both sexes. Over the course of the movement, they arrested some 390 individuals (277 of them women), many of whom were later prosecuted for having "obstructed the freedom to work." On the morning of 31 May, following the assaults on Renault and Reuilly, the five "ringleaders" from Salmson were swept into the dragnet. After a day's interrogation, the police let the women go.

Their reports make it quite clear that the police evaluated women and men according to very different standards. Male militants were investigated according to a political litmus test: Did they have any open ties to revolutionary or syndicalist groups? Had they been seen lurking about at such meetings, or were they simply so lazy they would rather be paid by German agents to stir up trouble than do an honest day's work building bombs? Women were evaluated by a set of "moral" criteria that were actually related to sexual conduct—behavior that was carefully spied upon and recorded. Were they married? Did they have children? Were they known to have many lovers? Were they cheating on soldier-husbands? Such behavior was evidence of a character wholly given to debauchery, incapable of sustaining any kind of loyalty, to husband, family, or nation. Further, a woman's open "debauchery" outside the factory gates was seen as translating into laziness and a lack of seriousness on the job: "Marie Testud . . . is a worker who is neither serious nor hardworking. Since her husband's disappearance [missing in action] she has openly abandoned herself to debauchery and many workers and soldiers visit her. She is a hotheaded character . . . [but] she has no known connections in revolutionary circles."[55]

In a neat piece of Aristotelian reasoning, the police observed that, since all husbands were absent, the rational part of the proletarian household was missing—the wifely "heart and soul" of the working-class home had lost her

[55] AN, F7, 13366, police report: "L'Agitation ouvrière . . . à Boulogne-Billancourt," 4 June 1917, pp. 11–12.

head.[56] As a result, the dark side of her "true," unchained nature was prone to erupt—"aggressive and insolent," "hotheaded" and "fierce": "Marie Louise Pouchet [is] aggressive and insolent, and proved one of the fiercest during the *débauchage* of the Boulogne factories. She has no known connections in syndicalist or revolutionary circles; we know only that she receives many men at her home, apparently workers, whom she takes as lovers."[57]

Sometimes police simply could not find an adequate explanation for individual action within the parameters of the strict political-male/moral-female polarity. Pauline Dantan, for instance, was a good worker, to judge by her earnings. Moreover, "her private conduct is good . . . [and] she is far less hotheaded than the others." But it was Dantan who had borne the red flag, leading that long and angry parade through the streets of Boulogne-Billancourt. Another of the original "ringleaders," Louise Piat, also enjoyed a good reputation; no amount of police snooping could uncover a single illicit affair. Her combative behavior therefore bewildered police investigators but did not lead them to question their foundational assumption: that among women, labor militancy (or any aggressively asserted political stance) sprang from an unchecked sexuality. Had they been interested in alternative accounts of women's activism, they might have listened to what Louise Piat herself had to say: "She complained bitterly that her two daughters, employed at the Lampes Iris factory, were now on layoff." In a time of acute hardship, Piat had become the sole breadwinner and could hardly absorb the cost of being fired herself. But Piat's interrogators, having duly noted her complaint, concluded that there was "no reason for her to have been mixed up in the movement of the past few days."[58]

This pattern was repeated time and again as police investigated the women they had rounded up outside Salmson's gates that morning. In their determined preoccupation with the women's household and living circumstances, they managed to uncover the one quality these five women had in common: all had been their families' sole breadwinners at the time Salmson had fired them.[59] This singular fact did not register, however, as police doggedly dug for

---

[56] See Aristotle, *Politics,* ed. Ernest Barker (Oxford, 1978), bk. 1, for an early statement of the argument that social hierarchy and levels of rationality dovetail in both the household and the polity, providing the means of establishing relationships of ruler and ruled. In the household, these relationships—between husband and wife, master and slave—are depicted as natural and fixed. The medieval church drew Aristotelian conceptions of social order into a larger portrait of the seamless, ordered chain linking heaven and earth, highest and lowest in an organic, tangible hierarchy. These Catholic notions of social-moral order turn up repeatedly in the notionally secular Third Republic.

[57] AN, F7, 13366, police report, "L'Agitation ouvrière . . . à Boulogne-Billancourt," 4 June 1917, p. 11.

[58] Ibid., pp. 12–14.

[59] Police also investigated three other "ringleaders" that day, women from other factories who had joined the original five at the head of the marchers in Boulogne-Billancourt. All eight

the kinds of "moral" information that in their eyes constituted an intelligible explanation for the leaders' aggressive behavior.

The neat link between political activism and manhood placed women outside the magic circle of rational-political action, and thus compelled police to construct nonpolitical explanations for women's manifestly political acts. In the cases of Pauline Dantan and Louise Piat, the police ultimately had to leave unanswered the question why these women had protested so vehemently, lest the boundary separating women from politics dissolve in the face of a more complex reality. But this dualistic conception, besieged as it was on the female-sexual side, could also break down on the male-political side—and so it did, in the case of a small band of nine deaf-mutes whom the police also investigated that day. Eight of the nine were men, yet the police applied the moral/sexual criteria usually reserved for women. The inspection of their personal lives was deemed relevant because several of the men in this group led a "private life [according to] special morals"; that is, they had been identified as homosexuals. For police and employers, concerned to root out the sources of this potent strike movement, the political was recast as personal if you were a gay man or a "hotheaded" (and therefore promiscuous) woman.[60]

The May–June movement was to represent the apogee of women's autonomous activism in the war factories. Women formed a strong and active contingent in the strikes that swept the aviation industry in September, during which they put forth their own demand for equal pay, grounded in their temporary status as head of the family: "As our husbands are all at the front, we have a right to the same wages as the men."[61] But the initiative was passing gradually from women to men, as men began to throw off the cloak of silence imposed by the sacred union (and the mobilization). By the spring of 1918,

---

were struggling to support themselves and their relatives and children on a rapidly diminishing real wage. Most of the women were in their thirties or early forties, widowed or married to soldiers who were listed as missing in action or prisoners of war. Only two were in their twenties. One was married to a man who was missing; the other—the only unmarried woman in the group—lived with her mother. The demographics of these militants are quite unlike those of the typically young (sometimes adolescent) unattached male militants who led the strikes that shook England and Germany in those last two years of war. See ibid., pp. 6–15.

[60] Ibid., p. 8. The identification of obstreperous women as promiscuous recalls some of the statements by the police who patrolled the *maisons de tolérance* (the state-controlled bordellos). See Jill Harsin, *Policing Prostitution in Nineteenth-Century Paris* (Princeton, 1985). See also Jacquelyn Dowd Hall, "Private Eyes, Public Women: Images of Class and Sex in the Urban South, Atlanta, Georgia, 1913–1915," in Ava Baron, ed., *Work Engendered: Toward a New History of American Labor* (Ithaca, 1991), pp. 243–72.

[61] AN, F7, 13366, police report: "Situation dans les usines de guerre," 22 September 1917, p. 1. During the war, most peasant and working-class wives took on the role of head of the family, de facto and de jure. As the Comité Intersyndicale d'Action contre l'Exploitation de la Femme argued, "Carrying the same burdens that the man previously carried, she must have a wage equal to his": *Travail de la femme*, p. 8.

when a more unambiguously antiwar movement swept the war factories, women made up only 30 percent of the audience at syndicalist meetings, compared with 40 percent the previous year.[62]

As the form and structure of the May–June movement suggests, however, unionization rates offer a distorted vision of women's militancy, for women looked to the unions only after they had initiated a protest, and then only sporadically. More important, women remained a prominent and vocal presence in the crowds that took to the streets during the vast insurrectionary strike against the war in May 1918. Thus, when the men at Thomson-Houston were ready to abandon the struggle after only a few days, it was their shop steward, Mme Martin, who urged them to stay out with the sharp reproach: "Enough of this war! Peace now and we'll strike until the end!" She then suggested that what was really needed was an assault on the works, to force out the treacherous *jaunes,* who were content to remain "idle" (that is, on the job) while their more courageous colleagues risked harassment and arrest in the streets.[63] The strikers adopted this plan with alacrity.[64]

As in 1917, police and employers watched the women activists carefully. They recorded their words and actions in hopes of controlling them, but their anxieties grew as women became more emboldened: "The women workers gather in groups on the streets, and feel free to call loudly for peace."[65] Yet they still shaped their observations within the contradictory framework of women as hotheaded yet apolitical wage hounds, and continued to ignore the politics of "equality in suffering."

This political vision still animated women strikers; indeed, its outlines had grown sharper and the tone more acid as the war took its toll. Thus, when Panhard fired a Mme Garnier for her militant role in the strike, she responded by listing her own sacrifices for the war effort. She had two children and a wounded husband languishing in a German prisoner-of-war camp; Panhard therefore did not have "the right . . . to put [her] out on the street."[66] Across the city at the Gnôme et Rhône aircraft plant, a Mme Martelet remonstrated

[62] By this time, mobilized men were coming out in droves. The army was ruthlessly combing out the mobilized workers, desperately seeking more machine-gun fodder to meet the final great German offensive that spring. Mobilized men no longer had much to lose by striking in such circumstances, since they were likely to end up at the front no matter what they did.

[63] Perrot notes that in the early twentieth century, "the strike was such a positive act, from the vantage point of working-class morality, that those who stayed out of it were called, by a significant twist of language, 'idle' ": "On the Formation of the French Working Class," p. 106.

[64] AN, F7, 13367, report of a strike meeting of 350 workers at Thomson-Houston, 16 May 1918. Mme Martin was one of nine women shop stewards (délégués d'atelier) on whom I found records in this period (1917–18). The unusually large number of women employed by Thomson-Houston perhaps explains why the firm had female shop stewards.

[65] Ibid.

[66] AN, F7, 13367, police report: "Une Réunion des ouvriers de la maison Panhard-Levassor," 19 May 1918, p. 2.

with equal vehemence: "As they've taken my husband to defend the bosses' profits, its's only right that they give me the means to live and raise my children."[67] Despite these sharp challenges to a system that had failed to distribute the costs of war equally, police investigators persisted in offering the standard interpretation of women's activism: although women were often "the first to want to strike" (hotheaded), they seemed "content to return to their munitions work, where their wages remain high, permitting them to lead a relatively pleasant existence."[68]

The May–June movement of 1917 had provoked very different reactions among police and employers, state officials and organized male labor. For the police and employers, the strikes disrupted the patriotic order of the sacred union and threatened the flow of arms to the front. Their first priority was to contain the women's "agitation" and to get everyone back to work before the dangerous aura of rebellion, freedom, and irresponsibility spread to the male workforce. "Whatever else they may be, these women's strikes are creating among the men themselves—mobilized or not—a spirit that the Government should look into."[69] The bureaucrats at the Ministry of Armaments were also concerned about ending the demonstrations and resuming production, but these were men of the left, broadly speaking (most were Radicals or right-wing Socialists). Though determined to end the upheaval and restore order in the streets and the factories, they had some sympathy for the material difficulties that workers faced. Hence, they received the news of the strike with an air of understanding; after all, prices had soared since 1914, and many industrialists had failed to apply the ministry's recommended minimum wages. The state thus supported the women's wage demands, stepping in to arbitrate on their behalf when necessary.

CGT men were of (at least) two minds about the women's action. It was, after all, the first serious rupture in their increasingly punishing agreement to lay down the weapons of labor militancy and join in the patriotic social peace. For the reformist partisans of the *union sacrée*, however, any break

---

[67] Ibid., "Une Réunion des ouvriers de la maison Gnôme et Rhône," 13 May 1918, p. 1. Mme Garnier based her right to work on a notional contract; the wartime state and defense profiteers clearly owed the Garniers for their visible contributions and sacrifices to the war effort. Garnier and Martelet were shop stewards at Panhard and Gnôme et Rhône, respectively.

[68] Ibid., report of 26 May 1918, p. 2. The *mouchard* (police spy) went on to report that after returning to work, one woman confided to her friend: "Today I made ninety pieces. I must make up the time lost last week." The spy further commented that such sentiments were common among the 2,800 women who had struck Delaunay-Belleville: "They work as hard as they possibly can, in hopes that their fortnightly earnings won't have fallen off too much as a result of the eight days' work stoppage."

[69] AN, F7, 13366, police report: "L'Agitation gréviste dans les usines de guerre," 1 June 1917, p. 1.

with that union threatened to nullify the measure of respectability that labor leaders had bought for themselves by their willingness to put their loyalty to the Republic first. For this reason, Jouhaux repudiated the women's action:

> As long as it was a matter of strikes among women garment workers, the CGT was able to distance itself from the movement. But now, with the eruption of women's strikes in the defense industries, the CGT must bring all movements under control, so that we will not be held responsible for any disorder.[70]

On the other hand, Alphonse Merrheim's more militant Fédération des Métaux threw its weight behind the movement; indeed, those who joined Merrheim in taking a strong antiwar stance muttered that the women had not gone far enough in opposing the war. Police and employer reports suggest, however, that the majority of male workers saw the strikes as a welcome departure from the self-imposed muzzle of sacred union and supported them by any means available, direct and indirect.[71]

Yet these diverse groups of men, who had such varied, even opposing stakes in the outcome of this struggle, were bound together by a common conviction that the women's strike movement issued from some realm other than the political. Despite their very different reactions to the strike, none of them interpreted it as a political event. As a result, one finds an odd convergence in the language of the police, employers, and organized labor on the subject of women's "unpolitical" nature.[72] On 24 May 1917 one union spokesman urged his fellows to create a more welcoming atmosphere at syndicalist meetings by focusing on "the questions that interest [women] . . . reducing the workday, raising wages, and winning the English week. . . . We must not mingle political issues in our speeches . . . when they are present."[73] A few weeks later André Citroën remarked that "one of the most striking differences between male and female workers is the latter's dislike of all mutualist and trade unionist efforts."[74] And, in the face of overwhelming evidence to the contrary, police and employers grimly adhered to the theory that the women

---

[70] AN, F7, 13617, speech by Léon Jouhaux before the Comité Confédéral, 2 June 1917.

[71] Many men joined the women in the streets; 12,000 of the 42,000 on strike were men, after all. Others (presumably mobilized men) stayed in the factories but crossed their arms and refused to work. Still others shouted encouragement to the women or suggested shops that were ripe for *débauchage*. See ibid., reports of 1, 3, and 4 June 1917. With the end of the war, strikes would swiftly revert to their sexually segregated pattern (according to GIMM's strike records, at any rate; see AN, 39 AS, 914–16).

[72] It would be interesting to know whether women concurred in this interpretation of their movement. It would not be terribly surprising if they did, yet there is no evidence in the police and employer reports to support even the shakiest conjectures regarding their self-perceptions.

[73] AN, F7, 13667, speech by L. Lefevre before the Comité Générale de l'Union, 24 May 1917. Lefevre was a member of the Executive Committee of the Fédération des Métaux.

[74] Quoted in Dubesset et al., "Quand les femmes entrent," p. 285.

had not acted on their own initiative but had been "advised to go on strike by certain leaders." For police, employer, and male worker alike, women's "corporate" identity as women—an identity resting in part on the notion that women and politics were disjoint entities—overwhelmed any other identity, such as worker, that women might also carry. The police thus spoke of "women, temporarily transformed into wartime workers,"[75] and they viewed this human mass as malleable (indeed, volatile) material in the hands of unscrupulous men, whether anarchist, syndicalist, or paid agent of the Kaiser's war machine.

French employers thus emerged from the upheavals of May–June with a limited understanding of their women workers' grievances, an understanding that reflected their own preconceptions about male and female nature more than it did any genuine coming to terms with what these thousands of women were calling for. Further, these preconceptions shaped what it was employers did learn from the strike: that women workers presented rather specific problems of discipline and control, problems that required new forms of intervention. Looking across the Channel, some saw the elements of a solution taking shape in the form of middle-class "lady" welfare supervisors, whom the Ministry of Munitions was pressing upon its contractors. The supervisors' main concern was intended to be ameliorating women's working conditions and limiting fatigue. Yet these women could just as easily aid the employers by tracking the workers and keeping an eye on shop-floor morale and discipline. And because they were women, but women of a higher class, employers might hope to reach, however indirectly, those who were doubly unreachable by virtue of both class and gender difference.

[75] AN, F7, 13366, police report: "L'Agitation gréviste dans les usines de guerre," 1 June 1917, p. 1.

CHAPTER 5

Welfare Supervision and Labor Discipline, 1916–1918

In 1925 Général Appert, director of the Alsthom electrical works at St-Ouen, looked back on the strikes of May–June 1917 with smug satisfaction, recalling that in his factory, "order and discipline reigned . . . despite the excitement and the threats" from women strikers.[1] He attributed this quiet to the anodyne presence of five *surintendantes d'usine* (women welfare supervisors), whom he had hired just weeks before to oversee the health, discipline, and productivity of Alsthom's enormous female labor force. By monitoring worker discontent and "gently rebuking" the more rebellious souls, the five had installed a harmonious matriarchal order that stifled any mutinous murmurings among the factory's 6,000-plus women.

The middle-class "welfare ladies" were especially unlikely travelers in the notionally all-male and distinctly proletarian world of the metals factory. Yet their presence in this world was no accident. Employers in both nations brought lady superintendents into their factories during World War I for the ostensible purpose of attending to the health and welfare of the new female workforce. Ultimately, however, their work went far beyond ensuring the physical and moral well-being of the nation's working mothers. Ever mindful of the connection between the individual worker's health and her productivity, metals employers were quick to call their welfare supervisors into more directly productive service. The "welfare lady's" expert and intimate knowledge of the woman worker's capacities and character made her a valuable ally in management's wartime campaign to tighten discipline and raise output.

The idea of factory-based welfare supervision first arose in England; the

---

[1] Général Appert, "Allocution du Général Appert,," *Bulletin de l'Association des Surintendantes* (hereafter *BAS*), 1925. Alsthom, already one of the largest factories in France, had tripled its female workforce over the course of the war, from 2,000 to 6,000.

French imported the idea in 1917, after observing British experiments. In both nations, the introduction of welfare supervision reflects employers' conviction that women posed a specific and novel challenge to labor discipline. Both the advantages and the disadvantages of employing women flowed from their innate (and collective) being; hence, employers had to find new, gender-appropriate methods of reaching and controlling this highly adept if somewhat troublesome workforce. The existing technical hierarchy (charge hands, foremen, shop chiefs), expressed in a language of skill/professional value ("the skilled elite versus the mass of the least competent," as the GIMM put it),[2] was perhaps adequate to the task of containing and directing male labor. But the particular indiscipline of women demanded that these workers be anchored not only through a technical chain of command but in a moral order as well.[3] It was the job of the lady welfare supervisor to implant that order.

The institution of welfare supervision thus permits us to explore the problems raised by the arrival of persons whom employers understood as not fully rational, and hence lacking an internal principle of self-control. The welfare supervisor represented a gender-specific answer to the problem, a woman of the employer's own class who might extend the kindly hand of woman-to-woman concern to these undisciplined and volatile beings. As a woman of the elite, the supervisor could tame the specific unruliness of creatures who existed at two removes of difference from their employers—that of class and that of gender—through the exercise and inculcation of middle-class and feminine virtue.

The Origins of Welfare Supervision in Britain

French women munition workers were not alone in seeking to better their lot by resorting to strikes. On 17 March 1916 some 6,000 women—about half the female workforce at Armstrong-Whitworth's Elswick works at Newcastle-on-Tyne—walked off the job in angry protest over the firm's miserly

---

[2] UIMM, 39/21/01, "Réflexions sociales sur la grève des métaux," 3 July 1919, p. 15.

[3] Many employers worried about the consequences of gathering women in groups, where they could talk among themselves and spread the contagion of moral corruption by exchanging stories (especially about sex) and information about birth control. Some employers sought to control these moral epidemics by placing older, married women in charge of young girls. "We attach great importance to an older woman being in charge of the girls to supervise them": PP 1918, Cd. 9073, *Report of the Departmental Committee Appointed by the Board of Trade to Consider the Position of the Engineering Trade after the War*, p. 16. Other employers sought to separate younger women from older ones, so that youthful innocence would not be corrupted by talk of sex and childbirth.

wages.[4] It was the largest and most important strike by women munition workers yet seen in Britain, and the women, though "controlled" and "well-behaved," showed "great determination and cohesion."[5] Unnerved by the extent and power of the movement at Elswick, the Ministry of Munitions' Wage Tribunal acted with uncharacteristic haste. They heard the case almost immediately, on 24 March and found in the workers' favor. The women returned to work, having obtained an across-the-board wage hike.

A few months earlier the Ministry of Munitions had suggested that Armstrong-Whitworth appoint a welfare supervisor to oversee the health, productivity, and discipline of the new female workforce. The director, D. S. Marjoribanks (who was, coincidentally, chief spokesman for the EEF), rejected the notion outright, certain that such a creature would only upset the workers and "fuss the management."[6] But the women took Elswick by surprise with their apparently sudden decision to down tools. Marjoribanks was determined that there would be no more such surprises. Within days of the return to work, he had hired the formidable Miss E. B. Jayne—a lady who would brook no "nonsense" from the girls in her charge—to monitor discontent and contain potential rebellion on the factory floor.

When she first arrived at Elswick, the atmosphere was still charged in the aftermath of the strike: "The girls were flushed with their recent success and inclined to take charge and to threaten another strike with or without the least provocation." She had few illusions about the difficulties she faced in her efforts to carry out her welfarist duty: "Supervisors appeared to them in the light of spies who were going to watch and report to the Management the ringleaders in the trade union organisation and endeavor to weaken their influence, or as goody-goody people who were going to poke their noses into the workers' private affairs and interfere with their liberty and independence." Of course, the "girls" were correct on both counts, for keeping a tight rein on personal conduct and trade union activity was precisely what Miss Jayne had been hired to do. But the hostile "stares and aloofness of shopfuls of men and women" were the least of Miss Jayne's difficulties. More challenging yet was the problem of carving out a sphere of independent authority for the welfare officer and her staff of assistant supervisors "amidst

[4] By 1918, 13,354 women worked at Elswick—Armstrong-Whitworth's gun and gun carriage plant—out of a total workforce of 45,087: IWM, Women's Work Collection, Mun. 24/4, dossier on welfare work at Armstrong-Whitworth. By the end of the war, Armstrong-Whitworth employed about 20,000 women, distributed across several factories in York, Newcastle, Manchester, and Glasgow. See PP 1919, Cmd. 167, *Appendices of Evidence to the Report of the Committee on Women in Industry,* testimony of E. B. Jayne, p. 208.

[5] IWM, Mun. 24/15, "A Résumé of Women's Welfare Work at Sir W. G. Armstrong-Whitworth & Co., Ltd., 1916–1919," by Miss E. B. Jayne, O.B.E. (head welfare supervisor), pp. 1–5.

[6] Ibid. In any event, his wife had already undertaken some of this work as a volunteer.

the suzerainties of charge-hands and foremen."[7] It was a situation laden with potential for friction and conflict between an entrenched male technical staff and the bourgeois lady interloper.

Advocates of welfare management had long argued that workers of every description—male and female, skilled and unskilled, adult and juvenile— would benefit from more careful attention to their health and well-being.[8] But none doubted that women and juveniles were "peculiarly helpless" and therefore peculiarly in need of the welfare lady's tutelage: "Women are more susceptible than men to outside influences which enormously react upon the ability of the producer to give the best that is in her."[9]

The welfarist principle that women and children come first gave Miss Jayne the entrée she sought into the structure of authority on the factory floor at Elswick. Armed with the notion that women workers have special needs, the lady supervisor and her many assistants (forty-odd women by 1918) took charge of selecting, hiring, and disciplining the entire female workforce at Elswick.

Up to this point, foremen had hired women workers as they needed them. Now applicants stopped first in the Welfare Office, so that Miss Jayne could weed out any obviously unsuitable types at the start. Only then could the foreman make his selection, at which point the supervisor passed through again to review his decisions and comb out any remaining "undesirables." If the foreman wished to dismiss or promote a woman worker, he could not do so without the supervisor's prior knowledge and consent.[10] The supervisor, however, had the power to transfer women unilaterally from one job or department to another, for reasons of health or shop discipline. In each case she was supposed to act in consultation with the male staff, but she had the final word on all matters related to the hiring, firing, promotion, and transfer of female labor.

The foremen were not at all pleased with this arrangement. Not only did it represent a real encroachment on their terrain, but it put them in the position of having to instruct and work with employees they had had only a small part in selecting. After the big strike, however, Marjoribanks was converted to the notion that keeping women workers quiescent demanded a different approach to labor selection. Simply applying to women the criteria that governed the hiring of men had been tried and found wanting: "It was felt that many undesirable characters had been taken on in the Works, who caused deterioration amongst other workers. . . . [Hence] the old plan of

[7] Ibid., p. 7.
[8] "In seeing to the health and well-being of the employees the welfare supervisor is thereby attaining the best possible results for the employer": Cmd. 167, *Appendices of Evidence*, testimony of Jeanie Lindsay, welfare supervisor at Beardmore's shell factory, p. 213.
[9] S. J. Woodward, "The Training of Women Employees," *System*, May 1915, p. 355.
[10] IWM, Mun. 24/15, Armstrong-Whitworth, "Summary of Departmental Supervisor's Duties," p. 19.

allowing foremen to engage their own female employees must be changed."[11] Marjoribanks was therefore prepared to give the Welfare Office broad authority over the female workforce, even if he had to tread on the toes of shop managers and foremen.

Miss Jayne arrayed her own staff in conscious conformity with the organization of the works itself, so that it might function as an "integral part" of the management.[12] Within each shop, alongside the charge hands and foreman, stood at least one forewoman, responsible for "all matters of conduct and breaches of discipline."[13] Wherever possible, Miss Jayne chose her forewomen and overlookers from among the "educated" women on the floor—"women with experience in handling women, such as Teachers, University women."[14] If such individuals were not available, she made do with "superior working class women," promoted to the job under the homelier title of "matron."[15] At the head of the shop stood the departmental supervisor, who dealt with the most serious breaches of discipline, and to whom the forewomen reported. The departmental supervisors reported to Miss Jayne, who was in turn directly responsible to the firm's managing director, Sir Percy Girovard.

Miss Jayne thus ordered her staff in vertical chains that mirrored the technical hierarchy in each of the shops at Elswick. In this fashion, she hoped to facilitate the separation of technical from welfare responsibility, a division that she underscored by confining her minions to what she termed the "non-production" side of production. The distinction was a nice one, difficult to draw, much less to uphold; but Miss Jayne was following the received wisdom of a nascent welfare "science" that prescribed a division of managerial authority along the familiar lines of the patriarchal family:

Where men and women are employed at the same operation foremen and forewomen are essential. This is no more dual control than that of father and mother. It is a combined, a more intimate and broader control. . . . The foreman's chief responsibility is production, and the quantity and quality of the work. The forewoman's just care is for the producers. She must keep her

---

[11] IWM, Mun. 24/6, Armstrong-Whitworth, "Female Labour Bureau Report," 24 July 1918, p. 1.

[12] As Miss Jayne later (1918–19) wrote: "A Welfare Staff was by this time [1916–17] recognised as a useful adjunct to the establishment, and it was desirable to see that it was so organized as to function in the workshops to its best advantage as an integral part of the management": IWM, Mun. 24/15, "Résumé of Women's Welfare Work," p. 8.

[13] IWM, Mun. 23/13, Cecil Walton, report on welfare work at the national projectile factory at Cardonald (Glasgow), 11 February 1919, p. 2.

[14] IWM, Mun. 29/15, Woolwich Arsenal, "Mode of Selection," n.d., p. 1.

[15] IWM, Mun. 21/11, "Memorandum on the Work of the Welfare Department at the National Projectile Factory, Dudley," p. 2. The use of working-class women for any kind of managerial duty, however limited, was strictly a tactic of last resort. The welfare supervisor at Dudley, for instance, found the matron "a well-meaning woman, but quite inadequate to deal with the situation."

squad up to the requisite strength, and each individual of it happy and fit. This is a natural division of responsibility, which makes for sweeter working and greater efficiency.[16]

The "natural" division of authority placed the welfare supervisor in a complementary and hierarchical relation to the male side of management. In theory, this arrangement should have eliminated any residual conflict. After all, the "familial" structure provided a model for resolving the problem of overlapping competencies. But the apparent clarity of the division masked an internal contradiction in welfarist theory. As a managerial strategy, welfare supervision explicitly linked workers' health and comportment to their efficiency on the job: "Welfare . . . is the surest way to speed up output. Swift praise, swift blame and punishment are as much essential parts of welfare as canteens and pianos."[17] However, if the "quantity and quality of production" rested on the health, contentment, and "moral discipline" of labor, at what point did the foremen/shop managers' technical authority leave off and the supervisor's health-and-welfare authority begin? As the endemic tension between foremen and supervisor makes clear, there was in fact no single, identifiable point where technical authority could be disentangled from its welfarist complement. Welfare theorists had drawn with one hand a gendered distinction in types of managerial rule, only to blur and erase that line with the other. It was perhaps inevitable, then, that despite her vehement assertion that welfare supervisors should never mingle in the business of production— it was "fatal in every instance"—Miss Jayne should have ended by molding her supervisory staff into a kind of shadow management.

As the supervisors gradually translated an underdeveloped welfare theory into concrete shop-floor practice, it would become painfully evident that the welfare hierarchy did not so much complement the technical one as constitute an alternative and competing locus of authority, at least where women workers were concerned. Miss Jayne's efforts to uphold the distinction between welfare and technical authority resulted in an independent and self-contained welfare hierarchy. Thus the welfare office was in a position to function as a court of appeal, a place where the disgruntled or harassed woman worker could lodge a complaint against her foreman or shop chief and perhaps even find some relief in the form of a transfer. Of course, if the woman's problems were work-related, the welfare office should be her last resort: "The foreman and shop manager should deal with it in the first instance and the Welfare Depart-

---

[16] Cecil Walton (manager of the national projectile factory at Cardonald), *Welfare Study— What It Is* (Glasgow, 1919), p. 10.
[17] Ibid., p. 6.

ment should only be appealed to if the matter remained unsettled."[18] But Miss Jayne's hasty addendum did not alter the fact that the welfare supervisor was positioned to alter the terms of conflict and authority on the factory floor, to recast the "class-and-gender" conflict between skilled male supervisor and unskilled woman worker in terms of gender division alone.

At the end of 1918, Miss Jayne recalled that when she first began her job at Elswick, "management . . . said they were terrified at welfare supervisors and what they were going to do, but now they do not know what they would do without them."[19] Few of her colleagues could look back on their own careers with equal satisfaction. Indeed, most ran up against a wall of indifference, if not active hostility, from their employers, who took a dim view of welfare supervision from the outset.[20] How useful could it be to place a woman with no industrial experience or formal qualification (except, perhaps, a degree in social work) in charge of the female workforce? Even if she did not prove a mere meddlesome nuisance, few were prepared to incur the additional expense.

Private industry's reception of welfare supervision was so unenthusiastic that the practice did not survive the Armistice in Britain, at least not in the metalworking industry.[21] However, the welfarist notion that employers could create a structure that promoted workers' active participation in the struggle to raise output did live on, though in markedly different form. After 1921, many employers would introduce a variety of elaborate efficiency schemes and work systems in a vain effort to escape the pinch of recession.

Welfare management was not without its exponents in Edwardian Britain. But it took the war emergency—the massive employment of women (many of whom were married) in the "rough," male business of metalworking—to give the concept broad currency in that distinctly unpaternalist managerial climate. The Ministry of Munitions played a crucial role in spreading the gospel of welfare to employers long accustomed to "getting along without

[18] IWM, Mun. 24/15, Armstrong-Whitworth, "Summary of an Assistant Supervisor's Duties," pp. 40–41. Nonetheless, "women workers might appeal to the Welfare Department on any question where difficulty arose."

[19] IWM, Women's Work Collection, Emp. 70, War Cabinet Committee on Women in Industry, "Minutes of Evidence," testimony of E. B. Jayne, p. W53.

[20] IWM, Mun. 19/4, "Report on Welfare Work in the National Shell Factories, 1916–17," p. 10: "The principle of Welfare has been accepted in National Projectile Factories. In these factories, *as in few others*, it has been possible to experiment with the complete cooperation of the Management. . . . The Managers themselves are interested in the work."

[21] In fact, outside the engineering trades, industrial welfare work burgeoned in the interwar period, maintaining its hold in such industries as food processing and spreading to department stores and other service industries as well. See M. M. Niven, *Personnel Management, 1913–1963* (London, 1967), for developments in industrial welfare work and an official history of the Institute of Personnel Management.

these new fangled notions."[22] As we shall see, the brand of welfare that the ministry disseminated was scored by the state's own interest in safeguarding workers' health, and especially the health of women, as a means of raising productivity. In the patriotic name of higher bomb output, the Ministry of Munitions put a distinctively productivist spin on wartime welfare work. It was this productivist aspect, and especially the fatigue-efficiency connection, that British employers would build on after 1920.

In September 1915 the ministry had appointed a Health of Munition Workers Committee to study the impact of the long hours and variable working conditions in defense factories on workers' "personal health and physical efficiency."[23] Where women were concerned, the committee broadened the definition of personal health to encompass the "health of the race," organizing its researches around a broad if rather formless set of anxieties over the potentially negative impact that munitions work might have on women's maternal capacity. The committee thus located its investigations in the larger context of safeguarding "the health of the people as a whole." In so doing, it focused particular attention on the welfare of the socially dependent: women, as the linchpin of the proletarian household, and juveniles, in whom the future of "the race" resided.

Public discussion of welfare work in Britain rarely turned on the kinds of natalist themes that were so prominent in France at the time. In fact, British government officials were notably reluctant to provide crèches and nurseries for working mothers, though the pressure of circumstances eventually drove them to do so.[24] Unlike the French, who saw in these collective installations a means of encouraging working women to procreate, British bureaucrats exhibited a classic liberal reluctance to sap individual initiative and responsibility through undue state interference in the sacred realm of the domestic: "A large increase in the number of crèches must necessarily neutralise to a large extent the efforts which have been made in recent years to secure a better care of children by their own mother."[25] If few pounded the pro-natalist drum in Britain, however, there was no lack of interest in "those contributions

---

[22] IWM, Mun. 18/9/4, "Intramural Welfare Work in National Factories, 1916–1917," p. 1.
[23] PP 1918, Cd. 9065, Ministry of Munitions, Health of Munition Workers Committee, *Final Report*, p. 5.
[24] By 1917, 108 day nurseries in Britain were caring for about 4,000 children: Adelaide Anderson, Ministry of Reconstruction, Women's Employment Committee, *Subsidiary Health and Kindred Services for Women* (London, 1919), p. 3. Cecil Walton reported that the women workers at Cardonald received the idea of day care with tremendous enthusiasm: IWM, Mun. 21/13, p. 3.
[25] PRO, Mun. 5/93/346/140, Health of Munition Workers Committee, "Welfare Advisory Committee: Notes and Report on the Advantages and Disadvantages of Crèches in Industrial Areas," n.d., p. 20. On wartime maternal and child welfare policies, see Jane Lewis, *The Politics of Motherhood: Child and Maternal Welfare in England, 1900–1939* (London, 1980).

which women alone can make to the welfare of the community." On the contrary, ministry officials believed that healthy families were the essential elements of moral and social order in the community. Those who formulated wartime labor and welfare policies never lost sight of the fact that women, as wives and mothers, were there to preserve the familiar contours of British family life: "Upon the womanhood of the country most largely rests the privilege first of creating and maintaining a wholesome family life, and secondly of developing the higher influences of social life."[26]

At the time the committee began its work, the welfarist creed had captured only a narrow segment of opinion in British managerial circles. Its most vocal proponent was Seebohm Rowntree, Quaker by faith, paternalist by conviction, and head of the ministry's new Welfare Department by appointment.[27] Rowntree painted a corporatist vision of a reformed factory community, socially and spiritually regenerated by the healing balm of welfare management. In his view, the mutual antagonism between worker and boss was not inevitable. The expanding size of the firm had destroyed the "personal relationship" linking employee to employer in the workshop of days gone by, but Rowntree believed that the welfare supervisor could restore that bond by fostering "those right relationships which are the basis of a well-ordered and harmonious community." Her timely interventions would "re-humanize" industrial conditions, sowing cooperation and mutual understanding where suspicion and enmity now dwelt. As the employer's goodwill ambassador in the reordered factory community, the supervisor could reach past the trade unions and deal directly with individual workers: "If the welfare workers have the confidence of the employees, and are always in touch with them, they will naturally be the medium whereby matters occasioning dissatisfaction or misunderstanding can be investigated and put right." Furthermore, because cooperation must inexorably lead to an increase in productivity, the "humanized" factory community would operate more efficiently and to the benefit of all: " . . . an increase in efficiency is important not only to the employers but also to the workers; for there cannot be a progressive improvement in wages unless there is a progressive improvement in methods of production."[28] Welfare work presumed a certain childlike dependency on the part of its beneficiaries. This attitude made such work problematic for male workers, whom welfare theorists

---

[26] Cd. 9065, *Final Report,* p. 20.

[27] Rowntree was owner and manager of his family's cocoa firm, a major employer of women and girls well before 1914. Rowntree is best remembered for his studies of poverty in the city of York; his public advocacy of welfare management suited him well for the job of director at the Ministry of Munitions' Welfare Department.

[28] Seebohm Rowntree, "Making a Success of the Woman Worker," *System,* June 1916, reprinted in *Bulletin of Labor* no. 222 (Washington, D.C., April 1917); and PP 1917, Cd. 8151, *Welfare Supervision,* p. 4.

also hoped to reach.[29] But it was an ideal strategy for women. Not only were women "more tractable than their brothers," they were, by definition, in greater need of the welfare lady's interventionist ministrations: "When she first enters a factory, the average girl is peculiarly helpless and almost lacking in resource . . . she is scarcely worth the meagre wage the . . . untrained worker commands." Careful attention to "welfare," in particular to regulating women's behavior both inside and outside the factory, was the only sure way to render the highly "susceptible" woman worker a reliable source of profit to the firm: "To foster . . . every right kind of activity and systematically to discourage and circumvent every unwholesome interest and feature outside of working hours no less than within is the only sound policy."[30]

Such intrusive guidance was completely inappropriate for male workers; indeed, efforts to regulate the behavior of adult men threatened to sap their dignity and initiative. Hence, even when an employer believed that "welfare is *not* necessarily for women only,"[31] his provisions for the two sexes took a sharply gendered form. Men were encouraged to join the "shop-club" (a company-based alternative to their trade union savings society), while women got the supervisor's sharp scrutiny. Both sexes shared the more gender-neutral provisions: restrooms, canteen, and infirmary.

Rowntree's corporatist conception of a harmonious factory community, restored through the welfare supervisor's kind ministrations, closely followed the solidarist and social Catholic visions of industrial order so popular with French paternalist employers. Yet Rowntree's welfarist pontificating won him few admirers in British managerial circles; indeed, it was the preaching of this voluble visionary that led most British employers to dismiss welfare management as the industrial equivalent of vegetarianism or theosophy. Employers thus responded with surprised irritation when the ministry's Welfare Department began to press for welfare supervision in munitions. In their view, the government had "no call to go mixing itself up with crank philosophy."[32] But if employers feared that the ministry was about to promote some "sentimental" managerial philosophy, they needn't have worried.[33] By the time the Health of Munition Workers Committee had finished its multiple investigations, welfare management bore scant resemblance to Rowntree's philosophy.

---

[29] Thus in 1921 Adam Kirkaldy remarked: "Where such [welfare] expense was necessary it is probable that much of it should have been undertaken before for the men": *British Labour, 1914–1921: Replacement and Conciliation* (London, 1921), p. 14.

[30] Woodward, "Training of Women Employees," pp. 356, 355.

[31] Walton, *Welfare Study*, p. 7. Trade unions resisted welfarist approaches to their members. "Men's trade unions looked on this work with suspicion": Cmd. 167; *Appendices of Evidence*, testimony of E. L. Collis, p. 206.

[32] IWM, Mun. 18/9/4, "Intramural Welfare Work," p. 2.

[33] The term is Walton's in *Welfare Study*, p. 6.

In concrete terms, the committee ruled that munitions employers should be providing basic sanitary and health facilities—additional lavatories, changing rooms, canteens, on-site infirmaries and first-aid stations—and recommended that middle-class supervisors be hired to oversee these installations.[34] But the committee devoted the bulk of its resources to studying productivity and industrial fatigue. This obsessive concern with efficiency and fatigue was especially influential in a nation where employers had little interest in or experience of welfare study. By linking individual workers' health to their efficiency on the job, ministry officials suggested that the study of industrial fatigue could promote the employers' pursuit of profits (through increasing productivity) while smoothing industrial relations by realizing workers' "just" demand for more healthful conditions at work. The committee thus stamped the nascent welfare movement with its own wartime productivism. In addition, by comparatively exploring the work/fatigue ratios for women versus men across a range of occupations, the committee lent an aura of scientific certainty to employers' conviction that "except on physical work men are not so quick as the women,"[35] and so placed women at the center of the movement to "rationalize" work. As welfare work moved into the war factories, then, Rowntree's generous hope that improving workers' health might stand as an end in itself was quietly undermined, reduced to the more instrumental link between health and productivity. Employers and welfare supervisors alike thus tended to women's "welfare" primarily as a means to enhance discipline and efficiency on the factory floor.

In recommending the appointment of welfare supervisors, then, the ministry added its official voice to the small but growing chorus of women and men who saw in welfare management a new, more humane and efficient approach to the problem of extracting a steady, intensive effort from the individual worker:

> . . . a worker's body may in one limited sense be likened to a machine and if a machine is not kept well oiled it cannot be expected to run swiftly and

[34] Welfarism prescribed male supervisors for men and boys and arrayed the supervisor-to-worker ratio on a scale reminiscent of the employers' boy/woman/man scale of individual responsibility and inner direction: it was recommended that employers hire one supervisor for every 100 boys, every 300 women, and every 500 men. See Cd. 8151, *Welfare Supervision,* 7; IWM, Mun. 18/9/4, "Intramural Welfare Work," p. 2. In practice, employers rarely hired male supervisors. What the lady superintendent could not handle was left to foremen and shop managers.

[35] IWM, War Cabinet Committee Minutes, testimony of Melville Smith, manager of Kings Norton Metal Works and the national filling factory at Abbey Wood, Birmingham, October 1918, p. D73.

smoothly or turn out perfect goods. But workers bodies being human flesh and blood need more than iron and steel, and cannot work efficiently without the oil of human kindness and consideration.[36]

Welfare supervision thus constituted an alternative managerial strategy, one that promised enhanced efficiency and tighter discipline through methods deemed especially appropriate to women. But the welfarist doctrine strained under its multiple and sometimes conflicting purposes. It was a project that strove at one level to reconcile health and efficiency and at another to reconcile the working class to the justice of employers' hierarchical rule in the factory. And at yet another level, welfare management was intended to bring together what had become increasingly antinomous in industrial Britain, women's factory work and the health and moral well-being of the nation. The entire reconciliatory project would turn on the character and qualifications of the women who realized these early welfarist initiatives, on their ability to harmonize the discordant elements of modern factory life.

"Molding Each Worker Aright"

In 1916 the Home Office ordered all munitions factories to appoint a welfare supervisor.[37] Private employers managed largely to evade the prescription, but the national factories were bound to accept it. By the winter of 1916–17, the Ministry of Munitions had dispatched twenty-eight supervisors to their new posts in national shell and fuse plants all across England and Scotland.[38] The ministry recommended that these women oversee the full range of welfare installations, such services as the canteens and infirmaries, whose benefits extended to male as well as female workers. But the heart of their work lay with the female workforce: hiring and deploying new workers, supervising the night shift, handling all breaches of shop discipline, keeping records of absentees and poor timekeepers, looking into complaints from the workers,

---

[36] IWM, Mun. 18/9/4, "Intramural Welfare Work," p. 1.
[37] Niven, *Personnel Management*.
[38] IWM, Mun. 18/9/4, "Intramural Welfare Work," p. 3. By the end of the year, several hundred women welfare supervisors were overseeing the health and work of women in munitions plants all across England and Scotland; by the end of the war, there were some 1,000. The ministry had appointed 275 more supervisors to look out for the welfare of young boys in munitions: Ministry of Munitions, *Official History of the Ministry of Munitions*, 8 vols. (London, 1920–24), vol. 5, pt. 3, p. 37. The ministry took responsibility for selecting and hiring the welfare supervisors, who remained in the ministry's employ throughout their tenure in the factories. Owners of controlled establishments were expected to hire supervisors on their own account. In both private and national factories, welfare provisions were financed largely through the excess profits tax.

and investigating "slow and inefficient work or incapacity arising from conditions of health, fatigue or physical strain."[39]

Hence the welfare supervisor was both to manage and to discipline the women workers while functioning as a friendly liaison between them and their employer. The fulfillment of this Hydra-headed managerial brief rested above all on the supervisor's class background and personal character. In order to guide and direct her proletarian charges, she had to be a woman of the middle or upper middle class, "accustomed . . . by habit and by social position . . . to supervising [her] inferiors." By the same token, she needed to be a person of discretion, tact, and sympathy, so that she could establish a bond of trust between herself and the workers. But that bond had to be forged from a distance. Employers, ministry officials, and the supervisors themselves agreed that the impulse to promote an "ordinary" working-class woman to this sensitive position was utterly wrongheaded and destined to fail. Such women lacked personal authority, that inborn ease in directing the activities of others which upper-class status carried. Moreover, working women were themselves "uncertain of their ability to control their equals"— or perhaps were merely unwilling to incur the anger, envy, and resentment of their peers. It was a moot point in any event, for whenever an employer tried to appoint a working woman to the job, she invariably refused the "additional responsibility."[40]

Lady supervisors thus rested their authority on class distance, "the decided difference in education, force of character and social position between them and their workers."[41] Yet a supervisor who sought to carry out her job solely on the ground of her class-based sense of entitlement could never form a creditable bond of sympathy. The workers would simply reject her overtures as the intrusions of an interfering busybody: "If she is a person of discernment and judgment almost any duties may safely be entrusted to her, but should she be tactless or unsympathetic, there is very little that is safe in her keeping."[42] The supervisor thus qualified for the job in her person rather than by any program of training or education.[43] As the manager of the Cardonald national

---

[39] IWM, Mun. 18/9/4, "Intramural Welfare Work," p. 2; Cd. 8151, *Welfare Supervision*, p. 6.

[40] Ministry of Munitions, *Official History of the Scottish Filling Factory at Georgetown* (London, n.d.), p. 147.

[41] Ibid.

[42] IWM, Mun. 19/4, "Report on Welfare Work in the National Shell Factories," p. 4.

[43] Indeed, welfare supervision in Britain required no formal preparation or any background in medicine or social work, although appropriate training programs did exist (both the London School of Economics and the University of Birmingham offered degrees in social work). The possession of a solidly middle-class or upper-middle-class background was deemed sufficient to the task. Just as employers understood women workers' abilities as innate, so the middle-class welfare supervisor/*surintendante* was qualified for her post by another kind of innate trait: her firm, bourgeois character.

projectile factory approvingly remarked, "above all the lady superintendant must be a student of human nature with a keen appreciation of sex peculiarities and difficulties."[44] At the same time, however, this sympathetic creature could not be a patsy, bowing to every tiny complaint. She had to possess the traits of an inborn leader, as tough and firm as Lilian Barker of Woolwich Arsenal, who left the welfare supervision business after the war to become governor at a women's prison.

The supervisor's authority thus perched uneasily atop a central contradiction in her role on the factory floor. Her dominion rested on class distance, which set her over and apart from her proletarian charges. Yet her ability to muffle shop-floor strife by establishing sisterly bonds with the women on the floor depended on narrowing the very divide on which her authority rested. The individual supervisors would succeed or fail according to how skillfully they managed to negotiate that difficult passage.

Like Miss Jayne, most welfare supervisors had originally been hired to monitor discontent on the factory floor, to nip any potential strife or conflict before it had a chance to blossom into full-blown trouble. Labor control remained a crucial component of their daily activity: "The Supervisors are women experienced in the handling of women and possessed of tact and a manner able to win the confidence of the naughtiest girl."[45] But good discipline demanded more than restraining the occasional troublemaker. The conscientious supervisor should ferret out all possible sources of disgruntlement, "investigating all serious complaints personally and keeping in close personal touch with grievances real and imaginary."[46] Foremost in the category of "real" grievances were wage issues, which formed an irreducible bone of contention between woman worker and foreman. Piece-rate earnings varied sharply from week to week and from worker to worker, and each woman's bonus rested on the foreman's assessment of her output. The Rowan, premium bonus, and other incentive wage systems were so complex that it was impossible for workers to predict their earnings or verify the foreman's judgment. More than one employer recalled that the moment of reckoning wages was a volatile one indeed: "There were sometimes disputes between women and foremen, and sometimes I could not get to the bottom of it."[47] One woman factory inspector estimated that 90 percent of the unrest among women workers might be resolved if employers placed supervisors rather than foremen

---

[44] Walton, *Welfare Study,* p. 7.

[45] IWM, Mun. 29/15, Woolwich Arsenal," Mode of Selection," pp. 1–2.

[46] IWM, Mun. 24/15, "Summary of Departmental Supervisor's Duties," p. 19. Some firms (such as Elswick) set up a system of shop committees, whose elected representatives met periodically to bring grievances before management. The supervisor was expected to facilitate the functioning of such committees.

[47] IWM, War Cabinet Committee Minutes, testimony of Mr. Horobin, p. D99.

in charge of monitoring women's output and wages: "This would enable her to help the management by explaining the system of payment to the workers."[48] Supervisors thus spent a good deal of their time tracking the women's wages, not only for productivist purposes but simply to ensure shop-floor harmony: " . . . we got a sympathetic woman who would . . . book up the women's work and wages and incidentally to talk to them and find out what the troubles were. . . . The difficulties with the women disappeared very soon."[49]

However, keeping an eye on wage disputes, trade union activity, and the obvious malcontents formed but a small part of the daily routine. In the welfarist vision, good discipline began with proper selection and deployment—a stipulation that the middle-class welfare lady interpreted to mean selecting and managing female labor according to bourgeois conceptions of feminine respectability: "False ideas of dress and conduct are gently but firmly discouraged . . . the great force of shop opinion is enlisted in the task of molding workers aright."[50] In some cases, the solution was to hire the working-class woman most familiar with middle-class ways and most familiar to the supervisor's middle-class eye: "The domestic servant is the best type of worker: she is an early riser and has endurance."[51] But supervisors also sought to attract women from the upper working class or even lower middle class— "girls with better education and from better homes." Such women were presumably more responsible and restrained than their "rough, unskilled" sisters, more promising raw material for a system of shop-floor discipline that turned on regulating women's behavior according to middle-class notions of appropriate feminine demeanor.[52]

The supervisors' determined application of these novel criteria generated considerable conflict between the welfare "lady" and the technical staff. On the one hand, foremen generally concurred with the supervisors on the matter of strength and endurance, and also chose women who looked as if they could withstand long, hard hours standing at the lathe or drill. On the other hand, foremen preferred to recruit the "rough" women of their own class.

---

[48] Cmd. 167, *Appendices of Evidence,* summary of testimony by Rose Squire, deputy principal lady inspector of factories at the Home Office, lent to the Ministry of Munitions as director of women's welfare during the war, p. 207.

[49] IWM, War Cabinet Committee Minutes, testimony of Mr. Horobin, p. D99.

[50] Woodward, "Training of Women Employees," p. 359.

[51] A welfare supervisor in a large engineering firm in Glasgow, quoted in Adam Kirkaldy, *Industry and Finance—War Expedients and Reconstruction* (London, 1917), p. 54.

[52] Rowntree, "Making a Success," p. 19. Once the women had been hired, supervisors joined in assigning them their posts in the factory. "Young and alert girls" were recommended for machine work, while "reliable, healthy girls with nimble fingers" were put in the danger sheds. "Sturdily-built women with a mechanical turn of mind" found themselves turning shells, while the "refined, alert, healthy girls, adept at the use of tools," were reserved for gauging, inspecting, fuse filling, and other close, delicate, or skilled tasks: IWM, Mun. 29/15, Woolwich Arsenal, "Mode of Selection," p. 1.

Not only did they find the more middle-class women an endless source of trouble, "apt to make much more fuss when displeased and to complain to higher authorities," but these women were not so easily intimidated as were their proletarian sisters. A threat of dismissal, so effective a tactic with women who were dependent on their own earnings, failed miserably with those who could get along quite well without the wage. As one foreman bluntly put it: "I should hate to have a girl in my shop I couldn't swear at!"[53] But the supervisors clung firmly to welfare theory's first principle of labor selection: "Rough, unskilled labor is seldom cheap in the long run."[54]

Having established a firm ground through careful selection, supervisors kept a watchful eye for any sign of erosion in individual discipline, be it lateness, absenteeism, or slackness on the job. Good timekeeping was particularly important. Under a detailed division of labor, lateness and unpredictable absences could cut sharply into the shop's productivity, as foremen scrambled to find women who could fill in for the absentees and keep the production chain running smoothly. Welfare supervisors thus placed special weight on devising schemes to improve women's attendance and timekeeping. At the national shell factory in Manchester, the supervisor discouraged latecomers with a system of hats: "I distinguished the best time-keepers in the factory by giving them a different coloured cap to wear." She then engaged the women's competitive instincts, "setting one shift to compete against another by putting up a list of the lost time of each shift weekly—marking it 'A. shift *v. good*, B. shift, *fair*, C. shift, *bad*,' and so on." The onus of time discipline thus fell on the work team: "Making it a shift matter often made a bad time-keeper mend her ways out of loyalty to her own shift, when she could not be got to do so from a personal sense of disgrace!"[55]

Secondary to her role as watchdog on the time clock was the supervisor's function as official recorder of all absences and illnesses among the women. By keeping careful account she could identify and follow up on frequent offenders, finding out which ones owed their problems to poor health "and putting them in touch with medical facilities." Some took this duty quite seriously, visiting the homes of women who had taken ill and using insights gained from the home visit to assist in their delicate managerial function in

[53] IWM, Department of Printed Books, "A Munition Worker's Career at Messrs. G, 1915–1919," Joan Williams, typescript, p. 10.

[54] Rowntree, "Making a Success," p. 19. Rowntree also maintained that welfare work could actually improve the workforce through a combination of conscious selection and improvement of the factory environment, allowing employers to attract a "better" class of labor: "Many employers can show how they have been able to obtain girls with better education and from better homes through the work of welfare supervisors at the factory."

[55] IWM, Mun. 23/14, "A Short Account of Welfare Work at the Manchester National Shell Factory, 1918–19," p. 5. See also IWM, Mun. 24/15, "Summary of Departmental Supervisor's Duties," p. 18.

the factory: "I found it a great help in the factory afterwards to have had a peep at their homes and home-life."[56] However meddlesome, such visits may well have helped individual women get much-needed attention to persistent health problems.

Middle-class standing thus secured for the welfare supervisor a place in the managerial hierarchy commensurate with that of a male supervisor. In their common class background, employer and supervisor often found a shared perspective on labor issues. In particular, both viewed the working-class woman as an almost childlike being, forever poised midway between a boy and a man. This adolescent nature manifested itself most strongly in her lack of discipline and self-control. A truly gifted supervisor, however, could direct and reshape this rough human material. Lilian Barker, head supervisor at the Woolwich Arsenal, accomplished some of this work during air raids: "She goes from factory to factory, and in the early days did much to steady the girls by her presence . . . she joined in their songs, laughed with them and talked with them. However, this is not so necessary now, as the girls have gained a great deal of self-control."[57]

This shared managerial perspective helped to guarantee the welfare lady's primary loyalty to the firm and counteract any inclination she might have toward overinterpreting her role as intermediary between employer and woman worker. Neither employers nor state officials wished to see the supervisor start playing Lady Bountiful, setting herself up as a genuinely neutral third party or, worse yet, as an independent worker advocate. In the early days, more than one employer sought to seal this allegiance by "employing" his wife as welfare supervisor. Lloyd George's men predicted disaster: "You cannot have a lady working under her husband." But it was a convenient arrangement from the employer's point of view, for, in the words of one Birmingham employer, "when I go home at night to dinner, I learn more about what is going on in the factory than I should ever know with any paid worker."[58] The ministry's Welfare Department soon put an end to this practice.[59] By 1917, the rule of wives had been supplanted by wifely surrogates, selected and supplied by the Welfare Department.

Most of the twenty-eight women appointed in the national factories were unmarried women of the middle and upper-middle classes. One had been a social worker in London before the war.[60] The language in which these women

---

[56] IWM, Mun. 23/14, "Short Account," pp. 5, 6.
[57] IWM, Mun. 29/21, Woolwich Arsenal, "Note on Air Raids," n.d., p. 1.
[58] IWM, War Cabinet Committee Minutes, Testimony of Melville Smith, p. D84.
[59] Cmd. 167, *Appendices of Evidence,* testimony of E. L. Collis, p. 206.
[60] IWM, Mun. 18/9/4, "Intramural Welfare Work," p. 3. At Woolwich Arsenal, Lilian Barker recruited many of the thirty-one women on her welfare staff from the helping professions—nurses, teachers, a welfare worker: IWM, Mun. 29, supervisor's report. "Welfare at Woolwich Arsenal." Welfare supervisors in the national factories were appointed and paid by

described themselves suggests that the supervisors may have been a bit older than the "girls" in their charge. Certainly, their method of managing the female labor force drew heavily on mother–daughter (or big and little sister) models of female interaction—models drawn from the family, where relations are structured by a natural hierarchy of difference (in age rather than class) and the whole is presumably bound by the common concerns of an organic community. Hence the pervasive tone of maternal condescension may well reflect this maternalistic style more than any real difference in age.[61] But on this question, as on so many others, the record is silent. What we know of the British welfare supervisor emerges only in her day-to-day interactions with upper management, foremen, and especially the women she supervised.

By and large, ministry officials were careful to speak the language of industrial self-interest when they urged defense contractors to invest in a welfare supervisor: "If, as in Newport, the Board [of Management] can say 'she is reducing the cost of our shell' or as in Swansea 'she has averted a strike' she cannot be considered superfluous."[62] But in the end, appeals to the profit motive failed to convince employers that welfare supervision was worth the bother and expense. Even those employers who believed their supervisors had done "good work among the women" could not deny that the welfare ladies had also managed to ruffle many feathers on the factory floor.[63] Foremen and charge hands often resented her intrusive presence. Not surprisingly, women trade union leaders also rejected her: "She is supposed to be the workers' friend—and she has become the tool of the unscrupulous employer. . . . If it is a question of slackness at work, she reports it; if it is a trade union meeting . . . it is very often she who will take the news to the employer and intimidate the girls . . . we can never place her; yet we find her everywhere."[64] Women workers often found the supervisor's well-meaning overtures intolerable, particularly when she sought to regulate their behavior by imposing her own notions of respectable demeanor. In one "rough" factory, the women quickly tired of the welfare lady's constant harping on their "irregular" domestic arrangements and vulgar taste in clothing. When she stood up one day and announced, "You want a club, you come from such overcrowded, dirty

---

the Ministry of Munitions; those in the controlled establishments were paid by the employers, though their appointment had to be reported to the ministry. As in France, the salaries of these women dangled perilously close to those of their charges: £2–3 a week, at a time when an adept woman worker, skilled or semiskilled, could easily take home that much.

[61] On the question of maternalism and welfare policy, see Seth Koven and Sonya Michel, "Womanly Duties: Maternalist Politics and the Origins of Welfare States in France, Germany, Great Britain, and the United States," *American Historical Review* 95 (October 1990): 1076–114.

[62] IWM, Mun. 18/9/4, "Intramural Welfare Work," p. 3.

[63] IWM, War Cabinet Committee Minutes, testimony of Mr. Horobin, p. D99.

[64] Kate Manicom, "The Welfare Supervisor," *Trade Union Worker*, June 1917, p. 7.

homes," the "girls" finally rebelled and, to her utter astonishment, threw their lunch at her.[65]

At the same time, supervisors were certainly capable of delivering genuine material benefits to the women in their charge, supporting their wage claims against a foreman's chary assessment, standing up against excessive overtime, and ensuring a supply of such basic necessities as soap, toilet paper, and sanitary napkins in the lavatories (more than one supervisor reported the utter lack of such basic amenities when she first arrived.)[66] Women workers sometimes looked back on the supervisor's iron rule with a fondness that suggests that on occasion she may have used her position to shield women from abuses by the male staff. "That Lilian Barker she was abrupt," said a bullet maker at Woolwich Arsenal, "—oh, ever so abrupt—but . . . she was a marvellous person as I say and she wouldn't have anything wrong in our factory. She was like a real old battle axe, you know, she'd fight for you."[67]

What told against the institution, in the end, was its power to disrupt the existing lines of command on the factory floor. Wherever welfare supervisors were introduced, events followed a course similar to the one that Miss Jayne had set at Elswick. In pursuit of her welfare responsibilities the supervisor inexorably moved onto the foreman's notionally distinct jurisdiction, hampering his freedom to select, deploy, and rebuke or reward the women who worked under his command. The ministry's firm belief that "all Welfare Superintendents should be a part of the Works Management"[68] simply institutionalized this tension, while the containment of welfare staff in separate but parallel hierarchies served to implant an alternative chain of female authority in the factory. The supervisors insisted that they had been hired merely to "assist in the working of the Factory, and not in any way to usurp authority."[69] Ultimately, however, the introduction of welfare supervision interfered with the rule of craftsmen, a rule that British engineering employers found largely satisfactory and were loath to disturb.[70] Worse, it splintered control over the workforce, leaving male workers under the command of foremen and shop managers while placing the women who worked alongside them under a largely separate jurisdiction. British employers thus rejected the institution as useless, state-sponsored meddling.

---

[65] "Women after the War," *National News,* 8 March 1917.

[66] See IWM, Mun. 21/11, "Memorandum on the Work of the Welfare Department at the National Projectile Factory at Dudley," p. 2.

[67] IWM, Sound Records Dept., accession no. 000566/07, Caroline Rennles, "War Work, 1914–1918," typescript, p. 65.

[68] IWM, Mun. 18/9/4, "Intramural Welfare Work," p. 3.

[69] IWM, Mun. 29/14, "Duties of the Supervisors," p. 4.

[70] See William Lazonick, "Production Relations, Labor Productivity, and Choice of Technique: British and U.S. Cotton Spinning," *Journal of Economic History* 41 (September 1981): 491–516, on employers' reluctance to disrupt craft control in the late-nineteenth-century mule-spinning industry.

Pro-natalism in the *Usine de Guerre*

By the winter of 1917, news of the English welfare supervisor had begun to travel back across the Channel. Employers, state officials, and a small circle of concerned middle-class women had watched with considerable interest as Britain's Ministry of Munitions sent up its welfarist trial balloons. Even the delegation of women workers that Thomas had sent to London in January 1917 singled out the lady superintendents for praise, and expressed the hope that French factories, too, might someday adopt a similar regime.[71] Factory-based welfare supervision won approval from such diverse constituencies in part because in its infancy it had that shapeless capacity to appear as all things to all people. To the bourgeois advocate of social reform, welfare supervision would improve working conditions and instill the "moral discipline" that ought to reign among women and men working together in dark, sweaty workrooms at all hours of the day and night. To the employer, a woman supervisor might tame the growing militancy among the female workforce and "calm the woman worker, who is so often embittered, crying injustice."[72] And to all who worried about the demographic future of France, welfare work could address the failure of women workers to produce enough children to replace the men sacrificed on the field of battle.

The unremitting slaughter at Verdun in 1916 pushed natalist concerns to the center of public debate on women's wartime employment.[73] Long-standing fears over the nation's dwindling birth rate now traveled under the urgent rubric of "national survival" and provided a common and patriotic language in which individuals at various points on the political spectrum could debate the issue of regulating women's factory labor. Even those employers who regarded any state interest in the labor contract as evil interference grudgingly conceded the need for regulation in the matter of maternal health.

Pro-natalist fears thus framed the discourse on women, work, and welfare in wartime France, and shaped the invention and introduction of welfare supervision in the *usines de guerre*. Outside the factory gates, the French public was acutely aware that women workers were abandoning their traditionally

[71] *BUG*, 19 February 1917, p. 343.

[72] Général Appert, "Allocution du Général Appert," *BAS*, 1929, p. 23.

[73] Pro-natalist sentiment won a permanent place in public discourse in 1896, with the formation of Jacques Bertillon's Alliance Nationale pour l'Accroissement de la Population Française. Natalist sentiment expanded steadily from that date until the outbreak of war, at which point unfavorable comparisons between the stable birth rate in France and the ever-increasing rate in Germany made the issue a matter of broad patriotic concern. See Laura Lee Downs, "Women in Industry, 1914–1939: The Employers' Perspective" (Ph.D. thesis, Columbia University, 1987), chap. 2; Monique-Marie Huss and Philip Ogden, "Demography and Pronatalism in France in the Nineteenth and Twentieth Centuries," *Journal of Historical Geography* 8, no. 3 (1982): 283–98; and Angus MacLaren, *Sexuality and Social Order* (New York, 1983).

feminine pursuits (textiles, garment making, and domestic service) and cross-ing into the harsh male world of metalworking. The war heightened existing concern over the health of French women, especially their reproductive health and moral capacity for motherhood. The discourse on women's war work entangled demographic anxiety with an uncomfortable awareness of the rap-idly shifting sexual division of labor. Indeed, women who did "men's work" threatened an already faltering birth rate and encouraged the tender, other-oriented sentiments in maternal hearts to give way to the greedy individualism of a mere wage hound: ". . . the child, that annoying impediment, remains for some less scrupulous women an obstacle to their freedom, a barrier between them and the maximum profit to be drawn from exceptionally well-paid work." Worse, if the lure of good wages threatened to corrupt the maternal spirit of self-sacrifice, the "moral" danger of working amidst an unsupervised band of unruly working-class women promised to corrode that spirit alto-gether: "Pro-Malthusian propaganda [that is, information about birth control] . . . can spread through the numerous groups of women gathered together at work. The workshop and factory offer an incomparable platform for un-healthy and antisocial ideas."[74]

In the eyes of the wartime state and an anxiously pro-natalist public, welfare management promised to reverse France's perilously low birth rate. Through careful attention to the health and maternal condition of France's working women, the lady superintendent (*surintendante d'usine*) would reconcile the conflicting national duties that had come to rest on the shoulders of women defense workers: their obligation to produce, simultaneously, more bombs and more babies.

Hence the institution of welfare supervision gradually took shape at the confluence of public and private, springing from the state's concern with the health of women munitions workers and from the broader moral/natalist anxieties of private philanthropists. The discussion of factory-based welfare work began at Thomas's Ministry of Armaments, which issued the first direc-tives on the subject and channeled welfarist energies in narrowly natalist directions. But the most lasting welfare provision—the *surintendante* her-self—came not from the state but from the independent action of middle-class feminists, eager to find an appropriate venue for their own patriotic and social activism. Long after wartime natalist installations had disappeared from the factories, the *surintendantes d'usines* remained.

[74] AN, F22, 444, Académie de Médecine de Paris, "La Protection des femmes et des enfants dans les usines," 1917, pp. 17, 18. In 1923 the Catholic writer Pierre Magnier de Maisonneuve warned that "the moral danger is greater still for women workers. If it is true that woman is subject to greater bursts of sentiment than man, it is also true that her descent into depravity—when it happens—is deeper and more complete": *Les Institutions sociales en faveur des ouvrières d'usine* (Paris, 1923), p. 217.

In the spring of 1916 Albert Thomas appointed a Committee on Women's Work to advise the ministry on the organization of welfare services for women in the *usines de guerre*. Thomas convened the committee in the collaborative spirit of sacred union, inviting participation by people across the political spectrum. Both the minister and his committee were convinced that industry's demand for female labor would only increase at the war's end. Thomas was certain that this increase could redound to the lasting benefit of industry and woman worker alike, yet most committee members anticipated it with some trepidation, doubtful that women's factory labor could ever be harmonized with healthy and prolific motherhood. As the demand for women's labor continued to rise, the committee thus turned its attention single-mindedly to the problem of protecting women's maternal capacity in the defense plants.[75]

In designing its protective mission, the committee was swayed by the persuasive words of one Dr. Bonnaire, chief obstetrician at the Maternité de Paris and fellow member of the Committee on Women's Work. Bonnaire assured them that so long as the pregnant woman could perform her work sitting down, she was no worse off than other women of her class. In fact, young mothers who worked within the rational order of the modern metals factory might well enjoy better health than those engaged in women's ordinary peacetime labors. Unpaid housework and unregulated occupations such as domestic service exposed women to a degree of "fatigue and organic debilitation" at least as great as that endured under the more "systematic" regime of the munitions factory.[76] By intervening directly at the point of production, then, the wartime administration could provide careful regulation of work and expert medical surveillance, thus rendering the defense factory a locus for intervention in matters hitherto closed to the state's protective scrutiny.[77]

With the help of Dr. Bonnaire, the committee soon devised a full-blown

[75] See Downs, "Women in Industry," pp. 552–54, for the composition of the committee, its plan of action, and its agendas over the thirty-two months it met (May 1916–February 1919). Twenty-one of forty-nine sessions were devoted to hours, hygiene, and safety, all in the context of maternal health, and a further ten sessions were devoted solely to the issues surrounding maternity. A scant two addressed the problem of women's wages—a problem that loomed quite large in the women's own view, if the strikes of 1916–17 are any gauge. See AN, F22, 538, Comité du Travail Féminin, "Programme de travail," 1918. For more on the wartime debates over women's work and maternity, see Downs, "Women in Industry," chap. 4; William Schneider, *Quantity and Quality: The Search for Biological Regeneration in Twentieth-Century France* (New York, 1990); Susan Pedersen, *Family, Dependence, and the Origins of the Welfare State: Britain and France, 1914–1945* (New York, 1993), chap. 2; Pauline Gemähling, *La Maternité ouvrière et sa protection légale en France* (Paris, 1915); and Gilles Bugeau, *La Prime d'allaitement: Oeuvre du "bébé-soldat"* (Lyon, 1920).

[76] "Rapport de M. le docteur Bonnaire, accoucheur-professeur en chef de la maternité de Paris . . . ," *BUG*, 25 December 1916, p. 276.

[77] Indeed, "protection of the mother and the nursing infant have never been so thoroughly assured as they are now, under the wartime administration": "Allocution de M. le docteur Bonnaire," in Gemähling, *Maternité ouvrière*, p. 5.

maternal health policy. Henceforth all pregnant women were to be taken off the night shift (which interrupted women's normal circadian rhythms, according to Bonnaire) and transferred to jobs they could perform sitting down, notably inspection and assembly work. Employers were to expand the factory medical services to include pre- and postnatal care, and were enjoined to strict observance of the eight-week maternity leave (four weeks before the birth plus four weeks after).[78] In addition, they were to provide some kind of maintenance in the form of either a birth bonus or a minimum wage (usually continuing the woman's basic time rate) throughout the maternity leave. But the centerpiece of the committee's policy was the factory nursing room (*chambre d'allaitement*). With the invention of this novel day-care arrangement, Bonnaire and his associates launched a program of mother-infant services that they hoped would form the cornerstone of future natalist policy.

Superficially, the nursing room resembled an ordinary municipal crèche. Only nursing infants were admitted, however, the bottle-fed being relegated to the crèches. To this room the young mother could retreat at regular intervals (usually twice each day) to nurse her newborn child. Yet from her perspective, nursing-room services were neither free nor unentailed. Not only did she pay a small fee for these services (usually about 25 centimes a day, deducted from her paycheck); she was expected cheerfully to accept the criticism of her child-rearing practices implied in the very structure of the nursing room's obsessive hygienic regulation. Each infant arriving in the nursing room was bathed and reclothed in "clean, disinfected clothing." Mothers were not permitted to enter the cradle room at all; rather, they were required to wash their hands, put on a fresh smock (which they were to leave behind when they finished), and wait outside in the vestibule until their child was delivered to them for the actual nursing. This process, too, was strictly supervised. Mothers were not allowed to carry in any "supplementary food" or little treats for their infants, for example. One suspects that worker-mothers did not always accept this treatment in a spirit of gratitude, for the nursing room regulation closes with an ominous reminder: "The mothers will be obedient and pleasant to the staff, in recognition of the care they give to their children."[79]

By extending factory day care to newborns, employers could actively promote breast-feeding and so participate in the patriotic campaign to reduce infant mortality. But pro-natalists sometimes doubted the employers' demographic zeal: "Under our current social order the mother who wishes to work

[78] Under the Strauss law of 1913, maternity leave could not be construed as a rupture of the woman's work contract; she had the right to return to her job four weeks after giving birth. The leave, however, was unpaid.

[79] BDIC, F 937, "Règlement de la crèche et garderie d'enfants de l'atelier de construction de Puteaux."

cannot nurse her child. . . . The employer has the social duty not merely to allow . . . but to encourage it by all possible means. . . . It is not just their social duty, but their national duty." Yet pro-natalist advocates could easily shift the blame from unscrupulous employers to the feckless mothers in their employ. The hyperpatriotic discourse swirled simultaneously around two poles: nursing-room advocates could in the same breath vaunt the working mother's right to nurse even as they doubted her will and capacity to do so: "The mother has the right and the duty to feed her infant. Any woman who voluntarily suppresses her milk is clearly stealing from her child, for the milk belongs to the latter; she is merely its manager." The middle-class supervisor in the nursing room could educate the ignorant young mother, giving her a more complete appreciation of her "managerial" responsibilities in the care and feeding of her child.[80]

The factory nursing room stirred more public excitement than all the other committee recommendations put together. It promised to harmonize motherhood with factory work while providing a point of entry for middle-class intervention in the care of working-class children. It was the only wartime natalist innovation that bore legislative fruit.[81] By the law of 5 August 1917, every employer of more than 100 women (over the age of fifteen) was legally bound to provide a properly equipped *chambre d'allaitement,* and to give young mothers two half-hour breaks each day, during which they could nurse their infants without suffering a severe loss in wages.[82]

Public response to this law ran the gamut from praise to warnings of doom. Ardent pro-natalists hailed with joy the dawn of a new custom, "inspired not only by the principles of justice but by those of hygiene and infant care. The mother's right to work is protected, as is the child's right to life: the wage is guaranteed to the one, while the milk is guaranteed to the other."[83] Feminist writers grimaced in wry amusement at a law that took so blatantly instrumental an attitude toward working women's bodies: "She is expected to bear millions of shells and turn dozens of children at the lathe."[84]

Male syndicalists offered a complex yet telling response. On the one hand,

---

[80] "Rapport de M. le docteur Lesage sur l'enfant de l'ouvrière d'usine," *BUG,* 1 January 1917, pp. 285–86. Dr. Lesage was an obstetrician at the Hôpital de Paris and general secretary of the League against Infant Mortality.

[81] Richard Tomlinson, "The Politics of *Dénatalité* in the French Third Republic" (Ph.D. thesis, Cambridge University, 1983).

[82] That is, the mother continued to receive her base rate; the main portion of her pay, the production bonus, was (obviously) interrupted. The two breaks were given in addition to the midday dinner break, which was generally an hour and a half.

[83] Gaston Rageot, *La Française dans la guerre* (Paris, 1918), p. 27.

[84] Marceline Cetival, *La Française d'aujourd'hui* (n.d.), quoted in Mathilde Dubesset, Françoise Thébaud, and Catherine Vincent, "Quand les femmes entrent à l'usine" (mémoire de maîtrise, Université de Paris VII, 1974), p. 210.

they rejected all company welfare, natalist and otherwise, as a ham-handed strategy to control working-class family and community life: "The man and woman in their factories, the children raised in their child-care center and educated by their institutions, and everyone fed by the company store, disguised as a cooperative."[85] Yet the syndicalist vision of family life could offer little else to the working-class wife. Lacking any critical perspective on the current sexual division of labor, leaders looked toward a socialist world in which working-class mothers would remain in the home, raising their children in the full understanding of the Marxist creed. Spokesmen thus invoked for socialist purposes the conventional views regarding the birth rate and the "proper" sexual division of labor espoused by the bourgeoisie. This perspective allowed such syndicalist patriots as Léon Jouhaux to dress their fear of women's undercutting men in the garb of demographic consciousness:

> Women, who are paid at lower rates . . . seek to raise their earnings by constantly overworking. . . . The long-term result is to completely disrupt women's health. . . . As a consequence, many will be unable to fulfill their social role in the future. And while today France suffers from a shortage of munitions, there remains for tomorrow the problem of the birth rate.[86]

But it was the employers' responses that ultimately determined the fate of the factory nursing room. They ranged from grudging (and minimal) compliance to fervent enthusiasm for the natalist cause.[87] Some of the larger employers—those who could best afford to do so—joined eagerly in the campaign against *dénatalité*. Contemporaries cited André Citroën as the "recognised pioneer in these matters, . . . an enthusiast for every sort of

---

[85] *L'Union des Métaux*, May–December 1917.

[86] Léon Jouhaux, in *La Bataille*, 11 February 1916.

[87] By the spring of 1918, a Ministry of Armaments survey revealed functioning *chambres d'allaitement* in twenty-one Paris-region defense plants, with two more under construction (only thirty-eight regional defense plants answered the survey, and ten of them employed fewer than 100 women). The survey also turned up six crèches and *garderies* (day care for children aged three to six). It did not mention the extensive municipal network or the collective "*maternité*" sponsored by a group of employers in the Levallois-Perret district. See AN, F22, 534, Ministère de l'Armement, Comité du Travail Féminin, "Enquête sur l'organisation des crèches," March–April 1918. The survey missed a number of large installations, including those at Puteaux and Renault. Before the law on nursing rooms was passed (August 1917), some 120 neighborhood crèches were the sole providers of organized day care to the working women of Paris. They were maintained and operated either by the municipality or by private philanthropic associations. Most of these institutions charged a small fee of 10 to 50 centimes a day (at a time when women earned about Fr 8–10 a day) and accepted children up to the age of three, according to a survey conducted in May 1917 by the Conseil National des Femmes Françaises (CNFF), quoted in Local Government Board, *The Welfare of the Children of Women Employed in Factories in Germany and France*, Intelligence Department report (London, 1919), p. 15 (BDIC, O 10188).

welfare, and particularly for maternity and child welfare."[88] M. Citroën, sparing no expense, built crèches, day nurseries, and a nursing room that could accommodate up to sixty newborns at a time (most nursing rooms could take five to twenty), all to the tune of Fr 500,000.[89]

Citroën's vast crèche–day nursery attracted plenty of attention, not only among pro-natalist activists but among his colleagues, who sometimes consulted the "pioneer" before constructing their own less lavish installations. But most defense contractors displayed a comparatively lukewarm dedication to the pro-natalist mission. Indeed, smaller firms often showed considerable ingenuity in evading the letter of the law. Many simply could not afford to build a full-scale *chambre d'allaitement,* and so advised their employees to use the neighborhood facilities instead. If the firm already had a crèche, the boss might set aside a few cradles for the nursing newborns. But nursing arrangements were often more makeshift still. Sometimes women who lived close by were allowed to return home during the nursing breaks. Others paid their visits to the concierge's house, the infirmary, or the canteen. One employer even offered his own apartment to the cause, a gesture that must surely have given the young mothers pause.

The arrangements at La Feuillette, an explosives firm, show how readily employers could integrate the new maternal services into an existing company paternalism. In 1917 management proudly inaugurated its own campaign to reverse the falling birth rate:

> So that France may be strong
> So that France may be happy
> So that France remains powerful
> She needs children, sons and daughters.[90]

Henceforth all women who had been with the firm for at least five months were to receive a nursing bonus of Fr 50 at the start of their maternity leave. A more substantial bounty followed the child's birth: Fr 200 to mothers who had borne sons, Fr 100 to the unfortunates who produced daughters.

[88] Lady Lawrence and Miss A. G. Phillip, Health and Welfare Section, Ministry of Munitions, "Report upon a Visit to France to Investigate the Arrangements Made in Munition Factories for the Care of Pregnant Women, Nursing Mothers and Young Children, October 14th–18th, 1918," appended to Local Government Board, *Welfare of the Children,* p. 54.

[89] The running cost was Fr 8 per child, according to Dr. Pinard's report, cited in Bugeau, *La Prime d'allaitement,* pp. 70–71. Citroën's expenditures can be traced not only to natalist conviction but to his plan to continue to employ all 5,322 women hired during the war. See AN, F22, 534.

[90] Poster from the workshops at La Feuillette de Meudon, quoted in AN, F22, 538, Comité du Travail Féminin, "Rapport de M. le professeur Bué sur les oeuvres de protection de l'enfance dans les usines privées," n.d., p. 2.

The pro-natalist fanfare that accompanied La Feuillette's apparently gener-ous offer masked a managerial sleight of hand. Through its multitiered bounty system, the firm never paid more than the equivalent of five weeks' wages throughout the entire eight-week leave.[91] Equally important, management apportioned the payments in Fr 20 installments, each contingent on the woman's continued service to the firm. After a year, if the child survived and if the woman still worked at La Feuillette, she received a "birthday present" of Fr 100 for the child. Employers thus integrated pro-natalist forms of welfare into an older paternalism that sought to stabilize labor turnover by buying workers' loyalty to (and dependency on) the firm.

Employers' weak and idiosyncratic application of the nursing-room law can surely be traced in part to working women's own reluctance to use the new facilities. Crèches were reputed to be hotbeds of contagious diseases, and mothers were reluctant to expose their young infants to them. Further, when it came to raising their children, few wished to endure the interfering counsels of a possibly nosy and certainly condescending supervisor. Finally, some women considered it "more respectable" to leave their children with a neighbor than to take them to the free crèche.[92] Traditional methods thus won the day. Some women did use the nursing rooms, but most continued to leave their children with a neighbor or relative each day, "abandoning" their babies to the scourge of bottle feeding.

Ultimately, then, the factory nursing room stands as a monument to the demographic anxieties of its founders, and not (as one journalist believed) the linchpin in the worker-mother's "charter."[93] By the autumn of 1920, the Paris employers' association (GIMM) was advising its members to close their nursing rooms and provide working mothers with a two-month paid leave instead.[94] Eighteen months later, the Departmental Commission of Labor, in an apt turn of phrase, pronounced the law on *chambres d'allaitement* "stillborn."[95] Employers were by no means opposed to the pro-natalist aim, as their continued provision of birth allocations indicates. But the state's wartime enthusiasm for nursing rooms had cost them heavily. There had to be another means of securing the desired demographic goal. Over the course

[91] Ibid., pp. 2–3. The initial Fr 50 bonus was the equivalent of a week's wages by the spring of 1918. The birth of a boy cost only four weeks' wages in addition; girls came even cheaper at two. Thus La Feuillete saved itself the full cost of the mother's base salary throughout her eight-week leave.

[92] Local Government Board, *Welfare of the Children.*

[93] Rageot, *La Française dans la guerre,* p. 27.

[94] See AN, 39AS, 403, GIMM to UIMM, "Chambres d'allaitement et allocations de gross-esse," 4 September 1920, p. 2: "We are convinced that from all points of view, notably the financial one, this solution would be infinitely preferable to the spread of factory nursing rooms."

[95] Dubesset et al., "Quand les femmes entrent," p. 226.

of 1917, that solution slowly materialized, though not in a form most employers would have expected.

Enter the *Surintendante*

The *surintendantes* first entered the defense plants in the spring of 1917. They were initially called to the factories to oversee the female workforce and manage the elaborate natalist provisions that the Ministry of Armaments pressed upon its contractors.[96] As time went on, however, employers came to find in their *surintendantes* the basis for a coherent and flexible company maternalism that reflected both pro-natalism and the employers' growing interest in forms of welfare aimed specifically at women.

In Britain the lady supervisors were the government's creatures, recruited by and responsible to the Ministry of Munitions. The French, by contrast, left the development of welfare supervision entirely to private initiative. Public concern for the health of working mothers had already impelled several employers' wives and daughters to organize canteens and infirmaries in the war factories.[97] The impulse to open out and elaborate factory welfare as a new sphere of social action came from a small band of republican feminists led by Cécile Brunschvicg.[98] In the winter of 1917 they founded the Association des Surintendantes de France, an organization whose avowed purpose was to train women to "create, oversee, or direct the social organization of working women in factories, from the point of view of material well-being and of moral preservation."[99]

Brunschvicg and her associates hoped to carve out a new and distinctly feminine profession, one that demanded the uniquely feminine (and bour-

---

[96] "There must be a French equivalent to the lady welfare superintendents who fill this role in England": "Voeux de l'Académie de Médecine," *BUG*, 19 March 1917, p. 370.

[97] Dubesset et al., "Quand les femmes entrent," p. 223.

[98] These women were all organized in the CNFF, the umbrella organization for the republican (i.e., nonsocialist) feminist movement and the largest feminist organization in France. Brunschvicg was a prominent figure in moderate feminist circles, having presided over the Union Française pour le Suffrage des Femmes (UFSF) since its foundation in 1909. With the onset of war, she assumed leadership of the CNFF's Section du Travail. For a detailed analysis of the shape and structure of France's tiny but vigorous bourgeois feminist movement, see Anne Kenney and Steven Hause, *Women's Suffrage and Social Politics in the French Third Republic* (Princeton, 1984).

[99] From the association's founding statutes, quoted in Maisonneuve, *Institutions sociales*, p. 268. Brunschvicg's associates in this venture included Nicole de Montmort and Marie Diemer of the Association des Infirmières Visiteuses de France; Marie Routier, director of L'Assistance par le Travail; and Mme Viollet of the Fédération d'Organismes du Travail. By the 1930s, Viollet would become head of the Association des Surintendantes. See Magdebourg Abril, "Les 'Surintendantes' dans nos usines," *Renaissance Politique, Economique, Littéraire et Artistique,* 22 December 1917, pp. 3–5.

geois) qualities of "empathy, tact, and discretion."[100] But feminist intentions also shaped the *surintendante*'s proposed interventions on the factory floor. Once inside the factory, Brunschvicg believed, the *surintendante* could use her position to secure better treatment of women workers, to shield them from ill use at the hands of foremen, and to support the principle of equal pay for equal work. At the same time, she could assist her employer in the struggle against *dénatalité*, protecting women's maternal capacity through careful administration of the factory's welfare and maternal services.

As we shall see, this mission was destined to founder on the very ambiguities that defined the *surintendante*'s position within the firm. On the managerial side, the *surintendante* self-consciously rested her professional standing on claims of parity with the employer—her class background made her the boss's "social and moral associate."[101] Moreover, the *surintendante*'s vision of a reformed and harmonious factory community dovetailed with the employer's conception of shop-floor order in important respects. Both she and he believed that the interests of labor were ultimately in accord with those of capital and that both were best served by the preservation of a strict hierarchical order in the factory, through which reforms flowed from the top downward. These larger shared convictions were in the end far more telling than any differences that divided the *surintendante* from her employer. To the extent that she shared the manager's vision of right order on the factory floor, the *surintendante*'s efforts to diminish gender inequality could be folded into and blunted by the employer's conception of her function. It was a swift and easy passage from employer's "associate" to novel instrument of his will.

When she turned to defining her connection to the women, the *surintendante* found that this aspect of her job also rested on contradiction. By entering the factory, the supervisor had breached a notionally impermeable class divide, yet her function on the shop floor demanded that she reconstitute that class boundary as the basis for her authority over her female charges. At

[100] Maisonneuve, *Institutions sociales*, p. 286. Twenty years later, Brunschvicg outlined her feminist philosophy before a meeting of the association, stressing the uniquely "feminine" mission of welfare work among factory women: "True feminism consists not of doing exactly the same things men do but of complementing their work. One can affirm that if they do certain jobs better than we do, we for our part can carry out better than they certain natural jobs that are essentially feminine or familial": "Allocution de Cécile Brunschvicg," *BAS*, 1937, p. 30. Brunschvicg was married to the eminent philosopher Léon Brunschvicg and was a public figure in her own right. She later became the first woman member of a French cabinet, serving as *ministresse* of education under Léon Blum.

[101] Bibliothèque Marguerite Durand (hereafter BMD), CNFF, Section du Travail, "Rapport de 31 March 1917." On the upper-middle-class origins of the first *surintendantes*, see Abril, " 'Surintendantes' dans nos usines." The etymology of the term *surintendante* is itself revealing, for in medieval and early modern times, the *surintendante* was the first lady-in-waiting to the queen: "La Surintendante d'usine," *La Femme dans la Vie Sociale* (published by the Union Féminine Civique et Sociale [UFCS]), no. 11, May 1928.

the same time, however, the *surintendante* needed to win the workers' trust, so that she might promote a more harmonious exchange between the boss and his employees. Gender identity formed a potential ground of solidarity between the woman welfare supervisor and her proletarian sisters, if only she could reach across that class divide on which her authority rested and establish the intimate bonds of sisterly contact.

In the spring of 1917, however, these contradictions and ambiguities had yet to surface. The notion of welfare supervision still gleamed bright with reformist promise, extending the hope of class conciliation, a more harmonious factory atmosphere, and professional advancement for middle-class *femmes de coeur*. Brunschvicg's association promptly opened a school to train the daughters of the bourgeoisie in factory-based social work. Candidates for admission had to be at least twenty-four years old and in possession of a nursing diploma (which enabled them to take over the crèches, nursing rooms, and infirmaries).[102] After two years spent studying industrial organization, managerial techniques, and the health and welfare problems of workers and their families, students went into the factory for their *stages d'usine*—two to four weeks spent as ordinary factory workers employed alongside their future clientele. At the end of their *stages, surintendantes* returned to the factory in their true incarnation, as middle-class welfare supervisors and labor managers.[103] It was an unusual and difficult program of study; of the first 300 candidates, only about 30 managed to complete it.

The school's extensive training program was of necessity quite abbreviated during the war; although the association never waived the age and nursing requirements, it did cram two years of study into several short months.[104] By August 1917 the school had already placed twelve *surintendantes* in the state

---

[102] One observer noted that the school preferred candidates of at least thirty, believing that authority increased with age: Maisonneuve, *Institutions sociales*, p. 271.

[103] They did not receive their diplomas, however, until the end of a full year's work in the factory. Very little of the students' education took place within the four walls of the school, for as Mlle Geoffroy (former *surintendante* and director of the school) later observed, "our school is in the factories, it is everywhere that men [*sic*] are working": Jean Botrot, "Femmes d'aujourd'hui: Secrétaires et surintendantes," *Le Journal*, 12 March 1931, quoted in Annie Fourcaut, *Femmes à l'usine en France dans l'entre-deux-guerres* (Paris, 1982), p. 42. The students' training was thus organized around a series of *stages*, or training periods, in the factory and in various municipal health services (crèches, dispensaries). For regular coursework, the young women were often directed to courses given by other institutions—political economy at the Musée Social, medical classes in the city hospitals, lectures on welfare and social assistance programs at the Collège de France. See Fourcaut, *Femmes à l'usine*, p. 28. The idea that one should train for a managerial post by doing a stint in the factory as an ordinary worker was not unique to France; Patrick Joyce notes that in Victorian Britain, Lancashire mill owners often trained their sons to take over the family firm by apprenticing them to a skilled weaver or spinner on the factory floor: *Work, Society, and Politics: The Culture of the Factory in Later Victorian England* (New Brunswick, N.J., 1980), p. 24.

[104] Abril, " 'Surintendantes' dans nos usines."

artilleries alone. By the end of the war, about fifty women had been placed, largely in the metalworking trades, and the school was poised for expansion.[105]

Albert Thomas, the Committee on Women's Work, and the Ministry of Labor all strongly endorsed Brunschvicg's initiative, for they consistently supported the idea of welfare for women, especially for the mothers and mothers-to-be who had been "torn from their homes" to labor on behalf of the national defense.[106] In Thomas's reformist vision, welfare supervision was precisely the kind of calculated intervention at work that would render women's factory labor an instrument of progress in the health and cultivation of the nation's working class. Beyond such hortatory statements, however, the state played no direct role in underwriting the school, structuring its curriculum, or placing its graduates in the factories.[107] The enterprise remained a private one from the outset, and *surintendantes* were directly responsible to the industrialists who hired and paid them.[108]

"And So We Second the Foremen"

"Dressed in her khaki uniform and wearing a veil barely shorter than those worn by nurses, the *surintendantes* circulate discreetly across the factory floor. . . . They pass through the workshops and, without ever intervening directly, let the shop chiefs know when the work is too taxing for the pregnant women or young mothers."[109] So wrote one enthusiastic woman journalist after paying a visit to the state arsenals, where the first *surintendantes* were employed. Employers had initially hired these women to look after the blossoming array of welfare and natalist services in the *usines de guerre,* but *surintendantes* also gradually assumed the role of welfarist labor manager vis-à-vis their female charges. Thus *surintendantes* were expected to oversee workers' health, main-

[105] The number of *surintendantes* employed in French industry rose rapidly after the war, from about 50 in 1919 to 101 in 1928, then doubling again in the 1930s: Fourcaut, *Femmes à l'usine*, p. 20. Nearly 300 *surintendantes* were working in France by 1939: "Les Surintendantes d'usines," *Revue de l'UIMM*, 15 February 1939, p. 100.

[106] Thomas to Paul Strauss, quoted in "Discours de M. Paul Strauss," *BUG*, 15 May 1916, p. 20. Thomas's many circulars reminded munitions employers that welfare supervision was no mere luxury; on the contrary, *surintendantes* could "relieve upper management of many difficulties of detail; they raise the factory's productivity even as they guard over the health, capacities, and happiness of the women workers": AN, 94 AP, 348, "Devoirs de l'inspectrice de bien-être," p. 4. The welfare policies of this right-wing socialist thus dovetailed neatly with those of the bourgeois feminists who made up Brunschvicg's association.

[107] The curriculum stressed health, *puériculture* (baby hygiene), and matters of "industrial organization" (e.g., Taylorist schemes for raising output) in equal measure. See Downs, "Women in Industry," p. 219.

[108] "Le Role de la femme dans le service social," *Revue de l'UIMM*, 15 April 1939, p. 237.

[109] Abril, " 'Surintendantes' dans nos usines," p. 4.

tain shop-floor discipline, and raise output: three distinct functions that the *surintendante* wove into a single, comprehensive managerial practice in the course of her daily activity on the shop floor.

In part, these women were elements in a new style of management, being developed to organize and control a redivided labor process. But they were also special managerial personnel brought in to address what employers understood as the "distinctive needs" of women workers for moral control and for particular attention to their health, especially their maternal well-being. Yet her arrival also signaled a new managerial concern with the health of workers, male and female, and its impact on productivity: "She ensures that the workshops offer the women every guarantee of health and comfort. This is very important to productivity itself. . . . Production rises in proportion to [the workers'] well-being."[110]

As it turned out, these managerial ambitions were not at all incompatible with the broader public concern over the health of working mothers, the concern that had drawn *surintendantes* into the factories in the first place. In fact, in stressing the link between women's physical condition and their efficiency in a deskilled work process, state and employers alike had conflated women's health with their reproductive capacity; "health" invariably translated as "maternal condition" where women were concerned. Within the shell of wartime pro-natalist discourse, then, unfolded a welfarist practice that was organized around raising productivity and aimed specifically at women, as workers and as mothers. Consequently, the more "scientific" management of women's labor in the war factory traveled hand in glove with the welfarist management of their maternity, actual or potential. Both spheres of management fell within the expert domain of the *surintendante d'usine*. Indeed, by connecting maternal health to productivity, welfare management effectively erased the line between public and private as far as the woman metalworker was concerned, opening her sexuality, personal health, and domestic arrangements to the sharp scrutiny of the employer's newest intermediary.

French employers and *surintendantes* shared with their British colleagues a view of working-class women as preeminently dependent beings. Outside their "natural" setting of home, family, and feminine occupations, they required a special kind of tutelage that could recreate and reinforce that domestic setting, providing a context in which they could be both disciplined and protected, even as industry tapped their unique productive potential. Where the British saw "peculiarly helpless" and childlike beings, however, the French saw creatures whose indiscipline could produce the tumultuous disorders of May–June 1917: "In the factory, as everywhere, there are bad souls, dubious

---

[110] AN, 94 AP, 348, "Devoirs de l'inspectrice du bien-être," p. 3, and Maisonneuve, *Institutions sociales*, pp. 57–58.

individuals who sow dissension and indiscipline, and cause amorality to reign. The '*surintendante*' knows how to avoid these 'undesirables' . . . at the moment of first hiring . . . she separates the wheat from the chaff."[111]

By implanting a figure of maternal authority in the factory, employers invoked the image of one who guards her flock even as she keeps it in line— "she who assures their existence," as one employer put it, while "strictly enforcing the rules of obedience."[112] Women workers, largely excluded from participation in the horizontal ties of syndicalist solidarity, were especially vulnerable to the overtures of management's newest emissary. By circumventing the male staff altogether and linking upper management directly to the women on the floor, *surintendantes* were able to assist employers in keeping women innocent of their brothers' syndicalist corruption. They were, in the words of one CNFF activist, the key to "avoiding the interference of outside organizations."[113]

Welfare supervision in both nations was predicated on the supervisors' use of familial imagery, in which factory hierarchies were metaphorically recast as a series of natural and reciprocal parent–child relations. But the strategy of painting the factory community as a family writ large operated a bit differently across national boundaries. Where the British welfare supervisor used class distance to set herself over and apart from her charges, the *surintendante* used class distance and the authority it lent her to reinforce the notion that she and her charges were connected by a kind of mother–daughter bond. The cultural distinction lay in the French emphasis on the connectedness of supervisor and working women. Though subtle, this difference seemed quite evident to French observers at the time: "The English Superintendant takes a more scientific approach to women's productivity; however, her relations with the women are stiffer, far less intimate."[114]

The perceived importance of class difference in structuring the *surintendante's* ersatz maternal relationship can be seen in the failure of the more democratically structured plan for welfare committees that Albert Thomas put forward in the spring of 1917. His proposal called for a system of shop-floor committees and female delegates, "consultative councils to management . . . on all matters relating to women's welfare."[115] Employer and council would act by mutual accord, raising to the post of welfare "representative"

---

[111] Abril, " 'Surintendantes' dans nos usines," p. 4.
[112] Appert, "Allocution," *BAS*, 1925.
[113] BMD, CNFF, Section du Travail, "Rapport de 31 March 1917."
[114] Maisonneuve, *Institutions sociales*, p. 264.
[115] Albert Thomas, quoted in ibid., pp. 265–66. The plan thus echoed on the narrow terrain of women's welfare the shop steward structure that Thomas had imposed on unwilling employers just weeks before. The welfare representative would presumably function either as a substitute for the *surintendante* or in harmony alongside her.

an actual working-class mother, a woman "of unimpeachable morals, who understands women workers' needs and working conditions, who has training in general hygiene, and who is both tactful and firm."[116] But Thomas was the first, and last, member of the war administration to imagine that women who had these qualities might be found on the shop floor. Indeed, the entire proposal, steeped as it was in the spirit of democracy and workers' self-determination, was destined to founder on employers' (and *surintendantes'*) belief that decisions about welfare and working conditions were the sole prerogative of management.[117]

Employers were by no means loath to use working-class women for limited and low-level supervisory functions. In fact, before the *surintendantes'* arrival, several firms had used forewomen to reinforce shop discipline, promoting them off the floor to positions of narrowly circumscribed authority, beneath the foremen and charge hands. One factory inspector remarked on the care with which managers selected these women, searching among the wives of clerks, low-level managers, and mobilized soldiers for workers who seemed "intelligent, firm, serious, and in possession of some authority over their comrades." Industrialists also looked back positively on these experiments. Not only did the forewomen come cheap (they were paid anywhere from 15 to 50 percent more than the women they supervised), they controlled the women more effectively than their male counterparts, for, as one employer put it, "women are more severe [with women] than men are."[118]

The forewoman's jurisdiction, however, was of necessity quite narrow, for, as one shell manufacturer pointed out, "it is very delicate to confer on one woman authority over her colleagues."[119] It would be far more effective to appoint a woman from outside the working class, for only class distance could confer that complete authority so necessary for controlling these dependent yet volatile beings. In proposing that employers engage working mothers for the work of welfare supervision, Thomas had (perhaps intentionally) missed the point. In order to accomplish her full task as welfare supervisor and labor manager, the *surintendante* had to have complete authority over the workers: "To be executed productively, the role of *Surintendante* demands women of the elite," averred the social Catholic publicist Pierre Magnier de Maison-

---

[116] Ministère de l'Armement, "Protection de la main-d'oeuvre féminine dans les usines de guerre," *BUG*, 16 July 1917, p. 91.

[117] The failure of Thomas's proposal for grass-roots welfare committees parallels the swift destruction of the shop steward system (*délégués d'atelier*) in the aftermath of the spring 1919 metalworkers' strikes. (In a campaign coordinated by the GIMM, Parisian employers chased known militants from the shops. See Downs, "Women in Industry," chap. 5.) After 1920, all shop-floor intermediaries (foremen, technicians, *surintendantes*) were appointed by management.

[118] *BMT*, January–February 1918, pp. 18, 19.

[119] Ibid., p. 18; director of a shell and fuse plant speaking.

neuve.[120] "Her education and social background must be up to the responsibilities of her job," declared Thomas's successor, Louis Loucheur.[121] However
motherly and upstanding she might be, a promoted worker could never forge
the appropriate relationship with her charges.

For the *surintendante*, motherhood was a trope for leadership and command, rooted in the firm soil of class distance; she was to be "mother" to
the women workers placed in her charge. The importance of middle-class
standing as a source of the *surintendante's* moral authority stands revealed
in the very different positions that forewomen and *surintendantes* occupied
on the factory floor. Forewomen invariably exercised their limited rule under
the watchful eye of foremen and charge hands; never did the foreman see
his own authority over women workers challenged by an ordinary forewoman.
It would be a different matter with the *surintendantes*.

At first French employers were not prepared to see their foremen undermined by middle-class women. Indeed, despite the rapid spread of welfarist
managerial strategies in the war industries, many employers were initially
quite cautious about the *surintendante*. Uncertain as to where her loyalties
truly lay, several industrialists expressed considerable ambivalence about the
idea of welfare supervision and, perhaps more important, the presence of
educated, middle-class women on the factory floor. Such women, imbued
with a sense of mission, might carry the bonds of sisterhood too far and
undermine the employer's authority in zealous pursuit of their own protective
project: "In daily contact with the woman worker, they might worry too
frequently about the exhaustion women workers feel; ultimately, they would
implant notions of fatigue in the worker's spirit by autosuggestion."[122]

Employers' early circumspection comes across especially clearly in the rules
that the industrialist Louis Loucheur recommended to his fellow employers,
defining the role and working conditions of *surintendantes*. On the one hand,
he secured her position in the shop-floor hierarchy by specifying that she be
placed "under the employer's direction, or that of his designated officer . . .
and not . . . under the authority of [his] subordinates."[123] On the other hand,

---

[120] Maisonneuve, *Institutions sociales*, p. 267.

[121] AN, 94 AP, 348, "Devoirs de l'inspectrice du bien-être," p. 1. See Philippe d'Iribarne,
La Logique de l'honneur: Gestion des entreprises et traditions nationales (Paris, 1989), for a
reflection on the importance of hierarchy and status in structuring the management of modern
industry in France.

[122] Interview with André Citroën in *La Vie Féminine*, 1 June 1918. Citroën must have dropped
his reservations rather quickly, for by 1919 the Ecole des Surintendantes had sent at least one
young trainee to the Citroën works.

[123] AN, 94 AP, 348, "Devoirs de l'inspectrice du bien-être," p. 1. See also Louis Loucheur,
"Dispositions générales régissant les surintendantes et les intendantes d'usines en service dans
les établissements de l'artillerie," circular issued 29 October 1918, reprinted in *BUG*, 25 November 1918, p. 245.

her salary—Fr 300 to 350 a month while training, Fr 400 a month for the fully trained *surintendante*—placed her in rather close proximity to those whom she managed.[124] Loucheur's careful specification of her rank (reporting directly to her employer) was probably designed to guard against what he feared most: that the *surintendante*, roaming freely across the factory floor, speaking with individual women at will, might become "a danger to his [the employer's] authority and that of the foreman."[125] As industrialists began hiring *surintendantes*, most adopted Loucheur's method and contained the potentially subversive impact of a roving workers' advocate by having her report directly to themselves.

Ultimately, this tactic reproduced the situation that already prevailed in England. Ensconced in her own welfarist domain, theoretically concerned solely with "the physical and moral well-being of the women . . . to the exclusion of all technical questions relating to work and wages,"[126] the *surintendante* formed a nascent new line of command, directly linking top management to the shop floor. The old chain of command, running through foremen, charge hands, and other technical staff, continued to function alongside this new line, though not without some friction between skilled male supervisors and the middle-class welfare ladies. And yet, because welfare management connects health and productivity, the sexual division of authority over women production workers could never be stably allocated; on the contrary, the pursuit of their welfarist duties continually drew the *surintendantes* directly into the foreman's notionally distinct bailiwick, hampering his freedom to select, deploy, and rebuke or reward the women who worked under his command.[127] The *surintendante* had the power to shift workers around on the line, or even to remove them altogether.[128] Although she was generally expected to consult with the foreman before taking such steps, her right to intervene in the deployment of labor represented a real encroachment on the foreman's territory. Indeed, the *surintendante* sometimes pitted her authority against the foreman's and on behalf of the women, transferring them from impossible jobs or helping them bypass a difficult foreman and carry grievances

---

[124] The average semiskilled woman earned about Fr 300 a month; her fully skilled male colleague earned between Fr 400 and 420 a month.

[125] Loucheur, "Dispositions générales," pp. 245–46.

[126] Ibid., p. 245.

[127] "The *surintendantes* must not ignore work-related questions and must circulate frequently through the workshops, exchanging views with the foremen": "Rapport de Mme Agnès Georges Jacob, surintendante-directrice de l'ecole," *BAS*, 1925.

[128] The *surintendante* "will transfer women from one workshop to another. . . . Also, in collaboration with the employer, she will arrange any job changes needed to place women on work that is appropriate to their age, strength, and health": AN, 94 AP, 348, "Devoirs de l'inspectrice du bien-être," pp. 1–3.

directly to the boss.[129] In these instances she was impelled to act by her sense of the workers' vulnerability to male authority in its proletarian incarnation—a more brutal form of authority to the bourgeois eye of the lady welfare supervisor.

As in Britain, then, employers could find no single point where the foreman's technical authority left off and the *surintendante*'s welfare authority began. Her power to intervene in the organization of labor, though consonant with the employer's wish to exert a more "scientific" control of labor, radically disrupted traditional authority structures. Yet in time, many industrialists came to see a distinct advantage in allowing their *surintendantes* to assume the role of "first foreman in the women's shops."[130] By the 1920s, these men would delimit a broad space for the *surintendante,* in which she shared— and sometimes appropriated—powers that formerly were the foreman's alone.[131] The rupture and redrawing of lines of authority was formalized in Loucheur's recommendation that employers consult their *surintendantes* before hiring or promoting foremen and charge hands, "for where the employer assesses the technical capacity of the [foreman], the [*surintendante*] judges his character and his probable attitudes toward his colleagues and his subordinates."[132]

Over time, then, the *surintendantes* gradually took up some of the discretionary powers hitherto concentrated in the hands of foremen alone. Hence the *surintendante*'s middle-class background was important not only for the power it gave her over her female charges but because it lent her the authority to dispute the foreman's judgment, if the need arose. Based in her own welfarist domain, the *surintendante* had become a key element in a new and gender-specific managerial strategy, concerned with husbanding the human and female factors. As such, she occupied a position that was both complementary to the technical hierarchy and yet outside and above it, threatening to supplant it by absorbing some of the foreman's former duties in her entirely distinct approach to labor discipline. Where the foremen often ruled by intimidation, threatening the recalcitrant with a fine or dismissal, the *surintendante* "managed" and directed by co-optation.

---

[129] The *surintendante* often received letters of grievance from the women. She passed on to the director those she deemed "justified" and held back the remainder. (Some were "unjustified," the vast majority merely "puerile": Abril, " 'Surintendantes' dans nos usines," p. 4.)

[130] UIMM, 69/54/13, "Le Travail des femmes dans les industries travaillant pour la défense nationale pendant la guerre de 1914–18," p. 20.

[131] *Surintendantes* hired, assigned, and disciplined the female workforce while directing the full range of factory welfare services, some of which reached male workers as well. See AN, 94 AP, 348, "Devoirs de l'inspectrice du bien-être."

[132] Ibid., p. 1. Loucheur goes on to note that although "this might seem to undermine or substitute for the authority of managers and forewomen . . . experience has shown that this has not been the case where the [*surintendante*] acts with tact" (p. 2).

In embracing the institution of welfare supervision, French employers permitted, perhaps even welcomed the disruption of traditional authority structures. In so doing, they allowed separate but overlapping jurisdictions to arise and the two styles of management to coexist. That French employers should have countenanced and even encouraged this development is, in itself, quite interesting. It suggests that, unlike their British colleagues, the French were not so content with a system of shop-floor rule grounded in the technical authority of foremen. Paternalist employers had long striven to curb these men's discretionary power by introducing engineers and other technocratic types into the factory.[133] Industrialists' recent willingness to implant a welfare hierarchy—a new kind of "moral" chain, directly linking the employer to the women on the factory floor—suggests that the *surintendante* was more than a strategic response to the influx of women metalworkers. Employers may well have seen in their new "moral associates" yet another means of limiting the foreman's "excessive" powers.

Hence, there seems to have been greater space for the *surintendante* in French factories, perhaps because the supplanting of craftworkers' self-directed rule by more centralized managerial structures had already partially disengaged the technical aspects of shop-floor rule from the political element.[134] In this context, it was clear that skill alone would not necessarily fit anyone, male or female, to assume a position of direct authority over other workers. In Britain the lines were not so clear precisely because of the way the social organization of the labor process linked the acquisition of skill to participation in the craftsman's collective authority and control over work. The war did not decisively interrupt this pattern in Britain. Not just craftsmen but employers remained attached to the practice of deploying skilled men to organize and direct the work process.[135] In France, where metalworking as a whole had moved further from a system of craft-based shop-floor management, the industry required fewer skilled workers but more middle-class managers.

Thus, by the early 1920s, when the institution of welfare supervision began to spread rapidly through France, the lady supervisors disappeared from British engineering plants. The demise of welfare supervision in Britain did not mean that engineering employers had abandoned the notion that managing women

---

[133] See Donald Reid, "Industrial Paternalism in France: Discourse and Practice in Nineteenth-Century French Mining and Metallurgy," *Comparative Studies in Society and History* 27 (October 1985): 579–607.

[134] See ibid., p. 591.

[135] See Lazonick, "Production Relations," on similar developments in the British mule-spinning industry. The question of women's entry into the industry, and especially of their training for skilled work, was thus intimately linked with changes not only in the technology and pace of work but also (potentially) in the lines of authority on the factory floor.

workers entailed gender-specific strategies. On the contrary, beyond making "suitable arrangements for their health and comfort," these men "attach[ed] great importance to an older woman being in charge of the girls to supervise them."[136] But if there was a moral aspect to managing women's labor that was best met by the use of female supervisors, it was also true that continued use of middle-class women for the job simply provoked the foremen's ire. For most engineering employers, this was too high a price to pay. British employers therefore abandoned the institution soon after the Armistice.

In France, by contrast, the early 1920s marked the opening of a new phase in the *surintendante*'s professional existence. As reconstruction fueled a boom in demand for metals and machinery, employers linked welfare more tightly to schemes for the rationalization of work. In so doing, they located the new techniques and technology of the modern industrial economy in a set of authority relations that had been recast by the deployment of middle-class women supervisors. But this development lay in the future. For the time being, the supervisor/*surintendante* was needed to assist state officials and employers in both nations, as they sought to effect a smooth transition from the wartime economy.

[136] PP 1918, Cd. 9073, *Report of the Departmental Committee*, p. 16.

CHAPTER 6

Demobilization and the Reclassification of Labor, 1918–1920

A week before the Armistice, the divisional commissioner for Paris's Sixth Police District suggested that among women munitions workers "the desire for a swift peace is not so lively as one might have once thought. . . . They have gained the habit of factory work. . . . Very few have saved, all have acquired a taste for spending. The return to old ways and the reclassification of the workers will be very difficult."[1] Long before the peace, Parisian employers had made it abundantly clear that in the event of economic downturn, foreign and female labor would be the first to go. The previous winter, for example, when shortages of raw materials had forced layoffs at several large firms in the region, employers had made no secret of their priorities: Lorraine Dietrich let 900 women go and Farman laid off 100. Three months later, Blériot trimmed its wage bill by eliminating all foreign and female labor, and firing all the apprentices.[2]

In Paris, then, women had already had a foretaste of the hardships that peace was to bring: as prices continued their relentless upward spiral, the era of well-paid work for women would most certainly come to an end. Across

---

[1] APP, B/a 1614, 4 November 1918. On the demobilization see Jean-Jacques Becker, *The Great War and the French People* (New York, 1985).

[2] *La Vague*, 26 February 1918, quoted in Mathilde Dubesset, Françoise Thébaud, and Catherine Vincent, "Quand les femmes entrent à l'usine: Les Ouvrières des usines de guerre de la Seine, 1914–1918" (mémoire de maîtrise, Université de Paris VII, 1974), p. 358. As instances of intermittent unemployment multiplied, Minister of Armaments Louis Loucheur decreed that in order to preserve public order, any worker laid off was to be paid unemployment compensation equivalent to her or his basic rate (without bonus) for an eight-and-a-half-hour day: circular of 4 February 1918, reprinted in *BUG*, 18 February 1918. Although it was better than nothing, this method of compensation cut women's wages in half at a time when the cost of living was rising relentlessly. In the spring of 1918, British munitions plants also began to reduce their workforces and women were generally the first to go.

the Channel, employers shared the conviction that women would be reluctant to return to their old occupations. One Birmingham employer spoke of munitions work as liberation from domestic servitude, and predicted that few women would willingly return to home and "feminine" pursuits: "I think a great proportion of the women at present employed in munitions . . . , having tasted the sweets of freedom and good wages, will be loath to go back to the humdrum, unpaid, household toil. . . . They like the freedom, the spirit of independence fostered by their new-found earning power, the social life."[3]

Both men were undoubtedly correct in observing that the return to old ways would be difficult, yet it never occurred to either of them to separate women's desire to work from the context of war. Rather, police and employers in both nations seem to have assimilated profound upheaval in the sexual division of labor by mentally confining that shift to the time-space of war emergency. Women's manifest desire to continue working outside the boundaries of prewar convention must therefore have emanated from some deep changes wrought upon their character by the experience of work in the war factories. In fact, observers were quite candid in connecting shifts in the sexual division of labor to issues of family life and social stability: "They seem quite willing to do without their husbands and as soon as the war is over, there will be a spate of divorces and disasters. The woman who has stood in for her husband and done her job well will no longer put up with his complaints and demands."[4] If the war had indeed transformed working-class women's expectations, it boded ill not only for the "reclassification of labor" but for the broader reordering of society, its restoration to the healthier outline of prewar days.

The Bid for Restoration

If nothing else, however, sheer economic necessity would drive women from the metalworking factory; with the war's end, employers in both nations were certain that demand would drop off precipitously, shrinking the industry rapidly to its prewar dimensions. Some even predicted that the revival of world trade, and especially competition from Germany and the United States, would further narrow French and British market shares.[5] Only the rare opti-

---

[3] Quoted in Adam Kirkaldy, *Industry and Finance—War Expedients and Reconstruction*, 2 vols. (London, 1917), 1:130.

[4] APP, B/a 1587, "Physionomie de Paris," 1917–18, quoted in Becker, *Great War*, p. 308.

[5] On 4 June 1919 GIMM reported to UIMM that "the mechanical engineering industry in the Paris region is on the verge of a serious crisis. . . . Its ordinary customers have been solicited by extraordinarily advantageous offers from our foreign competitors": UIMM, 39/21/01, "Au sujet des grèves qui viennent d'éclater parmi les ouvriers métallurgistes de la région parisienne," p. 4. British employers were also quite worried about German competition, and repeatedly invoked "cheap German manufacture" as justification for the engineering industry's increased

mist, a "progressive" modernizer such as André Citroën, took an expansive view of the industry's economic future; in January 1919 he grandly proclaimed the dawn of a consumer paradise in France, an economy in which all 5,000 of the women at his Javel plant would find employment on immense assembly lines, producing bicycles, automobiles, and sewing machines.[6]

But such men, however voluble, were few. In both England and France, the vast majority of metals employers were certain that their factories could not sustain wartime levels of employment. In the coming economy of scarcity, the key to a peaceful transition lay in persuading women to accept "reclassification" as housewives and as workers in those industries traditionally earmarked for feminine fingers: "In returning to your former occupations or to other peacetime jobs you will be as useful to your country as you were in devoting yourself to four years of war production."[7] So intoned Minister of Armaments/Reconstruction Louis Loucheur in a circular to the women workers employed in state arsenals. Having entered those factories in the Republic's hour of need, women were now being asked to answer another patriotic call, to "aid the national economy toward recovery" by accepting without a murmur the reconstruction of the prewar sexual division of labor. The men who managed England's "feminine demobilization" employed a similar vocabulary of national duty and patriotic sacrifice. For the past four years, women had stepped into the breach as needed. Now they were expected quietly to bow out again, "to be as splendid in this problem of demobilisation as they had been throughout the period of the war."[8]

In both nations, a palpable current of fear underlay the appeals to women's pliant patriotism. Open concern about the nation's long-term economic future twined with submerged though no less powerful anxieties about the capacity of coherent and stable social structures (family, factory hierarchies) to reassert themselves now that the upheaval of war had passed. "Can one now foresee how the home and factory will be linked? A capital question for the future of industry and of the race," mused one French journalist in the winter of 1919.[9] But any hopes for a simple return to the halcyon days of the Belle Epoque splintered on the rock of France's chronic labor shortage, a shortage

---

recourse to cheap female and child labor. See the interwar collective bargaining records of the EEF, Modern Records Center, University of Warwick (hereafter MRC); and Coventry District Engineering Employers' Association (CDEEA). For more on this issue, see Laura Lee Downs, "Women in Industry, 1914–1939: The Employers' Perspective" (Ph.D. thesis, Columbia University, 1987), chaps. 5 and 6.

[6] Reported in Léon Abensour, "Le Problème de la démobilisation féminine," *La Grande Revue,* January 1919, pp. 499–500.

[7] AN, F7, 13356, Louis Loucheur, "Circulaire aux ouvrières des usines et établissements de l'Etat travaillant pour la défense nationale," 13 November 1918.

[8] IWM, Mun. 29/25, "The Demobilisation of Women," p. 3.

[9] Abensour, "Problème de la démobilisation," p. 489.

made all the more acute by the appalling mortality in the trenches.[10] It was difficult to avoid the obvious conclusion: women would continue to work outside the home and perhaps even in industries where they had not been found before the war. The heavy wartime losses had ensured that simple restoration of the prewar division could not deliver both social balance and economic prosperity. Recovery of those goods would come only through a delicate weaving of the new with the old, a reconciliation of the glaring need for women's labor with the reconstitution of a healthy social and family life.

In Britain, where industry had rarely lacked labor before the war, the return to "normalcy" could proceed more straightforwardly, as the boundaries of custom were settled comfortably back in place:

> A call comes again to the women of Britain, a call happily not to make shells or fill them so that a ruthless enemy shall be destroyed, but a call to help renew the homes of England, to sew and to mend, to cook and clean and rear babies in health and happiness, who in their turn shall grow into men and women worthy of the Empire.[11]

War had turned the home front upside down, underscoring what one woman official termed "the social risks inherent in a widely extended and intensified employment of women in all great industries."[12] Recovery demanded that they swiftly revert to their proper places. In October 1918 the Ministry of Munitions/Reconstruction took the first step toward easing that passage when Stephenson Kent, head of the Civilian Demobilisation Division, ordered that the government's industrial training shops be closed to women. Kent justified his decision by declaring men's prior right to well-paid work:

> I think it both unwise and unfair to accept women at this moment as pupils under our present scheme. The resultant effect must inevitably be to increase . . . what is already in all probability an unabsorbable quantity . . . of women who, having had a taste of higher earnings and industrial conditions, may find themselves unable to continue in such occupations.[13]

---

[10] Gérard Noiriel places the human shortfall in the industrial labor force alone at about 10% in 1919: *Workers in French Society in the Nineteenth and Twentieth Centuries* (New York, 1990), p. 114. The 1.6 million men who emigrated to France in search of work after 1920 only partially made up the deficits of war. For data on France's human and material losses during the war, see Colin Dyer, *Population and Society in Twentieth-Century France* (New York, 1978), esp. p. 40; and Alfred Sauvy, ed., *Histoire économique de la France entre les deux guerres,* 3 vols. (Paris, 1968), esp. 1:21.

[11] IWM, Women's Work Collection, Emp. 80, Ministry of Labour, leaflet advertising government training programs, April 1919.

[12] Adelaide Anderson (head of the Factory Inspectorate), quoted in Sydney John Chapman, ed., *Labour and Capital after the War* (London, 1918), p. 85.

[13] PRO, Lab. 2/544/MWLS—347, memorandum on technical schools by Stephenson Kent (controller general of civilian demobilisation and resettlement), 25 October 1918.

Even before the Armistice, British officials were designing policies on the basis of a key, unexamined presumption: that "normal" social and economic life was constructed on a drastic differential between men's and women's right to the "higher earnings and industrial conditions" obtaining in such industries as engineering. Six months later, the Ministry of Labour built upon this edifice when it solemnly announced that it would assist unemployed munitions workers by training them for work in "normal women's trades" only, "and in the processes in those trades which were known as women's processes before the war. . . . In this connection domestic service will be included as a normal women's occupation. . . ."[14] In their haste to chase women out of the munitions and metalworking industries and back into more "normal" feminine pursuits, British bureaucrats pressed upon the unemployed a definition of normal womanhood which stressed domestic work, paid and unpaid, and automatically placed metalworking outside the bounds of acceptable feminine behavior.

On both sides of the Channel, then, pragmatic concern with the uncertain economic future joined with broader anxieties over the socially disruptive impact of a shifting sexual division of labor, prompting observers to urge a return to hearth and family. As the demobilization proceeded, the laudatory image of a woman "doing her bit" in the war factory rapidly shape-shifted. In her place appeared a menacing apparition: the wage-hungry woman muscling aside the honest veteran in the single-minded pursuit of "pin money" and "the free life of the factory girl": "In many cases, unhappily, the girl has made up her mind to remain as long as possible, with no thought for the fact that she is occupying a post which means the bread and butter of some discharged soldier and his dependents."[15]

Hence dark visions of economic constriction, revolutionary unrest, and women workers refusing to step aside informed the progress of industrial demobilization in both nations. With the growing threat of strikes at home and revolution already toppling regimes in the east, none dared imagine that demobilizing so many thousands of soldiers and workers could proceed as smoothly as it ultimately did. Fearful that further unrest might attend the transition from a controlled economy, state officials trusted that the best strategy for postwar prosperity was to return industrial affairs to private hands as quickly as possible.[16] With the resumption of business as usual, wartime

[14] PRO, Lab. 1222/TW—116, circular LAC 64, April 1919. Between June 1919 and March 1921 about 7,000 women were trained for "women's work" in government programs. About 2,000 of them received training for domestic service and laundry work.

[15] "Girl War Workers," *The Democrat*, 20 June 1919. (The Democrat was a rightist labor journal, unaffiliated with any particular trade union.)

[16] Hence in January 1919 Britain's Ministry of Munitions (now called the Ministry of Reconstruction) abruptly withdrew its controlling hand. See R. H. Tawney, "The Abolition of Economic Controls, 1918–1921," *Economic History Review* 13 (1943): 1–30. That same winter,

agitation might at last give way to the calm and familiar preoccupations of everyday living. But life could not be normal so long as women continued to take men's places at work. As they pressed women to leave the metalworking industries, then, postwar governments underwrote the reassertion of sexual division across the social landscape. In so doing, they helped to create a climate of hostility toward the woman worker turned selfish wage hound.

It was in this context of anti-female backlash that employers were to redivide labor in the metals and engineering industries of postwar France and Britain. In fact, women's orderly departure from the war factories ultimately facilitated the broader reshuffling of male and female job categories in the metalworking industries. Employers and state officials alike termed this reshuffling a "return to normalcy," to those familiar divisions of home and work, textiles and metals, female and male, which had scored the prewar world. But when the dust raised by returning feet had settled once again, in the early 1920s, the metalworking factory floor bore a new aspect. A significant change had scuttled in under the sheltering wing of "return to normalcy." Whereas prewar metals factories had employed women by exception and in small numbers only (5 percent of the 1914 metalworking labor force), the postwar industry bore the permanent imprint of wartime upheaval: at no time after 1920 did women's participation rate in this industry ever fall below 10 percent; indeed, after the early 1920s it expanded steadily in both nations, reaching 15 to 20 percent by the end of the 1930s. More important, employers had come to view women as a class of labor without which the industry could not function profitably. Though individual women might come and go, the class "female labor" was now a permanent stratum in this hierarchically ordered and internally differentiated labor force.

By 1920, then, employers had not restored the status quo antebellum, but neither had they perpetuated the wartime situation. Rather, they drew on a complex of wartime experience and convictions about male and female roles, on the factory floor and in the larger world outside. The result was a series of ideas about what it was women should be doing (stepping aside for men, producing a new crop of babies)—ideas that converged, even overlapped, with recollections of what it was women had actually accomplished, even excelled at, in the war factories. The outcome of this interpenetration was the postwar delimitation of a narrow niche of ill-paid employment earmarked for women. Of course, this move entailed the waste of a newly developed resource—the pool of highly trained women metalworkers.[17] At the time,

---

the French ended their wartime controls in a similarly abrupt fashion. See Richard Kuisel, *Capitalism and the State in Modern France* (Cambridge, 1981), for details of the French demobilization.

[17] Marion Kozak observes, "The post-war absorption of a greater number of women than before into the ranks of engineering repetition work was a continuation of pre-war trends and

however, the wastage passed unnoticed under the rubric of "return to nor-malcy."

Demobilizing the Wartime Workforce in Britain

Over the long term, postwar governments hoped to deliver prosperity and social stability to their war-torn nations through the rapid restoration of something resembling prewar conditions. The rededication to gender-appro-priate work roles which this restoration entailed dovetailed neatly with plans for addressing the more immediate question of public order. Within hours of the cease-fire, authorities were preoccupied with the problem of ensuring a swift and orderly passage from army to factory for demobilized men, and likewise a smooth return from male occupations to female ones for women. But as the number of unemployed mounted, some observers began to see the transition as a moment fraught with dangerous possibilities. Lilian Barker, whose final task as welfare supervisor at Woolwich Arsenal was the swift and orderly release of the arsenal's 30,000 women workers, warned her compatri-ots of the "great menace" posed by restless crowds of unoccupied women, "unemployed and therefore open to great moral danger." Deprived of income, thrown abruptly onto the streets, might not some of them succumb to the temptations of the street and the lure of easy money? Worse than the possible corruption of individual women, though, was the specter of their collective corruption by revolutionary propaganda. Of course, women had encountered many such ideas during the war, but they had been "too busy to heed them." With the return of peace, idle hands might do the devil's work, making thousands receptive to "dangerous and revolutionary theories."[18]

In the end, however, state officials did remarkably little to preserve women workers from the dangers and temptations of the street. The men at Britain's ministries of Labour and Reconstruction counted on women's rapid and voluntary withdrawal from their new occupations, and trusted that the existing labor exchanges were adequate for this sudden and massive transfer of labor— a shift far more abrupt than women's wartime entry, which had come over a period of eighteen to twenty-four months. As it turned out, only about half of those who had entered war factories elected to leave during that first

bore little relation to the semi-skilled tasks which many women had been trained to perform. Such waste of potential and actual manpower is striking": "Women Munition Workers during the First World War, with Special Reference to Engineering" (Ph.D. thesis, University of Hull, 1976), p. iv.

[18] PRO, Lab. 2/1223/TW—153, Lilian Barker to Women's Sub-Committee of the Demobili-sation Committee, 1 December 1918. The total number of women at Woolwich comes from IWM, Mun. 29/25, "Demobilisation of Women," p. 1.

postwar winter.[19] But over the following months, many more were driven from their jobs as employers reduced their workforces, generally letting the women go first.

The government's main contribution toward easing this transition was the temporary out-of-work "donation" (OWD) granted to all war workers and scaled to the familiar notion that women require less money than men.[20] Of course, not every woman eligible actually drew the unemployment benefit. When Lilian Barker inaugurated the demobilization at Woolwich, for example, she tenaciously guarded the public purse from the grasping fingers of those who, in Barker's estimation, were not in desperate need of support:

> When demobilisation came about it was realized that it would be a very calamitous thing if all those 30,000 women thought they could go on the unemployment donation without further parley, so I went round to every factory and pointed out to women . . . that if they took the 25s per week and gave nothing in return they were impoverishing the country. . . . We persuaded nearly 3,000 women to go back into domestic service.[21]

In urging the women to return to service, Barker encouraged them to take "a sensible point of view." Domestic work, she claimed, was no longer the restrictive servitude they had known before the war: "Mistresses, through the dearth of maids . . . had learnt to appreciate good maids and treat them with the consideration they should receive." But after the relative freedom of factory life, where the workday ceased with the end of one's shift, few women wished to settle back into a regime of household drudgery, toiling endless hours at another woman's beck and call. Barker persisted, however, reminding the women of their bleak and narrow options in the dawning economy of scarcity. If they were to accept domestic employment, "their food and accommodation, at least, would be assured."[22] After five months spent doing her part for a cheap demobilization, Lilian Barker finally resigned her post. Of the 30,000 women war workers at the arsenal, only 2,000 remained.[23]

---

[19] Arthur Cecil Pigou, *Aspects of British Economic History* (London, 1947); and Bentley Gilbert, *British Social Policy, 1914–1939* (London, 1970).

[20] The "donation" was 24s. for men, 20s. for women during the first thirteen weeks, then 20s. and 15s., respectively, for another thirteen weeks. The rates for adolescents were marked by a similar inequality, with boys receiving 12s. to girls' 10s., while men and women with dependents got an additional 6s. a week for the first child, 3s. for each additional child. All figures are from "Unemployed Workers and Self-Help," *Woman Worker* (NFWW newspaper), December 1918, p. 6. Finally, migrant women workers got free rail passes back home.

[21] IWM, Ministry of Labour, "Committee of Inquiry into the Out of Work Donation Scheme," 1919, p. 136.

[22] IWM, Mun. 29/25, "Demobilisation of Women," p. 2.

[23] By April 1919, sustained pressure from a host of Lilian Barkers had driven 296,000 women munition workers off the payroll in government establishments across the nation (this was

Lilian Barker was the faithful executrix of an official if unsystematic demobilization policy that combined miserly (and unevenly granted) unemployment compensation with a sustained effort to fill the emptied ranks of domestic servants with former munitions workers. But at the end of six months, women's unemployment had stubbornly refused to drop.[24] By March 1919 nearly half a million women (and 234,000 men) were claiming the benefit. Two months later, 75 percent of those still drawing the OWD were women.[25] Their persistent high unemployment led the minister of labour to conclude that women were living off their benefit and refusing to return to their old jobs. At 20s. a week, the OWD dangled well below the 35s. weekly minimum women had earned in munitions. Nonetheless, "the disparity between the amount of unemployment donation payable to women and the amount they were able to earn in many employments before the war, and can now, has created a very natural reluctance to go back to work so long as the donation lasts."[26] Perhaps it was time to adopt a more aggressive approach, to push off the dole those women who were using the benefit in order to "take a holiday at the National expense."[27]

In the spring of 1919 the Ministry of Labour began to withhold the benefit from people who refused to accept work offered to them at the local labor exchanges. Indeed, many officials used their control of the unemployment benefit as a kind of stick to drive women to accept reclassification as low-waged labor. One soldier's wife lost her benefit after refusing to accept a job that paid 8s. a week, the week being seven days long, ten and a half hours each day. Another woman, widowed with one child, refused laundry work at 17s. a week on the grounds that 17s. was too little for two people to live on. She was then offered domestic service, on the condition that she place her child in a home, or wood chopping at 17s. a week. If she refused again,

---

nearly half the number—600,000—employed in state factories in November 1918). See Kirkaldy, *Industry and Finance,* 2:103.

[24] Irene O. Andrews and Margaret Hobbes, *The Economic Effects of the World War upon Women and Children in Great Britain* (New York, 1921), p. 210. In January 1919 women's unemployment stood at 225,000, while men's was a mere 101,000. Three months later, 494,000 women and 234,000 men were drawing the OWD. In November 1919, when the ministry terminated the scheme, 29,000 women were still applying for the donation. These unemployment figures must be regarded as minimal, as they report only those women who applied for relief.

[25] Gail Braybon observes that no woman sat on the Committee on Out of Work Donation, despite the fact that by May 1919 three-quarters of the recipients were women: *Women Workers in the First World War* (London, 1981), p. 179.

[26] Sir Robert Horne, minister of labour and chair of the Labour Resettlement Committee, quoted in "Between Ourselves" (editorial), *Woman Worker,* March 1919.

[27] "The New Rest Cure," *Evening News,* 4 January 1919, quoted in Braybon *Women Workers,* p. 188.

the exchange would suspend her donation. The widow remarked bitterly that officials at the exchange claimed that these were "splendid wages, as they don't suppose we did any work before the war."[28]

Under the banner of sending women "back" to their homes, government officials were in fact articulating a demobilization policy that would systematically thrust working women back into the ill-paid and unregulated employments from which so many had escaped in 1914. In doing so these men reinforced the notion that women workers were by definition cheap labor. After all, these distinctively feminine job opportunities—laundry, wood chopping—clearly conflicted with women's domestic and maternal lives (asking that the widow place her child in a home) far more than well-paid and relatively skilled work in engineering had done during the war. It appears that the real criterion by which women's work was defined was not the ease with which it could be reconciled with their domestic labor but whether or not that work threatened a cherished social myth: that women were supported by male breadwinners, not by their own labors.

With the passage of the Restoration of Prewar Practices Act in October 1919, the British government kept its pledge to the ASE while setting the final piece of its demobilization program in place. By this measure the state undertook to enforce for a full year the status quo ante bellum on the metalworking factory floor.[29] The act provoked scant protest; on the contrary, the leader of the National Federation of Women Workers, Mary MacArthur, insisted that all wartime bargains with skilled craftsmen be upheld:

I am also certain that no individual woman would desire to retain the job of any soldier or sailor who may return to claim it. It is true that women will continue to demand a place in the sun, but that does not necessarily mean . . .

---

[28] "Some Bad Cases of Sweating," *Daily News*, 8 April 1919, quoted in Braybon, *Women Workers*, p. 182. Between 1918 and 1922 the Arbitration Board denied 81% of women's appeals against suspended benefits, claiming that the women who appealed had refused to accept "suitable employment." See Andrews and Hobbes, *Economic Effects*, p. 212. Applications for unemployment suggest that by the early 1920s, married women workers were dropping out of the employment pool, discouraged by the government's tendency to reject disproportionately the unemployment claims of married women workers ("double earners"). R. C. Davison notes that between 1925 and 1927 (when a Tory cabinet ruled) the Ministry of Labour turned down twice as many women's unemployment claims as men's: *The Unemployed: Old Policies and New* (London, 1929), pp. 115–18. By 1931, according to Sidney Pollard, many women had simply given up even registering as unemployed, "as they had exhausted their unemployment insurance benefits and considered it unlikely that they would ever be found work again": *The Development of the British Economy, 1914–1967*, 2d ed. (London 1969), p. 243.

[29] The restoration was to be implemented jointly by workers and their employers. Throughout the war, trade union officials had kept records of all process modifications and changes in the "manning" of machines. At the war's end, these records formed the basis for recreating the 1914 status quo, particularly in the area of skill and sex qualifications for specific jobs.

a place inside a ship's boiler before it is cold—one of the many undesirable positions in which women workers have found themselves today.[30]

In the fevered postwar climate, with promises of a heroes' reward for returning veterans issuing from all quarters, not even the women's trade union leaders could articulate a defense of women's right to work on an equal basis with men's. Small wonder, then, that government policy on the demobilization of women reflects no vision of such rights.

Engineering employers were perhaps the most divided about carrying through so complete a restoration, upheld by force of law. Some were reluctant to roll back wartime gains and developments, even if only for a year.[31] But the majority complied readily, "anxious to get their works re-started and fearful of the dislocation of [male] labour that might result from a refusal to implement their pledges."[32] The act was therefore quite widely applied, although the actual "restorations" that followed varied considerably from one region to the next, shaped by local custom and the more immediate pressures of labor demand. At one extreme lay the heavy engineering districts of the northeast (shipbuilding, foundry work), where enthusiasm for a full-scale reversion ran so high that employers occasionally removed women from processes on which they had been employed before the war. By 1920 the

[30] Mary MacArthur, "The Women Trade Unionists' Point of View," in Marion Phillips, ed., *Women and the Labour Party 1881–1932* (London, 1933), p. 24. Employers did not always receive the returning veterans with joy. The wounded "silver badge" men got an especially threadbare welcome, as employers anticipated that these "heroes" might pose problems of discipline and productivity. Even before the war had ended, national factory managers accepted these men only grudgingly, and indicated their opinion in a most revealing way. In 1918, when the Ministry of Munitions asked them to fill out returns indicating the number of workers employed, arranged by age, sex, and skill, some national factory managers listed the silver badge men as women. See IWM, Women's Work Collection, Emp. 70, War Cabinet Committee on Women in Industry, "Minutes of Evidence," testimony of Mr. Bean, manager of five national factories, 28 October 1918, p. D18.

[31] In the autumn of 1919, as the act went into effect, 228 of 764 firms surveyed by the Women's Industrial League indicated that they wished to keep women workers on; 97, fearing union opposition, elected not to do so. The remaining 439 were simply not interested. See *The Times Engineering Supplement,* January 1920, quoted in Braybon, *Women Workers,* p. 184.

[32] "In fact, most of the forms of dilution introduced during the War, while they afforded important lessons for further application to the technique of production, were not suited for direct and immediate application to the forms of normal production to which employers reverted. . . . Restoration was therefore carried through with far less friction than anyone had supposed to be possible. . . . Much to their surprise, the Trades Unions of skilled workers found most of their suspended rules and customs restored to them almost without opposition on the part of the employers": G. D. H. Cole, *Trade Unionism and Munitions* (Oxford, 1923), p. 196. Cole concluded (somewhat prematurely) that wartime conditions had not in fact been favorable to "large new industrial experiments," and that wartime expansion and transformation had been "abnormally rapid but also artificial. . . . Changes in the division and classification of labor . . . which were the results of war demand, did not form the foundation *at once* of a new capitalist era of mass production" (pp. 212–13).

Newcastle engineering industry, for example, employed fewer women than it had in 1913.[33]

At the other end of the spectrum lay firms that declared (and perhaps believed) themselves to be in compliance with the act while openly admitting that they had retained some portion of the women hired since 1914. Thus a Leeds firm that had hired no women before the war reported that in one shop 170 women were now working at "presses, lathes, preparation and soldering oil cans, lamps, etcetera, and they are considered in every way satisfactory." The manager hastened to point out that the presence of these women did not signify failure to comply with the law. On the contrary, though his particular factory had not employed women before the war, women had done similar work in other firms, "so it cannot be said that women are doing men's work, except perhaps in the case of the 'welders.'" Here the manager paused briefly, for welding was generally acknowledged to require some skill. The decision to continue employing women for this work must therefore have represented an especially glaring departure from the prewar order. Yet it, too, could be justified, not only because male welders were in short supply but because the switch from male to female labor had raised the firm's output. From management's point of view, the increase in productivity alone suggested that this work, though clearly skilled, was nonetheless more appropriate to women.[34] Under the rubric of "restoration," the firm had in fact installed a significantly altered sexual division of labor. In some factories, at least, it was already clear that the promised restoration would not survive long past the requisite year.

But whatever an individual employer's long-term goals might be, the government's determined application of the act did have a profound impact on the structure of wages and employment across the industry. After all, the restoration of prewar conditions, though occasionally incomplete, did force a sharp break with wartime practices at the national level. For women metalworkers there could be no continuity between the kinds of jobs and wages attained during the war and those that would be available to them after 1920. This rupture would only facilitate employers' reclassification of women as exclusively cheap and notionally unskilled labor in the metals industries.

A month after the Restoration Act was passed, official figures showed that the economy had at last reabsorbed all able-bodied men. Economists began

[33] Report from Newcastle cited in Adam Kirkaldy, *British Labour, 1914–1921: Replacement and Conciliation* (London, 1921), p. 29. One firm that had employed women as coremakers before the war discharged them all during the restoration.

[34] Report from Leeds, 1920, quoted in Kirkaldy, *British Labour*, p. 30. Even though bound by law to restore the prewar status quo, some employers were already citing local variations in the sexual division of labor to justify expanding their contingent of women workers.

to speak about full recovery, and some even termed it a postwar boom. But for women the picture was far less rosy. Some 579,000 of 819,000 women in munitions had lost their jobs, and at least 60,000 were still applying for the out-of-work benefit—all in the midst of what for men was a period of full employment.[35] After 1921 the demand for women metalworkers would begin to rise. From a postwar nadir of 9.6 percent in 1921 (well above their prewar rate of 5.8 percent) women's overall employment in the industry expanded steadily, reaching 13.4 percent in 1928 and 14.3 percent in 1931.[36] In the meantime, however, women were caught in a shrinking economy where state and industry alike were dedicated to restoring men and women to their prewar niches. Despite their reluctance to return to domestic service and other female employments, one young woman later recalled that such work rapidly became the only option: "I entered into a career of drudgery where long hours, low wages and very often inadequate food were accepted as standards of a life that was thrust on one out of sheer necessity."[37]

But domestic labor, paid or unpaid, was not the only space to which Britain's demobilization returned redundant munitions workers. Equally important was the effect the state's systematic devaluing of women's labor had on the redefinition of women's work in the metalworking industry. Within weeks of the Armistice, officials of the government's Wages and Arbitration Board reported that women were fast retreating to the most ill-paid niches in the industry (brass stamping and other nonmunitions work), often without even stopping to claim the OWD. One official threw up his hands in despair

[35] See M. L. Yates, *Wages and Labour Conditions in British Engineering* (London, 1937), p. 3, for global employment figures, and Kozak, "Women Munition Workers," p. 391, for numbers of workers still claiming the OWD. Contemporary accounts (e.g., Andrews and Hobbes, *Economic Effects*) suggest that these figures drastically underestimate women's real level of unemployment. Indeed, Andrews and Hobbes assert that throughout 1919–20, women's unemployment rates far exceeded those of men. In February 1922, government officials would finally "solve" the problem of women's unemployment by ruling that all married women workers would be excluded automatically from eligibility for the OWD. At the end of the decade, with widespread unemployment a structural feature of the British economy, married women would be excluded from claiming unemployment under the Anomalies Act of 1929. See Susan Pedersen, *Family, Dependence and the Origins of the Welfare State* (Cambridge, 1993), pt. 3. The gendered statistics of employment suggest that with the Armistice came a segregation in demand for male and female labor which produced distinct cycles of employment and unemployment for women and men.

[36] Overall figures conceal gross sectoral and regional disparities. Thus in 1923, when women formed only about 10% of the industry overall, they already accounted for 16% of engineering workers in Greater London, a region of light metals and engineering. Statistics from the Census of Population, cited in Yates, *Wages and Labour Conditions,* p. 3, and from the Census of Production, cited by Miss D. Elliott, negotiator for the National Union of General and Municipal Workers, MRC, EEF, Special Conference, "Women's Wages," London, 19 July 1935, p. 75.

[37] Winifred Foley, "general maid," quoted in John Burnett, *The Annals of Labor* (Bloomington, Ind., 1974), p. 221.

as he watched women accept jobs at starvation wages (7s. 6d. a week in one case, about one-fifth of women's basic rate in munitions): "It is difficult to circumvent this exploitation of the surplus female labour now available if the women themselves under-rate themselves."[38]

Concerned with the long-term effect that such systematic self-underrating might have on wages, this man castigated the women for accepting available work on the only terms offered them. Yet it was precisely the broader context set by the government's gendered demobilization policies that made it possible for engineering employers to impose such terms. By anchoring its demobilization policies in the call for women's rededication to domesticity, the government had created a discursive climate that stressed the need for a return to spheres sharply defined by sex. Government policy thus reinforced employers' own tendency to predicate a link between women's working lives and their duties in the home. This link provided a language for discussing women's work which was wholly separate from the language of wages and skills employed in discussions of men's work. Moreover, it supported the notion that behind each working woman lay her domestic life, constituting both her "real" work and a haven in times of unemployment.

The impact that this kind of reasoning would have on postwar employment policies emerged sharply in two industry-wide debates over the conditions that should govern women's employment. The first session took place in the fall of 1918, when the arms mogul Douglas Vickers convened a committee of engineering employers at the Board of Trade, so that they might discuss women's future in the industry. On the one hand, these men predicted that "there will remain considerable opening for the employment of female labour . . . [for] most employers will be anxious to continue to employ female labour on the lighter repetition work." At the same time, the committee believed that the majority of women would not be "permanently employed . . . [as] marriage has always been, and we trust will always be, a reason for the discontinuance of factory work by women." The solution to this conundrum lay not in excluding women from the industry but rather in making them a permanent source of labor as a class, while treating individuals within that class as temporary workers. Under these conditions, training women for skilled work became an uneconomic proposition by definition: "As marriage will in most cases take them out of engineering work it is of very little use for them to spend time acquiring all-around knowledge at the expense of the increased output attained by confining them to one or a few operations only." Yet in the committee's view, there was nothing burdensome or unfair in so narrowing the scope of women's employment. On the contrary, "it appears also to be

[38] PRO, Lab. 2/1779/MH Est. 1012/2, Wages and Arbitration Dept. Report, West Midlands area, 11 December 1918.

in accordance with their natural inclinations." Moreover, placing the burden of repetitive labor on women's shoulders would "free the boy apprentice for the general work that affords the proper training for the skilled man."[39]

The notion that married women should be employed by exception only laid the groundwork for a second and more protracted debate, in which employers and male trade union leaders wrangled over the level of women's wages and, more broadly, the principles that should govern them. In these struggles, employers' definition of women as primarily domestic beings provided the justification for paying them less than a living wage. By 1921, when the national Engineering Employers' Federation (EEF) finally rolled back women's wages, the reasoning that buttressed the definition of women as exclusively cheap labor was already in place.

The cuts came during the depths of the postwar trade slump that began in December 1920. Spurred by the sudden economic downturn, the EEF moved swiftly to dismantle wartime wage gains for workers of both sexes.[40] Proportionally, however, the reductions exacted a heavier toll on women, whose basic rate tumbled from 43s. 6d. in December 1920 to 36s. in March 1921, landing finally at 24s. in October 1922.[41] As it fell, the male–female differential, a mere 33 percent in 1919, widened steadily. By 1922, employers had reinscribed the gaping inequalities—50 percent or more—that customarily distinguished male and female pay levels.[42] W. T. Kelly of the Workers' Union inveighed bitterly against the cuts, arguing that the revised rate was subminimum and "does not enable a woman to maintain herself at anything like a reasonable standard." But it was employers' underlying principle—that a woman's wage was merely a "supplement" to a family wage—that Kelly

---

[39] PP 1918, Cd. 9073, *Report of the Departmental Committee Appointed by the Board of Trade to Consider the Position of Women in the Engineering Trades after the War*, p. 16.

[40] The wage cuts came in a period of rising unemployment in the traditionally male sectors of the trade, shipbuilding and heavy machinery, where unemployment reached 22.6% and 10.1%, respectively, by 1923, 22.0% and 11.8% by 1925. In the more consumer-oriented branches of electronics and autos, cycles, and aircraft, unemployment fell steadily, from 7.3% (electronics) and 9.7% (autos, etc.) in 1923 to 5.6% and 6.6% by 1925: Yates, *Wages and Labour Conditions*, p. 10. Already the sectors that employed women were proving far more recession-proof than those that employed only men. The automatic exclusion of married women from the unemployment insurance scheme no doubt exaggerates the gender gap in unemployment, but probably not much, given married women's very low participation rate in Britain's interwar economy.

[41] The 43s. 6d., first set in December 1919 (after most women had left their wartime jobs), was the basic time rate for women on work "not recognized as women's work prior to the war." On women's work, the time rate was 41s. 6d. See ibid., p. 155.

[42] Thanks to state intervention, the wage differential had been narrowed to 33% by 1918. State regulation of munitions wages, which was legally extended past the Armistice, finally ended in June 1920. The wage cuts that commenced the following winter widened the gaps between skilled and unskilled and between male and female until, by the fall of 1922, women's basic rate stood at about one-third of a skilled man's rate and just over half of the semiskilled man's rate. See Downs, "Women in Industry," chap. 5 and appendices, and Yates, *Wages and Labour Conditions*, chap. 9, for details on postwar wage adjustments.

denounced most vehemently: "Well, it is not fair. The woman performs work that is essential to the industry, and the woman ought to have a wage that does give her a better chance of maintaining herself properly."[43]

But the EEF was adamant. Women's wages were to be set not by the value of their labor to the industry but according to the laws of supply and demand that ruled female labor, as a generalized entity, across the industrial spectrum: " . . . what are we to do when firms in practically all other industries are taking on women at considerably lower rates of wages. . . . They can get female labour at 25s, 27s, up to 30s a week. . . . It shows you what we are fighting against at the present time."[44] In January 1921 the employers declared that in the miserly minimum rates set by the trade boards (government commissions established to curb abuses in the country's most sweated trades) one found the most reliable guide to the "true" value of female labor.[45] Two months later the EEF revised its women's wage list accordingly. The recommended schedule, which was to govern women's wages until 1935, stipulated a sliding scale, rising from 14s. 8d. a week for a girl of fourteen (8s. plus 6s. 8d. cost-of-living bonus) to 36s. a week for a woman of twenty-one (16s. plus 20s. cost-of-living bonus).[46]

W. T. Kelly continued to protest this unequal treatment, and even urged the employers to abolish women's separate wage base altogether: "Considering the industry and the work the women do . . . you can afford to pay a woman for the work she does."[47] But the employers would not be moved. Throughout the interwar period they continued to structure collective bargaining sessions around the theory that the man's wage was a family wage, set according to the value of his labor to the industry, while the woman's

[43] MRC, EEF, Central Conference, case 6, "Wages of Women Engaged on the Manufacture of Electric Lamps," York, 14 January 1921, pp. 4–5. Trade union representatives rarely put forth demands for equal pay between 1918 and the late 1930s. The equal-pay plan negotiated at Rover in 1930 (discussed in chap. 8) is a notable exception. When the Transport and General Workers' Union finally did demand the rate for the job in 1938, the tactic backfired as soon as the EEF pointed out that a single rate for the job might carry some unpleasant consequences for men. After all, if a woman who did a man's job should receive the man's rate, then was not the converse also true, that a man who did a woman's work should receive the women's rate? The union representative could only reply: "I do not know. Do not ask me." See ibid., Special Conference, "Women's Wages," 10 May 1938, p. 26.

[44] Ibid., case 6, "Wages of Women Engaged on the Manufacture of Electric Lamps," EEF chair speaking, p. 15. At that point, women were still getting 41s. to 43s. 3d. a week in munitions, 31s. 6d. to 36s. 6d. in other metals work.

[45] The Trade Board minimums "are and have been a guide in the assessment of the value of [female] labour": ibid., case 13, "Wages: Proposed New Scheme of Rates for Women and Girls," 14 January 1921, p. 3.

[46] See ibid., Special Conference, "Women's Wages," London, 17 March 1921. The cost-of-living ("bonus") portion of the wage fell sharply as prices tumbled in 1921–22, and women's weekly rate quickly fell to 24s., where it remained until the mid-1930s.

[47] Ibid., p. 5.

wage was a mere supplement, fixed according the general (low) price of women's labor, as determined by the trade boards.

The Reclassification of Labor in France

In the winter of 1918–19, the specter of mass unrest weighed heavily on French officials; more so, even, than on their British counterparts. The tempo of strikes and demonstrations had quickened in the last eighteen months of war.[48] Above all, they feared swelling the crowds of refugees, unemployed, and veterans who thronged the streets that first peacetime winter. "One cannot lay off 500,000 women, most of whom are utterly without resources, without running the risk of severe disturbances, warned the journalist Léon Abensour.[49] In hopes of averting such dangers, Minister Loucheur extended a month's severance pay to each woman who withdrew voluntarily from the state arsenals and returned to her "ordinary peacetime work."[50]

Receipt of the benefit was conditional on leaving the factory by 5 December. Each day a woman remained beyond that date, her severance pay fell by a day's wages. But demobilization was slow in France; men languished in the depots while sisters and wives still had to meet the ever-rising cost of living.[51] By 25 November so few women had quit their jobs that Loucheur was forced to adopt a different tactic: he instituted a five-hour day and spread the work among the thousands who still remained in the arsenals. As the five-hour day effectively halved the women's wages, Loucheur's measure did raise the exit rate, but it hardly cleared the arsenals of female labor. Indeed, women workers seemed not at all inclined to relinquish their jobs. For the first time since war had begun, women could earn wages (admittedly at a lower rate—Fr

---

[48] Police dossiers from the winter of 1918–19 are filled with anxious reports of mass meetings all across Paris in which women workers, "proudly calling themselves Bolshevists," combined protests against the mass firings with fierce revolutionary hopes and "frenetic bravos" for the "revolution that will come from the east": AN, F7, 13356, report on a mass meeting at the Salle Ferrer, 10 January 1919, p. 6. Police spies counted 2,070 women, 400 civilian men, and 30 mobilized women in attendance. See also APP, B/a 1614, report of December 1918, cited in Dubesset et al., "Quand les femmes entrent," p. 368.

[49] Abensour, "Problème de la démobilisation," p. 490.

[50] AN, F7, 13356, "Circulaire aux ouvrières des usines et établissements de l'état travaillant pour la défense nationale," issued by Minister of Armaments/Industrial Reconstitution Louis Loucheur, 13 November 1918. See also Loucheur's circular to industrialists, "Main-d'oeuvre féminine," 25 November 1918, in BUG, 9 December 1918.

[51] Despite increasingly determined wage interventions by the Ministère de l'Armement, the cost of living had raced steadily ahead of wages since 1914. By the end of 1920, the price index (Paris region only) stood at 452 while the index for women's wages had risen to a mere 390 (1914 = 100). Men were even worse off; their wages stood at only 354. See Roger Picard, Le Mouvement syndicale durant la guerre (Paris, 1927), pp. 113–14.

6–9 a day) and still find time for their "second shift" at home. Despite the deep wage cuts, then, Loucheur's demobilization measure simply facilitated continued employment among the many thousands of women who needed the work. At the end of December, anywhere from 20 to 33 percent of women hired during the war remained in the state's employ. The rest had departed, some with severance pay, some without; some to a new job, but many more to unemployment.[52]

Private industry was rarely so solicitous, for with the return of peace, women had become a largely surplus workforce, a burden that most industrialists hastened to shake off. "The employer who took steps to keep his women employed that winter was a rare man indeed," reported Abensour.[53] And although the government had encouraged employers to follow its example and extend women a month's severance pay, most ignored even this modest plea. By mid-December, police reports on the mood in the streets were filled with uneasy comment on the widespread misery caused by this rapid demobilization of women, laid off with no compensation and few prospects of immediate employment:

> The majority of women who have been laid off like this, many of whose breadwinners remain mobilized, are not finding work elsewhere. These women complain bitterly about the painful situation they've been thrown into, especially women from private industry, who were generally laid off without an indemnity.[54]

[52] By the end of December, two-thirds of the women at the Puteaux powder works (outside Paris) had taken their severance pay and left. Those laid off had been weeded out according to a hierarchy of need, with women whose husbands or brothers were working given lowest priority. Single women were the next to be let go, followed finally by women with several dependent children. (In fact, all who fell into the latter category were provided with work until the middle of January.) At Bourges, most women had returned to their former occupations (via the same placement offices set up in 1915), though 2,000 had been kept on in the chemical products division. Some 1,004 of the 1,633 women at the Bouchet powder works (near Versailles) left the works within six weeks of the Armistice. Most returned to their former jobs as field hands. See AN, F7, 13356, report from the Bouchet powder works, 5 January 1919. (The report further notes the reduction in mobilized male labor, from 1,354 to 569. Civilian, Arab, and Chinese men were, for the time being, holding steady at 376, 488, and 278, respectively.) Finally, 2,000 of the 2,500 women employed at Vincennes had left without even consulting the *surintendante*, and there is no evidence that they ever received (or even demanded) any severance pay. The 500 who wished to remain were given work at the arsenal. All figures are from reports by *surintendantes* in the state arsenals, cited in Abensour, "Problème de la démobilisation," p. 491.

[53] Ibid., p. 492. On 12 March 1919 the socialist newspaper *La Vague* reported that when six women workers at Gueret et Cie applied for the indemnity promised by the local labor controller, the director called the police, and four gendarmes came to haul the women off.

[54] AN, F7, 13356, "Licenciement du personnel et chômage dans les usines de guerre," police report from Bordeaux, 11 December 1918, p. 1. J. L. Thaon of the Fédération des Métaux estimated that about 80% of women munition workers had been laid off without an indemnity of any kind. See Dubesset et al., "Quand les femmes entrent," p. 364. Dubesset and her

With husbands and brothers dead, wounded, or still waiting at the depots (demobilization of soldiers lasted well into the following spring), the myth of women's familial haven offered hollow support indeed. As one woman bitterly remarked in April 1919, "I worked for four years in the war factories and I left my health there behind me. . . . My husband is still in the army and I can no longer stand it."[55]

Events at Citroën's Javel plant provide a revealing example of the demobilization "policy" that prevailed in private industry. The firm's long-term strategy was to shut down operations, retool, and then reopen on a peacetime basis. Ostensibly the firm was offering an indemnity (Fr 200–250) to all who would withdraw voluntarily. But the means of evasion were many. In late December one enterprising foreman gathered the women from his shop to warn them that they would be laid off the first week in January. He then added that a corsetmaker on the rue St-Augustin was currently recruiting. The women rushed off, only to discover that the shop in question had few openings. Upon returning to Citroën, they learned that by accepting the foreman's bait to seek work elsewhere, all had forfeited the unemployment indemnity.[56]

Within weeks this unlucky group had been joined by some 5,000 women, most of whom had managed to procure the indemnity, and several thousand men.[57] By February, Citroën's wartime workforce of 11,700, half of whom were women, had been pruned to a skeleton crew of 3,300 men, mostly skilled professionals, who were to convert the shops to peacetime production. Six months later, when the conversion was completed, the firm would hire back several hundred of these women to work on the factory's vast assembly lines.[58] In the meantime, they languished with no work and scant alternative means of support. "For six years my husband has been with the colors. I wore myself to the bone during the war, working at Citroën. There I sweated blood and

---

colleagues found a record of one strike in protest against the mass firing of women: some 1,000 shellmakers in St-Denis stopped work for one day (22 January 1919) to protest the release of their comrades ("most certainly women"). The strike failed and the 1,000 returned to work the next day (p. 366).

[55] A. B. to the Editor, *La Vague*, 22 May 1919, quoted in Dubesset et al., "Quand les femmes entrent," p. 371.

[56] *Le Populaire*, 27 December 1918.

[57] AN, F7, 13356, report on Citroën, 7 January 1919.

[58] These women represented about 10% of the 1919–20 workforce (down from about 50% during the war). Women's participation rate at Citroën would rise to about 14% by the late 1920s: Sylvie Schweitzer, *Des engrenages à la chaîne: Les Usines Citroën, 1915–1935* (Lyon, 1982). Thirty-one percent of these women were skilled, mostly welders and mechanics; 9% were laborers; and 40% were semiskilled "specialists," destined for production work on the firm's great serial production lines. All information from AN, F7, 13367, "Embauche aux usines Citroën," September–December 1919.

lost my youth and my health. Fired in January, I have known only misery. My child and I can afford to eat only bread, as we wait for them to release my husband."[59]

As the demobilization proceeded, similar tales were repeated in firms all across France. During the months that followed the Armistice, everything but labor was in short supply: steel, iron, coal, railway cars. With the abrupt cancellation of war contracts, employers scaled back drastically, sometimes shutting down altogether until times improved, or until the plant had been reconverted. Unemployment soared accordingly. As production slowly resumed on a peacetime basis, employers would recall some of the women they had dismissed so abruptly in 1918–19. By 1921, women would constitute 10 percent of the industry's workforce—twice their participation rate for 1914. In Paris the figures are even more striking, as women's participation in the local metalworking labor force rose from 5 percent in 1914 to 14 percent in 1921. Over the short term, however, the widespread plant closings threw thousands out of work. Once again, as in 1914, the layoffs struck women with especial force. A partial inquiry into unemployment in and around Paris revealed that by the end of April 1919 at least 35 percent of the wartime workforce had been laid off. For women alone, however, the comparable figure was 52 percent.[60]

Ultimately, then, the French "solution" to the problem of peacetime transition combined a swift and chaotic demobilization of women workers with the slower, equally disorganized release of men from the army. By the autumn of 1919, women's unemployment appears to have bottomed out, as firms either halted the dismissals or gradually reopened their doors.[61] But the dislocation had been sharp and severe, and in its own way it provided a break from wartime conditions as clean as the one occasioned by Britain's formal "restoration of prewar practices." In the absence of any such covenants, French employers could more freely declare their intent to continue employing "all orderly, dextrous, and docile women" on light assembly, machining, and mass-production work.[62] At the same time, however, they no longer had to concern themselves with training or deploying skilled women workers, and

[59] Mme Martin to the Editor, *La Vague*, 22 May 1919.

[60] Men's unemployment, then, must have been considerably less than 35%. See *BMT,* November–December 1918, pp. 548–51; and Dubesset et al., "Quand les femmes entrent," p. 370.

[61] One *surintendante* reported that after a precipitous drop from 1,440 in September 1918 to 400 in the fall of 1919, the number of women had stabilized and "the retooled workshops will employ women"; another reported that her firm intended to keep on all remaining women and children for its peacetime operations: UIMM 69/54/13, untitled report, fall 1919, p. 1.

[62] AN, F22, 534, Ministère de l'Armement, Comité du Travail Féminin, "Enquête sur l'organisation des crèches," March–April 1918, response from Ateliers Morin (precision instruments). This particular factory intended to deploy women on drilling and small assembly work.

this rupture with wartime practices facilitated employers' downward reclassification of women.[63]

But employers did not hatch their postwar production schemes in a discursive vacuum. Here, as in England, state policies and a broader public concern with the shape of postwar society played key roles, creating a discursive matrix within which metals employers reclassified labor and redistributed jobs accordingly. Of course, there were some important differences. French policy makers presumed that women would continue to work outside the home, and so focused on fostering a healthy relationship between factory and household. British officials, by contrast, behaved as though the woman worker were the unfortunate exception, and organized demobilization policies accordingly. But in both nations, government plans for postwar reconstruction established a discursive context in which the downward classification of women metalworkers would strike no one as particularly odd or significant. Indeed, the very act of reclassification—tightening the boundaries of women's labor, then slashing wages within these newly narrowed confines—dovetailed smoothly with the broader notion of wholesale return to the "natural" divisions that had structured prewar society. Consequently, employers were seen to be (and understood themselves to be) reconstructing gender-appropriate divisions at work. No one could see that the reclassification was in fact a moment of active creation, in which metals employers drew on their wartime experience (narrowly interpreted) to construct a new class of labor, unseen before 1914.

The discourse on restoration in postwar France stressed national recovery above all. The idea of regeneration, of rebuilding the devastated land and restoring lost population, formed a powerful core theme in postwar France, and one that was simply not present in Britain. France had endured greater wartime suffering and loss than any other combatant nation (with the possible exception of Belgium). At least 10.5 percent of the active male population had perished, compared with 5.1 percent for Britain, and a further 6.6 percent (at least) were so grievously injured that they could not hope to return to any kind of normal civilian life.[64] In addition, Germany's extraordinarily brutal occupation of the northeast, followed by a scorched-earth retreat in 1918, had

---

[63] This does not mean that employers were uniformly prepared to waste the women trained during the war. When the Comité du Travail Féminin surveyed firms in the Paris region, the management of Henri Lepaute (general engineering) declared: "It would actually profit us to retain the . . . semiskilled women [drillers, welders, cutters] if postwar production allows it": ibid.

[64] See Dyer, *Population and Society,* esp. p. 40; and Sauvy, *Histoire économique,* esp. 1: 21. The loss of so many young men had cut an already low birth rate (18.2 per 1,000 before the war) by half: by 1916 it stood at an all-time low of 9.5 per 1,000. Because the nation was slow to demobilize, the birth rate hardly rose with the return of peace: in 1919 it had risen to a bare 12.6 per 1,000. Only in the early 1920s did the French experience a mini–baby boom. See Dyer, *Population and Society,* p. 50.

left this once-rich region starving and in ruin.[65] Across the rest of France, fevered wartime production had run down plant and equipment. Active reconstruction was thus the order of the day. Unless the nation could reverse its historic "Malthusian" restraint, economically and reproductively, it would remain forever scarred by the losses of war.

Economists had long linked France's slow economic development to the sluggish birth rate, which made for low demand. Yet most of the prewar agitation for population increase had come from a vocal minority concerned with the social and military implications of continued demographic decline. By 1918, however, anxieties about "disappearing France" were no longer confined to an activist fringe. The devastating experience of war against a more prolific neighbor seemed to bear out the pro-natalists' grim forebodings. With the unsurprising news that deaths had outnumbered births throughout the final years of fighting, the long-standing fears of a minority moved to the center of public discourse.[66] Each time a feminist spoke hopefully of new civil and political rights to be granted in grateful recognition of women's wartime service, some pro-natalist stood ready to remind her that those rights belonged only to those who had paid their "blood tax" through the "horrors and suffering of childbirth." In a demographically conscious nation, women's social and political status should rest solely on prolific motherhood:

> What is woman's highest duty . . . the sacred task that the Nation expects from her? To bear children, bear them again, always to bear children. . . . If a woman says no to maternity, if she limits or suppresses it, then she no longer merits her rights; she is nothing . . . the price of the woman is the child . . . goal of life, honor, the only raison d'être of the woman.[67]

Though few took so narrow a view of women's social duties, pro-natalism acquired new salience in public debate as politicians and bureaucrats urged the nation to develop simultaneously both industry and the birth rate. Widely perceived as the most serious obstacles to a strong recovery, these two "Malthusian" questions were often viewed as twin aspects of a single problem. Ultimately, industrialists would entwine the two, linking Taylorist solutions to the problem of industrial productivity with pro-natalist answers to the birth-rate crisis. Women workers were to figure prominently in both schemes;

---

[65] See Duncan Gallie, *Social Inequality and Class Radicalism in France and Britain* (Cambridge, 1982), pp. 229–30, for an account of the devastation in the northeast.

[66] The law of 1920 banning birth control and abortion testifies to the broad fears of *dénatalité* in postwar France. See Mary Louise Roberts, *Civilization without Sexes: Reconstructing Gender in Postwar France, 1917–1927* (Chicago, 1994).

[67] Jacques Doléris and Jean Bouscatel, *Hygiène et morales sociales: Néo-malthusianisme, maternité et féminisme: Education sexuelle* (Paris, 1918), pp. 22–23.

indeed, throughout the 1920s employers would strive to combine the two into a single productivist strategy, aimed specifically at their female workforce:

> The woman worker . . . must be seen as the mother of future generations and the need to command a good output from her must not proceed at the expense of the birth rate. It is also part of a sound Taylorist policy to study the forms of work that are possible during pregnancy and nursing . . . in order to set a maximum level of fatigue and effort.[68]

During those years of extreme scarcity, the felt need to draw simultaneously on women's productive and reproductive capacities was so great that even those who took a conservative view of women's and men's social roles rarely suggested that women leave paid work altogether:

> For the health of the race and an increase in the birth rate, it is important not to perpetuate women's sojourn in the industries that exhaust them. . . . Among the jobs to which they should return are the fabrication of telephonic and telegraphic material, silkworking, the ribbon trade, garment making, luxury industries.[69]

Light metalworking (telephones, telegraphs) passed easily, almost imperceptibly into the realm of "traditional" feminine trades, harmonizable with women's reproductive duties.[70]

From the outset, then, French employers were thinking about national restoration and recovery in very different ways from their British colleagues,

---

[68] Commandant Emile-Auguste-Léon Hourst, *Le Problème de la main-d'oeuvre: La Taylorisation et son application aux conditions industrielles de l'après-guerre* (Paris, 1917), p. 57. Hourst, director of a state arsenal near Paris, was in peacetime a director of the Michelin tire factory.

[69] Georges Renard, quoted in Abensour, "Problème de la démobilisation," p. 497.

[70] Even industrialists who opined that all women should return to home and hearth were rarely prepared to make personal sacrifices for the sake of the broader social principle. At Bonvillain et Ronceray, whose management expressed formal dedication to the idea of returning women to the home, "except for those special cases who urgently need to work," all fifty-eight women hired during the war remained at the forges: AN, F22, 534, Comité du Travail Féminin, "Enquête." The twenty-two industrialists who responded to the survey accounted for only 8,138 of the 100,000 women working in the local metals industries. Two of these employers were unable to predict what they might do with their women workers and another planned to close his factory altogether unless he received new orders. Of the remaining nineteen, all ten who had employed women before the war intended to continue to do so, and four planned to employ at least as many as they had employed during the war. The other six in this group planned to keep two to four times as many women as they had employed *before* the war. Seven others that had hired no women before 1914 now planned to keep all or at least half of those taken on during the war. Finally, four of the twenty-two respondents had invested in retaining women by constructing nursing rooms on the premises, while Bréguet planned to develop courses to train skilled women in industrial design. See Downs, "Women in Industry," chap. 5.

especially when it came to women workers. After all, married women had long worked outside the home in France, and wartime slaughter had exacerbated the shortage of labor. Under these conditions, it made little sense to advocate women's "return" to domesticity. As one metal employer asserted: "It would be a very poor use of national [resources] to see male workers return to . . . jobs to which women could easily adapt themselves . . . work at metal presses, cutting machines, and at lathes on pieces light enough for women to handle easily." Such a radical revision of the sexual boundary was dictated not only by necessity but also by the cost-cutting logic of market rationality: "Within the limits allowed by the market for male and female labor, it will always be advantageous to replace male workers with females wherever woman's physical strength and her physiological characteristics permit it, and to reserve to men only the roughest jobs."[71]

In a nation whose industry had traditionally relied on women's labor power, industrialists could speak (and reason) far more straightforwardly than their British colleagues about their intent to continue to employ women. Even as they retooled their factories for peacetime production, men such as Citroën were already planning for the very specific role that women, conceived as a distinct kind of labor, would play in the redivided labor process:

> There are a number of . . . long mass-production series . . . small automobiles, bicycles, sewing machines, parts for railways and general locomotion; agricultural machine parts; and finally much of the handling of light pieces, which was done by men before the war and can henceforth be confined to women. . . . Far from planning to diminish their number, we fear a shortage of female labor.[72]

For the sake of the industry, employers agreed, the goal was not to banish women workers, married or single. Rather, one had to ensure an adequate supply, assuming they could be hired at an "economic" level of wages. Low pay was, after all, one of the defining features of female labor, and in the spring of 1918, employers hinted darkly at the shape of things to come in the event that the high wages granted in the heady wartime economy failed to fall: "At the current rates of women's wages in our industry, it is to our advantage to replace a large number of women with men," warned the management of the Société Industrielle des Téléphones. Yet at the same time, the firm announced that it would continue to employ all 297 women hired during the war. Further, in order to retain these workers, management planned to maintain the tiny nursing room that the factory had opened during the

[71] Hourst, *Problème de la main-d'oeuvre*, pp. 55, 53.
[72] Quoted in Absensour, "Problème de la démobilisation," pp. 499–500.

war.[73] It seems the threat to replace women was more in the nature of a declaration of principle: that women's future in the industry rested on the return of their wages to an "economic" level. In June 1919 GIMM hastened to meet this latter condition with new wage lists that restored that "economic" level by widening the male–female wage gap from 18 percent in 1918 to at least 30 percent.[74]

At those prices, Citroën was not alone in fearing a postwar shortage of women. Throughout the Paris region, industrialists anticipated difficulty in attracting and retaining sufficient numbers of women. During that first peacetime winter, firms were already pondering how they might reduce turnover among these workers—a perennial issue in this largely seasonal trade.[75] The management of the Ateliers Morin (precision instruments) planned to maintain the amenities and social services developed during the war: "cloakrooms, washrooms, meals taken in the workshop, in order to be certain of retaining the necessary [female] labor." Other firms (Vedovelli autos, the Société Industrielle des Téléphones) hoped that their factory nursing rooms would attract additional women workers. Still others believed that the "English week" would satisfy the women and so keep turnover at a minimum.[76]

For France, it seemed, the road to recovery lay not in exiling women from their newfound occupations but in finding a formula for the harmonious reconciliation of home and work. The broader discourse on national regeneration played a crucial part in organizing this radical shift in the sexual division of labor. It was a discourse crossed by at least two contradictory currents, as politicians and pundits alike advocated embracing modernity while recovering the stabler outlines of a more rural/artisanal (and fertile) France gone by. This Janus-faced vision produced some remarkable prescriptions for blending renewed prosperity with the regeneration of a healthier social organism. In one journalist's happy fantasy, the spread of electrification might permit the "reconstitution of the family workshop," a more "natural" setting in which the current "labor problem"—a shortage of men and debilitat-

---

[73] AN, F22, 534, Comité du Travail Féminin, "Enquête." Dard (small metal parts) also linked women's continued employment to wages ("It all boils down to wages"); Pillon et Cie (harness parts) announced that after the war "we expect to be able to employ 50% of our female labor force [i.e., 15 of the 27 employed in 1918] on the basis of 'equal pay for equal work.' "

[74] According to the final settlement between GIMM and the Fédération des Métaux, women were to receive a minimum of Fr 10.50 per day, unskilled men Fr 15, semiskilled men Fr 16.50, and skilled men Fr 18: UIMM, 39/21/01, "Projet Définitif," 23 June 1919. Women's rates would fan out a bit in the 1920s. See Downs, "Women in Industry," appendices.

[75] Especially autos and auto accessories, which closed for a few weeks near the end of each summer to retool for the new models. But airplanes and lamps seem to have observed an August closing as well. See Herrick Chapman, *State Capitalism and Working-Class Radicalism in the French Aircraft Industry* (Berkeley, 1991); and Ecole des Surintendantes, report from the Lampes Iris factory, 1923.

[76] AN, F22, 534, Comité du Travail Féminin, "Enquête."

ing competition between the sexes—could find resolution in a more "rational [that is, domestically structured] collaboration of male and female."[77] Throughout the 1920s, as the nation struggled to rebuild and repair its losses, "restoration" came to mean joining fecund motherhood with paid labor in new ways.

Redefining Skill, Reconfiguring the Workforce

Despite cultural and political differences and a growing divergence in their nations' economic condition, by the early 1920s metals employers on both sides of the Channel were deploying women workers according to remarkably similar principles. This structural similarity was forged in part from the common experience of war, from the shared exigencies of war production, and from the parallel organizations created to relieve them. But it emerged with startling force after 1919, as the common constraints of war melted in the reversion to peacetime practices. At this point, the two national histories, bound together by military alliance and a common economic fate, inexorably pulled apart once again. To cite but the most obvious example, the French economy blossomed after 1920, as industrial output grew at the unprecedented rate of 5 percent a year between 1924 and 1929.[78] During those same years, the British watched their staple industries sink into a recession that deepened yearly; at no point did the official unemployment figures ever drop below one million.[79]

As national particularity once again overtook the two economies, it is all the more striking to see the emergence of a common logic governing the restratification of the workforce in the two nations. Even as employers pared back their wartime workforces and reconverted tools and plant, they were restratifying labor in accordance with their understandings of the applicability of wartime technical innovations to peacetime production and of the ability of women to cope with new processes and machinery. The hierarchical and sexually divided structures that were to emerge in the early 1920s reflect a sharply restricted notion of women's "place" in the labor process, far narrower than women's wartime performance would dictate. Clearly, employers could assimilate only part of their wartime experience into their postwar plans

[77] Auguste Pawlowski, "La Main-d'oeuvre féminine pendant la guerre," *Revue Politique et Parlementaire* 10 (May 1917): 253–54. In addition, women would work "more happily if they were able to work alongside their husbands."
[78] Kuisel, *Capitalism and the State*, p. 84. This figure is double the already strong prewar rate—a steady 2.4% since 1896. See Sauvy, *Histoire économique*, and William Oualid and Charles Gide, *Le Bilan de la guerre pour la France* (Paris, 1931).
[79] Derek Aldcroft, *The Interwar Economy: Britain, 1919–39* (New York, 1970).

for recovery and renovation. Indeed, convictions of gender difference, as formulated within the evolving discourse on skill, dictated that they neglect one part of that experience (women as skilled labor) and build solely on the other. Ultimately, the newly gendered discourse on skill would provide metals employers with a rationale for altering the sexual division of labor—first for expelling women, then for recalling them on a highly segregated basis.

As employers redrew the horizontal boundaries that divided the labor process, they sought to locate the new female workforce along the existing, if now rather fluid, scale of skills. Though some interesting differences emerge in the French and British discourses on female skill, the similarities are striking. Employers strove to define women's particular qualities in all three arenas of work—skilled, semiskilled, and unskilled. Yet it was that rare creature, the fully skilled woman metalworker, who drew the most attention in the contests that raged over women's presence in the industry, the shifting content of job skill, and men's prior right to well-paid work. In their debates with skilled men over the rights and capacities of this minority, employers defined the limits of women's capacities as metalworkers. Furthermore, these debates reveal skilled men and employers both deploying the gendered language of skill to contain the threat of women empowered by skill itself and by the wages and shop-floor authority it carried.

Highly skilled women were thus prominent in the gendered discourse on skill after 1914. But the actual process of specifying and elaborating managerial conceptions of women's particular nature as a source of labor power took place on the less volatile terrain of semi- and unskilled work, where the vast majority of women metalworkers toiled. In this rapidly expanding realm of work one sees employers constructing a new, gendered language in which to discuss the kinds of capacities that these new forms of work required. By the early 1920s, employers had placed the semi- or unskilled woman worker in a niche of her own, distinct from that of the semi- or unskilled man. Whereas the handful of truly skilled women were interchangeable with their male counterparts by virtue of the fact that they performed the same tasks, most women metalworkers, though sharing a common designation (as semi- or unskilled labor) with their male colleagues, performed work that was classed not only by skill but also by gender.

The Asymmetries of Gender Complementarity

Throughout the war, employers had tried to identify women as a source of labor power by consulting the sociobiological "facts" of women's essential nature. These facts were constructed at the mental confluence of observation and prior conviction about the nature of gender differences. In other words, employers interpreted what women workers did in light of what they already believed to be true of women in general and of working-class women in particular. Thus French and British employers alike observed that women "work more carefully and more regularly [than men] . . . for women's precision of movement and visual acuity are superior."[80] Their "delicate fingertips" allowed them to excel at "jobs requiring quick and delicate manipulation"; indeed, on such jobs women consistently outproduced men.[81]

In the fragmented work process, where each person made only one small part of a final product, workers were no longer defined by what they produced—wood and metals for men, clothing for women, as the nineteenth-century French adage would have it—but by their movements on the line or at the machine.[82] As we shall see, metals employers soon came to believe that there was something inherently feminine about repetitive motion itself; indeed, employers regarded speed, dexterity, and regular, precise motions as specific to women, qualities whose origin, shape, and meaning were to be found in the household division of labor. Hence, when employers looked at women before their lathes, they did not see individuals, held to a new level of precision and regularity in motion by the unprecedented automatism of the new American machine tools. Rather, they believed they were looking at something they had seen before: women engaged in the timeless rhythms of household labor.

> The machines that the women operate function similarly to the men's but seem to run more continuously, at a more regular rhythm, because of the gentleness of women's movements, and because of their vigilance. There remains a housewife in every woman turning shells at the lathe, and women produce metal parts as they do sweaters.[83]

Whether the employer sought the explanation in the iron laws of physiology or in women's "universal" domestic function, he arrived at the same result: although women had rarely worked in this industry before the war, it was not really surprising, in fact entirely natural, that such creatures should consistently outproduce men on light repetition work.[84] Reasoning by analogy, employers

[80] Hourst, *Problème de la main-d'oeuvre* p. 55.

[81] Munitions employer from Leeds; quoted in Kirkaldy, *Industry and Finance*, pp. 87, 129–30. See also IWM, War Cabinet Committee on Women in Industry, "Minutes of Evidence," testimony of Major Ovans, 28 October 1918, p. D21.

[82] "To the man, woodworking and metals; to the woman, the family and clothing": nineteenth-century French adage, quoted in Schweitzer, *Des engrenages à la chaîne*, p. 56. The line that separated women's work from men's in nineteenth-century France was thus less a private-public divide than a distinction based on the resistance of the material being transformed.

[83] Gaston Rageot, *La Française dans la guerre* (Paris, 1918), p. 4.

[84] "On certain tasks, the output of a girl is greater than any average man could accomplish. Jobs requiring quick and delicate manipulation of the fingers are essentially women's jobs": a munitions employer from Birmingham, quoted in Kirkaldy, *Industry and Finance*, pp. 129–30.

arrived at an assessment of women's capacities which moved back and forth between the factory floor, where the idiom of gender difference was technical (women's accuracy and precision), and the domestic, broadly conceived as the realm of traditional female employment, inside the home and out.

Women seemed destined for deskilled production work not only by their "natural" endowment of speed and dexterity but by personal inclination as well; when employed on piecework, as nearly all women were, they proved exceptionally eager to earn as much as possible. One French employer observed: "Women produce to the extent their strength permits, in order to earn as much as possible."[85] They did not follow the example of their male colleagues and seek to control shop conditions by limiting output, nor did they resist the monotony of long production runs; on the contrary, the fewer variations in the work, the greater opportunity for earning production bonuses.

Employers in both nations were repeatedly struck by women's drive and capacity for hard work: "As soon as one pays them well, one gets more from women than he could from any man," remarked the director of the Loire iron works.[86] His British colleagues put it more bluntly: "Pay a woman by the piece and she'll work like the devil."[87] Women's zealous response to wage incentives led one French labor inspector to comment, with some acerbity, that "woman is thrifty, she is like an ant. Offer her a production bonus and you can work her to the point of complete exhaustion."[88]

Metals employers acknowledged that women would tolerate and even welcome the routine of a long, unvarying production series in order to keep their earnings high: "Girls who are paid by results prefer being on a job which runs all the week to having their work changed at frequent intervals."[89] Yet they persistently identified women's unflagging pace and apparent "love of routine" as natural features of female labor, not as the predictable outcome of their near-universal employment on piecework at half to two-thirds of the male rate. Skilled women's vigorous repudiation of the mind-numbing labor of their less-skilled sisters reminds us that, given the choice (as few women and many men were), women were no more "naturally" drawn to repetition work than men. One woman declared, "No wages would compensate me for

[85] AN, 94 AP, 348. "Note II: Le Recrutement de la main-d'oeuvre féminine," p. 2.

[86] Ibid. Another employer declared: "I would gladly replace all the men with women. [They are] more assiduous at their work and more eager to earn" (pp. 1–2).

[87] Birmingham munitions employer, quoted in Kirkaldy, *Industry and Finance*, p. 15.

[88] Marcel Frois, *La Santé et le travail des femmes pendant la guerre* (Paris, 1926), p. 43. Frois was a labor inspector for the Ministry of Armaments.

[89] A Birmingham munitions manufacturer, quoted in Kirkaldy, *Industry and Finance*, p. 129. This employer felt that repetition work had its own interest and incentives: "The monotony of repetition work is dispelled by the interest of counting results, of vying with the other operators, and of beating previous records."

having to grind away all day on a piece-work job, however skilled, doing one operation time and again, and no chance of learning new work, instead of the variety and interest got upstairs [in the air pump shop]."[90]

Women's excellence on repetition work was balanced by a presumed timidity and lack of initiative. Some employers judged women quite harshly for this alleged deficiency:

> Women are able to examine pieces as long as they're always the same, where all that's called for is a repetitive action, and not some initiative or understanding. It's like the stitches in their crocheting and lacemaking. But one must never demand an impromptu or unexpected vigilance from them; women draw parallels, they compare, but they are incapable of inventive thought.[91]

One employer concluded that women lathe workers were the factory analogue of those individuals who had learned to drive a car without ever mastering its inner workings: they "are incapable of handling an accident, if there is the slightest problem with the machine. They need a mechanic behind them."[92] Of course, semi- and unskilled men were no more capable of handling shop-floor "accidents," and often appeared equally diffident in the face of a jammed or malfunctioning machine. Yet employers interpreted their behavior as arising simply from ignorance. That same diffidence, when encountered in women, was recast as an appropriately feminine "passivity"; it sprang less from their unfamiliarity with the work than from that same gentle feminine nature which permitted them to turn shells with such rapid regularity at the lathe, "produc[ing] metal parts as they do sweaters."

Clearly, employers who invested in training women for skilled work did not feel that lack of ambition was an incurable condition of the species. In fact, one group of British employers used domestic analogies to argue that if women were only given the chance, they too could develop initiative, ambition, and a willingness to undertake responsibility: "It was evident from the extent to which [women] employed . . . these qualities . . . in their homes that they were not without them . . . given encouragement, they developed them in industry to a remarkable extent."[93] But the vast majority of employers, French and British alike, believed that lack of initiative defined female labor as a class; indeed, this passivity was the counterpart of their widely touted

---

[90] IWM, Department of Printed Books, Joan Williams, "A Munition Worker's Career at Messrs. G, 1915–1919," p. 40.

[91] Pierre Hamp (labor inspector), quoted in Dubesset et al., "Quand les femmes entrent," p. 91.

[92] AN, 94 AP, 348, unnamed employer quoted in "Note II: Le Recrutement de la main-d'oeuvre féminine," p. 3.

[93] Birmingham munitions manufacturer, quoted in Kirkaldy, *Industry and Finance*, p. 15.

ability to outperform men on light repetitive labors, "jobs that men would not tolerate."[94]

This presumed lack was not always seen as a drawback. Some industrialists—many of them men who intended to retain the more fragmented and mechanized labor process in which repetition work figured so prominently—found in women's alleged lack of initiative the wellspring of feminine excellence on the rationalized factory floor. Untroubled by men's grasping ambition, women could focus on the task at hand, no matter how dull. As one French employer put it, "A semiskilled man dislikes his work to the point where he does it as badly as would a less skilled man. By contrast, a woman, no matter how skilled, brings a constant level of attention to her work."[95] Whether they greeted women's alleged lack of initiative as inevitable or curable, vice or virtue, few doubted that the sex was in part defined by precisely this lack. Women's excellence on repetition work was the product both of what they were (swift and dexterous) and of what they were not (imaginative and ambitious).

Employers thus concluded that women's patient execution of rapid, detailed work sprang from some set of qualities intrinsic in women, and not from the structures of mass production into which new workers, male and female, were slotted. Further, the naturalization of women as repetition workers went hand in hand with employers' insistence that men were particularly unsuited to these new forms of work; the male's restless drive and imagination—the very qualities that made good skilled mechanics of (some) men—interfered with the ability of his less skilled brother to execute repetition work satisfactorily. Thus, while inexperienced workers of both sexes were initially placed on simple repetition jobs, employers declared a distinct preference for women: "It is far more simple to find qualified women than to find qualified men who, for the same wage, are at best capable of simple laboring."[96]

In staking out entire classes of repetition work as women's domain, employers distinguished the labor of unskilled women from that of unskilled men, assigning to women the "light operations that involve light fingering and that sort of thing," and reserving all "physical work" for men. "If [fuses and

[94] AN, 94 AP, 348, French employer quoted in "L'Oeuvre," an inquiry by Ennemande Diart. British employers similarly observed that "men . . . will not stand by a machine pressing all their lives but a woman will": IWM, War Cabinet Committee Minutes, testimony of Major Ovans, p. D33.

[95] AN, 94 AP, 348, M. Painvin, director of the Loire works, quoted in "Note II: Le Recrutement de la main-d'oeuvre féminine," p. 5. He further speculated that this happy circumstance arose from a woman's education, "which teaches her to perform monotonous work and, perhaps, to let her mind travel while her fingers fly."

[96] M. Lallemand, "Note sur les avantages et les inconvénients résultant de l'emploi des femmes comme pontonnières," Bulletin de l'Inspection du Travail et de l'Hygiène Industrielle, 1929, p. 253.

detonators] are made on capstans [semi-automatic lathes] she will do three times the work a man will do. . . . [On] fuse work, where you have a number of tiny parts, girls' fingers will do that and manage it far better than a man, whose fingers are stiff and clumsy."[97] By the end of the war, a distinction in types of work had become a distinction located in the workers themselves. Unskilled women had been defined as a "somewhat more delicate class of unskilled labor,"[98] and employers enshrined this distinction in a sexual division of labor that assigned women and unskilled men wholly different tasks. Unskilled men were employed on heavy laboring work—lifting and carrying loads, delivering materials to the line, cleaning heavy equipment—whereas unskilled women were invariably placed on simpler forms of machine or assembly work. If the unskilled man were to be promoted, his first step up would be to undertake the very machine work that "unskilled" women routinely performed. Nonetheless, this technical distinction found no expression in the wage structure. In Britain, women rarely earned more than half the unskilled male rate; in France, women's wages reached about 75 to 80 percent of the unskilled male level after 1925.[99] In both nations, employers justified the gap by their conviction that "normal" women, as dependent wives and daughters, had access to male wages, and so had no need to earn such rates themselves.

Yet where male workers were concerned, employers rarely invoked workers' needs as a basis for setting rates. Rather, they based wages explicitly on their assessment of the individual's worth to the firm. But in fact the wages of both women and men were grounded in a prior assessment of the skills and attributes that pertained to each class of labor, and it was at this level that women were delimited as a class apart. Employers in both nations were convinced that women's "natural" endowment included the technical capacity to accomplish, without training, tasks that lay beyond the reach of unskilled men. As their capacity came from "nature," and not from any program of apprenticeship, surely it should not be rewarded on the same basis as the hard-won skills of the male. The invocation of women's presumed lesser need for wages thus formed a rhetorical shield that masked a gendered distinction made at the moment when skills were assessed, and so rationalized and justified the unequal basis on which women and men were paid for similar work. Thus employers could see that when untrained women entered the factory, they were capable of executing jobs that untrained men could not. Moreover, they perceived that this facility was somehow related to the fact that under the

[97] IWM, War Cabinet Commitee Minutes, October 1918, testimony of Melville Smith, p. D67; of Major Ovans, p. D39; and of EEF, p. F60.
[98] AN, 94 AP, 348, "Note II: Le Recrutement de la main-d'oeuvre féminine," p. 3.
[99] See Downs, "Women and Industry," for detailed wage surveys over the period 1914–39 and a discussion of Britain's significantly wider wage gap.

broader social division of labor obtaining at that time, girls were trained to use their hands for household crafts—knitting, embroidering, lacemaking, sewing. But they seemed unable to separate these capacities from women's "eternal" (and unitary) being, and so naturalized their skills as qualities that women, as women, carried with them into the factory. This chain of reasoning fitted skilled work less easily, as workers of both sexes had to gain their training and experience after they entered the factory, before the employer's very eyes.

Women and Skill in the Stratified Labor Force

The classification of women as a source of skilled labor power took place in the context of the broader redefinition and specification of (male) job skill after 1914. As we have seen, dilution/rationalization was no simple, one-way process of deskilling. Rather than exerting a uniform downward pressure on skill levels throughout the industry, the mechanization and reorganization of work reconfigured skill, enhancing the skills of some men even as it decomposed and destroyed those of others. Repeated redivisions of labor gradually recast the role of the skilled craftsman, as employers progressively withdrew these men from directly productive work and reserved them for jobs as foremen or in the toolroom. Their broad knowledge of a variety of machines and processes made such men indispensable for the repair and regulation of an ever-expanding and increasingly complex range of semi-automatic machine tools.[100]

The same partial disaggregation of craftwork that redefined the role of skilled craftsmen also created a wide spectrum of repetition work, some of which demanded considerable technical address and some training and experience on the job as well. These skilled repetition jobs called for tremendous accuracy and judgment, as well as strength, precision, and dexterity in manipulating a variety of hand (as opposed to machine) tools.[101] It took several weeks simply to learn how to manipulate the gauges, micrometers, and hand tools required to make minute adjustments in the shape and dimensions of a metal part or tiny screw hole. It then took many more weeks, sometimes months on the job, before a worker would develop the "strong arm [and] delicate touch" without which she would lose control of the machine and damage

---

[100] In 1931 Sir H. Llewelyn Smith observed that "the skill required of both toolmakers and toolsetters is said to be on a higher plane, if more specialised, than that of craftsmen under the older type of production": *The New Survey of London Life and Labour*, vol. 2 (London, 1931), p. 135.

[101] The hand-vs.-machine distinction was very important in determining the level of skill involved.

both tool and shell.[102] Change in the labor process thus gave rise to a new technical distinction on the factory floor. Alongside the traditional, all-around "jobbing" work of craftsmen appeared the new category of skilled repetition: work that demanded skills of a more narrowly job-specific nature.[103]

This emerging distinction cut across older conceptions of skill, carving out and delimiting something entirely new that was then set in complementary relation to the older, craft forms of skill. But it was the employers who, in the course of elaborating new strategies for deploying labor in a reorganized labor process, placed the stamp of gender difference on this technical distinction, contrasting the "technical and initiative" skills of craftsmen with the "habituated, imitative skills" of women: "Women's specialized training was not designed to produce expert . . . craftsmen. . . . The object was to train women to a complete knowledge of only one machine or group of machines . . . thus . . . constituting habituated or imitative skill and not a technical or initiative skill."[104]

In the employer's mind, the qualities that made a good all-around skilled worker were diametrically opposed to those needed for efficient and steady performance on skilled repetition work. By the end of the war, these two types of skill had been defined in mutually exclusive and highly gendered terms:

> All work requires skill, but the skill required for repetition work is very much easier to acquire than the skill necessary for jobbing work. . . . You will have to have a very high class workman for jobbing work, making the gauges, the jigs, and what is wanted to enable repetition work to be done cheaply and quickly. A woman is ideal for repetition work and I call it women's work.[105]

While their descriptions of women's "highly skilled" repetition work sound remarkably like accounts of semiskilled men's work, employers adamantly refused to conflate the two categories. They preferred to gender the two forms of skill and treat them as complementary. Hence some (skilled) men

---

[102] Barbara Drake, *Women in the Engineering Trades: A Problem, a Solution, and Some Criticism* (London, 1917), p. 44.

[103] Employers and government officials were most apt to perceive the skilled nature of this work when it appeared in the context of entirely new industries, where technical and gender divisions of labor had not yet hardened into the fixed strata that ruled other branches of the engineering trade. Thus in June 1917, Gordon Campbell, director of the Women's Wages Section of the Ministry of Munitions, observed that the job of welder in the aircraft industry was a skilled one. Although a male welder might have a wider range of experience than his female counterpart, it was nonetheless "impossible to hold that all the work done by women is semi-skilled and not fully skilled work": PRO, Mun. 4/2213/MF 560, memo, 5 June 1917.

[104] PRO, Mun. 1/1276, T. Z. Zimmerman, "Report on the Training of Munitions Workers in Great Britain," 30 August 1917, pt. 2. Zimmerman was managing editor of London's business magazine *System*.

[105] IWM, War Cabinet Commitee Minutes, EEF testimony, p. F43.

were blessed with the exclusively male capacity to perform a broad range of work from start to finish, to move from one job to the next without missing a beat. The ambition, curiosity, and imagination that made these men into all-around mechanics—their "inherent" male predisposition to tinker with machines—rendered them incapable of delivering the sustained, concentrated effort needed to perform rapidly work requiring high levels of dexterity and manual expertise. By the same token, women's widely lauded excellence on the most delicate and highly skilled repetition tasks sprang not only from their uniquely feminine gifts of dexterity and concentration but also from that which women definitionally lack: initiative, ambition, and that "instinctive genius and love for machinery."[106] In the employer's eye, women's skill at repetitive labor was integrally related to their presumed inability to bond with machinery.

The two kinds of skill thus define two completely different and opposing human natures. The repetition worker is more closely assimilated to the machines she operates, executing her task with machinelike accuracy and regularity. The larger intent behind the job's performance is conceived as entirely separate from the woman who executes it—residing with the skilled man who set her tools, the managerial planner who designed the production flow, or the disembodied mechanical genius whose trace remains in the machine he created. As one British manager boasted: "We put the brains into the machines before the women begin."[107]

The kind of person who performs nonrepetitive work accomplishes a more fully human kind of labor, one that springs voluntarily from his independent will, the outward expression of an inner design and creative impulse. Questions of will, agency, and dependency were fundamental in the ordering of the shop-floor hierarchy, which, after 1914, came to rest on the gendered meanings given to skill, initiative, and repetitive action. It is therefore no accident that notions of skill and gender intersected in the distinction between repetitive and nonrepetitive labors. There is a powerful resonance between the repetitive, cyclical, and in some sense involuntary nature of women's domestic toil—in response to the needs and wills of others—and the repetitive work assigned to women in the metals factory. However much dexterity and experience such work may demand, it calls for little or no initiative, and the worker is

---

[106] British manager from the Midlands, quoted in *System,* April 1917, p. 250. The manager went on to comment that "women are not half so imaginative as men."

[107] Manager at a large ship-repair firm converted to shell production, quoted in Drake, *Women in the Engineering Trades,* p. 43. French employers in the machine-building trade conveyed a similar conviction: "The semiskilled worker ... minds a machine, and his output depends largely on that machine's degree of perfection and the tools with which it is equipped": AN, 39 AS, 914, "Rapport sur les revendications ouvrières concernant les salaires," Construction métalliques, 15 May 1918, p. 6.

bound to the "will" of a machine. Even the most highly skilled repetition work is ultimately defined by someone else; the judgment called for in wielding tools and making fine adjustments is circumscribed by the overarching intention of the managers who define the larger process within which her skilled task is located.[108]

It is perhaps not entirely surprising that employers gendered the two forms of skill even as the distinction between them first arose on the factory floor. As a trope of complementarity-in-difference, gender enabled employers to express the interdependent and hierarchical relationship between the new forms of skill and the old within a reordered labor process. But gender difference was more than a literary vehicle for expressing a new constellation of shop-floor relations. After 1914, gender difference, conceived as a system of fixed and natural antinomies, was woven through the system of division and hierarchy that ruled the factory floor. By the end of the war, employers had grounded the distinction between repetition skill and jobbing skill in "innate" biological difference, which ranked women's skills, however valuable, below those assigned to men:

> Owing to certain differences in mentality it is perfectly certain that, save in the most exceptional instances, women cannot become skilled mechanics. . . . On the other hand, a woman is quick to learn any particular job. She is intelligent, obedient and generally a good worker, and when she has become familiar with the details of a definite operation she will continue to repeat that operation satisfactorily.[109]

Henceforth, effective deployment of labor required the employer to distinguish the "imitative" skill of female production workers from the "initiative" skill of craftsmen.

During the war, workers of both sexes were occasionally promoted from skilled repetition work to jobbing in the toolroom. After the war, such promotions would cease altogether; indeed, in the discourse that developed around job skill after 1916, the distinction between jobbing and repetition skill hard-

---

[108] Maryanne Cline Horowitz puts it quite succinctly: "In the craftsman analogy, Aristotle implied that the male is *homo faber*, the maker, who works upon inert matter according to a design, bringing forth a lasting work of art. His soul contributes the form and model of the creation": "Aristotle and Woman," *Journal of the History of Biology* 9 (Fall 1976): 197. Aristotle employs the craftsman analogy (which first appears in Plato's *Republic*, bk. X) in his treatise "On the Generation of Animals" to express his understanding of male and female roles in reproduction, with the female as passive "laborer" (material cause) and the male as the active "craftsman," imparting form ("soul") to the embryo. See also Martha Nussbaum, "The Discernment of Perception: An Aristotelian Conception of Private and Public Rationality," in her *Love's Knowledge* (Oxford, 1990), pp. 54–105.

[109] PP 1919, Cmd. 167, *Appendices of Evidence to the Report of the War Cabinet Committee on Women in Industry, p. 54.*

ened into an unbridgeable divide: the "inherent" qualities required for the one were treated as incompatible with those demanded for the other. At the same time, the distinction between skilled and unskilled repetition work blurred; with sufficient training and experience, a woman could pass from unskilled to skilled repetition work. Hence managers' repeated protestation that the sudden "onslaught" of women posed no threat to craft: "Mechanics who are worthy of the name . . . who possess love of craft and a taste for finished work demanding knowledge, intelligence, and some technical capacity—will never see a competitor in the woman lathe operator. That would be absurd."[110] In both nations, the assimilation of skilled to unskilled repetition work found reflection in the narrower range of occupations designated female, and in the concomitant tendency for skilled and unskilled women's wages to gravitate toward a uniform rate.

The gendering of craft versus repetition work and the blurring of the distinction between skilled and unskilled repetition work led employers to place women in a wholly distinct relation to skilled work. Unlike the male worker, whose wages and role in production were defined by the skill required by his work, the woman worker was defined primarily by her gender, no matter what level of skill her work demanded. Hence, while some "remarkable work was done by women . . . the bulk of the products which excited the admiration of the public resulted from the novel methods of production rather than from the craftsmanship of the producers."[111] Throughout the interwar period, employers and their skilled craftsmen would continue to speak of skill as residing in the person of the worker, if the worker in question were male; if she were a woman, the skill lay in the work itself, and never in her. This attitude led to some contortions of logic, as when union members in Coventry demanded that "Female Workers, at present engaged on certain unskilled work, should be dismissed. . . . [The union] claimed that the particular work in question was appropriate for skilled workers only, and demanded the instant removal of the Females in question from the work."[112]

Work and the social identity of workers thus melded in the stratified labor

[110] Georges Calmès, "Note sur l'utilisation de la main-d'oeuvre féminine," *BUG,* 31 July 1916, p. 112.

[111] Ministry of Munitions, *Official History of the Ministry of Munitions,* 8 vols. (London, 1920–24), vol. 4, pt. 4, p. 82.

[112] CDEEA, Executive Commitee minutes, 10 February 1926, pp. 2–3. The French wage lists betray a similar prejudice: the male semiskilled worker was a "cutter, countersinker, or driller," depending on the machine he worked, but the woman was always a woman first—that is, "a woman on cutting, countersinking, or drill work." See AN, 39 AS, 914, Chambre Syndicale des Industries du Décolletage, "Tarif de base élaboré le 30 mai 1919." See also Downs, "Women in Industry," pp. 561, 571–72. Employers' belief that the skill required for less skilled work resided in the machine thus met with their feeling that a woman's status at work was determined more by her gender than by her particular occupation.

force. Labor stratification rested on the fundamentally Aristotelian presumption that social being dictates differential and complementary productive capacities. The differentiated classes of labor could, in a pinch, perform each other's jobs. In fact, employers often characterized war production in terms of confusion and boundary crossing among the various classes: "Boys will be men and girls will be boys," as one manager remarked.[113] Ultimately, however, these men believed that the several categories of labor were incommensurable. Although each was capable of filling in for the other, in the best and most efficient of all possible worlds, each would work only at the tasks most suited to her or his gender- and skill-specified qualities. Determining precisely where the dividing lines lay loomed large on the industry's postwar agenda. If, for example, the experience of war had revealed that repetition work was, in truth, women's work, then those firms that insisted on returning to a "men only" policy after 1918 were refusing to do the rational thing, stubbornly assigning men to tasks that by the laws of nature should be performed solely by women: "Most firms have been doing women's work by men and calling it men's work and that is a thing which has got to be gone into very carefully . . . and a line of demarcation laid down."[114]

Throughout the interwar years, employers in both nations frequently spoke as though company policies were intended to stabilize that line of demarcation. But given their successful defense of hierarchically stratified pay scales, these men's true advantage clearly lay in retaining the flexibility to lower labor costs by simply moving the line that divided men's work from women's work. Indeed, employers' insistence on the technical distinctions between male and female forms of skill dovetailed with the notion that women are, by definition, cheap labor. Together they formed a gendered discourse on job skill on the basis of which metals employers continuously shifted the sexual boundary dividing male from female on the metalworking factory floor.

These shifts were usually prompted by a change in the organization or technology of work. Yet employers could just as easily follow the example of one gearmaking plant in Laon, where simple reflection on "the qualities specific to this [female] source of labor . . . and the qualities demanded of those who operate these [machines]" led management to transfer the job of conveyor belt operator (*pontonnier*) from male hands to female ones. In making the transfer, management highlighted the unthinking, almost reflexive nature of the work: "It does not take much concentration . . . because it is the same or nearly the same motions that one repeats each day, and they rapidly become reflexive." In addition, the work was light; operators could occasionally sit down at their posts and in free moments (while the belts

---

[113] PP 1918, Cd. 9073, Board of Trade, *Report of the Departmental Committee*, p. 16.
[114] IWM, War Cabinet Committee Minutes, EEF testimony, p. F43.

remained stationary) "it is not uncommon to see *pontonnières* . . . knitting."
But the firm was most pleased about the way the shift from male to female
facilitated the transmission of orders along the chain of command: because
of their "technical ignorance" of work in the shop, the *pontonnières* had no
choice but to "passively follow orders . . . without having to take unfortunate,
even dangerous initiatives." On this point women were "especially appreciated
for their passivity and their dexterity in executing small motions." Indeed,
the firm was so delighted with the change that management decided that
henceforth it would employ only women for that work.[115]

Employers had responded to the challenge of war production by restratifying the workforce, assimilating gender to the old categories of age and skill.
But gender proved an intractable category; it did not blend smoothly into
the old system of divisions. Indeed, employers' notions of gender difference
formed a distinct criterion of selection, separate from skill yet operating in
conjunction with it to define a labor force that was divided simultaneously
along lines of sex and skill. In theory, these divisions appeared to shape two
parallel hierarchies, each arrayed in ascending order of age and skill, the
women's ladder mirroring the men's. But in real terms—job content, wage
levels, the types of skill required—the women's hierarchy bore scant resemblance to the male. Throughout the interwar period, gender and skill continued to interact on the metals factory floor, defining asymmetrical hierarchies
of male and female skill while maintaining women as a class apart.

I hope it is clear that the gendering of skill was no preconceived plan,
hatched in the minds of calculating employers. Rather, this unanticipated
outcome was immanent in the overall logic of the situation, in employers'
understanding of the meaning of gender difference, and in the particular
historical encounter between that understanding and the process of technical
transformation in the factory. In this process, gender masqueraded as a stable
and unitary category around which another spectrum of difference—skilled
to unskilled—shifted. But gender was simply a third dimension to that skilled–
unskilled polarity, a dimension that was also subject to change as participants
invested the category with new content or emphasized some elements (repetition) at the expense of others (women's skills, gained through training in
household crafts).

Skill thus gradually came to be mapped in subtle ways by distinctions of
gender. In the cross-national context of broadly similar changes in the structure and organization of work, one can see how local and contingent events—
regional patterns of female recruitment, particular struggles over distributing
work in the redivided labor process—influenced the division of work between
the sexes. With rapid technological change and repeated redivisions of the

---

[115] Lallemand, "Note sur les avantages," pp. 253–54.

labor process, management and workers of both sexes pressed constantly on these gendered boundaries, and frequently renegotiated the contours that distinguished men's work from women's work, men's skills from women's "special abilities." As the example of the *pontonnière* suggests, the specific content of the categories "men's work" and "women's work" often varied over national and even regional boundaries; what was a man's job in Paris might well be performed by a woman in St-Etienne.[116] But the principle of sexual division itself, and the managerial rationales on which the distinction rested, remained stable across those same boundaries. Hence the gendering of skill, however unintended, produced categories and distinctions that profoundly influenced the structure of opportunities for women throughout the metalworking trade.

The gendered language of job skill presents a deceptive unity of form across national and regional boundaries, a structure whose formal similarities—the nonparallel boy-girl skill ladders—contain and mask the considerable variation that locally specific divisions of labor actually exhibited. At the same time that the language of skill differentials provided a means of discussing and organizing difference, then, it elided local particularity, representing the multiple divisions of labor in metalworking as smoothly intersecting in a stable hierarchical order, built on "self-evident" distinctions in skill and gender. But this hierarchical system, constituted by a series of nonparallel binary oppositions (skilled/unskilled, male/female), produced a set of categories that were in fact incommensurable. Hence "woman" could be a trope for "unskilled labor" (though not vice versa); but employers could in the same breath speak enthusiastically of their skilled women workers.

The ostensibly coherent discourse on skill was thus riddled with internal instabilities in the meaning of its constituent elements, as concrete instances of women as skilled (and hence highly valued) workers vied with generalized conceptions of women as paradigmatically unskilled. Such multiplicity of meanings muddied the apparently crystalline distinctions of which the larger system was constructed. To workers and employers alike the sexual division of labor that was grounded in this unstable discourse on skill seemed perpetually on the verge of collapse. Yet the distinction endured, defining the horizontal and vertical structures that shaped gendered divisions of labor, occupational segregation, and relations of authority in the workplace.

---

[116] In 1921 Kirkaldy noted how rapidly the "indistinct line" dividing men's from women's work had shifted, and how variable the particular divisions were from one district to the next, especially in the new consumer-goods branch of the industry: *British Labour*, pp. 21–22.

The Schizophrenic Decades, 1920–1939

During the interwar years, the French economy underwent a profound restructuring in which women workers figured prominently. After decades of anemic growth, France had at last begun a process of rapid industrial development, beginning just before the turn of the century.[1] The demands of war had distorted but by no means halted that development, favoring highly localized growth in Paris and St-Etienne, privileging larger firms over small, and metals and chemicals above all others. After the difficult months of postwar transition, the upward trend continued with renewed force. With reconstruction fueling an especially strong demand for metals and machinery, the automobile, chemical, and electronics industries flourished. Here, at the very core of France's renewed prosperity, women's employment expanded without interruption. In metalworking alone the percentage of women workers tripled after 1914, rising from 4.2% to nearly 15% by 1939.[2]

---

[1] See Patrick O'Brien and Caglar Keyder, *Economic Growth in Britain and France, 1780–1914* (London, 1981); Jean-Jacques Carré, Paul Dubois, and Edmond Malvinaud, *La Croissance française: Un Essai d'analyse économique causale de l'après-guerre* (Paris, 1972).

[2] Evelyne Sullerot, "Condition de la femme," in Alfred Sauvy, ed., *Histoire économique de la France entre les deux guerres*, 3 vols. (Paris, 1968), 3:423. The figures are even more striking for the Paris region alone, as the contingent of women metalworkers rose over the interwar period from an already high 14% in 1921 to 14.8% in 1926 and reached 18% by 1936. The 14% in 1921 represented 39,741 women, whereas the 14.8% in 1926 represented 52,189 women; in other words, the industry itself was expanding rapidly, and women made up a disproportionate share of that increase. See Marcel de Ville-Chabrolle, "La Population active de 77 départements français en 1906 et en 1921," *Bulletin de la Statistique Générale de France* (hereafter *BSGF*) 16, pt. 1 (1925): 84; also two census reports of the Statistique Générale: *Résultats statistiques du recensement de 1926*, 3 vols. (Paris, 1929), vol. 2, pt. 3; and *Résultats statistiques du recensement de 1936*, 3 vols. (Paris, 1943), vol. 2, pt. 3; and AN, 39 AS, 830, GIMM to Ministère du Travail, "Répartition du personnel," 8 July 1936. The numbers for France as a whole are more restrained: 8% women metalworkers in 1921, nearly 11% in 1931, 15.3% in 1954: Françoise Gélaud-Léridon, *Le Travail des femmes en France* (Paris, 1964), table 3. (There are no national figures for the

Throughout this late industrialization, the staple trades of the nineteenth century (textiles, garments, domestic service) declined.[3] Many had been heavy employers of women, so women's overall participation in paid labor began to contract. The percentage of women workers in metals and chemicals continued to climb, but no amount of progress in new industrial occupations could make up for the enormous loss in traditional sectors.[4] After 1921, the percentage of women in the workforce gradually fell, from an all-time high of 46 percent in 1918 to 42.3 percent in 1921, then to 37.2 percent in 1926 and 37.1 percent by 1936.[5]

Paradoxically, a reaction against women's factory employment arose at precisely this moment. Even as the number of women workers began to drop, contemporaries trained uneasy eyes on their growing presence in the new and dynamic fields of autos and electronics and concluded that the numbers of women in industry were rising daily. This false impression was destined to acquire broad currency in those years of demographic anxiety. After all, women's transfer from a shrinking periphery to the highly visible center made it easy for the casual observer to misread the signs. Decline thus masqueraded as increase in interwar France. As time went on and the prosperous 1920s gave way to the stagnant 1930s, this illusory expansion would feed the worst fears of France's pro-natalist prophets of doom.

Vichy period.) Figures for Paris are consistently higher than national figures because the new and more consumer-oriented branches, in which women were most likely to work, were concentrated in this region. Thus the iron and steel industry, whose workforce was only 4.8% female in 1921, was concentrated primarily in the east and northeast of France (Lorraine, the Nord, and Pas-de-Calais), whereas firms that produced sewing machines, bicycles, and automobiles (11.7% female nationally by 1921) and electronics (15.6%) were concentrated in Paris and the *banlieue*. Here individual firms employed anywhere from 15% women (cars) to 30% or more (electronics). All figures are from *Résultats statistiques du recensement de 1921*, 3 vols. (Paris, 1926), vol. 2, pt. 3.

[3] Eighteen percent of all women employed in clothing and textiles in 1906 had left those jobs by 1921: Antonia Vallentin, "The Employment of Women since the War," *International Labour Review* April (1932): 495.

[4] In 1921 statisticians at the Statistique Générale recorded an aggregate decline of 23% in the cluster of "twelve typical women's industries," noting that "most of these 303,000 women who have been lost to the so-called essentially women's industries have gone over to other industries, where they are replacing men to an ever-increasing extent": Ville-Chabrolle, "Population active," p. 84.

[5] The 46% in 1918 is an estimate, as regular census data were not collected during the war. See Jean-Louis Robert, "Women and Work in France during the War," in Jay Winter and Richard Wall, eds., *The Upheaval of War* (Cambridge, 1988), p. 262. The decline in women's employment is delineated more clearly in the falling percentage of women who worked outside the home: an estimated 47% in 1918, 37.5% in 1926 (only 33%, according to Carré et al.), 34.2% by 1936 (only 30.5% according to Carré et al.). The decline continued after World War II, finally bottoming out in 1962, by which point only 27.5% of all women worked for pay. The 1968 census registered the first increase since the mid-1920s, a mere 0.5%. See Carré et al., *Croissance française*, p. 49. The decline was caused in large measure by the falling number of family farms, which diminished the number of peasant wives included among economically active women.

Britain's economy was experiencing a comparable restructuring, with staple industries (textiles, coal, ships) declining as the consumer-goods industries grew fat on a newly developing home market.[6] The context was rather different, however. In France the expansion in consumer goods lay at the heart of a larger leap forward, industrially speaking. In Britain, by contrast, people watched helplessly as this older industrial economy slid inexorably into a recession from which it would never truly recover.[7] On this bleak landscape, the new consumer industries formed islands of hope, small beacons in an otherwise gloomy portrait of relentless stagnation.

In both nations, the metalworking industries, and especially the new, consumer-driven sectors, hired disproportionate numbers of women after 1921. In Britain, however, the shift from textiles and domestic service to electronics and synthetic fibers masked no global decline in women's overall employment. On the contrary, despite the significant contraction in traditional sectors, the new industries provided more than sufficient counterweight; once the temporary bulge occasioned by World War I had passed, British women's participation in paid employment rose gently but steadily, from 29.5 percent in 1921 to 29.7 percent in 1931, reaching 30.4 percent by 1933.[8] This rise embraced industrial labor as well as clerical and sales work, and the decade 1921–31 saw a 10 percent gain in the number of women manual workers. Many of these new entrants flocked to metalworking and especially electrical engineering; over that same decade, the percentage of women engineering workers in Britain advanced from 10 percent to 14.3 percent.[9] Both countries thus saw a steady and significant rise in the number of women metalworkers over the interwar period.

Britain's slow increase in women's work had its own distinctive shape: with the war's end, older and married women withdrew once again from paid labor, continuing the trend established in the decade before 1914. Those who

[6] No comparable market, in which lower-middle-class and even blue-collar consumers clamored for such goods as radios, developed in France until the late 1950s.

[7] See Derek Aldcroft, *The Interwar Economy: Britain, 1919–39* (New York, 1970); Bernard Elbaum and William Lazonick, *The Decline of the British Economy* (Cambridge, 1987).

[8] Catherine Hakim, *Occupational Segregation*, Department of Employment research paper no. 9 (London: Ministry of Labour, 1979), p. 25, and *Ministry of Labour Gazette*, December 1938, p. 468. Hakim's figures reveal how stable British women's overall participation in paid labor has been over the first half of the twentieth century; the 29.7% reached in 1931 represents a recovery of their prewar position; the slight drop in 1921 resulted from postwar campaigns to drive women from industry and give their jobs to the returning heroes. Only in the early 1930s did the number of women workers begin to grow beyond this stable 29.7%.

[9] This growth becomes all the more impressive when one recalls that throughout the interwar period, the industry as a whole was expanding. See M. L. Yates, *Wages and Labour Conditions in British Engineering* (London, 1937), p. 3. Much of the impetus behind the increase came from the burgeoning electrical goods trade, where the figures delineate a more dramatic upturn: from 26.6% in 1921 to 32.4% in 1931 and a full 36% by 1936: Miriam Glucksmann, *Women Assemble: Women Workers and The New Industries in Interwar Britain* (London, 1990), p. 58.

230 Manufacturing Inequality

flooded the interwar labor market were overwhelmingly young and unmarried;
for a brief period (from 1919 to the mid-1930s) the female industrial workforce
in Britain became a workforce of predominantly single young (even adolescent) women.[10] Only 16 percent of these workers were married, whereas over
35 percent of women industrial workers in France were married.[11] This national
distinction would hold throughout the interwar period. In France the *mère-
ouvrière* of the nineteenth century remained a prominent figure, though the
work she performed had changed. In Britain, married women began returning
to industry only after the onset of the Great Depression.

Despite their differences, the interwar economies of both Britain and France
shared one crucial feature: the long-term industrial evolution that had brought
the consumer-goods industries to the fore had placed women workers at the
heart of the modern industrial economy. As one industrial crisis succeeded
another, politicians, journalists, sometimes even industrialists (generally those
who did not employ women) repeatedly demanded that women, especially
married women, step aside and hand over their jobs to unemployed men
(who were generally cast as "fathers of families"). In the flurry of polemic
that surrounded Europe's endemic and highly politicized recessions, few
people seemed to recall that the industry's careful redelineation of male and
female tasks in the war and postwar years had rendered a woman's work
noninterchangeable with a man's. She could not realistically hand her job
over to him without raising the wage bill and (worse yet) undermining an

---

[10] See Glucksmann, *Women Assemble,* p. 42. The number of older women began to rise
again after 1931, so that by 1951, 35% of all women aged 35–54 were employed. Glucksmann
believes that married women's return to paid labor began in the 1930s (p. 41). If so, it would
have started slowly in metals and engineering, as most firms maintained informal marriage
bars in this period. (At a conference in 1935, union representatives observed that by 1927, many
firms were refusing to hire married women. See MRC, EEF, Special Conference, "Women's
Wages," 19 July 1935, p. 73.) Of course, this did not mean there were no married women in
engineering. The bars were never official EEF policy, never were very rigidly applied, and did
not obtain in districts where women workers were in short supply.

[11] Thus married women, who accounted for 16% of Britain's female workforce in 1931 (Hakim,
Occupational Segregation, pp. 11–12), still constituted a full 35.5% of all women workers in 1921.
A further 13.5% of French women workers were widows or divorced. See Gélaud-Léridon,
Travail des Femmes, table 2. Interestingly, the French figures for metalworking alone reveal
an even greater proportion of married and widowed or divorced women; a 1933 survey by the
Catholic women's organization Union Féminine Civique et Sociale (UFCS) showed that 37%
of such workers were married, 17% widowed or divorced: UFCS, *Le Travail industriel de la
mère et le foyer ouvrier. Documents d'études. Extraits du congrès international de juin 1933* (Paris,
1933) p. 91. Jane Lewis notes that in interwar Britain, those married women who did work
were likely to be young women who had worked before marriage and continued at least until
the arrival of their first child. Thus the participation rate of married women aged 25–35 rose
from 9.9% in 1921 to 13.8% in 1931 and 25.2% by 1951. For those aged 21–24, the upward trend
is even sharper: 13.2% in 1921, 19.3% in 1931, and 37.7% in 1951. See Jane Lewis, *Women in
England, 1870–1950* (Lewes, 1984), p. 150.

efficient shop-floor order that, in the employers' eyes, rested on deployment of workers in jobs appropriate to their skill and gender.

The indissoluble link that bound women to rationalized work in the metal-working industry altered over the interwar years, as employers in both nations reformulated and scientized the bonds linking welfare and efficiency to the new female workforce. Under the mass-production organization of work, profits depended on women's ability to move swiftly and steadily with the machine, each motion ever more tireless and machinelike. In this setting, the concern for workers' "welfare" inevitably became a search for some means whereby human energy could be conserved and expended in accordance with a production process whose rhythm lay completely beyond the individual worker's control. By the late 1920s, a language of technocratic efficiency had thoroughly interpenetrated the welfarist's more "human" concern with workers' fatigue: "Intermittent violent action and idleness creates no rest. Constant action, with little fatigue, makes for efficiency."[12]

After 1919, French and British employers alike would resort to this newly scientized language of welfare and efficiency when they discussed women's work. Yet on each side of the Channel the link between women and rational-ized labor was articulated in socially different ways. French employers saw industrial rationalization as the key to economic development and expansion; indeed, those who failed to adopt modern methods would be "condemned to ruin," one industrialist warned.[13] As the gospel of "Americanization" spread through the interwar metalworking industry, the *surintendante* swiftly became one of its prime agents, implementing productivist strategies within a larger managerial tradition of a reinvigorated company paternalism, recast in light of wartime experience and the increased presence of women.[14]

This surrounding welfarist apparatus was entirely lacking in Britain, for with the war's end, employers had swiftly jettisoned the lady superintendents. But they did not give up the effort to control the rhythms and motions of work. The dream of co-opting workers into productivist structures and goals lived on in a series of unrelievedly technocratic time-and-motion studies, conducted in the vain hope that firms might escape the crunch of falling profits. As the economy slid from slump into outright depression after 1929, employers began to use strategies for the "rationalization" of work as a means

---

[12] Cecil Walton, *Welfare Study—What It Is* (Glasgow, 1919), p. 14.

[13] AN, F12, 8048, "Rapport Rateau" (1919), p. 38.

[14] On the enduring strength of paternalism in France see Donald Reid, "Industrial Paternal-ism: Discourse and Practice in Nineteenth-Century French Mining and Metallurgy," *Compara-tive Studies in Society and History* 27 (October 1985): 579–607; and Herrick Chapman, *State Capitalism and Working-Class Radicalism in the French Aircraft Industry* (Berkeley, 1991).

to effect cuts, to weed out the least efficient and hold down labor costs among the surviving remnant.

Yet French and British employers alike had created a discourse that placed images of the human as machine in uneasy juxtaposition with the express concern for the individual's organic well-being, physiological and psychological: "Where it [welfare discipline] is established it means that the employees are treated with as much consideration as the machinery, and just as highly valued."[15] The image of the woman worker as a well-cared-for machine does not appear to have troubled the British unduly. Not so with their French colleagues. As firms developed in size and complexity, employers turned to their *surintendantes* for assistance in reconciling the contradictions that growth inevitably entailed:

> The *surintendante sociale* is . . . the element that allows the modern enterprise *to function in the fashion of a small workshop*, both technically and morally. . . . A woman, *because she is a woman, and by vocation and training*, can ensure that liaison, that communication among all elements of the enterprise.[16]

Although the *surintendante* herself was a crucial element in the expansion and bureaucratization of the factory, it fell to her to humanize the rationalization project, to square the circle by pressing Taylorization on the one hand even as she created a more "human" context for the growing technocracy on the other.

[15] Walton, *Welfare Study,* and Amy Eleanor Mack, "Oiling the Human Wheels," *Pearson's Magazine,* February 1917, p. 134, quoted in Angela Woollacott, "Maternalism, Professionalism and Industrial Welfare Supervisors in World War I Britain," *Women's History Review* 6, no. 1 (1994): 39.
[16] M. Zérapha, in *BAS,* 1935, p. 21; emphasis in original.

Reshaping Factory Culture in Interwar France

Early one morning in the winter of 1919 a young student at the Ecole des Surintendantes stood outside the Porte du Versailles metro stop, shivering in the frigid gloom of dawn as she waited for the tardy tram that would deposit her before the gates at Renault. There Mlle Cailleux would begin her factory *stage,* the two- to four-week stint as an ordinary factory worker required of all aspiring *surintendantes* at the end of their second year at the school. Each student was required to keep a journal throughout her *stage,* reporting in some detail on the organization of work and ways it might be improved from the point of view of workers' health but also for reasons of industrial efficiency.[1] She was also to take note of all safety and welfare provisions, or lack of them, as this would be one of her prime concerns after she graduated to a post in the factory, and to comment more generally on the physical and moral condition of the workforce. The factory journals thus constitute a rich and remarkably interesting point of entry into the all but inaccessible world of factory labor in interwar France, for each student was expected literally to cross over into the world of her future clientele; to "put on the blue overall that will allow me to change class and mingle freely in the world of factory labor," as one student put it.[2] For nearly all these young women, this was their first contact with factory life.

[1] Twenty-nine of those journals survive from the period 1919–43, fourteen of which are from metalworking, automobiles, and electronics firms. All of the *surintendantes'* reports quoted in this chapter may be found in the archives of the Ecole des Surintendantes in Paris. Page numbers in the text refer to the journal of the *stagiaire* indicated.

[2] Report of M. Houssay, *stagiaire* at Renault, March 1920, p. 1. No one in the factory, including the employer, was to know that the student was not simply another worker. But the transition was rarely so easy as putting on an unfamiliar piece of clothing. For instance, foremen were often surprised and sometimes suspicious that women of such advanced age (25, 30, and even 35) had no factory experience: "The team chief looked at me with disdain: 'How

Thanks to the delayed tram, Mlle Cailleux arrived an hour late to work, at 7:30 A.M. instead of 6:30. It was not an auspicious beginning, but Cailleux persisted and was sent to shop 16, where the team chief put her to work rough-hewing valves at the lathe:

> That day I was to help another woman, and tomorrow I was to work by myself. It's very heavy labor, for the machine doesn't do everything. It does the hewing, but as it proceeds, I have to turn the valve while pressing against the machine tool as it does the rough cut. One must turn the valve a full forty degrees, and twisting to those forty degrees demands great strength. Each time, you have to fasten the valve with a monkey wrench, which is very taxing, lock it into place, turn the valve forty degrees while pressing against the tool, disengage the whole thing and unscrew it [with] the monkey wrench. The valve is then disengaged from the lathe by means of a lifting tackle that is bolted to the floor; thus one is continually lifting and heaving while at the same time twisting madly. I will most certainly have trouble making production. (pp. 6–7)

Not only was her work difficult, but Cailleux's lathe broke down repeatedly. Each time the machine jammed, her companion cried out in frustration, "What a pig of a job!" and they were forced to call on the setter for adjustment and repair. During these bouts of mechanical difficulty Cailleux and her more experienced partner chatted:

> "And you know, you must never miss a day," declared my companion. "He's a nasty piece of work, the foreman. The other day I missed the morning and he swore at me, oh he swore at me! And I had a sick kid. . . . Ah, he can't understand that. Children, he knows nothing about them. He can't have them, he's got potassium chloride in his . . . what you need in order to make babies!" Of course, she used the real word and not my delicate paraphrase. The vulgarity was unexpected and hardly banal! (pp. 7–8)

But Mlle Cailleux would hear no more diverting tales from this woman, for try as she might, the young student was simply not working out at the

---

is it that at your age you've never worked before?' Sensing his contempt, I told him I'd been a waitress in a hotel for many years. He responded: 'That's good, I thought you'd never done anything' ": report of Mlle Hilon, unnamed Paris metals factory, 1920, p. 2. Despite these difficulties, students spoke with some pride about managing to pass as ordinary workers: "I guess I've managed to adopt a proper working-class woman's manner, since no one seems to regard me with suspicion, as I feared they might, and my neighbors have already exchanged confidences with me": report of Mlle Nalon, Lampes Iris, 1923, p. 3. Yet one suspects that in more than one case, the mask of ordinary factory worker must have slipped. When Mlle Verneuil, *stagiaire* at Panhard in 1928, decided to confide her true identity to a trusted co-worker, the woman replied: "I could see clearly that you weren't .ke the others, but all this doesn't mean we can't be good friends anyway. You were right not to tell the others. They'd be more irritated [than I] to think you weren't like them" (p. 24).

Woman working in the winding shop at Thomson-Houston's Levallois plant, 1920–25. Cliché Thomson.

lathe: "My efforts were pitiful. I never managed to tighten the monkey wrench properly, and when I tightened it to the maximum, I couldn't loosen it again and had to call the setter. I think he found me stupid, that I inspired his profound contempt" (p. 7). After the lunch break, when she returned to her lathe, the team chief paused for a moment, watched her wrestle with valve and wrench, then shook his head in despair. " 'You must change jobs!' he said. 'Go over to the grinding wheel. Tonight we'll set you up and tomorrow you'll work on split shifts with another woman—you from 6:30 to 2:30, and her from 2:30 till 10:30. You'll each have your own work and your own boxes [for materials and finished pieces] on which you'll write your name. And there'll be no talk of wages!' " (pp. 8–9). It was an infinitely less taxing job. One had only to place the steel or nickel shafts properly, and the machine made the cut. "Not much physical effort, just careful attention, in order to cut each rod to the right length, and a certain adroitness, for if the piece isn't placed just right, the fragile chisel will break. It didn't take me long to learn that the cost of the tool would come out of my pocket" (p. 9).

As one of her new co-workers was quick to point out, this job transfer was not entirely to Cailleux's advantage:

"On the other machine, your forty sous [Fr 2] an hour come easily, one after the other, as if you were telling the beads on your rosary. You could go to the rest rooms without hurrying, if you weren't in a mood to rush." (Now that's a real pleasure!) "But on the grinding wheel," said my new comrade, "forty sous an hour—it simply can't be done; I could never make it, it doesn't pay enough!" (p. 9)

The next day Mlle Cailleux continued at the grinding wheel, struggling to succeed at work that, though not heavy, left her covered in the black dust of cut metal.

I work zealously, and a certain fever overtakes me as I begin to catch the rhythm of the job . . . and I work, I work furiously. . . . Now I've caught the rhythm, I've calculated my movements so that I only make those that are absolutely necessary; if I have no interruptions, then all goes well. But alas, the chisels break with maddening ease, and when they don't break, they wear out; at the end of about an hour, they have to be changed and you have to call on that powerful god the machine setter. Today's setter is less scornful than yesterday's, but all the same, it's hard to be cheerful about calling him for it's money out of my pocket—I lose a good quarter of an hour every time he comes.

Then the belt comes loose; I have to go chasing after the belt repair man, who sends me to find various tools and grows impatient with my slowness in finding them. "What do you want?" I ask, laughing. "I know nothing about all this. I don't even know the names of these gadgets!" This humility pleases him and he becomes more paternal and indulgent.

Then it happens that the current fails and we sit with our arms folded for an hour. The consternation is widespread. Finally one woman says: "Don't complain, there are factories where you sit idle two days a week for lack of electricity. Here at least they generate their own and it doesn't go down too often." After all these delays I return to work with such alacrity that my neighbors, male and female, grow terrified and tell me, "You don't have to work like that. You're pushing too hard! If you go too fast you'll lower your base rate and that's all you'll have gained for your trouble." I kept my moralizing to myself and simply responded, "But I'm not doing too much. I stop so often that I haven't yet made my forty sous for the hour!" In this case, there was nothing more to say; they bowed their heads with an air of approbation and returned to their work. (pp. 11–13)[3]

Mlle Cailleux was struck by the abundant and complex paperwork that paralleled the production process, accompanying each object as it traveled from the foundry through the shops, from one machine to the next, until the piece was finally finished. Renault used this intricate bureaucracy to control the flow of goods and materials while keeping careful account of the individual worker's rate of production. Cailleux's description of this elaborate work system reveals the young woman's surprise and curiosity at how easily the trail of paper tracked both labor and goods throughout the factory.

There are twenty separate operations involved in producing a finished valve. Every batch of valves (one hundred per batch) delivered from the forge is accompanied by its own red card, on which all twenty tasks are listed in a column. The person who is to execute a particular phase of the job—refining, cutting, polishing the head or the stem—marks her name in the next column, alongside the task she's about to perform. Just before beginning the job, you take the card to the time office and have it punched, to show that you're about to begin the job. (p. 14)[4]

The red card stayed with the carton of valves; hence, when a woman finished one operation, she passed both card and valves along to her neighbor, who then signed on and began the next phase. An entirely separate card followed the human producer through each one- or two-week pay period. This card belonged to the individual worker and listed the wage paid per hundred on

[3] At the grinding wheel one had to turn out a minimum of 100 perfect pieces an hour to get the famous 40 sous, the standard piece rate for women machinists in the Paris region in the early 1920s. In the gear shop, the minimum output was 1,000–1,500 pieces.
[4] Most of the *surintendantes en stage* reported similarly complicated paperwork associated with the piecework systems in their plants. In 1920 Houssay observed (p. 5) that in addition to all these time cards, one had a card for each machine tool she checked out from the tool shop.

each task she performed. One's entire weekly wage was computed on the basis of the record maintained on the second sheet; hence, at the beginning and end of each job, the worker punched in on both the red job card and her own pay card. Renault paid his workers a minimum hourly wage, based on the assumption that they would make the minimum amount (100 valves, in this case) during that time. The production bonus must have been sharply regressive, however, for Cailleux observed: "If you do too little in eight hours, you're paid just a bit above the minimum rate. And if you work swiftly and surpass the given minimum, it does you no good, you won't be paid much better. . . . In addition, the foreman can always fire those who habitually produce less than the minimum" (p. 14). Renault's wage system thus kept women and men working at a steady, swift, and predetermined pace. By 1919, then, the firm had already implemented one of Frederick Taylor's first principles by establishing a wage structure that enabled foremen to maintain a high and predictable output while systematically weeding out workers who could not keep up.

Eight hours of uninterrupted repetitive labor, even at less tiring jobs such as grinding valves, took a heavy toll on the worker, which Mlle Cailleux did not hesitate to record in some detail.[5]

> At the end of eight hours, I feel a terrible weariness, much worse than yesterday, when my eight hours were broken by a lunch break. Eight hours at a stretch are far more tiring and I feel a vague stupefaction come over me. . . . The fatigue will surely abate as I grow accustomed to the work, but the stupidity, the impossibility of thinking grows as I perform this mechanical labor. I've spent two days without an idea, without a thought, my eyes dully following the wheel as it turns, and because of this I well understand the animality, the bestiality brought on by this mindless labor. One is too tired, too bored, too brutalized to have the wherewithal to calculate, even to contrive some amusement or plan. Some brief, immediate pleasure, and then to sleep; that's all the body asks. (p. 15)

The juxtaposition of images is striking—the "intelligence" of the highly precise semi-automatic machines that demand a continuous, conscientious, and laborious effort and so ineluctably transform spirited humans into un-thinking beasts of burden. These images are not unique to Mlle Cailleux.

---

[5] In fact, hours at Renault were in accordance with the law of April 1919, which established the 8-hour day/48-hour week (44 in shops that gave the English week). But administrators gave many dispensations, especially to industries with furnaces and forges that ran continuously. In practice, then, industrialists frequently exceeded the 48-hour maximum. Annie Fourcaut finds that the large auto factories tended to observe the law, while smaller enterprises often boldly exceeded the maximum, working women 9, 10, even 10½ hours a day, 50 to 55 hours a week: *Femmes à l'usine en France dans l'entre-deux-guerres* (Paris, 1982), pt. 2.

Some fifteen years later, when Simone Weil went to work as a machinist at Alsthom, she observed in herself the same inner devolution as her capacity for reflection recoiled before the brutal onslaught of mind-numbing labor:

> Ultimately the exhaustion made me forget why I had ever come into the factory to begin with. What became almost invincible was the powerful temptation of which this life is made: to think no more, the only way not to suffer. It's only on Saturday afternoon and Sunday that memories return to me, glimmers of thought that remind me that I am *also* a thinking being . . . one day of work without the weekend's rest—and this could easily come to pass—and I would become nothing more than a beast, docile and resigned.[6]

Yet an eight-hour day was far from excessive, especially in comparison with the much longer shifts common in the smaller factories and workshops in and around Paris.[7] The now common practice of granting workers a half-day's shift on Saturdays made the long hours more bearable, and on Saturday morning the shops bustled with anticipation as women cleaned and oiled their equipment.

> Today, Saturday, I've felt a special excitement all morning. The women have been carefully cleaning down their machines, and the floor around them, since 11 o'clock. Walking through the shop I can hear them worrying about the time and speaking about trips out to the countryside, where some go to visit their children, sent out to a wet nurse, others go just to breathe the pure air and get a change of scene after a hard week.[8]

By her third day on the job, Mlle Cailleux was beginning to run up against the many restrictions that hedged workers' freedom of movement on the factory floor:

> I sat down for a moment on a high stool and saw that the job goes just as well sitting down as standing up but the chief has just told me that it's forbidden.[9] Forbidden also to go to the cloakroom during work. One must never leave one's machine. By noon I was dying of hunger, and was forced to eat my bread and chocolate at the machine, without being able to wash my hands. (p. 16)

[6] Simone Weil, *La Condition ouvrière* (Paris, 1951), pp. 67–68; emphasis in original. Between 1934 and 1936 Weil worked some eighteen months at three Parisian metals factories: Alsthom, J. J. Carnaud et Forges de Basse-Indre, and Renault.

[7] In some shops, management moderated the impact of long hours by granting workers a full hour and a half for lunch, so that those who lived nearby could go home and prepare a substantial midday meal for their families.

[8] Report of Mlle Wagner, Thomson-Houston electronics plant, August 1928, p. 9.

[9] Outside of assembly rooms in electronics plants, women and men always stood at their machines. Whatever stools might be scattered about a machine shop were there for brief rest pauses only.

Such tight strictures were by no means unique to Renault; on the contrary, it was quite common for firms to forbid workers to leave their machines, or the shop, once the shift had begun. The women at the Krieg & Zivy steel tube plant came up with a partial solution to the problem: "The workers are forbidden to take a snack break in the morning or evening, so they have to do it in secret . . . at the entry to the W.C."[10] Here, in the toilet, one's sole legitimate destination during the shift, workers could safely evade the shop rules against loitering or snacking during work.

But arbitrary shop rules were a minor affliction in comparison with the extraordinary power that a male hierarchy—team chief or tool setter,[11] foreman and shop chief—wielded in the everyday lives of the women. Mlle Ollier could "see more and more how the team chief or the setter can be a sultan, how much the women are at his mercy; if the setup is off even a bit, then the machine won't run, the job is botched, and hours are lost" (p. 17). *Surintendantes en stage* often remarked on these men's power over the women, in particular their control over the distribution of work. If you wanted a job that ran smoothly and paid well, it was best to stay on the team chief's good side. Sometimes simply doing one's job well was not enough. After a week spent drilling engine parts in a large factory near the Place Nationale, Mlle Hilon observed: "The foreman is a real hound. If he likes you, your machine always runs well, all your pieces turn out. But woe to you if you reject his overtures! Your machine will be silent. But it seems that the tool setter likes my face, and so my machine runs nicely" (p. 7).

It is clear from the *surintendantes'* reports that some of these men did not hesitate to use their positions of power to extract sexual favors. Mlle Cailleux heard one such tale within minutes of her arrival at Renault, as she stood in the hiring office waiting to be placed:

> One woman lost no time telling us that she had been forced to leave the factory because after she refused the setter's amorous advances, he made it utterly impossible for her to work at all. Worse, the foreman sided with his subordinate. He prevented her from switching shops, and wouldn't let her remain in the factory at all, unless she stayed in the same shop, with the same setter. (p. 17)

Stories of ill use and sexual harassment at the hands of male superiors surface regularly in accounts of shop-floor life. At the Panhard auto plant, for example, Mlle Verneuil observed that identification of the shop's wolves

---

[10] Report of Mlle Ollier, Krieg & Zivy (Montrouge), 1926, p. 5.

[11] The two terms were used interchangeably to designate those skilled men who performed what was essentially the same function, setting machines and distributing jobs to an assigned team (usually twelve to fifteen women and men) in the shop. Over these men stood foremen, and above the foremen, each shop had its chief.

Under the foreman's watchful eye, women work on the initial assembly in the valvemaking shop at the Société Radiotechnique (Suresnes), 1920–25. Cliché Thomson.

by more experienced colleagues seems to have been a veritable ritual of initiation for the female newcomer: " 'Watch out for the setter,' my companion warned, 'he loves to flirt with the women and soon gets too familiar. He's already gotten into trouble with the shop chief over this' " (p. 15). Such cautionary tales circulated freely among women workers. Significantly, they always involved a man in a position of direct power over women, be it the team chief or tool setter, the time-study man or some other "white shirt."[12] Whatever may have gone on between women and men who were positioned more similarly on the shop hierarchy apparently did not warrant mention, at least not in the same breath as the kinds of bullying and abuse laid at the

---

[12] The factory's petty officers—shop managers, foremen, and setters—wore white shirts or overalls to distinguish them from the workers, who wore blue. The term comes from Houssay's 1920 report from Renault.

door of these odious shop-floor "sultans." One wonders whether employers' practice of placing women workers under male supervision had perhaps begun to recast as gender conflict the tensions that arose partially from class difference, difference that was etched sharply in a shop-floor hierarchy that placed a highly skilled elite of men from the upper working class in positions of authority over a mass of proletarian women.[13] The shape that these tales invariably assume—women workers hectored, propositioned, and victimized by the men who controlled their labor and wages—certainly suggests that this was the case. As we shall see, employers' larger managerial strategy of painting the factory as a harmonious familial order—a strategy in which *surintendantes* played a crucial part—would only reinforce this trend, papering over divisions of class while underscoring those of gender.

The hiring of *surintendantes* to act as big sisters or even mothers to the women thus opened a new kind of space in which these women could intercede and mediate such conflicts. Here, then, was one vector along which *surintendantes* might potentially intervene, disrupting the foremen's unchecked rule on the factory floor. In practice, however, such radical ruptures rarely occurred, for on issues of sexual conduct and harassment, *surintendantes* were rarely prepared to take a woman worker's word. Mlle Cailleux, for example, took her informant's tale of unwanted advances followed by unfair dismissal with a grain of salt:

> It's possible, though not necessarily true. Women always give this reason for being fired, out of dishonesty or sometimes even believing it to be true. One must excuse them, they're not the only ones. We've all known the woman of the world who is convinced that all men are after her virtue and that she's bravely resisted the assaults of M. X, whereas M. X cries out in astonishment that he'd rather be impaled than to court this woman! (p. 17)

Alongside such stories surface two related phenomena—veritable tropes in the *stagiaires'* factory journals—which may help to explain the frank skepticism with which Cailleux (like many of her colleagues) greeted women's complaints of harassment. First, the students all seemed to regard working-class women as especially vulgar creatures, driven more by appetite than by intellect. Second, they tended to show more respect for male workers than for female ones. Although many *surintendantes* spoke warmly of women workers' kindness and generosity, they seem nonetheless to have viewed the women as more childlike and simple-minded than their male colleagues.[14] This attitude may

---

[13] The semiskilled and unskilled women and men who filled the metals shops of interwar Paris were generally from a less privileged stratum of the working class than the skilled male elite, and some were newly arrived from the countryside.

[14] Only one of the twenty-nine extant reports from the interwar period reveals the *surintendante* actively disliking the women workers: that of Mlle Basterra at Thomson-Houston, 1928.

well have inclined them to consider a man's word more reliable than a woman's.

On the first point, Cailleux observed that "their language . . . is . . . dreadful, openly coarse . . . the comparisons, the images are uniformly scatalogical" (p. 20). Ollier, too, was struck by the indelicate conversational proclivities of her future charges:

> I overheard [another woman at the assembly table] make improper overtures to one worker as calmly and naturally as though she had been commenting on the weather! Unfortunately, this is typical of all the women workers I've encountered. Most of their conversations and jokes indicate an utter lack of dignity and self-respect. They discuss the most intimate matters among themselves in great detail, unabashedly and with an unimaginable cynicism. It doesn't bother them in the least to have men join in these conversations; they'll even provoke the men to banter and make indecent gestures. (pp. 9–10)

The *surintendantes en stage* seem to have been most distressed by the fact that women workers could give as good as they got in exchanges with the men. Thus during the lunch hour at the Etablissements Dussé

> a few of the men traded sharp jests with the women. The women reacted, of course, for it was intended to make them laugh, and their retorts were bold and suggestive. These women baffle me. Don't they see how they degrade themselves when they speak like that, and that those same men, even as they laugh along with them, will be the very first to criticize them for their free and easy language?[15]

On the second point, the matter of valuing men's words above women's, it is clear that *surintendantes,* like the society that bred them, often rated working men's intelligence and breadth of vision more highly than that of women workers.[16] "The men are far more open-minded than the women when it comes to social issues," wrote Mlle Verneuil in 1928, during her *stage* at Panhard (pp. 21–22).[17] Given these values, one could see how a *surintendante* might trust a man's integrity more readily than a woman's,

---

[15] Report from the Etablissments Dussé (mechanical engineering), 1923, p. 6. The workers were given an hour for lunch (in a 10½-hour day), which they generally took in the workshop itself. The flirting and joking of which the *surintendante* writes took place during one such lunch break.

[16] Thus in 1920 Houssay observed that, thanks to their overly "narrow" conception of the working-class condition, the women at Renault had "less spirit of solidarity than the men" (p. 15).

[17] Of course, one of the "social issues" that she discussed with these men was the "problem" of women's work in metal factories, how it ruined their health and destroyed family life.

especially if the man in question were a highly skilled setter and the woman an uneducated machinist.[18]

Ultimately this vision of working-class women—vulgar, appetitive, and possessed of fewer moral and intellectual resources than their skilled male superiors—left no room in the *surintendantes'* conceptual vocabulary for the notion of sexual harassment as such. This absence emerges with startling clarity in Mlle Hilon's factory journal, in which the young *stagiaire* managed to dismiss harassment of which she herself was the object:

> The setter came by many times. He walked around me, hoping to get me to talk with him. He told me he lived in Boulogne, that he was married. . . . "Don't you have a guy, my little flea?" he asked, with some curiosity. "I'd be astonished if you didn't!" I told him I'd been married but my husband was killed in the war. He then took my hand and, eyes filled with tears, said: "Come, my pretty child, after a few months you'll get over it. You're a lovely girl and life is hard" (p. 9)

Evidently Mlle Hilon did not feel unduly pressured by the setter's persistence. Indeed, it is fair to say that his determined attentions did not weigh upon this young woman to the degree that they would have on her genuinely proletarian sisters; nor could they. Middle-class standing intervened, sheltering the young *stagiaire* and rendering her setter's behavior more charming than threatening: "I was deeply touched by his kind attentions, which proved once again that the people have a soul. . . . This little tool setter had a very kind heart, despite his appearance" (p. 9).

But the protective shield of class distance was a distorting mirror as well, for in combination with ingrained notions about working women's sexual mores, it made the very idea of sexual harassment impossible for a *surintendante* to conceive. Lacking any such concept, *surintendantes* would take other routes toward understanding factory hierarchies and defending the women caught within them. It is perhaps not surprising, then, that Mlle Cailleux quickly set aside the woman's bitter recriminations against her tool setter and turned to fulsome praise of her own team chief:

> In any case, no such criticism could ever be leveled at my team chief. He's a just man who keeps to himself and never jokes or trifles with the workers. Though he's handsome, he never flirts with anyone and he never wastes a minute. Calibrator in hand, he ceaselessly checks over our work. He's very

---

[18] Many *stagiaires* remarked on the women's "rudimentary" level of education—"a little primary schooling for the most part, one that left them with little taste for study," wrote one *surintendante* at the Etablissements Dussé. When Ollier asked a worker at Krieg & Zivy whether she knew about the company's maternal welfare plan, the woman replied, "I don't know how to read those posters about benefits" (p. 13).

organized and keeps an eye on everything; a truly conscientious and intelligent employee. (pp. 18–19)

Cailleux found it easier to fall in with the rhythm of social life at Renault than to catch the pace of her machine:

In the mornings, I've gotten in the habit of going with my comrades to get a cup of coffee at the bar across the street.[19] Here we talk and the newcomers learn the ropes. We pull our work coupons out of our pockets and ask an old hand what they're worth, and when and how we'll get paid: "You must figure your account for yourself," she urges. "You should do it at home, before payday. As for me, I always know exactly what I'm owed and I'll never let them fleece me!" (p. 20)

Mealtimes afforded workers those few moments of leisure otherwise forbidden in the factory and provided opportunities for instruction and amusement of all kinds. Professional singers strolled by the gates of Krieg & Zivy during the lunch break. "What fun this is for the women," wrote Mlle Ollier. "They learn all the latest songs and then repeat them throughout the afternoon as they stand in the doorway to the W.C., all the while munching furtively on the little snacks they sneak into the shop" (pp. 4–5). Political education, too, might proceed in the interstices, before the morning whistle sounded or perhaps during the lunch break.[20] Mlle Hilon recalled being gently rebuked by her mates for buying a "capitalist" newspaper.

I sat down and began to read. Two men, both quite courteous, sat down next to me, one on my right, one on my left. We shook hands. The comrade to my right . . . said, "But look now, we have to educate you. You're reading Le Journal, that's a capitalist rag. We've seen those guys, wearing their swallow-tailed coats while we're on strike. In the factory we only read L'Humanité— it's the only one that tells the truth. You have to get with the program or no one will know where you stand." (pp. 8–9)

---

[19] Not all surintendantes ventured so boldly onto workers' territory. Despite the terrible thirst that her work induced (turning, then drilling metal bars to make engine parts), Hilon sternly avoided the neighborhood cafés. "If I didn't have an aversion to entering a café, I'd have been sorely tempted" (p. 6).

[20] After the Confédération Général du Travail (CGT) split in the autumn of 1921, the syndical movement was effectively absent from the interwar factory, at least until labor's powerful revival in the wake of the May–June sit-down strikes in 1936. Under these conditions, whatever organizing went on took place outside the factory gates, and usually consisted of nothing more than the distribution of leaflets or copies of L'Humanité. In 1920, however, the power of the union movement was not yet fully broken, and workers could still exhibit their class-conscious politics without fear of reprisal.

Mlle Cailleux found the women at Renault a sympathetic lot, kind, well meaning, and always ready to help one another. She was especially charmed by their spontaneous solidarity in the face of adversity: "Yesterday the sweepers passed the hat for a worker, father of six children, who had been injured in an accident. Everyone gave something and they collected over Fr 200" (pp. 19–20). And Mlle Verneuil remembered the day she had to send a telegram:

> I asked a woman where I could find the nearest post office. After a moment's hesitation she said to me: "If you're going to ask for money from your family, don't worry; you can borrow it from me and pay me back next payday." And in the lunchroom, my neighbor always insisted on sharing her wine with me, for she believed that it was only to save money that I never bought any for myself. (p. 19)

Near the end of her *stage*, Mlle Cailleux finally caught the rhythm of her machine:

> My time in the factory is drawing to a close; today I have to settle up and ask for my wages. Just this morning, my work went beautifully, without a hitch, and I had one truly superb hour. So when I told the team chief that I would be leaving, he was outraged: "That's great! Now that you're making a two-seventy-five hour, that's the moment you choose to take off! It's always like that, and now some other boob will come in and she'll also set about breaking the chisels!" My neighbors and the foreman also seem scandalized. . . . It shocks them that I should quit this job when it's so hard to find work. I got myself out of it by saying that I had a sick child at home.
>
> I got my work certificate and left the factory filled with pity for my poor working sisters. Their lives are harsh and bleak, and they know so little, they have so few resources with which to think, to reflect. When I got back home, I thought about my life and those bitter days spent working [at Renault]. I compared this with the lives and homes of those poor women who are no less worthy than I, for I would surely do no better than they if I were placed in the same conditions since childhood, and this fired me with a great desire to help them a bit, if it is at all possible. (pp. 22–23)

When Cailleux and her fellow *stagiaires* next returned to the factory, they would exchange the blue overall of the ordinary worker for the khaki uniform of the *surintendante*. As each took her place in the managerial hierarchy, the cross-class sympathy stirred by their factory experience would (in theory) assume its proper place as the animating force within a larger managerial strategy of industrial rationalization as a collaborative and vertically ordered project. At times the *stagiaires'* reports reflect an uneasy awareness of the tensions that shaped their own role in that project. On the one hand, their training at the school and especially the *stage d'usine* encouraged them to encounter working-class women as fellow human beings. On the other hand, the khaki uniform moved each one away from the experience of work and upward into a niche in the hierarchy where her purpose was to maintain discipline, order, and productivity among those women.

This more coercive relation was deeply troubling to some *stagiaires*. Houssay found the job of machine tending "intolerable . . . when will an inventor figure out how to set the machines in motion by themselves, rather than condemning human beings to become nothing more than mechanical gears?" (p. 17). Mlle Nalon well understood "why these poor women [at Lampes Iris] are such terrible chatterboxes. If they didn't speak, wouldn't they be reduced to the state of mere things?" (p. 3).[21] But the transition to their full managerial position seems to have pushed many individual doubts to one side. Indeed, the solidarist philosophy of the Ecole des Surintendantes readily embraced the apparent contradiction between mutuality and hierarchy, casting cross-class solidarities as the reciprocal links in a factory hierarchy whose vertical order was justly determined by the neutral criterion of technical accomplishment.[22] *Surintendantes* thus took up their appointed task with a durable faith in its reconciliatory goals.[23]

Godmothers-Elect of Social Peace?

It is impossible to understand the power of rationalization as an ideological vision in France unless one recalls that its prophets and practitioners viewed

[21] Nalon was nonetheless surprised that management did not force the women to work in silence, "for the task would go more quickly if they did not chatter so" (p. 4).

[22] Solidarism, which the historian J. E. S. Hayward termed "the official social philosophy of the French Third Republic," is in many ways the secular analogue of social Catholic doctrine. Both philosophies deny the inevitability of class conflict and stress instead cooperation and collaboration among classes. Presumptions of vertical class order underpin both doctrines, with reciprocal obligations linking lower and higher. In the secular, solidarist version, these mutual obligations are imagined as part of an original social contract. See J. E. S. Hayward, "The Official Social Philosophy of the French Third Republic: Léon Bourgeois and Solidarism," *International Review of Social History* 6 (1961): 19–48. See also Karen Offen's enlightening discussion of the relationship between solidarism and republican feminism in her "Depopulation, Nationalism, and Feminism," *American Historical Review* 89 (June 1984): 648–76; Sanford Elwitt, *The Third Republic Defended: Bourgeois Reform in France, 1880–1914* (Baton Rouge, 1986); François Ewald, "A Concept of Social Law," in Gunther Teubner, ed., *Dilemmas of Law in the Welfare State* (New York, 1986), pp. 40–75, and *L'Etat Providence* (Paris, 1986); Judith Stone, *The Search for Social Peace* (New York, 1985). The idea that the war had forged a cross-class "brotherhood of the trenches" was yet another secular source for those collaborationist hopes.

[23] Hilon, for instance, ended her *stage* convinced that "most conflicts between workers and employers arise because they do not know each other" (p. 9).

enhanced efficiency not merely as an end in itself but also as a means of effecting a broader social transformation. Here the reformist, pro-rationalization wing of the labor movement[24] concurred with the more "progressive," modernization-minded employers: the installation of a rational order in the factory, answering to the rigorous and nonpartisan criteria of science, would improve efficiency and eliminate waste, enabling industry to raise output while lowering unit costs. The benefits could then return to all participants in the form of greater profits to the employer, higher wages to the worker, and more and cheaper goods to the consumer. Crucially, those who supported the idea believed that the benefits of economic growth would flow inevitably (and painlessly) from the more rational deployment of material and human resources, and not from any increased exploitation of labor. Industrial rationalization thus promised to realize what one scholar has termed the "society of abundance," and to distribute the rewards across the social landscape.[25]

But there was another element to the vision of social progress through technological development, an aspect more narrowly focused on the transformation of relations within the modern factory. Here *surintendantes* joined with their employers in imagining that under a more rational division of labor, the "unnecessarily" polarized relations of class against class might give way to a more harmonious structure, as all collaborated in the common productivist project of restoring and retooling the national economy.[26] Such faith in the socially regenerative powers of rationalization demanded that one adopt a sanguine interpretation of the impact that technical change had had on the structure of shop-floor relations and on the nature of work itself. Where its

[24] That is, Léon Jouhaux's noncommunist CGT. The communist wing objected to both welfare paternalism and the *surintendante,* "palliative for the abuses of a primitive Taylorism." Militants noted in particular her "infiltration" of working-class families, which was motivated, in their view, by patronal preoccupation with "the political tendencies of the father": untitled article signed by La Section d'Agit-prop du Quatrième Rayon de la Région Parisienne in *Cahiers du Bolchevisme,* no. 6 (August 1928), pp. 742–48. But the *syndicats* were far too weak to mount any effective opposition to the social services or to the *surintendantes,* and so tolerated both. See Fourcaut, *Femmes à l'usine,* p. 34.

[25] Richard Kuisel, *Capitalism and the State in Modern France* (Cambridge, 1981). On rationalization in interwar France, see Aimée Moutet, "Patrons de progrès ou patrons du combat?" in *Recherches,* nos. 32–33 (September 1978); Yves Lequin, "La Rationalisation du capitalisme français: A-t-elle lieu dans les années vingt?" *Cahiers d'Histoire de l'Institut Maurice Thorez,* no. 31 (1979); Sylvie Schweitzer, "Management and Labour in France, 1914–1939," in Steven Tolliday and Jonathan Zeitlin, eds., *The Automobile Industry and Its Workers* (London, 1986); Patrick Fridenson, "The Coming of the Assembly Line to Europe," *Sociology of the Sciences* 2 (1978): 159–78, and "L'Idéologie des grands constructeurs dans l'entre-deux-guerres," *Mouvement Social,* no. 1 (October–December 1972): 51–68.

[26] The idea that rationalization necessarily entailed class collaboration was not unique to France. This facet of the rationalization project, however, was particularly appealing to French employers, who stressed interclass cooperation far more than their British colleagues. "Rationalisation . . . requires the genuine collaboration of all factors of production": AN, 39 AS, 864, GIMM, "Déclaration sur la rationalisation et les salaires," April 1929, p. 1.

critics saw the intensification of work and more intrusive forms of managerial surveillance, rationalization's advocates envisioned a system that could "humanize" the factory by mechanizing brute labor and substituting the impartial rule of science for the arbitrary command of divine-right employers and their foremen.

Proponents of industrial rationalization saw in its technical innovations the opportunity to develop and improve the character of individual workers, and to recast shop-floor relations in a more cooperative mold. To some extent, the desired moral and social transformations would spring directly from the changed physical and social conditions of work. The scientific reorganization of labor demanded a different use of factory space, and often pressed employers to construct brighter, roomier shops and assembly halls. They brought in new machines and rearranged the old ones, so that production flowed continuously, with each task feeding automatically into the next. Rationalization thus ameliorated the physical conditions of work, and the cramped, ill-lit workshops of fin-de-siècle Paris gradually gave way to vast, airy, sunlit spaces, equipped with the most modern tools.[27] Mechanization also eased the individual worker's task, substituting rapid hand movements for heavy twisting and laboring. Finally, the random placement of workers at machines was superseded by the "scientific" selection of labor, in which women and men were assigned to specific tasks after a careful assessment of technical capacity and individual character.

Clearly employers hoped that rationalization's multiple reforms would not only deliver prosperity but facilitate the reconstitution of an imagined productive community, an organic social whole that had been torn apart in the futile and destructive industrial conflicts endemic to industrial France. But few believed that the restoration of community would flow from technical change alone. Such changes provided the material ground for social renovation. Further, the victory of a neutral ethic of efficiency over the competitive structures of laissez-faire's "excessive individualism" made it possible to redefine the terms on which labor encountered capital. Henceforth the two could set aside the blanket presumption of antinomous interests and meet on the common terrain of a mutual, productivist project. But even the most optimistic

---

[27] *Surintendantes* often spoke admiringly of the well-ordered spaces and streamlined managerial hierarchies characteristic of the modern factory. Of course, not every interwar metals factory was a miracle of the modern imagination; indeed, for every bright, high-tech space that opened in the 1920s, dozens of dark, dirty, ill-organized shops continued to limp along. Nalon wrote scathingly of conditions at the Lampes Iris factory: "Today I made a truly revolting discovery: W.C.s in a state of unimaginable filth. They had been properly designed—six *cabinets à la Turque* giving onto a well-ventilated room with large transoms and a washbasin at the entrance. But the flushing mechanism must have stopped working, although people still use the toilets, and when their condition becomes too disgusting, management closes them off by nailing a board across the doors!" (p. 7).

technocrats believed that some kind of active managerial intervention was required in order to locate and reconstruct the "lost" community of face-to-face relationships in the vast, technocratic landscapes of modern industry. Only then could the twin promises of technical and social transformation be realized on the factory floor.

Here, at the confluence of two streams in interwar managerial practice—the social and the technocratic—employers and their *surintendantes* opened out and defined the space in which welfare supervision would develop. The *surintendante* became a central figure in the elaboration of new managerial strategies for rationalizing labor, adapting the workforce to a steady and intense pace of work. At the same time, however, she stood at the heart of the larger reconciliatory project entwined in the effort to rationalize labor. Through her "maternalistic" management of the women entrusted to her care, the *surintendante* projected an image of the factory as a family writ large, a realm in which relations of reciprocity and mutual concern replaced and effaced the polarized structures of prewar days.

Although metals employers first began to hire *surintendantes* during World War I, it was in postwar years that the institution of welfare supervision spread most rapidly. During these years France faced a massive task of reconstruction, rebuilding farms and railways, coal mines and factories in the desolate wasteland that had once been France's richest region: the Nord–Pas-de-Calais, ruined and hovering on the brink of starvation after four harsh years of German occupation. The French were eager to restore the devastated regions to their customary state of industrial hyperactivity. Yet work proceeded in a climate of fear and uncertainty, as industrialists fretted about economic competition from a Germany resurgent; an upcoming economic "war" in which the enemy would deploy subtler but no less destructive means to bring France to its knees.

France's short-term economic problems looked all the more alarming in the context of this anticipated trade war. Industrial reconversion proceeded, but in slow and halting fashion, with firms hampered by a lack of raw materials and frequent interruptions in the power supply.[28] The shortages and general economic dislocation lasted well into 1923 and hindered all efforts to retool and recommence production on a peacetime basis. This prolonged and difficult transition fostered widespread uneasiness about the country's economic future: "Surely we can only end in ruin if things continue like this," cautioned

---

[28] Raw materials, especially steel and coal, were in perpetual short supply until the end of 1921. It was therefore difficult to generate a steady stream of electrical current and so ensure continuous production. Worse, the transport system barely functioned, for the nation's entire rolling stock had been driven into the ground by years of heavy use and scant repair.

Mlle Nalon in 1923, as she watched the Lampes Iris factory temporarily shut down operations for lack of raw materials (pp. 13–14).[29] As we have seen, industry's continued reliance on women mingled with an urgent pro-natalism to produce an obsessive discourse on France's need to develop its birth rate in tandem with its industry.[30] Yet the heavy losses of war—at least 2.5 million men killed or badly wounded—had produced a serious labor shortage.[31] After 1920, metals employers had no choice but to turn to women and immigrant labor to make up the deficit.[32] By 1936, nearly 15 percent of the industry's workforce was female, closer to 20 percent in the Paris region.[33]

As employers strove to reconcile motherhood with women's work in the factories, welfare supervision spread rapidly across the industry; by the late 1930s, more than fifty surintendantes were employed in metals and electronics factories, largely in Paris and its suburbs.[34] But industrialists did not view their contribution to postwar natalism as pure philanthropy. Rather, they

[29] This was Iris's second closing since 1919–20 (aside from the regular annual closings in late summer and early fall). The earlier closing was undoubtedly due to the raw materials crisis that affected industries throughout France after the Armistice. By 1923, however, supplies of steel and coal had stabilized, and Nalon did not hesitate to identify management's poor organization as the main culprit here.

[30] Françoise Thébaud aptly terms dénatalité a "leitmotiv" of interwar discourse: Quand nos grandmères donnaient la vie: La Maternité en France dans l'entre-deux-guerres (Lyon, 1989), p. 228. Like the grim discussions surrounding France's economic future, pro-natalist discourse was dominated by militarized images of patriotic struggle against the ruthless (yet admirably productive) Teutonic foe.

[31] At least 10% of the industrial workforce had been killed. See Gérard Noiriel, Workers in French Society in the Nineteenth and Twentieth Centuries (New York, 1990), p. 114.

[32] Women who did their factory stages in the immediate postwar period, when employers drastically reduced the percentage of women workers, remembered how hard this time was on the women. Houssay wrote: "It's ten o'clock and we're still at the gates with a long line of women waiting ahead of us. Throughout the long wait, they agonize, fearing they won't get hired, for now it's no longer wartime, when all hands were equally desirable. Now it's hard to get hired. . . . The high cost of living has brought these women here, although many of them are mothers" (pp. 3–4).

[33] AN, 39 AS, 830, GIMM to Ministère du Travail, "Répartition du personnel," 8 July 1936, states that 18% of the workers in affiliated firms were women. (At the time, GIMM embraced some 3,120 firms—about 80% of the local metals industry—employing 87% of the Paris region's metalworkers.)

[34] The number of surintendantes employed in all branches of French industry more than quadrupled from 1919 to 1937, rising from about 50 to 218. In the mid-1930s these women were concentrated overwhelmingly in the metals, automobile, and electrical goods industries. See Fourcaut, Femmes à l'usine, p. 21. Surintendantes were also prominent in administering the employer-organized social services and family allocation funds. See Mlle Hardouin, "Les Surintendantes d'usine et des services sociaux," in "L'Hygiène sociale," Cahiers du Redressement Français 17 (1927): 119–35. As the surintendante became a fixture in the interwar factory, the number of grandes dames drawn to the profession fell sharply; interwar recruits were more solidly middle-class in origin. See "Les Surintendantes d'usines," Revue de l'U.I.M.M., 15 February 1939, pp. 100–101.

made a virtue of necessity, placing the *surintendante* at the center of elaborate welfare schemes that linked the establishment of order in the home to good work discipline among the women:

> We are currently obliged to call upon the female labor force, and will be obliged to do so to an even greater extent in the future. . . . However, from the necessary evil of women's employment in the factory some good can come, for the woman who is advised and guided by the *surintendante* gradually develops moral ideas, and from this woman, exposed to the corruption of the big cities, you can make an excellent mother and a good worker.[35]

In these years of demographic "crisis," metals employers could celebrate their welfarist labor discipline as both socially conscious practice and sound business sense.

As the economy of scarcity at last gave way to a continuous, reconstruction-driven expansion, employers greeted the *surintendantes* as welcome collabora-tors in the struggle to modernize industry and raise output: "The *surinten-dantes'* return to our factories will harmonize with the larks of the spring: they return as the heralds of a new prosperity."[36] Employers were to realize the new spring-time of prosperity by adapting wartime methods—redividing work, fragmenting tasks, introducing more automatic machinery—to peace-time production. Further, they hoped to cut costs by driving workers to a more intensive effort through the application of highly coercive work systems that purported to assess the energy and effort expended in production.

These systems, which traveled under the rubric of "industrial psychophysiol-ogy" or "psychotechnique," drew their authority from wartime and postwar studies of the relation of effort expenditure, output, and fatigue.[37] Psychotech-nique promised to "rationalize" the labor process by distinguishing necessary motions from wasted ones, productive time from nonproductive time. Em-ployers seized on the idea, confident that they had at last found a means to identify and eliminate all nonproductive time (and workers) from the factory floor. Piece rates were now tied to effort inputs as well as output, and the pace of work raced frenetically ahead.

Because industrial psychophysiology correlated output with the workers' physical condition, the employer often gave his in-house welfare expert much

---

[35] "Rapport de M. Niçaise [director of the Lorraine-Dietrich factory]," *BAS*, 28 February 1922.

[36] Ibid. Many employers had dismissed their *surintendantes* during the demobilization, unwilling to pay their salaries when the future looked so bleak. Most factories were not ready to welcome back the peacetime workforce until 1921–22.

[37] See "Rapport de Mme Catelet sur la sélection professionelle," *BAS*, 21 February 1928, pp. 26–28.

of the responsibility for operating the new effort-measurement systems.[38] The *surintendante's* detailed acquaintance with the habits and abilities of individual workers made her an important ally in organizing assembly lines, redistributing jobs, and imposing the ruthless speed-ups that the scientific management of labor entailed.[39] Her stopwatch measured effort inputs of male and female workers alike, but her surveillance focused most heavily on women, who so often performed the rapid, deskilled tasks that were especially subject to intrusive time-motion management and speed-ups.[40] In 1935 Simone Weil described the heavy cost that this streamlined labor process extracted from the individual: "The constraint. To do nothing, even in matters of detail, which might take the least initiative. Every motion is simply the execution of an order. . . . One is merely a thing attached to the will of another. . . . How one would love to leave her soul in the box by the door, and reclaim it upon leaving!"[41]

As dedicated partisans of the rationalization project, *surintendantes* viewed the mass-production organization of work from a radically different perspective: that of shop-floor managers who applauded employers' bold efforts to drag French industry into the twentieth century.[42] One hears in Mlle Wagner's voice a frisson of sheer aesthetic pleasure at the ordered calm and efficiency she saw on the factory floor:

[38] Though concerned to create a "human" context for these systems, *surintendantes* nonetheless embraced their newly scientized role. They swiftly adopted the arcane and often convoluted language of psychophysiology, perhaps because it allowed them to don the mantle of science as the basis for broader claims to a specific professional expertise: "The psychotechnician studies not absolute but relative individual values. He compares biological values and classes them according to the labor market": ibid., p. 27. On the broader convergence of scientific discourses with "human factor" management in interwar Europe, see Anson Rabinbach, *The Human Motor* (Berkeley, 1992).

[39] Thus at Thomson-Houston, foremen routinely consulted the *surintendante* before arranging women on the line: "One of [the team chiefs], organizing a new mass-production team, placed the women in standing and seated stations at random. Then he asked the *surintendante* to come take a look: 'I still don't know, tell me whether or not they're well placed.' I suggested a few changes on the grounds of serious health considerations, and he adopted them on the spot": Le Service Sociale, Thomson-Houston, Usine des Piles, "Rapport du Service Sociale," 7 March 1928, p. 5 (Ecole des Surintendantes).

[40] *Surintendantes* often concurred in the employers' assessment of what constituted appropriate work for women in the industry. Thus at the highly rationalized Jaeger factory, Mlle Dieterlen wrote in 1930: "The work in this shop demands the qualities of care, precision, and dexterity that are completely suitable to a semiskilled female workforce" (p. 4).

[41] Weil, *Condition ouvrière*, pp. 227–28.

[42] The *surintendantes'* criticisms, when offered, were generally reserved for those factories that failed to implement an intelligent organization of machinery and human material. Nalon's report of work at Lampes Iris, for example, describes a primitive and perpetually bottlenecked assembly line whose defects could be traced to poor organization and management. The flow of work through the filament shop depended on one highly skilled woman, whose frequent absences brought the entire shop to a standstill. Management had failed to organize a back-up supply of stand-ins, skilled women who knew each phase of every job and so could fill in for anyone who was absent.

Radio valve shop at the Sociéte Radiotechnique (Suresnes), 1920–25. Note foremen (in white coats) standing at the left of the assembly hall. Cliché Thomson.

From my glassed-in office I can watch the activity in the shop and I admire the discipline that reigns there. The women work without disruption, and at times their motions are quite lovely to see. From time to time one or another lifts her head, and seeing that my eyes are upon her, makes a little sign of friendship. (p. 8)

Occasionally *surintendantes* glimpsed in this highly coordinated labor process a darker, more distressing side to industrial progress: "Perpetually repeating the same motion simply makes a machine of the woman worker," wrote one *stagiaire* of work in a brand-new electronics plant whose bright and commodious spaces she had praised fulsomely not two pages earlier.[43] But most saw in scientific management a promise to ease working women's burden,

[43] Report of Mlle Collot, Cie Lorraine des Charbons, 1928, p. 11.

as further rationalization would "simplify" factory work and match the individual to the task. One *surintendante* asserted that industrial psychophysiology

is also and *especially* in the interests of the working class, for whom "psychotech-
nique" affords a measure of protection against the risks of a poor psychomotor
adaptation. . . . If each worker is in his place, industry will fulfill its social role.
Rather than grow more deadly, it will permit each worker to develop his
personality, instead of wearing out his physical and moral force at a job incompatible with his constitution.[44]

In matching the individual to her task, the *surintendante* relied on the
"scientific" principles invoked in interwar manuals on labor selection. By
lending a pseudo-scientific verisimilitude to notions of gender difference,
this literature ensured that *surintendantes* would conjoin worker and task in
gender-appropriate ways: "The woman's ergographic force is proportionally
more developed than the man's . . . therefore women are more able to repeat
a moderate effort than to give a maximal effort once."[45] As the expert agents
of the new work science, *surintendantes* upheld the not-so-new boundaries
of sexual division even as they redivided the labor process. Although they
were all uncomfortably aware of the gap that yawned between men's and
women's wages—a gap that hovered between 20 and 30 percent after 1918—
these women never questioned the sexual division of labor within which that
wage differential was inscribed.[46] They might balk at the breadth of the gap;
some even recognized that it was upheld by a wage policy that penalized
women for being adept at their work: "As soon as management sees women
on piecework making more than Fr 18 or 20 a day, they lower the rate,"
observed M. Houssay during her *stage* at Renault. "It seems completely unjust
that women should be paid less simply because they work quickly" (p. 17).
Yet having grasped this fact, Houssay looked away from its source, in the

[44] "Rapport de Mme Catelet," p. 28; emphasis in original.
[45] Paul Razous, *La Sélection des travailleurs* (Paris, 1924), p. 11. The ergograph was a machine
that purported to measure muscular effort. On the origins of ergonomy, see Rabinbach, *Human
Motor*, chap. 5.
[46] Yet every report mentions women's lower wages on similar or identical work. In 1920
GIMM set women's rates at about 70% of men's. After some fluctuation, women's wages then
began to climb faster than men's, reaching about 80% by 1930. Here they stayed, more or less,
until the end of the decade. These figures elide some interesting particularities. Women and
men in the same skill classifications never earned the same wages. Beginning in 1930, however,
semiskilled women's rates equaled and sometimes slightly surpassed those of unskilled men.
Such boundary crossings never occurred in Britain, where employers resolutely held the interwar
wage gap at about 50% and lumped all women in a single category, gently graded by age alone.
British employers never acknowledged women's skills in the formal structure of wage scales.
At best, an individual firm might concede a few extra shillings to women employed on skilled
work. See M. L. Yates, *Wages and Labour in British Engineering* (London, 1937), p. 120; and
Downs, "Women in Industry," appendixes.

hierarchical sexual division of labor, and turned instead to a detailed consideration of the punishing impact that this inequality had in perpetuating the
struggle between labor and capital:

> Moreover, they [women workers] limit their own output, saying that there's
> no point in wearing themselves out; they know that as soon as they produce
> more, the work will be retimed and the minimum piece rate will be lowered
> once again. Thus the struggle never ends between capital, which wants an
> intensive effort at the lowest possible rate, and labor, which defends itself,
> limiting and doling out its energies. And one cannot blame them because such
> intensive production is in truth nothing more than systematic and terrible
> overwork. (p. 24)

Houssay recognized the gross inequalities that shaped the factory floor at
Renault—between women and men, between worker and employer. Yet here,
as elsewhere, the *surintendantes'* deepest ambition—to forge lasting bonds
of cooperation across an unnecessary (and falsely conceived) class divide—
cut off any nascent feminist or class-conscious stirrings at their very root.[47]
The spectacle of shop-floor injustice might cause the *surintendantes'* attention
to flicker briefly, and male–female inequalities were especially likely to catch
her eye. Yet in the end, even the most earnest concern was diverted by the
surintendantes' overarching faith in the prospect of forging class harmony.
Houssay thus closed her report with the fervent declaration that in her future
work, she would strive to realize her "vivid desire to bring our class closer
to theirs" (p. 33).

In hopes of bridging that divide, *surintendantes* cast themselves in the role
of mother to the woman worker. In so doing, they created an appropriately
domestic context for labor discipline, shaping what was meant to be a warm
yet firmly hierarchical relationship: "This intermediary between the women
workers, the employers, and the foremen [has] a considerable moral influence

---

[47] In general, the earlier reports reflect more knowledge of class-based issues, more awareness
of and sympathy toward a class-conscious perspective. This awareness, couched in the language
of class difference, jostles uneasily against these women's equally powerful hopes for class
harmony through social services and face-to-face encounters between workers and their employers, represented by the *surintendante*. Thus Houssay expressed the desire to go to some trade
union meetings (p. 30), and her colleagues referred to the other women as "comrades," spoke
of reading *L'Humanité*, and commented on the solidarity of male workers. As the 1920s wore
on, this desire to encounter working-class politics and culture on their own terms tended to
fall out of the reports. Any proto-feminist stirrings visible in the *stagiaires'* earlier reports—
their anger at women's lower wages, for example—also fell from view as students trained in
an atmosphere of rising pro-natalist anxiety expressed more open ambivalence about women's
presence in the factory at all. By the late 1920s, the *stagiaires* seem to be framing their
observations about women and working-class life in a more exclusively social Catholic/solidarist
discourse of class collaboration.

over the worker-mother: a kind of familiarity springs up between them, a familiarity engendered only by [one of] the same sex."[48] As the *surintendantes* pried further into the women's home lives, this "familiarity" deepened:

We chat about everything, health, family life, their painful secrets, we talk of marriage, career, and work, of debts to be paid and sometimes of more serious matters, very serious . . . we have utter trust in each other. Sometimes they don't understand when I am strict, but this does not hurt our mutual confidence: "Why did you say that, Mademoiselle?" and the explanation brings us another step toward friendship.[49]

During these sessions, the *surintendante* often garnered information about the women's private lives that could prove useful in efforts to impose discipline on the shop floor. In 1933 one Mme Vialette, *surintendante* at Michelin, reported with some satisfaction that she had successfully driven three "lazy" women to work more quickly by giving them a stern lecture about the serious financial difficulties each of their families faced. Her veiled threats of dismissal proved sufficient chastisement, for as Mme Vialette well knew, none of these women could afford to lose her job. To no one's surprise, all three "understood and became very good workers."[50]

The *surintendante's* multiple managerial functions were thus embedded in a broader framework of personal, woman-to-woman interventions in the everyday lives of her occasionally wayward proletarian charges: "Isn't this the *surintendante's* role," wrote Mlle Collot, "to gently warn the woman that, since her work is not sufficiently productive, it might be necessary to transfer her. As she is paid on a bonus system, this is as much in her interest as in the firm's" (p. 12). Général Appert, director at Alsthom electrical works, grew misty-eyed as he imagined his *surintendante* making her daily rounds: "Who better than the *surintendante* to intervene and alert management to the abilities of a woman worker? Who better than she to look into their little weaknesses, their problems? [Who better than she] knows how to give them joy in their work, which is necessary for a good output?" Yet Appert's tender vision was also animated by hard-nosed practicality; in an industry plagued

---

[48] Jacques Doléris and Jean Bouscatel, *Hygiène et morales sociales: Néo-malthusianisme, maternité et féminisme* (Paris, 1918), p. 255. The *surintendantes* cherished the notion that the women participated wholeheartedly in the familial fiction. Thus the *surintendante-directrice* of the school recalled that "one day a woman worker, more than 60 years old, wrote to me about her *surintendante*, aged 28: 'My *surintendante*, I love her like my mother' ": "Rapport de Mme Agnès Georges Jacob," *BAS*, 1925.

[49] Service Sociale, Thomson-Houston, "Rapport," p. 2.

[50] Mme Vialette, "L'Embauche et le travail qui en derive pour une surintendante," *BAS*, February 1933, pp. 29–30.

by high turnover, "it is she who brings back the good workers when they're wanted. Thanks to her intervention, they remain attached to the factory, which does not abandon them, which follows them during the [annual] unemployment. Doesn't this help achieve a stable female workforce—so sought after and yet so difficult to achieve in the Paris region?"[51]

In the *surintendante* employers believed they had at last found an answer to the problem of reconciling women's work with their maternal function: "We expect a great deal of the *surintendante*—neither nun nor worker nor woman of the world, or perhaps all three things together, she stands as the strongest link between the working class and our class: the godmother-elect of social peace."[52] Industrialists used the language of motherly concern and face-to-face intimacy to characterize the *surintendante's* work in part because such images constructed a model of factory relations that denied the inevitability of class conflict without abandoning the central fact of hierarchically structured authority relationships. The *surintendantes* shared this vision, and saw themselves in a familial and essentially maternal relation to women workers and to the "male" side of management. Indeed, they spoke of themselves as "mistress of the house, nurse, and teacher" and as "liaison between employers and workers," blending the technical with the social in a single web of welfare relations.[53] Hence *surintendantes*, like their employers, rarely saw any incompatibility between productivist goals and efforts to improve the workers' physical and mental state. Indeed, most believed that raising output and tending to the workers' welfare were complementary elements in modern factory management; the former could not help but flow from the latter. From the *surintendante's* standpoint, then, there could be no tension between her technical role as labor manager and her welfarist concern for women's physical and moral condition.

Welfare supervision was thus predicated on the belief that fragmented and polarized social relations were not the inevitable outcome of industrial expansion and the fragmentation of work. On the contrary, *surintendantes* endeavored to heal that rupture through their maternalistic management of labor, offering an alternative, familial image of factory relations where reciprocal obligation, mutual concerns, and a common productivist project enabled the reconstitution of the "true," organic and harmonious factory commu-

[51] "Allocution de Général Appert," *BAS,* February 1929, pp. 24, 25. Turnover rates were high for workers of both sexes in this period, suggesting high levels of discontent in factories that they continued to describe as *bagnes* (prison camps).

[52] René Doumic, speaking at the Académie Française as the Académie awarded its Prix de Vertu to the Association des Surintendantes in 1921, quoted in Pierre Magnier de Maisonneuve, *Les Institutions sociales en faveur des ouvrières d'usine* (Paris, 1923), p. 291.

[53] "Rapport de Mlle Geoffroy sur ce que font et peuvent faire les surintendantes pour 'l'Education Familiale' et 'l'Enseignement Ménager,' " *BAS,* February 1928, p. 33; and "Rapport de Mlle Duponchel," *BAS,* 1929, p. 14.

nity.[54] The iconography of family and domestic industry—the modern enterprise as small workshop—provided a model of social relations that denied the possibility of irreconcilable class difference, rooted in the socioeconomic structure outside the factory and reproduced in the sharply vertical command structure within. Instead, the *surintendante,* animated by the solidarist/social Catholic conviction of organic community, bound by ties of mutual affection and duty, linked the technical to the welfarist in a seamless structure of control that was exercised for the woman worker's own good.

Clearly the movement to reshape and restore a more harmonious factory community was saturated by images of women as workers and as mothers. In a nation obsessed by its birth rate, pro-natalist sentiment mingled with Taylorist strategies to produce a patronal policy that regarded women's work in a rationally ordered factory as compatible with motherhood. The interpenetration of natalist and Taylorist ideas reminds us once again of the cultural particularity with which the French wove together the social and the technocratic aspects of modern managerial "science."

Surintendantes and the Regulation of Proletarian Domesticity

In postwar years, employers gradually discarded the more narrowly natalist wartime installations, such as the factory nursing rooms. Costly to maintain and underused in any event, the nursing rooms did little to advance productivity on the shop floor.[55] But the disappearance of these rooms did not signal the abandonment of welfare management as a labor strategy in France. On the contrary, in these years of ongoing demographic crisis and rapid industrial growth, metals employers took up a more direct regulation of proletarian family life through intensified supervision of the female workforce. Through a series of new initiatives—offering home economics classes for the women (after hours, of course) and sending the *surintendantes* directly into workers' homes to help order proletarian domesticity—employers sought to extend their influence beyond the factory walls and into the notionally private realm of the working-class household.

Clearly their heightened concern with the structure of workers' family lives grew out of pervasive middle-class anxiety over the proletariat's stubbornly

[54] Maisonneuve tellingly described that idealized community as "an uninterrupted chain, guaranteed in part by social services": *Institutions sociales,* pp. 57–58.

[55] In 1920 GIMM adjured adherents to close their nursing rooms and simply let young mothers stay home for a month before and a month after childbirth, at half or perhaps full base pay. GIMM noted that this solution was cheaper and "infinitely preferable to the spread of factory nursing rooms": AN, 39 AS, 403, GIMM to UIMM, "Chambres d'allaitement et allocations de grossesse," 4 September 1920, p. 2.

low birth rate. But it also reflected the qualitatively different sort of control to which "progressive" employers aspired. No longer content simply to prod individuals with wage incentives, employers sought to implant in each worker an inner principle of self-discipline that would make her an ideal complement to the swift and powerful American machine tools that filled the machine shops and assembly halls around Paris.[56] Antonio Gramsci characterized the efforts of these modern managers as nothing less than a campaign to redefine the worker:

> It is worth drawing attention to the way in which industrialists (Ford in particular) have been concerned with the sexual affairs of their employees and with the family arrangements in general. One should not be misled by this concern. The truth is that the new type of man demanded by the rationalisation of production and work cannot be developed until the sexual instinct has been suitably regulated and until it too has been rationalised.[57]

Uniquely poised to monitor women's family lives as well as their productivity on the job, the *surintendante* took on the task of reshaping the worker, extending her "maternal" influence beyond the factory gates and into the heart of the proletarian household.

On the factory premises, the *surintendante* sought to lead the women by example. In her daily management of the factory's welfare and maternal services she found an ideal venue for reinforcing the factory's "familial" hierarchy while instructing her charges in the stern disciplines of motherhood. If the crèches and infirmaries were maintained in a state of "perfect cleanliness" and run with "unwavering discipline [and] equal concern for order," then the young worker-mother would "see the care her infant requires, and this cannot help but awaken in her a more precise sense of her duties."[58]

Of course, women workers had to be using the crèches if they were to glean any benefit from contact with that disciplined and orderly world, and it seems that few of them did so voluntarily. One *surintendante* after another ruefully reported that the factory crèche stood empty or very nearly so, that women workers preferred to rely instead on neighbors, relatives, even the concierge.[59] The crèche remained an option of last resort, as one student discovered during her *stage* in La Villette:

---

[56] For an account of retooling in the postwar metals and automobile industries, see Patrick Fridenson, "Automobile Workers in France and Their Work," in Steven L. Kaplan and Cynthia J. Koepp, eds., *Work in France: Representation, Meaning, Organization, and Practice* (Ithaca, 1986); and Schweitzer, "Management and Labour in France."

[57] Antonio Gramsci, "Americanism and Fordism," in *The Prison Notebooks*, ed. Quintin Hoare (New York, 1971), p. 297.

[58] "Rapport de Mlle Geoffroy," p. 30.

[59] Like many of her colleagues, Mlle Ollier believed that the crèche offered better care than the women themselves knew how to give. At the crèche children "blossomed, largely sheltered

I asked one young mother, "What would you do if you didn't have your mother-in-law to take care of your baby, how would you handle things?" Her friend Rosalie interjected, "She'd do as I do and use the crèche." The young mother then replied: "Yes, I would be forced to use the crèche of course, but I've heard that babies are poorly cared for in the crèches." And Rosalie did not contradict her.[60]

To reinforce the salutary impact of domestic instruction on the factory premises, the *surintendante* made periodic visits to individual women's homes, armed with sound advice for pulling those homes into better order.[61] By virtue of her sex, class standing, and education, the *surintendante* was, in her own mind as well as that of the employer, ideally poised for the transmission of domestic virtue: "The experienced *surintendantes* know which steps to take in order to lead a turbulent and noisy group of young workers . . . released after hours of nervous tension in the factory, to a state of calm, attentive to a delicate and exacting task. . . ."[62] *Surintendantes* did not doubt for one minute that women workers were in grave need of these lessons: "I have seen many young girls reading cheap romances that distort their understanding, twist their judgment, make them forget women's duties, and give them no real idea of the natural role to which they are called in society."[63] Yet if her instruction was to achieve its intended purpose, the *surintendante* required a receptive audience, and it seems that women metalworkers, married and single, had little interest in rounding out an eight- or nine-hour shift with a few hours of sewing and cozy chat with the welfare lady.[64]

Employers understood the value of extending their control from the public world of work to the private lives of their workers. Under the *surintendante's*

---

from life's evil influences . . . here the staff applies a [child-rearing] method that leaves nothing to chance, a method developed through extensive research" (p. 3). Although most *surintendantes* concurred, they generally upheld the mystique of the mother's care. The best solution, therefore, lay in educating these women for motherhood.

[60] Report from Etablissements Dussé, 1923, p. 9. The sole recorded exception I found was in Verneuil's report from Panhard (1928), in which she mentions a co-worker who left her one-month-old daughter in Panhard's crèche "and is very happy with the care they give her there" (p. 20).

[61] As Mlle Wagner's report reveals, *surintendantes* were hardly dispassionate in their approach to these visits: "It pleases me to imagine sweet, happy little proletarian households but the manner of some of these women makes me think that irregularity and debauchery are just as likely. How much of their ill conduct arises from never having been taught properly, and for how much of the vice that so often suffices to explain their misery are they alone responsible?" (p. 9). Carola Sachse, *Industrial Housewives* (New York, 1987), gives an account of parallel developments in the German metals industries.

[62] "Rapport de Mlle Geoffroy," p. 33.

[63] Report from Etablissements Dussé, 1923, p. 10.

[64] " . . . the idea of following home economics courses holds little appeal for the young girls and women": Union Féminine Civique et Social (hereafter UFCS), *La Mère au foyer: Ouvrière de progrès humain. Documents d'études. Extraits du congrès international de juin 1937* (Paris, 1937), pp. 244–45.

guidance, women workers could create a more orderly home life for their husbands and children, and so ensure the maintenance of a healthy labor force. Equally important, training women to accept the arduous and routine labors of domesticity was an inexpensive and gender-appropriate means of instilling self-discipline and a taste for order in the often "unruly" woman worker: "Employers have observed important changes in the overall attitude of women workers. They have been able to approach the most difficult groups of women, and the impact is noticeable not only in the women themselves, but in the households and at the heart of the factory itself."[65] Home economics classes honed women's "innate" ability to perform swiftly the monotonous taskwork of mass production by schooling them in the virtues of patience and attentiveness to a boring and thankless job. Moreover, these classes constituted an excellent forum in which to spread the gospel of social renewal through industrial rationalization. After all, as one *surintendante* observed, there was a happy coincidence of national/social interest and private capitalist interest in training women to run their homes more efficiently: "The industrial and social viewpoints agree. . . . The woman who wears herself out at home has low output."[66]

In addition, many *surintendantes* believed that working-class family life was such a fragile plant that it required a great deal of propping up if it was to survive. The social consequences of its dissolution were dire:

> The married woman spends very little time at home, returns home exhausted, and little by little lets the housework lapse. If her husband doesn't help her with the cleaning, the home is badly kept. . . . If there are children, they are poorly cared for, grow sickly and stunted. Tuberculosis is forever at the threshold. . . . The wife becomes bitter and her husband no longer takes pleasure in returning home. He gradually abandons this neglected home, takes refuge in a nearby café, and . . . gives himself up to liquor, to cards, and soon falls into the abyss.[67]

[65] AN, 39 AS, 402, "Note sur le mouvement familial ménager," 8 July 1926. Annie Fourcaut reminds us that workers generally paid a small fee for the privilege of taking these home economics courses—about Fr 3 a month (at a time when women earned about Fr 25–30 a day). If they wished to eat the food prepared during these classes, they paid an additional Fr 7 per meal: *Femmes à l'usine*, p. 203.

[66] "Rapport de Mlle Gros-Croissy," *BAS*, 1925. In addition, home economics would teach women to stretch their wages further: "A woman who does not know how to cook or put the linen and clothing in order can never balance the budget, *even with higher wages*," wrote the manager of the Forges d'Haironville in response to a UFCS survey on returning mothers to the home, 19 October 1936, UIMM, 69/54/03.

[67] Report from the Etablissements Dussé, p. 11. The effort to refurbish proletarian domesticity was dogged by the workers' severe lack of resources. Housing was ancient, cramped, and often in hideous disrepair. Plumbing was primitive (many apartments still lacked running water) and domestic consumerism was quite limited. On interwar housing in Paris, see Tyler Stovall, *The*

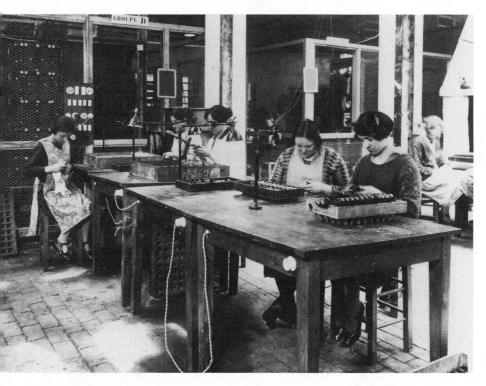

Placing the bases on the valves, Société Radiotechnique (Suresnes), 1920–25. Cliché Thomson.

The *surintendante* could arrest and even reverse the course of this grim trajectory by addressing timely counsel to the worker-mother, linchpin of that essential if precarious social body, the working-class family.

In the eyes of the faithful (industrialist and *surintendante* alike) the kind of class collaboration that productivism, welfare management, and home economics classes could create on the factory floor had the power to transform individual character:

Many things could be cited as evidence of this notable transformation. The most immediate is the better use of wages, and perhaps most striking is the moral and social change observed. . . . Finally, there is . . . an atmosphere of

Rise of the Paris Red Belt (Berkeley, 1989); and Susanna Magri and Christian Topalov, eds., *Villes ouvrières, 1900–1950* (Paris, 1989).

relaxation, of mutual confidence in these courses, produced by the study of things so closely related to family life. . . . Properly guided by readings and conversations, this inclination toward healthy ideas can affect not only their morality, as women and as workers, but also the moral welfare of the entire factory.[68]

When the long boom of the 1920s gave way at last to depression and stagnation in the 1930s, the *surintendante*'s familialist interventions acquired added weight.[69] Through this, "her most delicate role, but also the most beautiful," she strove to uphold family values and support the working-class household, beleaguered by falling wages and unemployment.[70]

The Campaign to Return Working Mothers to the Home

In the autumn of 1930, industrialists saw the first slight signs that France's unprecedented industrial prosperity might be starting to ebb. In June the monthly index of production had reached its postwar peak of 144 (1913 = 100). In October unemployment began to rise. Two months later retail prices started falling. Over the next twelve months the French economy slipped gradually into a depression from which it would not recover until after World War II. By the first quarter of 1932, overall industrial production had fallen 25 percent, and there it more or less stayed through the remainder of the decade.[71] After 1931, unemployment and short time became permanent features of the French economy.

For the metalworking industry, the crisis was delayed until the winter of 1931–32. But in metalworking, as elsewhere, decline, once it arrived, settled in for good.[72] Overall unemployment for the industry, 6 to 7 percent in the

[68] AN, 39 AS, 402, "Note sur le mouvement familial ménager," and Mlle de Robien, "Rapport," in *Congrès de l'Enseignement Ménager* (Paris, 1922).

[69] Familialism and pro-natalism are analytically distinct movements that went hand in hand at this time, as activists in both camps worked to raise the birth rate. Pro-natalists were ready to back any course that promised to make more French babies, while familialists were concerned to raise fertility within the patriarchal family. *Surintendantes* were rarely extreme partisans of either doctrine, although the general air of urgency surrounding the birth rate clearly affected their management of women workers, especially in the stagnant 1930s. I am indebted to Miranda Pollard for pointing out this distinction.

[70] Unnamed *surintendante* quoted in Mathilde Dubesset, Françoise Thébaud, and Catherine Vincent, "Quand les femmes entrent à l'usine: Les Ouvrières des usines de guerre de la Seine, 1914–1918" (mémoire de maîtrise, Université de Paris VII, 1974), p. 196.

[71] Julian Jackson, *The Politics of Depression in France, 1932–1936* (Cambridge, 1985), pp. 23–24.

[72] The index of production for the industry as a whole stood at 138 in 1928 (1913=100). After 1930 production fell off sharply, reaching a low of 96 in 1932. Over the next two years production recovered somewhat, reaching 101 in 1934, where it remained until 1939. See Great Britain, Department of Overseas Trade, *Economic Conditions in France*, Report by Robert Cahill (London, 1934), p. 628.

mid-1930s, conceals the considerable hardship that metalworkers endured, for at least 40 percent of those who retained their jobs were working on short time after 1932.[73] Throughout the 1930s, women appeared to be weathering the Depression better than men: although 36 percent of all employed persons were women, women made up at most one-quarter of the reported unemployed.[74] This widely discussed phenomenon helped foster the notion that male unemployment might be "solved" if married women were removed from the workplace and sent back to home and family.

The arrival of the Depression coincided with the news that the French population was failing to reproduce itself: in 1929 the number of deaths had actually exceeded births by 9,000. Things would only go from bad to worse in the 1930s, for in these years the "hollow cohorts" born during the war came of age, demographically speaking. Between 1935 and 1939 the death rate consistently outstripped the birth rate, which at 14.6 per thousand was one of the lowest on the planet.[75] These grim tallies rekindled pro-natalist fears of a "disappearing France" and widened the ranks of those receptive to the notion that both economic and demographic depression could be solved by "returning" working mothers to the home.

> Aside from all the social, moral, and sanitary considerations . . . is the fact that the maintenance of the woman in the home frees the job she would have occupied and so contributes to reabsorbing unemployed men and single women. . . . The country cannot wait much longer for the application of the most efficacious remedy against the discouragement of families, the falling birth rate and unemployment.[76]

During the early 1930s, the movement to expel mothers from industry rapidly gained momentum. By 1932, pro-natalist activists in the Catholic feminist Union Féminine Civique et Sociale (UFCS) began to hound industri-

---

[73] The entire Parisian auto industry, whose production index had dropped from 627 in 1929 to 400 in 1935, was put on a 32-hour week in 1932: *BMT*, January–March 1936, p. 14.

[74] Usually about 23% of those listed as unemployed were women, thanks to widespread underreporting of women's (especially married women's) unemployment and employers' preference for retaining cheaper workers in a time of falling profits. According to a factory inspector for the Paris region, unskilled men and laborers bore the brunt of male unemployment during the Depression, because firms cherished their skilled men: Gabrielle Letellier, *Le Chômage en France de 1930 à 1936* (Paris, 1938), pp. 66–68. In metalworking, where women made up nearly 20% of the Parisian labor force, they accounted for only 14% of the unemployed: *BMT*, January–March 1939, p. 11.

[75] See André Armengaud, *La Population française au 20ᵉ siècle* (Paris, 1973), p. 60.

[76] Georges Bonvoisin, "Les Allocations familiales et la présence de la mère au foyer," in UFCS, *La Mère au foyer*, p. 138; and UIMM, 69/54/03, UFCS, "Article-type pour la presse," December 1938, p. 2.

alists to take a stand on the issue of mothers' employment in their industries.[77] Often pressure was most intense in such "nontraditional" arenas as metalworking, where turning back the clock seemed easiest. In the face of shrill opposition, metals employers came to a considered (and determined) decision to continue deploying women workers, single and married alike.[78]

These men realized that there was no going back on redivisions of labor drawn during the war and elaborated since. What had started as a temporary, stopgap measure had become a structural feature of the industry, especially in those branches that had moved furthest from a craft-based division of labor. Firms could not just turn around and replace their women with the unemployed fathers of families:

> We only began to hire women during the war and because the normal workforce was lacking. . . . This [female] labor force has proved equally indispensable since the war, during which supply has never kept up with demand. It has become part of the factory. In numerous cases it has shown psychomotor aptitudes that one never finds among male labor: dexterity, quick reaction time, adaptability. Many times we have tried to fill vacancies by placing men on jobs formerly held by women . . . in order to give work to fathers of families. We have had to end this practice for [men's] lack of adaptability and low output.[79]

In industries such as electronics and to a lesser extent automobiles, the work process had come to rest on the particular kind of labor power that, in the employers' view, only women could deliver.

[77] The UFCS was a Catholic organization dedicated to improving women's civil and political status within the cautious framework of Catholic doctrine on the family. Its primary goal was to return working mothers to the home, or, more precisely, to make it economically possible for working-class mothers to choose *foyer* over factory by putting their incomes on a par with those of mothers who earned wages. They would do so by adding a bonus (*prime de la mère au foyer*) to the family allocation payments that GIMM members already paid to their workers. (Allocations were one tactic for keeping wages low, and metals employers were quite clear on this point; in the event of a strike, for instance, GIMM often instructed members to hold the rate steady and raise the family allocations instead. See AN, 39 AS, 915, GIMM to Etablissements Vachette, 30 November 1923.) In the 1930s the UFCS held two conferences on *la mère au foyer*, carefully preparing the way for each by surveys of industrial opinion on the employment of mothers. The following discussion is based largely on the results of these two surveys (one in 1932–33, the other in 1936). All of this material is preserved in the UIMM archives. For more on the UFCS and the campaign to return mothers to the home, see Henri Rollet, *Andrée Butillard et le féminisme chrétien* (Paris, 1960); Naomi Black, *Social Feminism* (Ithaca, 1989); and Susan Pedersen, *Family, Dependence, and the Origins of the Welfare State* (Cambridge, 1993).

[78] Whatever individual employers may have thought about married women working in the "ideal republic," they quickly circled the wagons in the face of the *mère au foyer* campaign and rallied around the claims of individual liberty and the freedom to work: "Any social measure that aims to grant allocations to mothers on condition that they not work would be a hindrance to the freedom to work. The taste for domestic life must be given through training in home economics": UIMM, 69/54/03, response of Pont-à-Musson to UFCS survey, 20 October 1936.

[79] A metals employer quoted in Mlle Delagrange, "Le Travail de la femme mariée" (results of a survey on women's work in the Depression), *BAS*, 1934, p. 36.

Throughout the campaign to return mothers to the home, the category "mothers" continually threatened to expand to embrace first married women, then all women. Industrialists, feeling the pressure, struggled to hold the two categories apart. This was not an easy task for men who treated women workers as a single class, undifferentiated by skill or occupation. In firms that relied heavily on women workers, however, managers were more likely to draw these distinctions. In such firms, married women were the last women workers an employer would relinquish, not the first, for "the married woman, having more reason to work than the single woman, is a better-quality worker."[80]

Most important, married women were often the most skilled women workers in the factory, thanks to formal training, or at least to their longer and more varied experience. When asked what they thought about a legal prohibition on married women's employment, managers at one general engineering firm wasted no time in mouthing pro-natalist pieties. Instead, the several department heads crafted a long and detailed response explaining in no uncertain terms that the firm would have a very hard time of it if the government enacted any such ban: "It would be very difficult for us if we were deprived of the labor of mothers."[81]

If such a law were passed, the firm would try to replace the mothers with young girls. This course would be far from ideal, however, for the work that married women did (and here "married" clearly means "skilled") required a long apprenticeship. In the filemaking shop it took five years at least for a worker to reach "average capacity" on handwork, and two to five years if she cut files with the help of a machine:

> Replacing mothers with young girls is not as easy as it seems . . . the term of apprenticeship is relatively long . . . [and] if at the end . . . the young girl whom we have trained marries, the law would force her to leave the factory, and thus we would lose the profits that we had a right to expect from that worker.

Under no circumstances would the company consider hiring men for this work. Not only was it technically unsuitable for them, "demanding proficiency

---

[80] Ibid., p. 42. It was quite the opposite in heavy metallurgy, where married women were always the first to go. In the 1920s, many of these firms had hired women because of the labor shortage. With the onset of the Depression, some knew that "at the slightest upswing in economic activity, we will be forced to hire all available labor, women included": UIMM, 69/54/03, response of the Société Métallurgique du Périgord to UFCS survey, 10 October 1936. Others pontificated on women's place in the home (see, for example, the response from the Société Anonyme d'Escaut et Meuse: "Our opinion is that the place of married women, and even young girls, is in the home. In a pinch they can work in lingerie and women's shops, but never in the office or factory": ibid., 24 January 1933).

[81] Ibid., "Lettre de la Société Anonyme des Hauts-Fourneaux, Forges et Aciéries du Saut-du-Tarn," 14 March 1933.

and rapid execution," but men were simply too expensive: "On fuse work we would have a clear jump in costs on the order of 60–80%." (The estimate was based on the projected combined effects of higher wages and lower output.) Ultimately, the firm could contemplate no scheme of replacing "mothers" with men, for "on certain light jobs such as cutting small files . . . the professional competence of women is far superior to that of men in terms of quality as well as output."[82]

Outside the heaviest metallurgical plants, women had come to hold a permanent and specific place in the interwar division of labor. The jobs they held were no longer "men's jobs," pro-natalist claims to the contrary notwithstanding. Since 1914, successive redivisions of labor had rendered this work appropriate for "feminine fingers" only; it could not now revert to men.[83] In these factories, then, the socially conscious practice of Depression-era France—firing the "mothers of families" so that the fathers could replace them—could not be reconciled with sound business sense. And so it was not followed.

As the country's malaise deepened, some metals employers adopted the more rabidly pro-natalist rhetoric of mothers in the home and made it their own. This development led to the odd spectacle of industrialists turning a blind eye to their own substantial contingents of women.[84] In 1936 Peugeot's director general, Maurice Jordan, offered a classic example of the newly fashionable familialist double-speak: "The woman who needs to has a right to work, but it is essential that we do all we can so that the wife and mother can in the normal course of things remain at home." His own workforce was over 40 percent female at the time.[85]

The public attack on married women's work forced the *surintendantes d'usine* to examine their beliefs about women's work in the factory and the "problem" of proletarian motherhood. By the mid-1930s, this soul-searching ended with the *surintendantes'* reaffirming their commitment to women's right to work, despite the pro-natalist convictions that most of them shared. Crucially, their stance dovetailed with their employers' decision to continue

---

[82] Ibid.

[83] "Certain jobs can be done only by feminine fingers, notably wire winding in our profession [radios and electronics]. But for work demanding technical knowledge, such as assembling radio sets, we prefer young men, who are interested and teach themselves through their work, while young girls, with rare exceptions, think of other things altogether": metals employer quoted in UFCS, *La Mère au foyer,* p. 314.

[84] Fridenson, "L'Idéologie des grands constructeurs," provides an excellent discussion of the contradictory currents that crisscrossed these men's conceptions in the 1930s.

[85] Maurice Jordan, *Quelques Remarques sur des sujets d'actualité et sur un exemple d'économie dans une société anonyme* (Montbéliard, 1936), p. 28. The figures on women's employment at Peugeot are quoted in Fourcaut, *Femmes à l'usine,* p. 200. According to the UFCS, 37% of women who worked in the metals industries in 1933 were married and about 85% of those women had children: UFCS, *La Mère au foyer,* pp. 90–91.

to employ women workers. One wonders what they would have concluded had the employers not taken the stand they did, for the *surintendantes'* internal debate over women's work was laced with an ambivalence all its own.

This ambivalence sprang from the *surintendantes'* own conceptions of women's nature, their domestic responsibilities, and the nature of factory labor. As the welfare supervisors grew familiar with the factory world, these conceptions knocked repeatedly against a fact that nearly all the *surintendantes* found surprising and worthy of comment: women workers, though often fatigued by the heavy labor, seemed to enjoy their work. They liked the money and the social life; "They have little to do at home and they enjoy life in the factory, with its gossip, its little adventures and camaraderie," reported Mlle Verneuil (p. 21). But they also seemed to like the work itself, and showed particular fondness for their machines: "After being out sick a few days, [my co-worker] could not wait to return to *her machines* which *are everything* to her."[86]

Though initially baffled by this attachment to the machine, many *surintendantes* came to understand it as one aspect of women workers' pride in their skills and their ability to excel in tough, traditionally male occupations: ". . . the woman worker at her job, with her skills and her professional conscience . . . now seems cloaked in a new dignity that it has been a joy to discover," wrote Mlle Wagner at Thomson-Houston (p. 14). Yet these women, carefully oiling and adjusting their machines, proud of a job that brought in such good wages, also seemed alienated from that which was most feminine, in the *surintendantes'* bourgeois eyes: the love of home. "Speak to these women of a normal life, of the cares of housekeeping, of linens to repair, and they will snort with laughter, with an imperturbable aplomb."[87] Of course, the *surintendantes* worried about the effect that heavy machine work might have on these women's childbearing capacities: "You have to pull with all your might to operate the lathe," wrote Mlle Hilon. "With every tug you feel the fatigue in your abdominal muscles. . . . I cannot imagine a pregnant woman engaging in such acrobatics . . . without miscarrying immediately" (pp. 10–11). But the real danger lay less in the workers' wombs that in their hearts and minds. So long as they stayed in the factory, *surintendantes* feared, the love of home would never be awakened in them.

When she has her first child, the young woman who had worked outside the home feels a connection to the home by the awakening of maternal sentiment. If this propitious moment is not seized, there is a serious risk that no second

---

[86] Report of Mlle Basterra, Thomson-Houston, 1928, p. 8; emphasis in original. Annie Fourcaut comments that the *surintendantes* often remarked on the number of women who seemed to love their machines: *Femmes à l'usine*, p. 62.

[87] Report from Etablissements Dussé, p. 10.

Women workers displaying some of the larger valves produced at the Société Radio-technique (Suresnes), 1920–25. Cliché Thomson.

child will arrive, for as these mothers say, "one doesn't have children only to place them in the crèche or day-care center."[88]

Women had some perfectly understandable reasons for choosing factory over home. One *surintendante* observed that the woman metalworker enjoyed "a relatively easy existence, one that [was] less resigned" than that of the woman at home. Not surprisingly, they were loath to give it up for a life of isolation and self-sacrifice. "They want no children, or just a few," wrote Verneuil. "Not because they don't like them but because the arrival of children is the renunciation of work, or at least the beginning of a divided, harried existence with factory work superimposed on the [children's] care and education. They want an easier life" (p. 21). But it was the desire for money, above

[88] UIMM, 69/54/03, UFCS, "Projet de proposition de portant modification à la loi du 11 mars sur les allocation familiales," p. 2.

all, that lured working women from the quiet path of housewifely self-sacrifice. The evidence for their easily awakened greed could be heard each day in conversations such as one Houssay overheard: " 'Renault is already a million-aire, but when I go on to piecework, I'll hit the big time myself; with my husband, we'll be making Fr 60 to 65, and then we'll drink champagne every day' " (pp. 10–11).

Here the *surintendante* faced the antinatalist threat at its very root, for women's "appetite for gain" could easily lead them away from the austere beauties of the home. Too often the pursuit of money turned them toward the gay life of the factory and (more dangerous still) the transient pleasures their wages could buy. In the worst-case scenario, the ambition to earn more money and spend it wildly could displace any desire for children: "Here everyone agrees: 'No kids—they're a bother and they cost too much.' Maternal sentiment seems to have been supplanted by the love of fine lingerie, good meals, movies, and sometimes camping."[89] The idea that one chose between luxuries and children was a familiar trope in pro-natalist discourse. "We see young couples hesitate a moment between having a child and buying a car," lamented one economist. Worse yet, "Some young women . . . put their dog in the place of the child."[90] At any time, love of things—fine lingerie, movies, or perhaps one's machine at work—might push aside the tenderer sentiments, leaving no space at all for love of home and children.

In the *surintendantes'* minds, a woman's right to work always jostled uneas-ily against her (primary) responsibilities as mother and homemaker. This produced an unstable discourse that opposed the gay, luxury-loving factory worker who refuses maternity to the woman who accepts the humble, austere, yet more profound duties of motherhood. Although interwar industrial policy had turned on reconciling the two (and would continue to do so), under the stress of the 1930s it became clear that at some level the *surintendantes* were not entirely sure that such a reconciliation was possible.[91] But they continued to make the effort, for however much they might worry over the birth rate or the "desertion" of the working-class hearth, *surintendantes* believed that women had the right to work outside the home.

Usually they defended that right in its most minimal incarnation: the right to work as breadwinners. In a period of falling wages and persistent unemploy-

---

[89] Report of Mlle Bellier, Compteurs de Montrouge, 1942, p. 7.

[90] Georges Risler, "La Dénatalité mortelle," *Musée Social,* May 1939, pp. 123–24.

[91] Thus in 1935 one *surintendante* wrote hopefully: "The married woman has everything to gain from staying home. First, she acquires a taste for domestic life, she economizes. She makes the home more welcoming and her husband finds himself staying home—he stops going to the café before dinner. The moral state of the household benefits. . . . The woman who raises her child herself has a stronger attachment to it; she cares for it better than any nurse could": Mlle Combes, quoted in Delagrange, "Travail de la femme mariée," p. 43.

ment, *surintendantes* could justly point to the inadequacy of male wages that in some areas could not ensure "even a modest standard of living," even if the couple had no children: "The only working-class homes that have a suitable standard of living are those in which man and wife work and where there are no more than two children," wrote one *surintendante* in 1935. Moreover, "the husbands are quite happy to have their wives work. They prefer helping with the housework and laundry to seeing the household go without her wage." This situation did not seem to affect domestic harmony in the least; on the contrary, "we know many women who work because their husbands wish it adamantly: to them, a woman at home is doing nothing; she is 'a loafer.' "[92]

Surintendantes thus saw few reasons to remove married women from the factories and several compelling reasons not to: "Women get bored at home and go visit neighbors. *The result is always the same: an ill-kept home, meals composed almost solely of canned food.* These women are often quite lively in the factory and lazy at home."[93] At least in the factory, these laggards might be exposed to the *surintendante*'s good example. Home economics training had a key role to play here, for in these years of retrenchment, *surintendantes* found that "the state of women's homes depend[s] far less on external circumstances than on the character, temperament, and physical strength of the housewife. And, we would add, her education. . . . Frequently the homes of working women are better kept than those of women who stay home."[94]

In no case would a *surintendante* declare that women's right to work was absolute. This is not terribly surprising; after all, their defense of that right rested on an unstable opposition between the voluntarily childless luxury hound and the mother who graciously bows to necessity. It produced a rather thin safety net for women's threatened rights. But it served well enough, especially since employers' decision to continue to employ married women— a decision taken for their own profit-maximizing reasons—stretched a less threadbare safety net below the *surintendantes'* qualified defense of women's right to work.

Welfare management thus continued to blur the distinction between the worker's private, domestic existence and her public function in the world of work, although the emphasis had shifted away from pure natalism and toward control over the structure of family life. Indeed, by linking an increasingly

[92] Ibid., p. 45.
[93] Ibid., p. 40; emphasis in original.
[94] "La Crise" (results of a survey on working-class households in the Depression), *BAS*, 1936, p. 25.

intrusive paternalism with the techniques of scientific management, French metals employers hoped to gain access to workers' motivational core. Practitioners of this "modern paternalism" saw the relationship between home and work as clearly reciprocal, especially in the case of women. Their strategies for control thus centered on the regulation of women's values and behavior not only on the shop floor but in the notionally private domestic sphere as well. At the heart of this new strategy stood management's emissary to the proletarian home, preaching order, cleanliness, and thrift in the household as a means of promoting those same values on the shop floor.[95]

By her own lights as well as those of her employer, the *surintendante* constituted a human link between rationalized labor, a new social harmony in the factory, and a more rational order in the proletarian home. She occupied a pivotal position in the "true" factory, a community of reciprocally ordered relations that, in her own mind, underlay the false and unnecessarily polarized relations of modern industry. By exercising her "disinterested" influence—softening the strictures and discipline of the employer's rule, explaining the "just" demands of individual workers—the *surintendante* could reunite an alienated labor force with its stern yet benevolently paternal employer.

Nonetheless, the welfarist aspect of her role demanded that she be alive to the actual impact of intensified labor on the women and men she managed, even as she sought to reconcile their well-being with the increased pace of work. On occasion she could not escape from the contradictions that her dual function entailed: " . . . one is almost overcome," wrote Houssay, "when one imagines that for years, throughout their entire lives, women will perform the same motions . . . nailed down to one place, with no power to move for eight hours, performing movements that are utterly devoid of all interest but on which one must nonetheless concentrate, for fear of doing it badly" (pp. 17–18).

But she was ill placed to draw anything but reformist conclusions. Houssay thus stayed on at Renault, convinced by her education—and by her position at the foot of the employer's table—that the contradictions she had observed were mere appearance. Beyond them she could discern a deeper reality of mutual interest and eventual harmony, and she concluded her report with

---

[95] If, as Donald Reid argues ("Industrial Paternalism: Discourse and Practice in Nineteenth-Century French Mining and Metallurgy," *Comparative Studies in Society and History* 27 [October 1985]: 582), paternalism constitutes a discourse on the creation of the employee, then the *surintendantes'* newly technocratic language of welfare supervision is a discourse on creation of the worker-mother in the modern, rationalized factory. See also Gérard Noiriel, "Du 'patronage' au 'paternalisme': La Réstructuration des formes de domination de la main-d'oeuvre ouvrière dans l'industrie métallurgique française," *Mouvement Social*, no. 144 (July–September 1988), p. 17, in which he points out that during the 1930s the metals industries presented "the most highly developed and fully theorized forms of paternalism" in French industry.

Woman worker at the Société Radiotechnique (Suresnes) placing filaments in radio valves, 1920–25. Cliché Thomson.

the idea that some profit-sharing scheme might eventually resolve "this terrible struggle between . . . capital and labor whose fates are now not so different" (p. 24).

The man who had hired her viewed the matter somewhat differently. Though he agreed that the working class, and working women in particular, had much to gain from contact with the *surintendante*, he had not hired this woman to instruct him in labor relations. Throughout the interwar period, employers happily used *surintendantes* to further their own social policies, domesticating the workforce and Taylorizing the factories. But their autocratic rule of factory relations continued, undisturbed by any moderating influence from the women they had employed to monitor productivity and welfare.

The *surintendante*'s ability to assist her proletarian sisters was thus severely circumscribed by her employer's conception of her responsibilities and by the relentlessly reformist vision she brought to her work. In the end, her viewpoint could not be meaningfully distinguished from that of her boss. Thus she believed in the importance of a hierarchical authority in the factory, agreed that working-class women were peculiarly vulnerable and in need of special care and moral tutelage, accepted the "natural" authority of middle class over working class, and embraced the notion that industry had to raise its productivity at all costs. Employers therefore had little difficulty in containing the reformist impulses of the *surintendante*. Although she saw herself as a mediator between labor and capital, she remained in reality an employee of one side, hired to manage and discipline the other.

CHAPTER 8

The Limits of Labor Stratification in Interwar Britain

In the late 1920s, the Dutch radio firm of Phillips opened a highly mechanized radio assembly plant on the site of an old valve factory in Mitcham. The main assembly shop consisted of seven lines, each with forty-five positions stretched over a quarter-mile span. Every assembler was female, as were the four spare hands (popularly known as "piddle breakers") who were held in reserve at the edge of each line, ready to replace women who failed to show up, fell behind on the job, or simply needed a moment to pay a visit to the toilet. The inspectors, foremen, casers, and repair workers were all men.

Seating on the line was staggered, so the women worked in isolation, heads bowed in concentration over tasks that were finicky and repetitive. From the moment the belt was switched on, at 7:30 A.M., until 5:00 in the evening, women remained tied to their posts, attaching components and soldering joints at the rate of fifteen joints per minute. Every three minutes a new radio set traveled down the line, demanding immediate attention to its forty-five joints. If an operator fell behind, the evidence of her failure mounted steadily behind her, where she piled the unfinished sets as she struggled, often vainly, to catch up. "Forty-five joints in three minutes was hard work," recalled Jessie Evans, one of the faster workers at Phillips. "You had no time to look up even and there was no time to talk. The whole belt was timed to do so many sets an hour and you had to keep up with the belt. If you didn't then you were really no good and you were put out—sacked. It was awful really— some women used to be carried out screaming hysterics."[1]

At the end of 1929, the British economy slid from the protracted slump of the 1920s into outright depression. Unemployment, already hovering around

---

[1] Quoted in Miriam Glucksmann, *Women Assemble: Women Workers and the New Industries in Interwar Britain* (London, 1990), p. 177.

10 percent, crept steadily up toward 15 percent while industrial production plummeted. In the north of England, center of the old staple trades—coal, ships, and cotton—factories closed their gates, the docks lay empty, and entire towns stood idle as local unemployment reached 30, even 50 percent.[2] The southern districts were more fortunate. Greater London and the Midlands, home to the growing automobile and bicycle trades, saw the rise of mass-production industries after 1920—the electronics and synthetic textiles factories where so many young women would find employment.

As in France, unemployment in the interwar period was a gendered phenomenon. In 1931, for example, 12.7 percent of insured men were unemployed, while women's unemployment stood at 8.6 percent.[3] The gap was even more pronounced in the engineering industry, with women's unemployment rates ranging from one-quarter to one-half of men's.[4] In 1934 the economist Francis Hirst concluded that the numbers reflected employers' effort to cut costs by dispensing first with more expensive male labor.[5] Individual employers undoubtedly made precisely this sort of calculation when they pared back their workforces. Nonetheless, women's apparently greater resistance to unemployment stemmed less from the collective impact of such decisions than from the profound restructuring going on in the interwar economy. As a result of that restructuring, women workers were clustered in the one sector of the engineering trade that, even in the midst of the Depression, enjoyed uninterrupted expansion: electrical engineering and, to a lesser extent, automobile construction.[6]

Since the end of the war, the industrial center of gravity had shifted steadily

[2] Britain's staple trades never recovered from the loss of foreign markets during the war, and so remained in a state of underemployment throughout the interwar period.

[3] W. H. Beveridge, "An Analysis of Unemployment, Part III," *Economica* 4 (1937): 168–83. The dramatic gap in male and female unemployment rates probably stemmed in part from systematic underreporting of women's unemployment, to which the 1929 Anomalies Act (which denied unemployment benefits to married women) undoubtedly contributed. In fact, Beveridge's report also indicates that married women's unemployment (insofar as it could be determined) was a good deal higher than unemployment among single women: 17.2%, as opposed to 6.9% in 1931.

[4] Timothy Hatton, "Female Labour Force Participation: The Enigma of the Interwar Period," discussion paper no. 113, Centre for Economic Policy Research, London (June 1986).

[5] Francis Hirst, *The Consequences of the War to Great Britain* (London, 1934), p. 288.

[6] Thus in 1937, electrical engineering enjoyed a 10.2% increase in output; the comparable figure for the automobile industry was 10.1%, and growth for the British economy overall stood at a poor 1.9%: Sidney Pollard, *The Development of the British Economy, 1914–1967*, 2d ed. (New York, 1969), pp. 96–97. The percentage of the engineering workforce employed in the electrical sector mushroomed from 5% in 1907 to 15.4% in 1924 and then 22.5% in 1935: James B. Jefferys, *The Story of the Engineers* (London, 1945), p. 198. One scholar has termed the electrical engineering industry "one of the most important sources of growth in the economy throughout the interwar period . . . experiencing 'super-normal expansion' ": Miriam Glucksmann, "In a Class of Their Own? Women Workers in the New Industries in Interwar Britain," *Feminist Review* 24 (Autumn 1986): 23.

away from the old, craft-based trades, where skilled men built customized machines and equipment to order, toward the very differently organized industries of the nascent mass-production economy. At the same time, employers in mass-production factories (aside from the automobile industry) showed a clear and growing preference for women workers and juveniles for most production and assembly work. The statistics on male and female unemployment in the engineering industry as a whole thus reflect two simultaneous and contradictory movements: the contraction of male-dominated sectors (ships and heavy machinery) and the startling growth in new, feminized branches. As new industries such as electrical engineering increased their share of productivity and profits, the percentage of women employed in these factories rose without interruption, from 26.6 percent in 1921 to 32.4 percent in 1931 to a full 36 percent by 1936.[7]

After 1920, then, the percentages of women workers in British engineering trace a steady upward trajectory whose shape recalls the parallel trajectory being limned in France. These similar patterns of growth suggest that despite the very different directions in which the two national economies were moving, a clearly gendered restructuring was taking place within the postwar metals and engineering industries.[8] This restructuring, which transcended national boundaries, was rooted in the decline of the craft-based organization of work and the rationalization and mechanization of the industry over the twentieth century, developments that were sharply gendered after 1914. But this restructuring produced a more nuanced result than the simple dualism of rationalized factory (women) versus not-rationalized workshop (men). Over the long term, the slow disintegration of craft can be read in the shift from an all-male metals industry to one that exhibited at least three identifiable sexual/technical divisions of labor, ranged along a spectrum that was visible in both nations.[9] Each of the three sexual/technical divisions—heavy, barely rationalized; intermediate, partially rationalized; and light, highly rationalized—was associated with a distinct market position in the interwar economy.

At the barely rationalized end of the spectrum lay forgework, shipbuilding, and the heavy branches of mechanical engineering. All remained overwhelmingly male-dominated, employing 2 to 5 percent women at most in the interwar period. In these sectors employers treated women as a reserve army, to be drawn into their plants when male labor was short, then expelled when demand contracted.[10]

---

[7] See Glucksmann, *Women Assemble*, p. 58.
[8] On the gendered nature of this restructuring, see ibid., p. 51; and *BSGF* 16, pt. 1 (1921): 84.
[9] I've constructed this tripartite scheme with the benefit of hindsight. In practice, the categories tended to overlap.
[10] In France the sole exception to the "reserve army" rule in heavy industry was the job of *pontonnière* (conveyor-belt operator), which employers agreed was especially suited to women.

Midway between heavy and light industry lay those partially rationalized industries in which the frontier of mechanization was constantly shifting: mechanical engineering, lighter forgework, and the automobile industry (which was, by and large, not a mass-production industry in interwar France and Britain). In these factories, women formed a small but indispensable fraction of the workforce, usually 10 to 15 percent. Here employers consciously deployed workers on the principles of labor stratification, doling out the shop's repetition work to women and adolescents of both sexes while reserving all other jobs for semiskilled and skilled men.[11] Thanks to the practice of labor stratification, employers could not replace women without raising the wage bill and upsetting the careful balance of gender and skill on which (they believed) efficient production rested. After 1929, as the Depression turned thousands of men out onto the streets, the employers had to remind anxious union representatives of this fact:

> Now with regard to men being out of work and the girls employed, does anyone say that the men were pushed out of work and the girls taken on? . . . The work the girls were wanted for was available, and the work the men were wanted for was not available. . . . If the girls were not there at all . . . they would both be idle.[12]

Finally, there were the new "light" industries—mass-market, mass-production factories where a workforce that was about 30 percent female produced electrical goods for such industries as cars and airplanes, and increasingly for home use as well—telephones, radios, lamps and light bulbs, batteries, electric irons, and cooking apparatus.[13] The organization of work in light industry was structured around a hierarchical and sharply gendered division of labor that from the outset was quite stable. Unlike factories in the intermediate classification, where any technical change might well prompt employers to move the sexual boundary, mass-production industries were characterized by

---

See UIMM 69/54/03, response of Société Métallurgique du Périgord to UFCS survey, 19 October 1936.

[11] "In an intermediate state between small scale and mass production however there are now semi-automatic lathes, . . . which . . . can in some cases be worked by women or girls, but in others require considerable skill and the constant attention of the worker": Sir H. Llewellyn Smith, *The New Survey of London Life and Labour* (London, 1931), 2:132–33.

[12] MRC, EEF, Central Conference, no. 12, Barrow reference, York, 12 June 1931, p. 10; William Watson speaking on behalf of the employers. The women in question were making airplane engines and propellors.

[13] The global figure conceals dramatic variation in the percentages of women employed. Depending on the extent to which the shops had been organized for serial machining and assembly, women made up anywhere from 20 to 80% of the total workforce in the electronics plants of interwar Britain and France, about 30% for the electrical engineering branch as a whole in the 1930s. See M. L. Yates, *Wages and Labour Conditions in British Engineering* (London, 1937), and Françoise Gélaud-Léridon, *Le Travail des femmes en France* (Paris, 1964).

a rigid two-tier structure. Skilled men regulated and repaired the machinery, supervised the women's work, and performed any process work deemed too heavy or complicated for women. On the line, where the actual work of production and assembly took place, the workforce was often 100 percent women. This steep pyramid was fixed through differences of both age and gender, as "the vast majority of the workers are girls, but men are employed as supervisors and maintenance engineers for the machinery."[14]

Miriam Glucksmann argues persuasively that assembly-line work made for a new and distinctive set of labor–capital relations, and that women, as the premier assembly-line workers, were the first to experience these novel conditions. Each line assembled its women into a "collective worker," whose constituent elements were paid according to the line's productivity.[15] Further, the detailed division of labor and the unforgiving pace of the conveyor belt subjected women assemblers to direct managerial control; the design, content, and speed of their work was externally determined by the factory's engineers and time-study men. As mass production extended its grip on the interwar and postwar economy, more of the working class would be subjected to the new forms of domination. For the time being, however, women were the pioneers. Gathered at the line, the hub toward which all productive chains flowed, they swiftly assembled components, building the cheap consumer durables—radios, irons, vacuum cleaners, lamps, bicycles, car accessories—on which the nascent mass-production economy depended.

Hence the long-term restructuring of the metals industry that brought new, feminized sectors to the fore also signaled that the core workforce in metalworking was gradually shifting its center of gravity from skilled male craftworker to less skilled female, juvenile, and immigrant labor. This seachange was common to the metals industries of both Britain and France. Yet the particular shape that the crisis took in Britain made this shift painfully visible, as the collapse of the old shipbuilding and heavy machine trades put thousands of men on short time or threw them out of work altogether. Of course, not everyone was out of work. Thanks to the growth of mass production, "the daughter is offered a job whilst the father is kept unemployed."[16] The bitter invocation of patriarchy inverted—young girls ("daughters") working while men (always "fathers") languished on the dole—became a standard trope of protest among craft unionists as they struggled to defend a position

---

[14] Smith, *New Survey*, p. 165. Smith is writing about the lampmaking industry, which was heavily feminized in France as well.

[15] As Smith observed, "The girls in these teams are paid on piece-rates varying with the output of the group as a whole, so that one slow worker may reduce the earnings of the others": *New Survey*, p. 165. The wage form thus imposed a collective self-discipline on the women grouped around each assembly belt.

[16] MRC, EEF, Central Conference, no. 12, Barrow reference, York, 12 June 1931, p. 5.

already badly eroded by years of trade depression. At the center of their defense stood an old protagonist, job skill. The revived debate over skill—whether the new work was skilled, whether women possessed genuine skill or not—reveals how muddled the entire picture remained. As events at the Rover automobile plant demonstrate, the employers who engineered these changes were no more certain about their consequences than were the women and men who had to live with them.

The Resilient Structures of Occupational Segregation

Observers of women's work in the electrical engineering industry were genuinely confounded by the question whether this work was skilled or not. In 1928 the Balfour Committee on Industry and Trade remarked that although "girls" who worked in the lamp trade served no formal apprenticeship, they nonetheless "achieve a high degree of dexterity and the most highly skilled are transferred . . . to thermionic valve manufacture in which the pay is higher."[17] No formal apprenticeship, but clear evidence of skill—a paradox that Sir H. Llewellyn Smith tried to untangle. "Women workers in the engineering trades are not 'skilled,' in the craft sense of the word, but many of them acquire great skill and speed in particular processes."[18] Well, were they skilled or weren't they, and what was meant by "skill," anyway?

Much of the uncertainty stemmed from the technical transformation of the industry. "The progress of this mechanical evolution . . . is fast making obsolete the old bipartite distinction between skilled and unskilled labour, and a graduated series of specialised workers are becoming the most characteristic figures in mechanical industry."[19] Before these men's very eyes, rationalization was fast rendering the old binary opposition between skilled and unskilled meaningless. Along the new "graduated" hierarchy of more specialized workers, the Balfour Committee, Sir H. Llewellyn Smith, and others found skilled women.[20] They were not craft-skilled, but craft skill was itself changing, becoming more narrowly specialized and less important, or at least far less prominent in the more streamlined mass-production process.[21] At the apex

[17] Board of Trade, Balfour Committee on Industry and Trade, *A Survey of Industries*, 4 vols. (London, 1928), 4:320–21.
[18] Smith, *New Survey*, pp. 137–38.
[19] Ibid., p. 5.
[20] For instance, "Captain Wilks said that he thought that the work in the Rover Company's Female Trimming Department was very highly skilled—much more skilled than Machine shop work": CDEEA, Executive Committee minutes, 10 September 1930, p. 3. Wilks was Rover's managing director.
[21] Smith underscored the changing function and content of craft skill. "The skill required of both toolmakers and toolsetters is said to be on a higher plane, if more specialised in character, than that of craftsmen under the older type of production": *New Survey*, p. 135.

of Smith's "graduated series" stood women who were skilled in new ways, ways that fitted the rationalized work process.

With the further mechanization and rationalization of labor, "skilled repetition work" acquired a new salience, on the factory floor and in the changing discourse on job skill as well: "Mere skill is not the most generally demanded quality. In all process and repetition work, and in such productive work of a skilled type, the chief industrial virtues are steadiness and care."[22] Hard enough to keep up with the changing definition of "skill" through all this "mechanical evolution," but the fact that the workers who achieved a "high degree of dexterity . . . and skill" were women made it all the more difficult for men to apply the label "skilled" to them and have it stick. If Smith, a fairly neutral observer, had trouble holding the ideas "woman" and "skilled" in his head at the same time, imagine the problems experienced by angry, defensive craftsmen and their determined employers. Granted, the definition of "skill" was evolving along with the labor process; but could women's evident abilities really be called skills?

Old arguments were taken out of mothballs and rehearsed yet again. Surely women's "industrial virtues" sprang from aspects of female nature that were present from the time they were very young: "their suppleness of fingers made them more suitable than boys for certain occupations."[23] Certainly their employers believed this was the case. Hence they continued to justify women's extraordinarily low wages (still about half of men's)[24] by saying that small assembly, which was always done by women, is in essence mindless: "The whole thing require[s] not any more knowledge of putting things together than the great majority of housewives engage in when on Tuesday morning they assemble the kitchen mincing machine and disguise the last part of Sunday's joint for the delight of the family."[25] Each time the barrier separating women from skill threatened to dissolve—and this danger was immanent whenever employers moved the sexual boundary at work—employers swiftly resurrected these time-worn assertions in order to reset the distinction once again.

---

[22] Ibid., p. 143.

[23] John Gollan, *Youth in British Industry* (London, 1937), p. 237.

[24] Women's wages were still governed by the EEF's national scale for women, promulgated in March 1921. On this wage sheet the women's scale was far narrower than the men's. From a basic rate of 24s. per week—half the wage of unskilled male laborers—women could rise only 7s., to a top rate of 31s. On average, women earned no more than 27–28s. a week throughout the 1920s, while men were averaging 52–56s. Further, the average male wage concealed a far wider range of rates, as skilled men earned at least 70s. a week throughout the decade, whereas unskilled men averaged 48s. All wage averages are based on Ministry of Labour inquiries cited in Yates, *Wages and Labour Conditions*, pp. 120, 124.

[25] MRC, EEF, Central Conference, no. 11, Leeds reference, York, 13 April 1934, p. 5. The work in question was small-scale assembly in a textile machine factory.

At times trade union representatives tried to catch their employers in a contradiction, asking why, if women's work was so mindless, it was necessary to have skilled men take their places on the night shift.[26] This was a point the employers preferred to sidestep, however, usually by invoking the familiar contention that if women did a job well, the credit was due solely to the machinery: "Engraving . . . is work which is entirely suitable for their deft fingers, and does not call for any stress or strain. The skill is in the machine and the girl does the routine work."[27] The women-skill conundrum thus had a simple if circular solution: The work that women do may be skilled, but women themselves never are; they are simply women.

Here things generally rested, for trade union leaders, craft or no, accepted the circumscription of women's skill implied in the logic of such statements. It seems that organized (male) labor also believed in the fundamental presumption of labor stratification—that something irreducible distinguishes women's labor power from men's and women's skilled work from skilled men's work.

Thanks to this shared presumption, craftsmen were forced to fall back on weak moral arguments when they faced a demarcation dispute:

The introduction of female labour into the factory is anti-Christian [and] immoral. . . . None of the Employers would put their own daughters into an Engineering shop. . . . You are a man of the world, old enough to know what it means to a woman to stand at a machine, and, from the very environment she is in, what it must make her.[28]

But labor stratification carried more dangers yet, for women's ambiguous relation to skill made them flexible instruments in the stratified labor force. As the unions well understood, gender and skill might at times uncouple altogether: "We are not arguing the skill or lack of skill required in the thing. It is an introduction of a class of labour that never worked there before."[29]

---

[26] "In places like Lucas' they [women] are grinding component parts to fine limits, working to a thousandth; and as some indication of the type of work they are doing, when they go off at the end of the day and men come on for night work, skilled men are employed on those jobs": ibid., Special Conference, "Women's Wages," 16 December 1936, p. 17; representative of the Transport and General Workers' Union speaking.

[27] Ibid., Central Conference, no. 12, Barrow reference, York, 12 June 1931, p. 12.

[28] Ibid., pp. 4–6. Faced with this singular attack, the EEF found itself in the unexpected position of defending women's right to work. "There is nothing new about girls being employed alongside your members. The sisters, daughters and even the sweethearts of the Engineers are found engaged in the Engineering Industry without detriment to their morals, without reduction of their charms, without removing from them any of the attributes of womanhood that we should like to see them possess. . . . It would be very difficult to say 'You were born a woman; you shall not touch this at all' " (pp. 8–9).

[29] Ibid., no. 11, Leeds reference, 13 April 1934, p. 1.

These demarcation disputes rarely arose in mass-production industry, where the technical and sexual division of labor were one and the same, a single division that was vertically ordered and discontinuous. But in such industries as automobiles, organized by an intermediate division of labor, the sexual divisions were horizontal as well as vertical; that is, women and men often did similar or identical work.[30] Substitution of one sex for the other was fairly frequent in these shops, although it drew comment (and stirred protest) only when men were being supplanted by women.[31] Paradoxically, then, the threat of feminization lurked closer to the surface in factories of the intermediate classification, even though such factories employed many fewer women than the mass-production plants of the electrical engineering trade. Indeed, demarcation disputes regularly punctuated the rhythm of production in these shops throughout the interwar period. It was precisely these kinds of tensions that underlay the Bedaux conflict at Rover.

The Rover Auto Works was located in Coventry, a major engineering center in the East Midlands. The entire district had a long tradition of female employment and the interwar records of the Coventry District Engineering Employers' Association (CDEEA) reveal a continuous and steady demand for women workers and a perennial concern for ensuring the local supply.[32] Women, a "class" of labor that was in short supply from the early 1920s on, constituted a highly specific form of labor in the district's carefully stratified engineering workforce. In the automobile industry, women often worked in the trim shops. Here they performed some classic "feminine" tasks, such as sewing upholstery. But women also did some of the finishing work on the car bodies. Conflict first erupted in these shops in the mid-1920s, when skilled male vehicle builders protested a technical change in the process of painting

---

[30] As Steven Tolliday aptly put it, "The frontier of mechanisation was, therefore, continuously shifting, tasks were regularly re-organised and even in the most advanced flow systems of the 1920s and early 1930s, the separate operations at each stage still needed time and attention for efficient completion": "The Failure of Mass Production Unionism in the Motor Industry," in Chris Wrigley, ed., *A History of British Industrial Relations* (London, 1986), p. 301.

[31] In the late 1930s, industrialists in the north tried to ease that region's high unemployment (30% or more) by transplanting the Midlands miracle: mass-production organization of "light industry," along with its "essential equipment," female labor: if "you put half a dozen Ward machines in Birmingham and put women on them [it] would not cause a ripple on anybody's mind, because it is the custom, but it does . . . if you do it on the Tyne and the Clyde. . . . If we want those industries to be established there, . . . we have to permit the establishment of what is a common practice in other parts of the Country": MRC, EEF, Central Conference, no. 12, North West reference, York, 11 February 1938, p. 5.

[32] By 1923 the local employers' association had decided to eliminate the informal marriage bar, "as the single women had now all been absorbed in this District": CDEEA, Executive Committee minutes, 17 December 1923, p. 5. The CDEEA had installed the bar after the war as part of a broader effort to give demobilized soldiers priority in the postwar scramble for for jobs.

car bodies—a switch from an oil-and-varnish to a cellulose paint finish—which allowed employers to transfer the work from skilled male hands to female ones.

The use of cellulose paint allowed firms to dispense with the final varnishing step (necessary to set the oil paint) and finish car bodies with a simple hand or machine polishing. Manufacturers soon found that "women are better adapted to this type of work than men."[33] Without abandoning the gender-based division of labor, Coventry auto firms gradually ceased to uphold the old boundaries, which had confined female trimmers to the appropriately feminine tasks of sewing upholstery, and increasingly employed women for finishing processes that had been the sole province of skilled men.

When the all-male National Union of Vehicle Builders (NUVB) sought to reinstate the boundary, the employers invoked the logic of labor stratification: "The use of 'cellulose' paint [is] an entirely new process and as such appropriate for unskilled, semi-skilled or female labour."[34] The association then repudiated the NUVB claim as an illegitimate interference with employers' "right to manage."[35]

The vehicle builders continued to resist the employment of women, and their protests abated only when Coventry's auto employers conceded a strict physical separation of male and female trimmers. The Employers' Association "advised the undesirability of firms endeavoring to press the use of female labour on trimming work, unless the firms are prepared, in each individual instance, to open a Department for this work, absolutely separate and distinct from the male trimming department."[36] The provision of segregated trim shops granted the NUVB men some small protection from the immediate threat of undercutting (or replacement) by women workers. But it did not limit or even hamper the employment of women, who continued to work as trimmers throughout the Coventry district. The NUVB's struggles around the sexual division of labor thus eased somewhat when the employers retreated from directly substituting women workers for skilled men and began to confine women to their own shops. This solution opened up a whole new tactic, however—that of piloting new managerial strategies in the all-female trim shop—and set the stage for Rover's later difficulties.

[33] MRC, EEF, Darracq Motors, "Objection to the Employment of Female Labour on Operations in Connection with the Process of Car Painting Known as 'Cellulose Finish,'" Executive Committee minutes, 6 July 1926, p. 82.

[34] CDEEA, Executive Committee minutes, 20 September 1926, p. 2.

[35] In fact, the association maintained that "the operations now being performed by female workers . . . had, in fact, been performed by this class of labour before the War": ibid., 25 January 1926, p. 3. Women's employment on trim work was thus a matter of custom, and so was not subject to negotiation.

[36] Ibid., 20 September 1926, p. 2. See also 25 January 1926, pp. 3–4, and 1 March 1926, p. 4, for the earlier stages in this dispute.

The Foundations of the Bedaux Strike at Rover

By 1929 Rover was beginning to feel the limits of its semi-Taylorized, "quantity flow" production process. Faced with an unstable and shrinking market share and ever-narrowing profit margins, managers cast about for new ways to raise output and increase their control. The solution, it seemed, lay in abandoning altogether their traditional market strategy—making quality cars in small production runs—and moving toward a mass-production system that would enable the firm to break into a broader domestic market.[37] In order to make this transition, the firm needed to reorganize production, cut costs, raise individual productivity, and establish more direct control over its production workers. Rover's management hoped to do all these things by adopting a popular interwar rationalization scheme, the Bedaux system of labor management.

"Rationalization" was a term whose broad power to sway the interwar imagination stemmed largely from the shadowy promise of painless economic growth conjured by its vague prescriptions for installing a "rational" and "scientific" order in the factory. As this growth would result from a more rational organization of work rather than from increased exploitation of labor, the technocratic and utopian vision captured the imagination of men on both sides of the labor–capital divide. In these years of chronic industrial malaise, the captains of industry and of organized labor could meet on the apparently neutral terrain of a hoped-for economic recovery, inspired by the American model of industrial efficiency.[38]

When labor leaders spoke of rationalization, images of Henry Ford's $5 day danced before their eyes.[39] Under Ford's system, workers received a high

---

[37] Throughout the interwar period, three large firms (Austin, Ford, and Morris Motors) dominated Britain's quasi-luxury-car market, accounting for nearly two-thirds of national car production. Throughout the 1920s, Rover jockeyed with other smaller producers—Rootes, Vauxhall, and Standard—for its share of the remaining third. By adopting mass-production methods, Rover hoped to penetrate the broader market controlled by the "Big Three." See Roy Church and Michael Miller, "The Big Three: Competition, Management, and Marketing in the British Motor Industry, 1922–1939," in Barry Supple, ed., *Essays in British Business History* (London, 1977), p. 180.

[38] In the aftermath of the disastrous General Strike of May 1926, reformist labor leaders and a group of "progressive" employers met for the first time in 1928 at the widely publicized Mond-Turner conferences. The talks continued through 1929 but produced no concrete agreements or policies on rationalization or the industrial cooperation that was expected to form the context for any rationalization scheme. The talks did, however, open a labor–management dialogue on rationalization as the solution to Britain's economic difficulties, and helped establish a base for consensus on this issue between reformist labor leaders and managerial "progressives." See Howard Gospel and G. W. McDonald, "The Mond-Turner Talks, 1927–1933: A Study in Industrial Co-operation," *Historical Journal* 16, no. 4 (1973): 807–29.

[39] On Fordism and scientific management in the United States see David Montgomery, *Workers' Control in America* (New York, 1979); Harry Braverman, *Labor and Monopoly Capital* (New York, 1974); Alfred Chandler, *The Visible Hand: The Managerial Revolution in America*

daily wage in return for an intensive effort on the assembly line. Unlike European employers, Ford paid a flat rate that was not linked to one's output, in the expectation of a consistently high level of effort. This was a reasonable expectation, for by controlling the speed of the assembly line, managers gained direct control over the pace of production, and so could dispense with piecework wage incentives. Ford's strategy also provided cheaper goods; the Model T lay within the grasp of the very men who produced it. It was the dual prospect of high wages and the development of working-class consumerism that drew organized labor into the Fordist camp and made individual leaders receptive to the American model of rationalization. Indeed, many union leaders welcomed the opportunity to collaborate in the national effort to revitalize British industry via rationalization. "I do welcome rationalisation, and I make no apology for so doing," declared Ernest Bevin (head of the Transport and General Workers Union), at the Trades Union Congress in 1928. "I would rather see a real organised attempt by rationalisation than I would see a long-drawn weary road from the small employer to the big."[40]

But though Britain's engineering employers favored a more productive organization of work, they adamantly opposed Ford's system, particularly his "promiscuous" wage policy. And in fact Ford's overall production strategy—turning out a very few models in long production runs—did not translate easily into the British context. In the United States a large market of farmers eagerly awaited the thousands of cheap, durable Model T's that poured off the assembly lines each year; Britain offered a far narrower if somewhat wealthier market to automobile producers.[41] The key to securing a toehold in this less stable, quasi-luxury market lay not in imitating Ford's competitive pricing strategy, grounded in mass-production-based economies of scale, but rather in continuously improving model design in order to meet the demands of the upper-middle-class consumer.

Tied to a market that demanded frequent changes in model and design, British manufacturers could not afford to adopt Ford's production structure, with its attendant rigidities in car design and its premium on quantity over quality. Employers therefore adopted a more flexible "quantity flow" production strategy, in which they embedded Fordist techniques for raising individual

---

(Cambridge, Mass., 1977); Michael Burawoy, *Manufacturing Consent* (Chicago, 1979); Charles Sabel, *Work and Politics* (New York, 1982); William Lazonick, "Technological Change and the Control of Work: The Development of Capital–Labor Relations in U.S. Mass-Production Industries," in Howard Gospel and Craig Littler, eds., *Managerial Strategies and Industrial Relations* (London, 1983); Lazonick, "Strategy, Structure, and Management Development in the United States and Britain," in Kesaji Kobayashe, ed., *The Development of Managerial Enterprises* (Tokyo, 1986). Ruth Milkman's *Gender at Work* (Urbana, 1982) has some interesting things to say about Fordism and women workers during World War II.

[40] Trades Union Congress, *Annual Report*, 1928, p. 451.

[41] See Tolliday, "Failure of Mass Production Unionism"; Church and Miller, "Big Three."

productivity.[42] Ford's central wage strategy—the high, flat daily rate, on which Britain's labor leaders had pinned their hopes—was simply out of the question, for it would have eliminated management's main means of raising output: driving labor to work harder by cutting piece rates. Mechanized assembly lines remained quite rare in the labor-intensive factories of interwar Britain, and management continued to rely on regressive piecework systems to drive labor.[43] The ideology of industrial renewal through a "rational" reorganization of work might extend hope of prosperity for all in the United States, but in Britain's narrow automobile market in these Depression years, rationalization could only redistribute the costs of economic contraction.

Shop-floor workers seem to have understood this, and often opposed their leaders on the issue of rationalization. Where union leaders saw in the rationalization movement a means of restoring the trade union movement's power and prestige, severely damaged by chronic unemployment and then defeat in the General Strike of 1926,[44] production workers saw a new weapon for accelerating the pace of work. Indeed, rationalization came to Britain not as Fordism but in the guise of schemes for cutting costs by weeding the workforce and intensifying the labor of those who remained. Women and men had to work ever more rapidly and intensively at tasks that had been further routinized and opened to closer managerial scrutiny. Moreover, during these years of permanent underemployment, rationalization schemes provided employers with a set of "rational" (and therefore just) criteria for weeding out the slower workers. No wonder the semi- and unskilled women and men, whose working lives were directly altered by the operation of the new, "scientific" management policies, bitterly opposed such plans. Many of them understood more

[42] See Tolliday, "Failure of Mass Production Unionism," p. 301. In fact, throughout the interwar period, workers were far more receptive than employers to the notion of a Fordist reorganization of wage and managerial structures. See Wayne Lewchuck, "Fordism and British Motor Car Employers, 1896–1932," in Gospel and Littler, *Managerial Strategies*, and "The Motor Vehicle Industry," in Bernard Elbaum and William Lazonick, eds., *The Decline of the British Economy* (Oxford, 1987).

[43] Scholars disagree on the precise moment at which moving assembly lines made their debut in England. Lewchuck argues that the moving line first arrived in 1917, with the Associated Equipment Company's construction of a "mechanised moving platform . . . designed to hold ten chassis": "Fordism and British Motor Car Employers," pp. 101–2. In 1928 Austin's production manager, C. R. F. Engelbach, claimed to have installed Britain's first "mechanically driven track," for chassis and car body assembly, at the Longbridge Works: "Some Notes on Reorganising a Works to Increase Production," *Proceedings of the Institute of Automobile Engineers* 23 (1927–28): 517, quoted in Church and Miller, "Big Three," p. 186.

[44] Overall union membership in Britain dropped from 8.3 million at its peak in 1920 to 4.9 million in 1927: *British Labour Statistics: Historical Abstract, 1886–1968*, Table 196. In addition, skilled engineers had suffered defeat and lockout in the spring of 1922, after a protracted struggle to limit overtime work. Parliament dealt organized labor a further blow in 1927, when, in the aftermath of the General Strike, the punitive Trades Disputes Bill circumscribed the political activities of trade unions more narrowly than ever.

clearly than their leaders that rationalization carried threats of redundancy and overwork rather than the promise of high wages.

Perhaps the most popular of the interwar "scientific management" schemes was the Bedaux system of time-motion study. In certain respects, it was no different from other interwar labor management systems. All of the most popular ones were coercive, intended to extract a more rapid, intensive effort from individual women and men by speeding up the line or altering the relationship between wages and effort. The system's originator, Charles Bedaux, added several novel features. First, the system purported to reward workers for effort expended rather than for actual output. Second, Bedaux cloaked the process by which effort inputs were established in the apparently rational language of science, lending an essentially arbitrary procedure the aura of scientific truth. Finally, the system was installed not by the employers but by Bedaux's own staff of time-study "engineers." These men entered individual firms in the guise of neutral third parties, bringing the benefits of Bedaux's "labor science" to worker and employer alike. But behind the technocratic language of the time-study engineer lay the reality of Bedaux's coercive work system, which raised productivity by driving women and men to work intensively and without respite.

Bedaux's system grew out of his dissatisfaction with Frederick Taylor's theories on labor management, which, he believed, failed to specify the relationship between effort and fatigue.[45] As long as this relationship remained murky, employers would have no precise means of controlling the time workers took to execute particular tasks. Drawing on wartime studies of industrial fatigue, Bedaux created an instrument he believed would deliver such control to employers: a formula for determining precisely the level of strain imposed by any given type of work. "For a muscular effort of a given power the duration of work and rest periods is inversely proportional to the rapidity of motion."[46]

Bedaux's law of strain offered a "scientific" method for calculating the appropriate ratio of work time to necessary rest time in the performance of any task, regardless of its actual content or of who actually performed it. In

[45] See Frederick W. Taylor, "Principles of Scientific Management," in Taylor, *Scientific Management* (New York, 1964). On the diffusion of scientific management in England, see Lyndall Urwick, *The Meaning of Rationalisation* (London, 1929); Urwick and E. F. L. Brech, *The Making of Scientific Management*, vol. 2 (London, 1948); Craig Littler, *The Development of the Labour Process in Capitalist Countries* (London, 1982); Edward Cadbury, "Some Principles of Industrial Organisation: The Case for and against Scientific Management," *Sociological Review*, 1st ser., 1914, pp. 99–125. See also the Management Research Groups Archive, London School of Economics, sec. I (Labour), Box 12, esp. dossier 474, "Confidential Results of a Survey of Employers Who Have Used Bedaux for a Number of Years," 2 August 1938.

[46] Charles Bedaux, *The Bedaux Efficiency Course for Industrial Application* (New York, 1917), p. 274.

fact, applying this law demanded that one ignore a job's particular aspects and focus on its general characteristics; that is, the muscular expenditure and rapidity of movement demanded by each cycle of work activity. By comparing different tasks on the basis of these shared general features, employers could root their effort norms in the objective basis of how taxing the work really was, expressed in a "universal" work unit, the Bedaux:

> . . . all human effort may be measured in terms of a common unit, that unit being made up of a combination of work and rest, with the proportions dependent upon the nature of the effort and the subsequent relaxation required to compensate for it. As tasks vary, the ratio of work to rest within the unit varies, but the unit itself remains constant.[47]

As each Bedaux minute comprised a minute of work and relaxation in the proportions deemed appropriate to each task, 60Bs represented a minimum hourly effort below which workers fell at their peril.[48] Moreover, the notional integration of relaxation into each Bedaux unit enabled employers to eliminate all rest breaks and turn each moment clocked by the worker into an optimally productive "Bedaux minute." Bedaux thus removed from the worker all discretion over the time taken to complete a task and placed it in the hands of the employer. In fact, he proclaimed, the Bedaux unit gave employers a single measuring stick by which they might "scientifically" assess the relative efficiency of workers, monitoring individual effort inputs without regard to the specifics of the task or the skill, age, or gender of the person who performed it.

Yet the common standard cut two ways. In striking down the qualitative distinctions among tasks, Bedaux's system razed the barrier between men's and women's work. Employers who adopted this scheme thus unintentionally laid a new basis for an old claim: equal pay for equal work. But this potential escaped employers' attention until the Bedaux strike at Rover.

The Bedaux system was enormously popular among interwar employers, largely because it called for no costly overhaul of tools and plant. Rather than demand that employers invest in a more productive work organization or purchase new equipment, Bedaux placed the responsibility for raising productivity squarely on the workers' shoulders. His consulting "engineers" stood by the machines and assembly lines, observing women and men as they worked and offering suggestions for accomplishing individual tasks more quickly. Then, on the basis of their observations, the Bedaux men assigned each job a standard production time, or "B-value." Once they had set these production norms, the Bedaux men withdrew, leaving management to operate the system.

---

[47] Charles Bedaux, *Bedaux Labor Measurement* (New York, 1928), p. 3.
[48] Ibid., p. 4.

As much as Bedaux's "labor science" appealed to employers, it was universally detested by workers, who saw in Bedaux's scheme a system of "intensive scientific slavery . . . an inhuman system of speed-up that sought to turn people into machines."[49] Indeed, from the perspective of the shop floor, Bedauxism meant speedups on the production line, rate cutting as productivity rose, layoffs for workers who could not keep up, and the loss of predictability in one's week-to-week earnings. And, as the system conflated the "standard" effort level of 60B with a "normally attainable" level of 80B per hour, it was virtually impossible to resist overwork; those who could not consistently achieve the extra 20Bs were threatened with dismissal.[50] In these years of chronic underemployment, workers correctly suspected employers of using the Bedaux system as an instrument for the Darwinian weeding of the workforce.[51]

Worse, the Bedaux system rendered labor a passive object by excluding workers from the process of establishing effort norms and minimum wage rates. As the Engineering Employers' Federation observed, the scientific expertise of the Bedaux consultant justified speedups as a matter of technical necessity, and enabled employers to bypass the unions when they set production norms: "The Bedaux system is different . . . in that the unit of measurement is not fixed by mutual arrangement between the employers and workers concerned. . . . The Bedaux engineers . . . form their opinion by observing and judging whether the workers are working reasonably hard."[52]

Finally, Bedaux introduced an unwelcome observer into the workshop, the consulting engineer. Though only a temporary addition to factory life, his

---

[49] A. J. Caddick of the all-male Amalgamated Engineers Union (AEU), speaking before the Trades Union Congress (TUC): *Report of the Proceedings at the 64th Annual Trades Union Congress* (London, 1932), p. 421. See also Steven Tolliday, "Militancy and Organisation: Women Workers and Trade Unions in the Motor Trades in the 1930s," *Oral History*, Autumn 1983, p. 48.

[50] The minimally productive worker, moving at a swift 80B per hour, found her employer counting one-quarter of her "normal" effort in bonus points ("premium Bs") and so paying 25% of her wage in the form of Bedaux's sharply regressive production bonus. Her weekly earnings were thus even more difficult to predict, as the wage was paid on the basis of two scales, each of which was shrouded in the mysterious terminology of Bedaux's system. In fact, the scales of "B-values" amounted to nothing more than a roundabout means of counting the number of pieces produced, which continued to form the only tangible entity employers could measure.

[51] This suspicion was reinforced by the practice of publicly posting individual B-attainments, with all B-levels under 60B highlighted in red ink. In theory, this measure enhanced productivity by appealing to the worker's pride and encouraging her to enter into "friendly" competition with her fellow workers. "The worker takes new interest in his daily routine. His record speaks for itself as compared with that of a less competent neighbor, and he has opportunity to prove fitness for promotion. In times of low production and lay-offs, the better workmen are retained": Bedaux, *Bedaux Labor Management*, p. 10.

[52] MRC, EEF, 237/3/1/235, Assistant Secretary to Lt. Col. H. B. Sankey of Messrs. Joseph Sankey & Sons, Ltd., 15 May 1934.

intrusive presence was deeply resented. Workers often switched off their machines when the time-study man came to observe them, and one group of women chased the Bedaux consultant up to the roof and threatened to hurl him down into the street below.[53]

With so little to recommend it, the Bedaux system rapidly acquired an evil reputation among British workers, and the NUVB protested vehemently at the first hint that Rover might introduce the scheme:

> It is a damnable pernicious system to be forced on the workers. It is so damnable that we are prepared to fight it for all we are worth. You might as well have it straight out. You have been had; you have bought a white horse and you want to put it on the workers and we are not having it. That is straight English.[54]

Management therefore decided to pilot the scheme on the female trimmers.

The Genesis of the Strike at Rover

Concentrated in their own shop and almost certainly not unionized, these 150 women must have seemed the obvious point of entry for this unpopular system. Yet when the company floated its Bedaux proposal in mid-March 1930, representatives of the Female Trimming Department "stated emphatically that they declined to work the Bedaux system of piecework which it was proposed to introduce."[55] Rover, however, was determined to adopt a mass production strategy and leave the old ways behind. In the event that workers could not be coerced into accepting the Bedaux system, management was prepared to try a Fordist scheme of enhanced daily rates.

The CDEEA was horrified by the prospect that, failing Bedaux, Rover might take the "retrograde" step of a high-wage strategy. John Varley, CDEEA secretary, lost no time in warning the firm against such a venture, underscoring in particular "the harmful effect which the giving of enhanced day rates would have on the industry of the district."[56] As far as the CDEEA could see, the Bedaux system posed no such threat to the established wage structure. Quite the contrary; upon investigation, the employers concluded that by basing wages entirely on effort, Bedaux's scheme promised a more "scientific" control of labor, even as it promised to keep district wages low,

---

[53] Harold Nockolds, *Lucas: The First Hundred Years*, vol. 1 (London, 1976), p. 261.

[54] MRC, EEF 237/3/1/235, Ted Buckle (NUVB district official), "Notes from a Local Conference between the NUVB and CDEEA," 14 April 1930.

[55] CDEEA, Executive Committee minutes, "Report of a Works Conference Held at Rover, 19 March 1930," 31 March 1930, p. 3.

[56] Ibid., p. 4.

because "output . . . depend[s] on the extent to which waiting time and waste time are eliminated, and the degree to which the ability of the labour itself can be raised above the average by progressive selection." On the grounds of "progressive" labor selection, CDEEA officials applauded Bedaux's system, welcoming in particular its capacity to drive labor through the promise to "distinguish between the increased output which comes automatically from eliminating avoidable waste time, and that which can only come from an increase in the operator's individual effort."[57]

They did not expect organized labor to take kindly to its "progressive selection," for "Official Labour has never been sympathetic towards any proposal that a man should be dependent upon harder work in order to get greater earnings." But the association was determined to uphold managers' "right" to use the Bedaux system to sort the sheep from the goats on the factory floor. In fact, enthusiasm for Bedaux's system ran so high that the association decided to "resist any attempt by Official Labour to reject the Bedaux system" and to "give its firm support to any member who is seeking by aid of Bedaux or otherwise to arrive at a more scientific appreciation of its managerial responsibilities."[58] With the CDEEA behind them, Rover's managers launched a campaign to bring the recalcitrant women around to their view.

By this time (early April 1930) the women had approached the NUVB's Coventry officers and informed them that they were "solidly determined to resist the desires of the firm."[59] Though the NUVB opposed the introduction of Bedauxism into the district, union rules barred them from actually bringing the women into their organization.[60] Caught between their historic policy of resisting women's employment in the car industry and their desire to join the women's struggle against a system that promised to degrade the wages and working conditions of NUVB trimmers as well, the union could offer the women no genuine support. After pledging them all possible assistance, the NUVB Executive sent the female trimmers to the local of the Workers' Union, recently merged with the Transport Workers to form the Transport and General Workers' Union, or T&G.[61] The conflict at Rover gave the

---

[57] Ibid., "Report by the Special Committee on Payment by Results," in "The Bedaux System of Payment by Results," 7 July 1930, pp. 3–4.

[58] Ibid., pp. 3–4, 1.

[59] Quoted in Tolliday, "Militancy and Organisation," p. 46.

[60] As recently as 1929, the NUVB Executive had voted against the proposed admission of women and opted to continue to fight against the expansion of women's employment in the auto industry.

[61] The persistence of a Workers' Union local in Coventry may be explained by the union's exceptionally strong roots in the area, dating from before the war, when the union had stepped in and helped to organize a successful strike of semi- and unskilled women and men metalworkers. See Richard Hyman, *The Workers' Union* (Oxford, 1971).

T&G an opportunity to gain a foothold in Coventry's engineering shops and break the craft unions' monopoly on organizing engineering workers. This ominous precedent was not lost on the NUVB leadership. As one official gloomily remarked: "We could not help them other than by moral support, and the Workers' Union gladly took the opportunity of immediately enrolling them into membership."[62]

But enrolling in the T&G hardly solved the women's problems. Though ready to fight tooth and nail against an unreconstructed Bedauxism, the T&G leaders had long been enchanted by the prospect of joint participation in the project to revive industry through rationalization. Hence these men were prepared to accept precisely what their new female members hoped to avoid—the imposition of a coercive work system and general speedup—so long as some part of the profits thus accrued trickled down into the women's pay packets.

Rover was hoping to entice the women and their union representatives into a joint investigation of the Bedaux system, as a preliminary to installing the scheme. The T&G refused any such investigation on the grounds that Rover had no compelling reason to alter its wage system. By denying that the firm had any legitimate basis on which to tinker with "the present simple system of payment by results for the purpose of substituting what on the surface appears to be a very complicated system," the union hoped to deflect the issue before an unreformed Bedaux could get a single toe through the door. Yet the employers stubbornly insisted on their right to organize this investigation, and after much wrangling and failure to agree at both the works and the local conference level, the entire issue was referred to a national conference in May. There Andrew Dalgleish, secretary of the T&G's new Metals, Engineering, and Chemicals trade group, explained: "Now our people fear . . . that this new system is going to bring along at least three evils with it: one, the elimination of workpeople; two, a reduction of earnings; and three, that there would be an unnecessary and fatiguing speed-up." The employers stood their ground, however, and Dalgleish must have realized that his arguments were falling on deaf ears, for toward the end of the conference he agreed to participate in the investigation, provided that Rover resisted the temptation to begin Bedaux time studies on the women until the inquiry was finished.[63]

Dalgleish and the eight others deputed to investigate the scheme met with

---

[62] *NUVB Quarterly*, April 1929, quoted in Tolliday, "Militancy and Organisation," p. 47.
[63] MRC, EEF, Central Conference, case 21, "Refusal by the Union of the invitation of the firm for a joint investigation of a suggested System of Payment by Results to operate in certain departments of their Works—Messrs. The Rover Company, Ltd.," York, 9 May 1930, p. 7.

the Bedaux consultants and toured two engineering firms where the system was already being implemented.[64] He also met several times with Rover's managing director, Captain Spencer Wilks. At some point Dalgleish and the other T&G people appear to have convinced themselves that with certain crucial amendments, Bedauxism might be interpreted as conforming to the "customs and agreements" maintained between the union and the Engineering Employers' Federation.[65] By late July, Dalgleish and Wilks had worked out a revised version of Bedaux's scheme that the union, without consulting its new female members, was willing to accept.

The revisions included two vital concessions by Rover. First, all "premium B's" (bonus earnings, above the minimal 60B per hour) were to be paid directly to production workers, with no 25 percent skimmed off for "the bosses." More important, the union succeeded in shifting the establishment of B-allowances (effort norms) away from Bedaux's technocratic "experts" and back into the employer–employee negotiating arena. Since Rover was prepared to operate the system with these modifications, the T&G "could not see that there was anything to object to in the system as proposed to be worked by the Rover Company." The Employers' Association was also quite satisfied with this arrangement because the system's "great advantage"— "that all non-productive time is booked, which gives firms an opportunity of eliminating waste"—remained undisturbed by the amendments that Wilks and Dalgleish had agreed upon.[66]

The only dissatisfied parties were the female trimmers. As they were not consulted, their objections went unrecorded and, in all likelihood, unremarked. As far as Dalgleish and the T&G were concerned, Rover had offered them the opportunity to negotiate a version of Bedauxism more favorable to the workers and so to establish a T&G role in the rationalization of British industry. That assent to Rover's Bedaux plan utterly contravened the explicit wishes of the union's new members did not trouble Dalgleish unduly. Indeed, at the EEF's request, he returned to Coventry to try to persuade the women to go along with it. "Dalgleish saw the work girls last night," the chair of the EEF reported, "but in spite of all he told them, they won't have it."[67]

If the T&G had no intention of forcing a confrontation over Bedauxism, the NUVB stood firm in its opposition, at least so long as their men were not

---

[64] MRC, EEF, 237/3/1/235, 23 July 1930. The EEF sent the delegation to Hoffman's Ball Bearings plant in East Anglia and to Carreras & Enfield Cable Company in Manchester.

[65] CDEEA, Executive Committee minutes, 23 June 1930, p. 1.

[66] Ibid., p. 2; "Report by the Special Committee on Payment by Results," 7 July 1930.

[67] MRC, EEF, 237/3/1/235, Sir Allan Smith to R. Campbell (EEF joint secretary), 23 July 1930. The T&G's abrupt reversal on this issue has led Tolliday to accuse Dalgleish of being "soft on the Bedaux scheme from the start": "Militancy and Organisation," p. 46.

directly involved. For the time being, this opposition ruffled few managerial feathers: ". . . the NUVB . . . were quite adamant in their refusal to work this system, but as it was not yet intended to introduce it into the departments using skilled labour, this refusal did not raise any serious difficulty at the moment."[68] But the NUVB men employed at Rover felt particularly uneasy about the beachhead for Bedauxism that management had so easily secured. When the female trimmers finally struck work in mid-August, they found their staunchest allies among their skilled male colleagues.

By late July, Rover had grown impatient with the women's obstinate refusal to work the Bedaux system. On 22 July John Varley informed the EEF that Dalgleish had failed to win the women over. The phone call ended on a warning note: Varley's "people in Coventry were not going to have any more of this dilatory method and were going straight ahead with their scheme." Chairman Smith agreed that Rover's "only course" was in fact "to proceed with the introduction of the system as far as the girls were concerned, leaving them to take such action as they saw fit."[69] As long as the female trimmers formed the sole node of opposition, the CDEEA continued to back Rover. All parties to the conflict seem to have forgotten that, by local agreement, all systems of pay had first to be accepted by employers and the workers actually affected.[70] The T&G's accession to Rover's imposition of Bedaux was by itself insufficient.

Because summer was a slack time in the car industry, it was several weeks before Rover introduced Bedaux into its Coventry works.[71] The first eight female trimmers who were called to work under the Bedaux system refused to do so, claiming it meant a speedup and more work in shorter hours. When the company responded by firing all eight, the entire shop of 150 women abruptly downed tools and joined their comrades in the streets. At this point the T&G officially acknowledged the strike and dispatched a local officer, Alice Arnold, to help organize it. When Rover sent to the Labour Exchange for new workers, Arnold helped the women to organize the picket lines. Despite harassment from the local constables, who kept moving the pickets on, the trimmers policed the streets so effectively that the area around Rover became workers' territory. Only one or two blacklegs actually found their

---

[68] CDEEA, Executive Committee minutes, 7 July 1930, p. 1.

[69] MRC, EEF, 237/3/1/235, "Note of a Phonecall," Varley to Campbell, 22 July 1930; Smith, 24 July 1930.

[70] This agreement, dating from April 1920, gave "freedom to the Employers to introduce systems of payment by results satisfactory to the men and the Employers concerned": MRC, EEF, Central Conference, case 21, "Refusal by the Union," p. 2.

[71] Firms typically retooled for the new models in the late summer. All but a skeleton staff of skilled men were temporarily laid off or put on short time during this period, then brought back in the fall, when the new models went into production.

way into the works, and Arnold declared, "The girls are splendid. They know their work and are carrying out their duties well."[72]

The Struggle Escalates

During the first week of the twenty-day conflict, Rover confined itself to approaching individual strikers and urging them to work under the new system. The company eventually managed to bring in six new women, all of whom were started on trimming. Rover then asked a group of male (NUVB) trimmers to take over jobs normally done by the women. It was the firm's first major tactical blunder. The thirty-four men refused, and when the firm threatened to dismiss them, they joined the strike.[73] The struggle escalated rapidly, with more NUVB men coming out each day. By early September, some 70 vehicle builders were picketing alongside the female trimmers.

When Rover took on twenty male replacements for the striking vehicle builders, the NUVB leadership grew anxious over its members' involvement in this "women's business." Like other craft unions, the NUVB enjoyed a special relationship with local employers: in return for adherence to the disputes procedure—a procedure that had effectively curbed the militancy of skilled men since the disastrous lockout of 1922—members' wage rates were sheltered from the full impact of Depression-era wage cuts. NUVB leaders were extremely reluctant to endanger this arrangement in a showdown over conditions in the women's shop, and began to disavow their members' "unconstitutional" and spontaneous act of solidarity with the women. In a phone call to Sir Allan Smith, Mr. Nicholson, of the NUVB Executive Committee, disparaged the men's involvement in this dispute: "We should never have been mixed up in this beastly thing, it was something which we had nothing to do with."[74] As the conflict wore on, the NUVB Executive began to fear, with some justification, that the men's refusal to return to work might ultimately provoke a Coventry-wide lockout of NUVB workers—an outcome that would undoubtedly rupture the favorable arrangement the union had won for its men. Its leaders therefore cast about for a way out of their embarrassing position.

The most direct solution—to call their men back to work immediately—

[72] Quoted in F. W. Carr, "Engineers and the Rise of Labour in Coventry, 1914–1939" (Ph.D. thesis, University of Warwick, 1978), p. 475. See MRC, EEF, 237/3/1/235/1, Varley to Smith, 17 August 1930.

[73] MRC, EEF, 237/3/1/235, Smith, "Note of a Phonecall," 26 August 1930.

[74] Ibid., "Note of a Phonecall from Nicholson," 10 September 1930. Nicholson's use of the term "unconstitutional" refers to the EEF's rather lengthy procedure for settling disputes.

was out of the question, for the NUVB men at Rover disagreed completely with their leaders over the significance of the women's struggle. From the outset the men understood that the women's battle was their own. They saw in Bedaux's system a threat that was too powerful to ignore, and recognized that its current confinement to the women's shop was a purely tactical maneuver; its imposition on the women was simply a prelude to the Bedauxization of the entire works. Despite considerable pressure from on high to abandon the "women's" cause and guard their own relatively privileged position, the vehicle builders' sympathy strike remained solid.

Rover, in no position to endure a protracted conflict, looked to its fellow employers for support. Captain Wilks urged the CDEEA to threaten the NUVB leadership with what it feared most: a Coventry-wide lockout. But Rover had not reckoned on the division that opened up between the union's leaders and the seventy men on strike. However anxious the leaders were to extract their organization from this situation, they had lost touch with their men on the Bedaux issue. When the employers pressured the Executive Committee to call for a return to work, it became clear that they had lost control of the situation: "Mr. Nicholson said quite frankly that he knew their men were in the wrong, but at the present he could not get them back. He said it was very difficult to prove to the men that they were not blacklegging the girls"; "To put the whole thing bluntly, I am satisfied that Mr. Nicholson is fully aware that his men are out of order, but up to the present he has not been strong enough to get them back to work."[75] Lacking any alternative, the NUVB's national officials contacted the top-level leaders of the T&G and began to lean on them to settle quickly and end the entire conflict.

Unintended Consequences: Equal Pay for Equal Work

Unbeknownst to the vehicle builders, Captain Wilks was having some difficulty of his own persuading the CDEEA to call for an NUVB lockout. The men's solidarity strike had raised the stakes considerably. As no one else in the district was contemplating any drastic changes in production strategy, a district-wide lockout of NUVB men seemed an unnecessary disruption of their own production schedules. One after another, association members began to recall the terms of the agreement with workers regarding the introduction of systems of payment by results. These recollections raised doubts about the manner in which Rover had forced the Bedaux issue.

[75] Ibid., "Note of a Phonecall to Nicholson" and discussion between Smith and Campbell regarding Smith's phone call to Nicholson, 11 September 1930.

Mr. Oliver (Humber Ltd.) said he personally was not satisfied that the strike of the Female Trimmers was unconstitutional because he had never yet understood that the Rover Co. or any other Company were entitled to introduce a new system of payment by results without the consent of the individual workpeople concerned.[76]

Despite its recent affirmation of the employers' "right" to introduce systems of payment by results, the association was not prepared to back Rover's unilateral imposition of the Bedaux system. Unable or unwilling to bear the cost of supporting Rover with a lockout, the association turned to the EEF in the hope that the federation could tame the unions and insist on an immediate return to work.

Rover's abandonment by the CDEEA was paralleled by the T&G leadership's readiness to abandon the female trimmers and negotiate the introduction of Bedauxism at Rover. Untrammeled by the traditional interests of their respective and antinomous constituencies, Spencer Wilks and the T&G's general secretary, Ernest Bevin, hammered out an agreement at London's Transport House on the morning of 10 September, twenty days into the strike. Wilks emerged from this session feeling satisfied with the accord they had reached and convinced that Bevin was "a very clever man."[77] At that moment the labor conflict ended and a more deadly fraternal struggle began.

Wilks passed the afternoon far less pleasantly. Closeted with the EEF general secretary, R. Campbell, Wilks stubbornly defended the memorandum of settlement that he and Bevin had drafted that morning. The memorandum, which Wilks intended to sign the following day, secured labor's cooperation in the Bedaux time study in return for a guaranteed weekly minimum wage of £2.15.0 and the closing of male–female wage differentials: "the value of the unit of measure of any one operation shall be equal irrespective of age or grade."[78]

Both the guaranteed minimum and the elimination of the male–female wage gap ran completely against local and national wage policies:

> . . . the Secretary [of the CDEEA] pointed out [that the memorandum] was contrary to recognised practices in that they [sic] implied the abandonment of the Employers' well-established practice of varying piecework prices according to the grade of labour employed. He further warned Captain Wilks that it was contrary to the recognised practice of the Engineering trade to guarantee

---

[76] CDEEA, Executive Committee minutes, 8 September 1930, p. 3. This was the first Executive Committee meeting held since 23 July, before the strike began.

[77] MRC, EEF, 237/3/1/235, Campbell, "Notes from a Meeting with Spencer Wilks," 10 September 1930.

[78] Ibid., Memorandum of Settlement, clause 1, "Proposals for a Settlement of the Dispute Agreed between Wilks and Bevin," 11 September 1930.

anything in excess of the agreed base rate specified in the Coventry Women's Scale.[79]

But as far as Captain Wilks was concerned, Rover's future depended on making the transition to mass production. He therefore countered Campbell's argument by pointing out the contradiction between Bedaux's system and unequal pay: "Captain Wilks said that for the life of him he could not see why a piecework price should be any different for a man, woman or boy. His line is that a B is a unit of measure of effort and therefore should be of the same value for everybody."[80]

Campbell refused to contemplate the possibility that any basis for wages might exist other than that inscribed in the practice of labor stratification. He spoke bitterly of Wilks, as though the man had turned traitor before his eyes.

> Captain Wilks . . . is suffering from some rather ill-digested views with regard to Capital and Labour. He is a great admirer of Mr. Ford and American methods. . . . His idea is that everybody should receive a high flat day rate and then be compelled to work as hard as possible and if they do not do so then they are to be fired.[81]

In fact, Bedaux's system, which notionally collapsed actual differences in work and compressed these distinct forms onto a single scale of effort input, was fundamentally inconsistent with a qualitatively stratified wage structure, where the different classes of labor were regarded as incommensurable. But Campbell's shock and outrage at Wilks's fairly obvious point is understandable. In its previous applications, Bedauxism had simply been grafted onto the existing stratified wage structure, pressing downward on the wage/effort ratio within each class but not leveling the barriers between them. It was only when labor shifted tactics, from refusing to work the system in any form to negotiating a single Bedaux time rate, that the system's comparable-worth potential surfaced. This potential has been forgotten—indeed, it has been completely ignored in recent literature on the Bedaux system[82]—perhaps

---

[79] CDEEA, Executive Committee minutes, 18 September 1930, pp. 1–2.

[80] MRC, EEF, 237/3/1/235, Campbell, "Notes from a Meeting with Spencer Wilks," 10 September 1930.

[81] Ibid., Smith, "Notes from a Discussion of Campbell's Meeting with Wilks," 10 September 1930. Wayne Lewchuck has observed that British managers typically interpreted Fordism as "a disease or mental deficiency": "Fordism and British Motor Car Employers," pp. 105–6.

[82] See, for example, Littler, *Development of the Labour Process*; Lewchuck, "Fordism and British Motor Car Employers"; Tolliday, "Militancy and Organisation."

because the one time its equal-pay implications found their way into management's plans for implementing it, the system never made it to the shop floor. Wilks was very angry with the Employers' Association for its refusal to lock out the entire NUVB, and does not appear to have cared much what his colleagues thought of the memorandum of settlement. His overriding concern seems to have been to forge ahead with his Bedauxist mass-production plan, a strategy that had grown more Fordist with each successive amendment. This evolution had culminated in Rover's minimum wage, which guaranteed the female trimmers twice the weekly rate paid to women elsewhere in the Coventry district. Here, in the assimilation of the women's pay scale to that of unskilled men, lay the real danger in Wilks's accommodation with Bevin. If their traditional instrument of labor control, low wages, were abolished, how could management drive women to work at high speed? "This . . . rate was so high that there was a probability of the girls being satisfied with £2.15.0 and the question then arose what would happen if the girls did not do £2.15.0 worth of work in a week."[83] Certain that Rover's new pay scale would drive up the price of female labor and destroy the structure of inequality on which local wages rested, Varley lost no time in censuring Captain Wilks: "[This agreement] poses a very real danger . . . an *agreed time rate* for Female Labour of 1s 2d hour, as against the recognised district rate of 6½d per hour only . . . must create serious difficulty for our local industry."[84] Ultimately, the CDEEA angrily rejected Wilks's settlement and over the next few months came very close to expelling Rover from the federation. Under threat of banishment, Wilks finally withdrew the amended Bedaux plan and scrapped the entire mass-production venture.[85]

Bevin fared little better with his constituency. In trading off intensification of effort for increased rewards, he managed to negotiate a version of Bedauxism that actually would have delivered high wages to women rather than function as a complicated sweating system. Yet he signed and sealed this trade-off without ever consulting the women involved, and they were hardly inclined to accept Bevin's deal. Though aware that it would double the earnings of those who managed to keep up, the trimmers steadfastly opposed the introduction of a

[83] MRC, EEF, 237/3/1/235, "Note of a Phonecall from R. Campbell to J. Varley," 15 September 1930.
[84] Ibid., Varley to Wilks, 12 September 1930; emphasis in original.
[85] Ibid., Varley to EEF, 6 November 1930. Despite the CDEEA's stab in the back on Rover's Bedaux plan, Wilks must have blanched at the prospect of losing the association's collective support. In an era of fairly powerful organization on both sides of the labor–capital divide, exile from the Employers' Association would have isolated the firm from industry-wide bargaining procedures and from exchange of information. Caught between the adamant female trimmers and his equally unbending colleagues, Wilks must have felt he had no choice but to abandon the entire project.

system that would enable management to maintain a swift pace on the shop floor and to weed out those who could not or would not keep up. Three days after Bevin's fateful meeting with Wilks, the women bowed to necessity and reluctantly assented to the T&G's action on "their" behalf.[86]

The NUVB had conspicuously failed to seize the opportunity on which Bevin had capitalized. Not only had they lost a group of car workers to a rival organization, but the union's failure to keep pace with its people on the issue of Bedauxism at Rover had come close to rupturing the vehicle builders' privileged relation with the Coventry employers. For some weeks after work had resumed at Rover, NUVB officials continued to approach the employers with some trepidation, and never missed a chance to disavow the "wildcat" strike of vehicle builders at Rover: "I know full well the irregularity of the action of our men," wrote a member of the union's executive committee to the EEF general secretary, "but the circumstances were extraordinary, and in this period of women butting into most things, their action actually, for the first time, I think, drew us into conflict with your Association."[87]

The T&G's inroads into NUVB territory as a result of the dispute at Rover catalyzed an about-face among the vehicle builders on the question of admitting women. In December 1931 the NUVB reversed its resolution against organizing women in the car industry. This reversal signaled the adoption of a new tactic for dealing with women workers. No longer did it appear possible to circumscribe the extension of their labor in auto shops. Rather, the union had to acknowledge the permanence of women as workers, at least in the trim shops, and search for a more direct way to control their use as cheap labor. "The development of female labour in the production of the motor car has gone beyond our power to erase. . . . It is not anticipated that this will develop beyond the motor car centres but it will give us a control that now belongs to others."[88]

In the end, Rover's mass-production plan foundered on organized resistance from both workers and employers. The female trimmers refused to accept an unreformed Bedauxism, and their skilled male colleagues refused to blackleg the women, despite their leaders' willingness to abandon the women to the hated system. But it was the collective opposition of Rover's colleagues that decisively blocked the mass-production plan. Committed to traditional methods of controlling labor, the CDEEA could not allow Rover to disrupt the structure of stratified labor and low pay on which that control depended.

Rover abandoned its efforts to shift over to mass production, and the female

---

[86] CDEEA, Executive Committee minutes, 15 September 1930, p. 2.
[87] Ibid., Nicholson to Campbell, 22 September 1930.
[88] "Report of the Annual Conference, December, 1931," *NUVB Quarterly*, January 1932.

trimmers continued to earn 24s. to 31s. a week. The firm appears to have retained both its former division of labor and its old system of payment by results. But the local employers were particularly unforgiving of Rover's flirtation with equal pay for equal work. Despite Rover's capitulation in the Bedaux conflict, relations with the CDEEA remained quite strained; it was five years before Rover appeared at a single association meeting.

The struggle at Rover reveals how narrowly the range of possible managerial action was circumscribed in Britain's interwar engineering industry. Of course the economic crisis limited all industrialists to some extent; often the money for substantial investment in retooling or reorganizing plant and machinery simply was not available. But, ironically enough, employers themselves further restricted the range of managerial response to the crisis by their stubborn adherence to a stratified labor force.[89] The decision to weather the Depression by clinging to wage stratification trammeled not only the conservative firms but those that were prepared to innovate as well.

The most remarkable aspect of the strike at Rover is the way it moved from a labor–management dispute to an intramural battle among employers over which labor strategy would prevail in the district. Each of these strategies contained its own bizarre presumptions—the idea that a single unit could reliably measure effort inputs across a broad range of jobs, or the notion that socially constructed ideas about males and females are central to organizing the labor process. On the basis of these presumptions, the two systems created their own sets of equally arbitrary wage standards.

Yet the fundamental opposition between the two systems was never fully articulated in the confrontation at Rover, for the Coventry employers were ideologically committed to the efficiency that rationalization schemes such as Bedaux's promised to deliver. Thus, when Bedaux's pseudoscientific effort unit confronted the traditional order of stratified labor with the claim that all work and all workers were the same, Coventry employers applauded the introduction of a "scientific" basis for measuring effort and controlling non-productive time, without acknowledging that the very standard of measurement, the Bedaux unit, denied the validity of a labor strategy built around the notion of essential distinctions in work and workers.

This failure to see the implications of Bedaux's scientism is not in itself

---

[89] In 1938 the National Employers' Federation reaffirmed its commitment to stratified labor and to the asymmetrical positions that women and men held in that structure. Women "do not fit into the economic structure of the industry at all in the same way as men do. The women in engineering have their particular place and a valuable place it is, but . . . their activities in the industry are of a particular character and not subject to the same general expansions and reservations and incidences as in the case of men": MRC, EEF, Central Conference, "Women's Wages," 22 February 1938, pp. 403–5.

surprising. Elsewhere employers had simply grafted the system onto the existing stratified wage structure and used it to raise output within that structure. The contradiction between the two systems emerged only when the T&G, whose members' interests were consistent with seeing the point, observed that if all work and all workers were the same, then all workers must be equally valuable. Captain Wilks was willing to concede this point, and apparently felt that the gains in productivity that the new system promised would more than cover the cost of raising women's rates to the (unskilled) male level. Rover's colleagues, by contrast, welcomed Bedaux's pseudoscientific system of labor control without ever seeing that it undermined the basis of stratification as a means of deploying, controlling, and remunerating the workforce.

Because labor stratification in any one firm depended on the stratification of the entire local labor force, there was never any hope for peaceful coexistence between the traditional strategy and Rover's revised Bedaux plan. If the worst fears of Rover's colleagues had been realized, and women workers had all flocked en masse to Rover or struck for parity, the traditionalist firms could not simply have replaced the women with other forms of labor. In a qualitatively differentiated labor force there are no ready substitutes for each specifically constituted source of labor. Men were too expensive and adolescents lacked the requisite speed, dexterity, and steadiness. In a market situation in which few industrialists could afford to follow Rover's lead and switch over to mass production, their only recourse lay in preventing Rover from implementing equal pay. For the majority of firms, survival depended on maintaining a wage hierarchy that held women's pay at half that of men.

Rover's troubles did not discourage other engineering employers in the region from experiments with Bedauxism. Indeed, two years after the conflict at Rover had ended, Bedaux consultants were touring the shop floor at Lucas Aircraft Factory in Birmingham, measuring and timing the women as they worked. Resistance was swift, spontaneous, and sharp.[90] Knowing Bedaux's system by reputation, the women at Lucas never gave it a chance. Years later Alice Roach, who had worked at Lucas in 1932, remembered the scene vividly:

And . . . the rumour started to fly around. The Bedaux system is coming to Birmingham. Coming to Lucas's . . . and then they said "It's in! . . . They started it in [shop] G6 and it's terrible, it's awful! We're going to be like slaves." . . . [We were] working away, and talking to each other about it, and all of a sudden the door opened in the middle of the shop, and a girl run in, she says, "Come on we're all out!" We all run out except the few . . . and there was hundreds of women down in the yard . . . and the excitement was terrific.

[90] By 1932, hatred of the Bedaux system ran so high that even at Lucas, where most of the women were the sole support of families laid low by the Depression, hundreds fled the shops and filled the streets in angry protest against the system. See Jim Crump's interview in R. A. Leeson, *Strike: A Live History, 1887–1971* (London, 1971), pp. 128–30.

. . . Then we came in the next day, then the excitement blew up again, and out we went again . . . there was shouts, stamping their feet, cheering, singing out there the commotion was terrific . . . we went in again the next day, and the excitement . . . there was no work being done. And the men didn't back us up you know, Oh no, the men didn't back us up. And the rumour came around: "They're dropped it [sic]! They're putting it out, they're not putting it in, they're decided to drop the whole thing!" So of course everybody started to sing, the excitement was terrible. Thousands of women singing and dancing in the street. It was really, well, we really enjoyed it. But you know what they done. We came back to work, we carried on just the same as usual, and then they started to slip it quietly into one shop under another name, and gradually we got it. They didn't call it that but that's what it was.[91]

We have no record of what Rover's female trimmers felt about their own struggle, about the final outcome of the conflict, or about their own role in bringing about that result. Alice Roach's recollection of a similar struggle implies that Rover's women may well have been satisfied with themselves for having kept Bedaux out; certainly their reluctance to accept the negotiated version, equal pay notwithstanding, supports this surmise. Further, Roach's tale suggests that women workers throughout the engineering industry were unwilling to accept Bedaux's "scientific slavery," whether or not their employers were prepared to offer equal pay in exchange for greater managerial control and enhanced productivity.

The struggle between Rover and the CDEEA reveals a vital conflict between the more traditional production strategies employed in the partially Taylorized factories of the interwar engineering industry and the new mass-production strategies. Ultimately, one company's pursuit of the new strategy directly threatened the capacity of traditionalists to adhere to their old ways. This element of struggle between traditional and innovative employers, a struggle whose outcome would determine how local labor markets were structured, is often overlooked in the literature on British industrial decline. Yet it is evident that Rover's failure to innovate on the eve of the Depression owed at least as much to the opposition of conservative employers as to labor's refusal to bear the full cost of raising productivity.

---

[91] Quoted in Tolliday, "Militancy and Organisation," pp. 50–51. The very different nature of the struggle at Lucas, in particular the lack of support from skilled men, may be due to broad structural differences between Rover and Lucas, especially in the organization of work and shape of the workforce. Lucas had mushroomed since the war and by 1932 was ten times the size of Rover, with nearly 20,000 workers, 80% of them women. Most male workers were isolated from the women, working either in the toolroom or as laborers, rarely on the assembly lines. Rover, by contrast, employed women solely for trim work, and no more than 10% of its 1,800–1,900 workers were women. Bedauxism must have presented a more proximate threat to Rover's skilled men; clearly management would not go to the trouble and expense of altering the work system in only one shop. As a result, skilled men took a direct interest in the female trimmers' struggle and helped to shape that conflict.

Epilogue

By the mid-1930s, widespread unemployment in both France and Britain had put renewed pressure on metals employers to turn back the clock and restore the all-male workshops that had prevailed throughout the trade a scant generation before. In the face of such pressures, employers staunchly upheld their Depression-era labor strategies, defending the new sexual division of labor in nationally specific idioms that reflected the distinct ways in which the changed organization of work had been assimilated to common industrial practice on both sides of the Channel. Thus British industrialists countered demands that women be replaced by men by observing not only that such substitutions were technically unfeasible, women and men being noncommensurable forms of labor, but that women, too, had some right to their jobs, a right that with the passage of time was beginning to acquire the weight of custom. Hiring women for work in engineering "has gone on for a long time," one employer observed, "and it cannot be stopped: our competitors all over the world are doing it. As citizens of the State, entitled to get a livelihood out of industry, I suppose it would be difficult to deny it to them. They have the vote the same as you and I have got."[1]

Faced with a broader, more overtly political assault on women's right to work, French employers were more inclined than their British counterparts to underscore the unique skills and abilities that women alone were presumed to possess. Hence, when a group of *mère-au-foyer* activists grilled the management of one engineering company about the firm's unwavering commitment to employing married women as file cutters, management explained that because "one rarely thinks of male labor for certain small jobs comparable to fine sewing, where the entire job demands more dexterity than effort,"

[1] MRC, EEF, Central Conference, no. 12, Barrow reference, York, 12 June 1931, p. 12.

306

women were in fact the only kind of skilled labor that the firm could profitably place on this work.[2] But if French employers were more likely than the British to emphasize women's particular skills, they also tended to champion women's beleaguered right to work as a matter less of right than of industrial necessity— the industry's urgent need for labor that was both cheap and skilled. In 1933, that usually meant married women.

It is interesting and significant to see here the return of the unrepressed domestic analogy, invoked to sustain a policy of deploying only married women on the highly skilled work of cutting files by hand to fine specifications. In truth, file cutting has no more in common with fine sewing than microsurgery does; the domestic analogy cannot purport to describe what it is workers are doing when they cut and shape these precision tools. As we have seen, however, such analogies had a deeper function in articulating and reinforcing a social/technical order that could retain the appearance of stability even as employers repeatedly revised the technical and sexual divisions of labor. After 1914, the use of domestic analogies allowed metals employers in both nations to produce an account that justified such radical revisions to their own satisfaction and that of their male workers.

Such an explanation must have been especially vital in cases like this one, for the first thought to enter a contemporary observer's mind was very likely not that file cutting was "comparable to fine sewing" but that the work these skilled women were performing had been the sole province of apprenticed craftsmen twenty brief years before. As we have seen, a similar chain of reasoning bound women to less skilled forms of work as well, for as one female factory inspector put it, "women link themselves more easily to a machine."[3] At all levels of skill, then, employers continued to weave domestic analogies through the newly reformulated language of job skill, seeking, perhaps, to lend the appearance of stability to an order of technical and social relations that was in fact continuously changing.

I have suggested that employers' citing of the domestic in their discussions

[2] UIMM, 69/54/03, UFCS survey, 1932–33, "Lettre de la Société Anonyme des Hauts-Fourneaux, Forges et Aciéries du Saut-du-Tarn," 14 March 1933. The firm opened the defense of its policy by describing in some detail the five-year apprenticeship required to become fully skilled at filemaking. At the time of the UFCS survey, there were no young, single women working in the file-cutting shop. Indeed, the female workforce consisted largely of married women (53.5%) and widows (23.2%). These were precisely the workers—older, fully skilled women—whom management was so concerned to keep on despite the pressure to return mothers to the home. Overall, women made up 12.3% of the workforce at this firm.

[3] Gabrielle Letellier, Le chômage en France de 1930 à 1936 (Paris, 1938), pp. 66–67. Letellier observes (p. 68) that with further rationalization, "industrial labor, having lost much of its technicality and demanding nothing more than mere manual dexterity and an automatism of motion more frequently found among women than among men, could be entrusted to a female labor force. . . . One could expect to see employers seek to lower their overall costs through more intensive employment of women."

of women workers, though extraordinarily common, was singularly unsuited to describing the work women actually performed in metalworking. Moreover, I have suggested that neoclassical models of capitalist reason cannot adequately account for the pervasiveness of such imagery in employers' discourse. Indeed, theorists who operate within this framework would dismiss this way of talking about women metalworkers as ultimately uninteresting, perhaps even beside the point.[4] They would do so in one of two ways. First, the neoclassicist might construct metals employers' overall labor strategies as rational a priori— these profit-driven men must have done the rational thing ipso facto, and any particular sexual division of labor arrived at must therefore reflect the operation of a clear, untrammeled capitalist perception. But as we have seen, the geographic mutability of any given gender division of labor in this period— what was defined as a man's job in Barrow might well be given over to women in Newcastle—argues against the proposition that gender divisions of labor were determined by the simple operation of a singular and pure capitalist reason.

Second, our neoclassical theorist might argue (more cogently) that employers' potentially clear vision of the rational course of action was in fact obstructed by their own awkward burden of conviction that women have a categorically distinct nature, and that this nature is relevant even to the task of cutting metal or building machinery. This burdensome faith in the meaning of gender difference held industrialists back from taking full advantage of women's labor, as they might have done had they been able to break with their own time- and culture-boundedness, lift their blinders, and jettison the weighty baggage of gender prejudice.

What the two neoclassical scenarios share is a lack of interest in the specific

---

[4] The "human capital" school argues that discrimination as such occurs not in the workplace but in social arenas outside the factory (the family, in the case of women), creating humans who arrive in the factory underendowed with human capital—that is, skill. This account of women's inferior position in the workforce closely matches the rationale for lower wages offered by interwar metals employers. See three works by Gary Becker: *Human Capital: A Theoretical and Empirical Analysis with Special Reference to Education*, 2d ed. (New York, 1975), *The Economics of Discrimination* (Chicago, 1971), and *An Economic Analysis of the Family* (Dublin, 1986). See also Jacob Mincer and Solomon Polachek, "Family Investments in Human Capital: Earnings of Women," *Journal of Political Economy* 82 (1974): 76–108. The radical critique of human capital theory, the theory of structured, segmented, or split labor markets, seeks to describe and explain what human capitalists are uninterested in exploring—the ghettoization of underprivileged workers in a second-rate stream of the labor market. The proponents of a segmented labor market argue that employers stratify the workforce in a kind of divide-and-rule strategy. Though this account is descriptively persuasive, it ultimately flattens the complexity of employers' thought into an unreflective will to power. See Peter Doeringer and Michael Piore, *Internal Labor Markets and Manpower Analysis* (Lexington, Mass., 1971); David Gordon, Richard Edwards, and Michael Reich, *Labor Market Segmentation* (Lexington, Mass., 1975) and *Segmented Work, Divided Workers* (Cambridge, 1982); Lester Thurow, *Generating Inequality: Mechanisms of Income Distribution in the U.S. Economy* (New York, 1975).

ways in which employers spoke about, managed, and deployed their women workers. I return, therefore, to the odd and unsettling juxtaposition of images produced by employers' repeated invocation of domestic analogies when they discussed women workers: women turned shells as they might knit sweaters; they assembled machinery as they might set up the meat mincer and transform Sunday's joint into Tuesday's hash. Taken seriously, these images are, I think, one visible sign of a partially submerged logic of social being, a logic in which social being is seen to be manifested in the particular skills and abilities possessed by distinct categories of human: female, skilled male, unskilled laborer, young boy. It is a logic that is fundamentally Aristotelian in nature, in that it casts social difference in the more essentialist terms of categorical (versus individual) differences in ability, and then welds the resulting diversity into a coherent whole by arraying all on a vertical chain. It is a logic whose overtones resound in the vocabulary that metals employers themselves used to talk about who their new female workers were, what they could and could not accomplish, technically and morally, and the consequences this all carried for recasting productive hierarchies in the newly rationalized labor process.

But in suggesting that those hierarchies were undergirded by an Aristotelian social logic, I seek not only to identify the kind of command structures that ruled factory production in the early twentieth century; ultimately, I hope to open up the whole question of social order in the factory. This is an issue on which neoclassical economic theorists have been remarkably silent. Yet productive orders are always social orders, whether the language exists to discuss that fact directly or not. Hence, even in the early twentieth century, when the industrialists' discourse was dominated by talk of market calculation, of costs, profits, and losses, they were also discussing the socioproductive hierarchy that allowed anything at all to happen on the factory floor. Further, although these discussions proceeded overtly in the market language of political economy, they were informed by and even predicated on an Aristotelian logic of social being and social hierarchy, an older language that twined through the numeric language of the market and is episodically audible to the attentive listener.[5]

Upon reflection, the presence of this Aristotelian social logic is not quite

---

[5] One could go further and observe that the Aristotelian linkage of socioproductive being and social order has also shaped the modern system of political economy, which, as Jean Baudrillard trenchantly observes, "produces the very conception of labor power as the fundamental human potential . . . the system is rooted in the identification of the individual with his labor power and with his act of transforming nature according to human ends": *The Mirror of Production* (St. Louis, 1975). Karl Marx, too, spoke in this vein: "Men begin to distinguish themselves from animals as soon as they begin to produce the means of their subsistence, a step which is conditioned by their physical organization. . . . What they are, therefore, coincides with their production, both with what they produce and with how they produce": *The German Ideology*, ed. C. J. Arthur (New York, 1970), p. 42.

so startling as it may at first appear. As a comparison of early-twentieth-century French and British factories suggests, the industrialist's central challenge was (and is always) to bring together the various agents of production; to assemble and activate particular individuals who bring to their relationship with capitalist production their own powerfully held beliefs, loyalties, commitments, and constraints regarding gender, family and communities of skill. One needs a social logic of human particularity and diversity (and Aristotle's is but one such logic) to speak meaningfully and concretely about the innately social nature of production—the fact that the employer's central task inside the factory is to mobilize and direct a conglomerate of active, willful, dreaming, soulful individuals.

The language of market encounters, based on a belief in an abstract, rationally ordered economy inhabited by economic men and women, is simply insufficient to encompass this complexity of social relationships. Market rationality and language are organized around a single scale of value, a single goal: profit. In this language, only one kind of human excellence—job skill—is overtly valued, even articulable. Aristotelian social theory/language, on the other hand, is plural and particular; that is, it comprehends and accepts, even anticipates difference, and provides ample latitude for articulating that difference.

The Aristotelian solution to the problem of forging a coherent social order from that human diversity—inequality, hierarchy—seems worlds away from the egalitarian and individualistic realm of market relations. And indeed it is, for (as Marx reminds us) the factories of nineteenth- and early-twentieth-century Europe constituted social orders of an entirely different kind. Once a worker had signed her labor contract, she left the egalitarian realm of the marketplace behind and crossed over into a world where relationships were structured around order, constraint, and hierarchy, where all activity took place along sharply vertical orders of command. Here, inside the "hidden abode of production," a rather different ethos from that of the market was required to shape and command those vertical orders. In the Aristotelian logic of hierarchy and difference employers found a language that harmonized well with this vertical organization; one that, moreover, allowed them to speak about the particular differences they perceived among workers, instead of merely arraying labor along a singular, quantitative scale, as market logic dictates.[6]

Aristotelian language thus endowed employers with a vocabulary of order

---

[6] My distinction between singular and plural languages of value rests heavily on Martha Nussbaum's discussion of plural values and noncommensurability in her essay "The Discernment of Perception: An Aristotelian Conception of Private and Public Rationality," in her *Love's Knowledge* (Oxford, 1990), pp. 54–105.

and command in an environment where strict hierarchy was presumed to be the condition of efficient production. In addition, this vocabulary enriched the overly narrow portrait of human motivation, drive, and desire that is all that political economy can offer. Finally, the Aristotelian logic both supplemented and underwrote productive hierarchies in the factory. Hence employers used the older vocabulary to express their understanding of the relevant differences among workers. These men then built hierarchies from the complementary skills and capacities that, in their view, bound workers together along productive chains that were at once horizontal (the technical division of labor) and vertical (the technically grounded line of authority). Yet as we have seen, the capacity of the Aristotelian language to convey a range of perceived differences constantly threatened to destabilize factory hierarchies, which purportedly were structured according to the unitary scale of skill attainment.

Nonetheless, through this composite language employers and workers found ways to talk about social organization, human needs, and the relationship between the factory and the broader society. By contrast, the pure market language of neoclassical economics cannot, on its own, address or even recognize the social nature of production. The neoclassical theorist therefore draws a veil of silence around this crucial dimension, a silence that has profound consequences. First, it renders phenomena that are endemic to capitalist production, such as gender discrimination, articulable only as errors in the system, blots on the operation of pure economic reason, rather than as elements of which productive hierarchies are constructed in the factory. But the refusal to come to grips with production's social aspect presents further problems of language and understanding, problems that are, finally, intractable.

This refusal ultimately springs from the neoclassicist's desire to preserve a strict division between the material (that is, the realm of the social, the "real") and the ideal, for the possibility of pure capitalist reason, unpolluted and unblinkered by particular cultural allegiances, rests on this division. So long as it holds, one can transmute the problem of capitalist production—a problem that is ultimately one of power (creating and policing a factory order)—into a problem of perception: the reasonable employer has only to look past the obfuscations of cultural attachment (even and especially his own) to discern the most rational economic choices, shimmering just beyond the slippery world of noneconomic value. But there is something deeply wrong with a model of economic analysis that imagines it possible to jettison one's cultural baggage, as the struggle at the Johnson Controls battery plant reminds us.

In the fall of 1990, the issue of fetal protection in the workplace briefly captured public attention when the United States Supreme Court agreed to hear the case of *United Automobile Workers* v. *Johnson Controls, Inc.* The Automobile Workers were challenging the company's fetal protection policy on the grounds that it violated women's right to work, protected under the Civil Rights Act of 1964. Throughout the case, debate entangled women's right to work with questions of motherhood while studiously downplaying the risks that the same work might pose to men. Embedded in the entire dispute, however, was a deeper problem, one that lay at the heart of the conflict and yet could never be fully articulated in the discursive context of fetal protection: the issue of women's access to well-paid jobs in this traditionally male industry.[7]

Johnson Controls manufactures lead batteries for the big automobile suppliers—Sears, Goodyear, and the like. The air inside the plant is laced with tiny particles of lead and lead oxide, "indisputably toxic substances" but (according to company claims) not present in such high density as to be dangerous to adults.[8] No one denies, however, that the levels are excessive for children and fetuses. In 1982 the company passed a fetal protection policy whose effect was to all but ban the employment of women in this high-wage industry.[9] Under the terms of the policy, only those women who either were too old to bear children or had been surgically sterilized were eligible to work on the production lines, where Johnson's best-paid jobs all lay. By September 1990 a mere 12 of the company's 280 production workers were women. "The issue is protecting the health of unborn children," claims a company statement. And as there is no "economically feasible" way to reduce the levels of lead in the air, in Johnson's view, the firm decided it had no choice but to bar from production anyone who might someday bear a child.

News of the fetal protection plan enraged the workers at Johnson Controls. Women were furious over the policy's direct and negative impact on their wages and opportunities, since all the best opportunities for promotion originate on the production line. Some men were angered as well by the evident lack of concern for male reproductive futures, not to mention the casual stance that the fetal policy betokened toward the men's own health and comfort.[10] Joanne Leard, health and safety monitor for the union, observed

[7] Susan Faludi notes that fetal protection plans often appeared in the early to mid-1980s in industries that had faced "intensive federal pressure to hire women a decade earlier," such as AT&T and American Cyanamid: *Backlash: The Undeclared War against American Women* (New York, 1991), p. 438. Although Europeans treat battery making as a clearly "feminine" occupation, American manufacturers have long viewed this work as more suitable for men.

[8] My account is drawn largely from Peter Kilborn, "Who Decides Where Women Work When a Job Can Endanger Fetuses?" *New York Times*, 2 September 1990, pp. 1, 12. See also Faludi, *Backlash*, pp. 437–40.

[9] Kilborn notes that in September 1990, workers at Johnson Controls earned up to $15 an hour, as compared with $6 to $7 paid in other local factories: "Who Decides," p. 12.

[10] No definitive studies have demonstrated the long-term deleterious impact of lead on the viability of sperm, but it turns out that the studies on which the company based its female-centered reproductive protection policy are not reliable: all are either out of date or nonexistent. See Faludi, *Backlash*, p. 439.

that workers of both sexes find Johnson's allegedly safe levels of lead difficult to tolerate on a daily basis, and told of one young man whose lead level rose so high that the company had to send him home for five months at full pay (as the law required), until the lead in his blood had fallen back to the allowable maximum. "He came back to work when it was down, but it's back up again even though he works in a low-lead area. He now has dizziness, aches in his joints and constipation. They're so concerned about protecting the female. They should protect the men as well."[11]

The women at Johnson Controls were quick to protest the new fetal protection rule, arguing that its adoption obstructed their access to well-paid work and so was in violation of the 1964 Civil Rights Act. Over the next eight years, as the case worked its way through the judicial system, the union put forward the same argument, but without success. In March 1991, however, the case won a favorable hearing at last, when the U.S. Supreme Court upheld the women's right to work.

The unfolding of events at Johnson Controls reminds us that as in the metalworking plants of the early twentieth century, employers and workers continue to struggle over complex issues of power and human needs in a composite language that speaks overtly of individuals, skills, and rights, and can acknowledge the social dimension of production at best indirectly. Political economy thus continues to mystify its own Aristotelian predicates, denying its systematic reliance on a social language of power/order in order to uphold the claim that in a market society, all receive socially neutral treatment—a guarantee of equal opportunity. But protecting this claim has its costs. Hence, when struggles such as the one at Johnson Controls arise, conflicts in which the social dimension of production assumes such salience, employers and workers alike are left to address the social aspect as something separate, as though it existed apart from the real business of making batteries. An important dimension of human existence in the modern world thus remains hardly articulable.

[11] Kilborn, "Who Decides," p. 12.

Bibliographic Note

Considerations of economy prevent me from listing all the materials used in the preparation of this book. Readers interested in the specialized bibliography of particular issues will find full citations in the footnotes at appropriate passages. But it seems useful to say a few things here about the primary sources available to those who would pursue further research in this area.

On women workers and the reorganization and rationalization of industry, one may usefully combine material in public and government archives with the records of private employer organizations. In France, the most important public sources include the papers of Albert Thomas (Archives Nationales, series 94 AP), which deal with Thomas's administration as undersecretary for artillery, then minister of armaments. This rich collection offers a detailed view of wartime projects for industrial transformation: volumes of correspondence and reports on the interrelated issues of job training, wages, technical organization, working conditions, and the integration of the new female workforce. The series also contains a full set of the ministry's weekly *Bulletin des Usines de Guerre*, a gold mine of information on both the technical and social aspects of the "scientific" reorganization of work endorsed by Thomas and his associates. Equally valuable are the records of the Ministries of Labor (AN, series F 22) and Commerce (AN, series F 12), which include material on the organization of war industry and on the demobilization and plans for a postwar reorganization of the French economy. When read alongside the records from the employers' associations—the UIMM (whose collections remain private) and its Paris affiliate, the GIMM (which has deposited its records at the AN, series 39 AS), a clear picture of French industrial culture starts to emerge: a preference for centralized authority, sharply hierarchical managerial structures, and paternalist and welfarist strategies of labor control as means of circumventing workers' (and state authorities') wish to implant mechanisms of collective bargaining.

The GIMM's records offer an exceptionally full and detailed portrait of the *groupement* strategy: detailed wage scales for the region (so that affiliated firms might know what constituted a "reasonable" wage demand), lists of known militants or "troublemakers," extensive material on industrial social policy (family allocations, which were organized by the GIMM, company housing schemes, factory-based maternal welfare provisions, leisure programs for young workers). The UIMM's records, though patchier, also reflect employers' interest in the relationship between industrial welfare and the suppression of labor conflict; indeed, they are especially rich at moments of widespread labor unrest (1919–21 and 1936). Of particular importance for this study are the dossiers on women workers in the interwar metals industry, gathered and preserved in the late 1930s by one Mlle Boumier, a *surintendante*-turned-UIMM-functionary.

On the British side, government material on wartime and postwar industrial reorganization can be found in two places: the Public Record Office, which holds the papers of the Ministries of Munitions and Labor, and the Imperial War Museum, whose extraordinarily rich collections are the essential starting point for any study of Britain during World War I. Of primary importance for this book are the materials gathered in the Women's Work Collection—records from the national factories, reports by women welfare supervisors, contemporary autobiographical accounts by women munitions workers, and the exhaustive minutes of evidence taken by the War Cabinet Committee on Women in Industry in October 1918. In addition, there is the more personal and individual evidence of women's memories of war work recorded some fifty years after the Armistice in a series of oral interviews conducted by the IWM's Sound Records Department.

When one reads this material alongside the records of the Engineering Employers' Federation, one begins to discern the central lineaments of British industrial organization, namely, the enduring power of skilled craftsmen and the concomitant willingness of employers to bargain collectively with them, a willingness that over time extended grudgingly outward and downward to less skilled and women workers. The EEF thus adopted a distinct strategy for organizing and controlling labor: by co-opting skilled men into a formal bargaining procedure, the federation sought to minimize work stoppage and contain labor militancy, to maintain industrial peace via consensus with the unions, and with skilled men above all. This system generated a range of records that proved enormously valuable for this study: detailed wage lists, numerous collective bargaining transcripts, and minute books from the federation's executive committee, as it met to prepare for these sessions. The EEF holds transcripts from national conferences only; records of local conferences are held in the district offices of the federation's local affiliates.

The shape and structure of industrial and public archives in France and Britain thus underscores crucial differences in national industrial cultures and conceptions of authority. But these sources are equally revealing of similarities in the "deep structures" of the two economies, similarities that are etched most visibly in the gendered hierarchies of skill that organized wage lists, and the entire labor process, on both sides of the Channel. An equally significant similarity—employers' inability to reconcile their understanding of women's "distinct" capabilities with the idea of craft skill—emerges quite sharply in transcripts of collective bargaining sessions in the two countries. At the same time, it is important to note that common concerns about women and job skill, technical change and industrial training, were often articulated in somewhat different contexts in France and Britain. The lack of parallelism in the location of these debates is itself quite revealing. Thus British discussion of these issues tended to occur either in the course of collective bargaining or in the context of the state's efforts first to revise and then to restore the prewar division of labor over the period 1914–21. French discussions were likely to arise in the course of broader conversations about industrial organization, mechanization, and the provision of maternal health and welfare facilities on the factory premises, revealing the broader tendency in French industrial culture to link social and technical issues of production, especially where women workers were concerned.

French employers' concern with neo-paternalist strategies of labor control brings me to the final bodies of evidence I want to discuss, namely, the records of factory welfare supervisors (*surintendantes d'usine*), the police, and the press. Of course, welfare supervision of women workers emerged in war factories on both sides of the Channel. But it was French employers who, in the interwar era, placed a system of maternalist and pro-natalist welfare discipline at the heart of their strategy for controlling the female workforce. Accordingly, I have relied heavily on records from the Ecole des Surintendantes d'Usine, where the daughters of the bourgeoisie trained for careers in factory-based social work. Here one finds material on the founding of the school, a near-complete run of the Association des Surintendantes' annual *Bulletin*, and a thick dossier of twenty-nine journals (covering the period 1919–43) kept by students during their *stages* as ordinary factory workers. The association's *Bulletin*, published annually from 1920 on, contains the full proceedings of the association's yearly general assembly—an annual report and budget for the school, testimonial speeches by employers and public figures praising the school and the *surintendantes* for their work among women factory workers, and a selection of reports "from the field," sent in by *surintendantes* in factories across the nation. These materials, in particular the *surintendantes'* reports and journals, offer a kind of middle-class "ethnography" of the all but impenetrable world of factory labor in interwar France.

Finally there is the press, a source I have used rather sparingly, in part because of the heavy censorship under which the press labored in wartime France. For instance, news of the May–June 1917 movement of women munitions workers was almost entirely suppressed in the Parisian newspapers of center (*Le Petit Journal*), right (*L'Eclair*), and left (*L'Humanité*); in all three cases, very full, day-to-day reportage on the *midinettes'* strike of mid-May broke off abruptly and quite visibly when the initiative passed to women arms workers. By May 31, columns such as the *Petit Journal's* "Les Grèves à Paris" had been reduced to an incoherent patchwork of half lines and large empty swatches—all that remained after the censor had passed through with his scissors. The book therefore relies on police and employer records to reconstruct strike movements, and to recapture the widespread labor militancy that attended France's slow and difficult demobilization. And this recalls a central irony in labor history, that the records of a repressive state may be most helpful in reconstructing the actions (if not the motives) of those being repressed.

Archives and Government Publications Cited

ARCHIVES

Britain

Coventry District Engineering Employers' Association (CDEEA)
    Complete minutes of Executive Committee meetings
    Three cartons of "Historical Documents," including a few transcripts of collective
      bargaining sessions at local works conferences
Imperial War Museum (IWM)
    Department of Printed Books
      Joan Williams, "A Munition Worker's Career at Messrs. G. 1915–1919."
    Women's Work Collection
      Complete minutes of evidence taken by the war cabinet committee on women
        in Industry, 1918
      Records of welfare work in national shell and projectile factories, 1916–1919
    Department of Sound Records
      Oral History Recordings. War Work, 1914–1918
    Department of Photographs
Management Research Groups Archive, London School of Economics
    Minutes of meetings held throughout the interwar period
Modern Records Centre, University of Warwick (MRC)
    Full records of the Engineering Employers' Federation (EEF) (wage books, corre-
      spondence, committee minutes, collective bargaining transcripts)
    Arthur Young Papers
Public Record Office, London (PRO)
    Series Lab.: Ministry of Labour
    Series Mun.: Ministry of Munitions

France

Archives Nationales, Paris (AN)
  Series F7: Ministère de l'Intérieur
  Series F12: Ministère du Commerce
  Series F22: Ministère du Travail
  Series 39 AS: Groupement des Industries Métallurgiques, Mécaniques et Connexes
    de la Région Parisienne (wage lists, correspondence, administrative records,
    factory welfare and family policy, strike activity and employer defense)
  Series 91 AQ: Renault automobile factory
  Series 94 AP: Fonds Albert Thomas
Archives de la Chambre de Commerce, Paris
  Records of metals industries not working under defense contracts
Archives de la Préfecture de Police, Paris (APP)
  Series B/a 1375: Strikes in war factories, 1916–18
Bibliothèque Marguerite Durand, Paris
  Press cuttings on women's work since the late nineteenth century (including
    several folders on the *surintendantes* in series 360 ASS and 331 ASS SUR 360)
Ecole des Surintendantes d'Usine, Paris
  Bulletin de l'Association des Surintendantes (published annually from 1920 on),
    1922–39 (the issues for 1920 and 1921 can be found at the Bibliothèque Nationale)
  Dossier of journals kept by students during their factory *stages,* 1919–1943.
Union Féminine Civique et Sociale, Paris (UFCS)
  Complete series of the UFCS journal *La Femme dans la Vie Sociale,* 1925–39
  Material on Andrée Butillard
  Origins and early years of the UFCS
Union des Industries Métallurgiques et Minières, Paris (UIMM)
  Series 39/21: Strike movements in 1919 and 1936
  Series 69/54: Women metalworkers during World War I and the interwar period

GOVERNMENT PUBLICATIONS

Britain

Board of Trade, Balfour Committee on Industry and Trade. *A Survey of Industries.*
  4 vols. London, 1928. Vol. 2, *Further Factors in Industrial Efficiency,* and vol. 4,
  Survey of the Metal Industries.
Dilution of Labour Bulletin.
Hakim, Catherine. *Occupational Segregation.* Department of Employment research
  paper no. 9. London: Ministry of Labour, 1979.
Home Department. *Report to the Right Honourable the Secretary of State for the
  Home Department by the Departmental Committee on the Employment of Women
  and Young Persons on the Two Shift System.* London, 1920.
Ministry of Labour. *British and Foreign Trade and Industry Statistics, 1924–1930.*
  London, 1931.

Ministry of Munitions. *Official History of the Ministry of Munitions*. 8 vols. London, 1920–24.

——. *Official History of the Scottish Filling Factory at Georgetown*. London, n.d.

——, Health of Munition Workers Committee. *Employment of Women and Juveniles in Great Britain during the War*. Reprinted in *Bulletin of Labor* no. 223, U.S. Department of Labor, Bureau of Labor Statistics, April 1917.

Ministry of Labour Gazette.

Parliamentary Papers (PP). Individual sessional and command papers are cited in the notes.

France

Bulletin de l'Inspection du Travail.

Bulletin du Ministère du Travail.

Bulletin de la Statistique Générale de la France.

Bulletin des Usines de Guerre.

Ministère de l'Armement. *Crèches et garderies d'enfants: Règlements et inventaire*. Paris, 1917.

——. *Salles d'allaitement*. Paris, 1917.

——. *Supplément aux tarifs et réglementation des salaires applicables pour les fabrications de guerre de la région parisienne*. Paris, 1918.

——. *Tarifs et réglementation des salaires applicables pour les fabrications de guerre de la région parisienne*. Paris, 1917.

——, Comité du Travail Féminin. *Protection et utilisation de la main-d'oeuvre féminine dans les usines de guerre*. Paris, 1917.

Ministère de l'Intérieur. *Rapports mensuels sur les grèves de 1918*. Paris, 1918.

Index

Abhervé, Bertrand, 19n
Abortion Law of 1920, 207n
Accampo, Elinor, 6n
Aircraft industries: Gnôme et Rhône, 131,
143–44; Gwynne's, 45, 96–98, 103; Han-
riot, 130–31; Lucas, 292, 304; Salmson,
129–30. *See also* Strikes
Alberti, Johanna, 31n
Aldcroft, Derek, 211n, 229n
Alsthom (electrical), 147–50, 239, 257
Amalgamated Engineering Union (AEU),
187–90
Amalgamated Society of Engineers (ASE):
and attitudes toward women workers,
43, 195, 116; and collective bargaining,
195; and equal pay, 115–18; and rational-
ization, 32, 43, 110; and strikes, 195; and
wages, 106–18
Anderson, Mary, 31n
Apprenticeship, 20, 91–94. *See also* Craft;
Job training; Skill
Argenteuil, factory in: Gnôme et Rhône,
131, 143–44
Aristotelian language: and neo-classical ar-
guments, 8, 309–10; and social order, 8–
9, 140–41, 309; and technical/sexual
division of labor, 8, 102–3, 220–23, 308–9
Armengaud, André, 265n
Armstrong-Whitworth (munitions), 148–53
Assembly lines, 247–50, 286–92. *See also* Sci-
entific organization of work
Association des Surintendantes, 166–74,
177–85, 317. *See also* Surintendantes
Austin (automobiles), 104, 286n
Authority: and class, 94–100, 174–77; as
component of skill, 2–8, 17–21, 39–40,

94–100, 211–12; and gender, 2–4, 147–85,
211, 315. *See also* Foremen; Welfare super-
vision
Automobile industries: Austin, 104, 286;
Citroën, 61, 104, 130, 210, 286; Clément-
Bayard, 57n, 59, 133n; Daimler, 65n, 105;
Delaunay-Belleville, 23, 24n, 91, 134, 144n;
Dion, 126–27; Morris, 286; Panhard-Le-
vassor, 61, 133, 143, 234, 240–43; Re-
nault, 23, 56–60, 129–31, 237–39, 255, 271;
Rootes, 286; Rover, 284–305; Standard,
286; Vauxhall, 286; Vedovelli, 129, 210.
See also Strikes

Banbury National Shell factory, 66, 99
Barker, Lilian, 160–65, 192–94
Baron, Ava, 3n, 8on
Barrett, Michèle, 107n
Bataille, 171n
Baudrillard, Jean, 309n
Becker, Gary, 7n, 308n
Becker, Jean-Jacques, 51n, 186n, 187n
Bedaux, Charles, 289n
Bedaux system, 11, 286–305. *See also* Scien-
tific organization of work
Beechey, Veronica, 3n
Berg, Maxine, 8on
Berlanstein, Leonard R., 18n
Bernard, Philippe, 22n, 23, 25n, 54n, 131n
Bertillon, Jacques, 166n
Billaud (munitions), 50n
Birth control, 167. *See also* Maternity;
Natalism
Black, Naomi, 266n
Bordeaux Agreement, 22–23, 26, 30–31
Bordeaux conference, 22–23

323

The Wilder House Series in Politics, History, and Culture